THE EU AND SOCIAL INCLUSION

Facing the challenges

Eric Marlier, A.B. Atkinson, Bea Cantillon and Brian Nolan

First published in Great Britain in 2007 by

The Policy Press
University of Bristol
Fourth Floor
Beacon House
Queen's Road
Bristol BS8 1QU
UK

Tel +44 (0)117 331 4054
Fax +44 (0)117 331 4093
e-mail tpp-info@bristol.ac.uk
www.policypress.org.uk

North American office:
The Policy Press
c/o International Specialized Books Services (ISBS)
920 NE 58th Avenue, Suite 300
Portland, OR 97213-3786, USA
Tel +1 503 287 3093
Fax +1 503 280 8832
e-mail info@isbs.com

© Eric Marlier, A.B. Atkinson, Bea Cantillon and Brian Nolan 2007

Transferred to Digital Print 2009

British Library Cataloguing in Publication Data
A catalogue record for this book is available from the British Library.

Library of Congress Cataloging-in-Publication Data
A catalog record for this book has been requested.

ISBN 978 1 84742 419 8 paperback

Cover design by Qube Design Associates, Bristol
Printed and bound in Great Britain by Marston Book Services, Oxford.

Contents

List of figures, tables and boxes

Figures

Tables

Boxes

List of abbreviations and acronyms

Country abbreviations

AT	Austria
BE	Belgium
CY	Cyprus
CZ	Czech Republic
DE	Germany
DK	Denmark
EE	Estonia
EL	Greece
ES	Spain
FI	Finland
FR	France
HU	Hungary
IE	Ireland
IT	Italy
LT	Lithuania
LU	Luxembourg
LV	Latvia
MT	Malta
NL	The Netherlands
PL	Poland
PT	Portugal
SE	Sweden
SI	Slovenia
SK	Slovak Republic
UK	United Kingdom
US	United States

Other abbreviations and acronyms

CERC	Conseil de l'Emploi, des Revenus et de la Cohésion sociale (France's "Council for employment, income and social cohesion")
DG EMPL	Directorate-General "Employment, Social Affairs and Equal Opportunities" of the European Commission

DG SANCO	Directorate-General "Health and Consumer Protection" of the European Commission
EAPN	European Anti-Poverty Network
ECHP	European Community Household Panel
ECHP UDB	ECHP Users' Data Base
ECOFIN	EU Economic and Financial Affairs Council of Ministers
EEC	European Economic Community
EHSS	European Health Survey System
EPSCO	EU Employment, Social Policy, Health and Consumer Affairs Council of Ministers
ESSPROS	European System of Integrated Social Protection Statistics
EU	European Union
EU-10	The 10 "new" EU Member States, who joined the EU in May 2004 (CY, CZ, EE, HU, LT, LV, MT, PL, SI, SK)
EU-15	The 15 "old" EU Member States, before the May 2004 Enlargement (AT, BE, DE, DK, EL, ES, FI, FR, IE, IT, LU, NL, PT, SE, UK)
EUROSTAT	Statistical Office of the European Communities
EU-SILC	Community Statistics on Income and Living Conditions
FEANTSA	Fédération Européenne d'Associations Nationales Travaillant avec les Sans-Abris (European Federation of National Organisations working with the Homeless)
GDP	Gross Domestic Product
HBS	Household Budget Survey
HDI	Human Development Index
ICT	Information and Communication Technologies
ILO	International Labour Organisation
ISCED	International Standard Classification of Education
ISG	Indicators Sub–Group (of the EU Social Protection Committee)
JIM	Joint Memorandum on Social Inclusion
LAP	Local Action Plan
LDP	Local Development Plan
LFS	Labour Force Survey
MDGs	Millennium Development Goals
METR	Marginal Effective Tax Rate
MISSOC	Mutual Information System on Social Protection
NAP/inclusion	National Action Plan on social inclusion
NICs	Newly Industrialising Countries
NSR	National Strategy Report
NSR/health	National Strategy Report on Health Care and Long-Term Care
NUTS	Nomenclature of the Statistical Territorial Units (in French: Nomenclature des Unités Territoriales Statistiques)

OECD	Organisation for Economic Cooperation and Development
OMC	Open Method of Coordination
PISA	(OECD) Programme for International Student Assessment
PPS and PPP	Purchasing Power Standards and Purchasing Power Parities. On the basis of Purchasing Power Parities, Purchasing Power Standards convert amounts expressed in a national currency to an artificial common currency that equalises the purchasing power of different national currencies (including those countries that share a common currency). In other words, PPP is both a price deflator and a currency converter.
PROGRESS	Programme for Employment and Social Solidarity
RAP	Regional Action Plan
RDP	Regional Development Plan
RTD	Research and Technological Development
SDS	Sustainable Development Strategy
SPC	(EU) Social Protection Committee
TSER	Targeted Socio-Economic Research
UN	United Nations
UNDP	United Nations Development Programme
WI	Work Intensity of households

Foreword

With some 16% of its population at risk of poverty, one of the most important challenges that continues to face the European Union (EU) is the need to achieve a significant reduction in the level of poverty and social exclusion. This is not a new challenge. Since the March 2000 European Council in Lisbon the EU has been committed to taking steps "to make a decisive impact on the eradication of poverty" (Presidency Conclusions). The EU Social Inclusion Process, the Open Method of Coordination on poverty and social exclusion, has been the means used to achieve this objective.

This Social Inclusion Process is of great importance. Given that more than a quarter of those who are at risk of poverty are at work, it is clear that there is no automatic link between more jobs and a reduction in poverty. Furthermore, access to a job is not a realistic solution for many of those who are living in poverty and are outside the labour market. Thus it is essential that we accompany our efforts to promote growth and jobs with strong social inclusion policies.

In 2005, after five years of the EU Social Inclusion Process, Member States and the European Commission agreed it would be timely to review the effectiveness of the Process with a view to making proposals for its further strengthening and to ensuring a greater coordination with the other social "processes" launched in the context of what has become known as the *Lisbon Strategy* – the Pensions Process and the Health Care and Long-Term Care Process. The Luxembourg Government strongly supported the need for such a review. It thus decided that making a significant contribution to this *mid-term review* of the social processes launched at Lisbon would be a key priority for its Presidency of the Council of the European Union.

A particular concern of my Government was that the effectiveness of the Social Inclusion Process had been limited, both in Luxembourg but also in the Union more generally, by a lack of consistent monitoring and evaluation of the Process. Indeed, the need for Member States to enhance social monitoring of national performance had already been highlighted in the Conclusions of the Spring European Council in 2004. I thus decided to organise a major conference in June 2005 on "Taking Forward the EU Social Inclusion Process" with the aim of contributing to the review of the Social Inclusion Process and in particular to the issues of social monitoring and policy analysis. This book is based on the excellent independent report written for that conference by Tony Atkinson, Bea Cantillon, Eric Marlier and Brian Nolan.

At the same time as the review of the Social Inclusion Process was taking place, the wider political environment was also changing. At their Spring 2005 European Council, EU Heads of State and Government decided to re-focus the overall Lisbon Strategy with an enhanced emphasis on economic competitiveness and more and better jobs. In the lead-up to this meeting there had been, therefore, some uncertainty and well-founded concern about the place intended for the social pillar of Lisbon in the framework of the revised Lisbon Strategy. Happily EU leaders, encouraged by the Luxembourg Presidency, acknowledged the continuing importance of the Lisbon objective of greater social cohesion and the need to promote greater social inclusion. In particular point 36 of the Conclusions of the European Council stressed that "Social inclusion policy ought to be pursued by the Union and the Member States with its multidimensional approach". However, at the time of the Luxembourg Presidency Conference, a key issue that remained to be resolved was exactly how the Social Inclusion Process, and the other social Processes initiated at Lisbon, would be positioned in this new political framework. This repositioning of the Social Inclusion Process thus became an important theme in the background report and during the discussions at the conference.

Over the past year since the Luxembourg Presidency Conference, many of the issues raised at the conference and in this book have been extensively debated. In the second half of 2005 the UK Presidency carried forward the discussion. The future of the Social Inclusion Process was a key issue discussed at the Round Table Conference on social inclusion in Glasgow in October, hosted by the Presidency. Then, at an informal Summit at Hampton Court in November, the Presidency stimulated a debate on how to maintain and strengthen social justice and competitiveness in the Union in the context of globalisation. In December 2005 the European Commission issued a communication proposing new streamlined objectives and working arrangements for the Open Method of Coordination on social protection and social inclusion. These stressed the importance of ensuring close links between the Social Protection and Social Inclusion Process and the revised Lisbon agenda on jobs and growth.

The political momentum was maintained under the Austrian Presidency in 2006, first at an informal meeting of EU Ministers for employment and social affairs in Villach in January and then at the *Employment, Social Policy, Health and Consumer Affairs (EPSCO)* Council meeting in March. There was extensive discussion of the Commission's proposals by Member States but also involving other stakeholders, particularly Non-Governmental Organisations (NGOs) and the social partners. Several important changes and additions were agreed. This culminated in the endorsement at the 2006 Spring European Council of new objectives and working arrangements for the Open Method of Coordination on social protection and social inclusion. It is my view that these new arrangements provide a strong basis for the future development of the Union's efforts to promote greater social inclusion and for reinforcing the struggle against poverty and social exclusion.

I would particularly stress and endorse five things about the new arrangements which I think are also well supported by the arguments made in this book. First, the EU Social Protection and Social Inclusion Process is of central political importance. The Heads of State and Government have reiterated that promoting greater social cohesion and making a decisive impact on the eradication of poverty by 2010 are fundamental goals of the Union and of the overall Lisbon Strategy. The challenge for us all now is to respond to this high-level political commitment by intensifying our efforts to reduce poverty and social exclusion and by ensuring that we mainstream social inclusion goals at all levels of governance – European, national, regional and local.

My second political message is to stress the interdependence of the Union's economic, employment, social and environmental goals. This has been emphasised in the Conclusions of the last Spring European Council, in March 2006. It is also reflected in the revised objectives for the EU Social Protection and Social Inclusion Process, which highlight the importance of ensuring effective and *mutual* interaction between these policy areas. In this regard a key challenge in the coming period will be to ensure that the future National Reports on Strategies for Social Protection and Social Inclusion and the National Reform Programmes for jobs and economic growth prepared by Member States are mutually reinforcing. As is evident from the European Commission's report on the first round of National Reform Programmes, this interconnection was not very evident in 2005. It is essential that it becomes a key element of the next round later this year.

The third point that I would stress is the importance of strengthening arrangements for monitoring and reporting of progress. At the time of the Luxembourg Presidency Conference I emphasised the importance of reporting processes coming together each year in the Joint Report on Social Protection and Social Inclusion, which is, in the words of my Belgian colleague, Minister Demotte, the "product of the Open Method". I believe that it is very important politically that the Spring European Councils should be fully informed by these Reports. The Luxembourg Presidency already established this principle by transmitting the first Joint Report on Social Protection and Social Inclusion to the 2005 Spring European Council. I am delighted that this precedent was maintained this year under the Austrian Presidency. Furthermore, the conclusions of the European Council of March this year state that in future the Joint Report will be submitted to "each Spring European Council".

My fourth point is to stress that, although we now have a streamlined Social Protection and Social Inclusion Process, it is also important to maintain and build on the distinctive strands of social inclusion, pensions and health care and long-term care. I welcome that the new arrangements provide for the continuation of National Action Plans on social inclusion (NAPs/inclusion). As we move forward it will be important to continue to be vigilant in ensuring that the distinctive identity and profile of the social inclusion strand is maintained at both national and EU levels. It must not become submerged in the wider Process. This also needs to be evident in the Joint Report each year.

The final point I would stress is the importance of the NAPs/inclusion becoming more strategic, focused, and placed further in the mainstream of national policy making. This is essential if we are really to achieve the objective of making a "decisive impact on the reduction of poverty and social exclusion by 2010", as reaffirmed by Heads of State and Government at their last Spring Summit. In this regard the Guidelines that have been agreed between Member States and the Commission for the preparation of the first National Reports on Strategies for Social Protection and Social Inclusion, and in particular the section on the NAPs/inclusion, are encouraging. They both invite Member States to focus, on the basis of a thorough diagnosis, on three or four key issues and to outline in very concrete terms the actions they propose to take and to monitor their implementation carefully. They also invite Member States to outline how they will ensure stronger governance on social inclusion issues, in particular by mainstreaming social inclusion goals in national policy making. Given the multidimensional nature of poverty and social exclusion, it is vital that all policy areas and all actors contribute to the efforts to create greater social inclusion. It will of course be important to ensure that the Union's social inclusion objectives are mainstreamed into all relevant policy areas at European level as well as at the national and sub-national levels.

It is clear that the new arrangements that are now in place benefited significantly from both the background report as well as the thorough discussions that it stimulated at the Luxembourg Presidency Conference. The challenge now is to ensure their effective implementation. As the 2006 Joint Report on Social Protection and Social Inclusion has made clear, there has been a gap between the objectives and aspirations of Member States and the actual implementation of policies and programmes aimed at bringing about a decisive impact on the eradication of poverty and social exclusion. That is why I believe the publication of this book is most welcome and also very timely. It contains a wealth of analysis and suggestions that should be of great assistance to the Member States and the Commission over the next few years. In particular I believe it can be particularly helpful in three key areas: strengthening policy analysis and the monitoring and evaluation of the NAPs/inclusion; revising and strengthening the common indicators which underpin the Social Inclusion Process, especially in the new policy context; and enhancing the focus on child poverty.

Finally, I would like to thank everyone who participated in the Luxembourg Presidency Conference. By doing so they contributed to both the new objectives and working arrangements on social protection and social inclusion and to the preparation of this book. A special word of thanks is due to the Luxembourg-based research institute, CEPS/INSTEAD, particularly to Eric Marlier, who provided the scientific coordination of the event, and to the President of the institute, Gaston Schaber, who supported the initiative.

Last, but not least, my thanks go to the four authors of the background report for the conference and of this book: to Tony Atkinson and Eric Marlier, who coordinated its preparation and to Bea Cantillon and Brian Nolan who were co-authors. They undertook a similar task at the outset of the Social Inclusion Process in 2001, preparing a report for the Belgium Presidency Conference on "Indicators for Social Inclusion: Making Common EU Objectives Work". That report and subsequent publication by Oxford University Press proved to be an invaluable and influential resource for the first phase of the EU Social Inclusion Process. I am quite sure that this book will play a similar central role in the next phase of the Process.

Marie-Josée Jacobs
Minister of the Family and of Integration
Government of Luxembourg
June 2006

Preface

This book is based on an independent report written at the request of the Luxembourg Government, in the context of the Luxembourg Presidency of the Council of the European Union during the first semester of 2005. It does not represent in any way the views of the Government of Luxembourg. Equally, although the original report was prepared with the cooperation of the European Commission, neither the book nor the report represent in any way the views of the Commission or the European Union (EU). We, the four authors, have written in a strictly personal capacity, not as the representative of any Government or official body. Thus we have been free to express our own views.

In the preparation of the original report we were advised by a Steering Committee (see list of members in Appendix 3) whose views have been of considerable value in preparing the report. We should like to thank, in addition, for their most helpful comments and suggestions, Gabriel Amitsis, Lidija Apohal Vučkovič, Laura Bardone, Iain Begg, Fred Berger, Jasper Bloem, Jonathan Bradshaw, Chris Burston, Laurent Caussat, Anne Clémenceau, Ian Dennis, Didier Dupré, Olivier Dutheillet de Lamothe, Isabelle Engsted Maquet, Chantal Euzéby, Michael Förster, Hugh Frazer, Alessio Fusco, Bernard Gazier, Tim Goedeme, Liz Gosme, Anne-Catherine Guio, Krzysztof Hagemejer, Anne Hartung, Richard Hauser, Petra Hoelscher, Marie-Josée Jacobs, Pierre Jaeger, Jana Javornik, Bruno Jeandidier, Balázs Krémer, Peter Lelie, Michèle Lelièvre, Jean-Marc Museux, Hanna Nicholas, Ramón Peña Casas, Muriel Rabau, Jean-Claude Ray, Stijn Rottiers, Sylvia Rybárová, Armindo Silva, Elaine Squires, Holly Sutherland, Raffaele Tangorra, Johan Vandenbussche, Philippe Van Kerm, Tim Van Rie, Vijay Verma, Jérôme Vignon, Robert Walker, Brigitte Weinandy, Daphne White, Dorota Wijata, Elise Willame, Donald R. Williams and Vytas Žiūkas. We would like to give a special word of thanks to Hugh Frazer for his most helpful suggestions and wise advice when drafting the original report, and for his important assistance in editing and updating the report for publication. Isabelle Bouvy, Mireille Coos, Begoña Levices and Lin Sorrell have provided invaluable secretarial and bibliographical help. It should be stressed that the book and the report on which it is based do not represent the views of members of the Steering Committee, nor of those thanked above. We take full responsibility for the judgments made about past and current policy and for the recommendations for future policy.

The original report was presented and discussed at the high-level Conference on "Taking Forward the EU Social Inclusion Process", organised by the EU Luxembourg Presidency with the support of the European Commission (Luxembourg City, 13–14 June 2005). The report and conference were a project established as an initiative of Marie-Josée Jacobs, Luxembourg Minister of the Family and of Integration. The scientific coordination of the whole project was entrusted to the Luxembourg-based CEPS/INSTEAD research institute, and was the responsibility of Tony Atkinson and Eric Marlier. The report was finalised following the conference, taking into account the very valuable comments made by participants. Since then the text has been substantially revised to take account of EU policy developments in the social area in the year after the conference, and of the most up-to-date comparable statistics available at EU level.[1]

The conference report aimed to be complementary to the activities of official bodies in reviewing the Lisbon Agenda, the Social Inclusion Process, and the Open Method of Coordination (OMC) in the social field. We were anxious to avoid duplication of the work that was being undertaken by the Commission, by the EU Social Protection Committee and its Indicators Sub-Group, and by other EU bodies. In preparing the report and in this subsequent book we have taken the position of outside, but informed, observers, assessing some of the strengths and weaknesses of the current processes, and considering how they may be advanced. Thus, a key aim of the original report was to provide an external assessment as a hopefully helpful input into the 2005 official review procedure which, subsequently, resulted in the revised objectives and new working arrangements for a streamlined OMC on social protection and social inclusion which were adopted at the European Council in March 2006. However, the original report was intended not only to be a contribution to the review process but also to provide suggestions and ideas for the future implementation of the Social Inclusion Process. Thus we felt it would be worthwhile to produce a new version of the report as a resource for the many people who will be active and interested in the future implementation of the Process. Given the nature of the new arrangements that have now been put in place, we are more than ever convinced of the relevance of the issues raised in this book.

A.B. Atkinson (Nuffield College, Oxford, United Kingdom)
Bea Cantillon (University of Antwerp, Antwerp, Belgium)
Eric Marlier (CEPS/INSTEAD Research Institute, Differdange, Luxembourg)
Brian Nolan (Economic and Social Research Institute, Dublin, Ireland)
Luxembourg, June 2006

Note

[1] Full information concerning the conference can be obtained from the CEPS/INSTEAD address: http://www.ceps.lu/eu2005_lu/default.cfm. This includes the conference programme and the list of participants as well as the conference conclusions and all the conference interventions made available by speakers.

A one-page summary of contents

- Chapter 1 sets the scene, and introduces the context and contents of the book.
- Chapter 2 provides a brief historical account of the development of EU cooperation in social policy from the Treaty of Rome to the re-focused Lisbon Strategy post-March 2005 and the adoption of new working arrangements and revised objectives for the Open Method of Coordination on social protection and social inclusion in March 2006, leading up to the proposed designation of 2010 as the "European Year of combating poverty and social exclusion".
- Chapter 3 examines what can be learned about poverty and social exclusion from the rich body of evidence provided by the social indicators that have been commonly agreed at EU level, investigating the impact of Enlargement and the inter-relation between income and other dimensions of deprivation.
- Chapter 4 suggests how policy analysis in the Social Inclusion Process can be deepened, to help learn "what works", using model families analysis and micro-simulation modelling to develop a "common analytical framework" to accompany the common indicators.
- Chapter 5 contributes to the dynamic process of developing the common social indicators, in the context of Enlargement, a new EU data source (EU-SILC) with a new income concept, a streamlined OMC on social protection and social inclusion, and new policy concerns. It emphasises the development of non-income-related indicators on deprivation, housing quality/adequacy and homelessness. It discusses the need to balance the development of indicators to cover several areas currently not adequately covered against the dilution that might ensue if there were to be a proliferation of indicators.
- Children mainstreaming, in the sense of viewing social inclusion from a child's perspective, is a theme linking Chapters 3, 4 and 5, and suggests new approaches to both analysis and indicators.
- Chapter 6 considers the challenge of advancing the Social Inclusion Process in the context of the re-focused Lisbon Strategy, and of embedding the Process in domestic policies and implementing a *social inclusion mainstreaming* through establishing a scheme of systematic (*ex ante* and *ex post*) policy assessments at EU, national and sub-national levels. It proposes the setting of targets, fundamentally restructured NAPs/inclusion, and working towards more "joined-up" Government, on the basis of committed administrative and political leadership, and parliamentary scrutiny. It also stresses the importance of raising awareness of the Social Inclusion Process, and of further mobilising the different actors involved in the fight against poverty and social exclusion at the sub-national, national and EU levels.

"'A social Europe in the global economy: jobs and opportunities for all', this is the motto of the second phase of the Social Agenda covering the period up to 2010." (European Commission, 2005d, page 1)

"At its heart, the Lisbon Strategy promotes the idea of a positive interaction between economic, employment and social policies. It aims at promoting a model of sustainable development for the Union which raises the standard of living of all European citizens by combining economic growth with a strong emphasis on social cohesion and the preservation of the environment. In so doing, it stresses the need to improve EU level coordination mechanisms in order to foster consistent and mutually reinforcing policies in the economic, employment and social areas." (European Commission, 2005b, page 2)

"Social inclusion policy should be pursued by the Union and by Member States, with its multifaceted approach, focusing on target groups such as children in poverty." (Presidency Conclusions, European Council, 22–23 March 2005, paragraph 36)

"The new strategy for jobs and growth provides a framework where economic, employment and social policy mutually reinforce each other, ensuring that parallel progress is made on employment creation, competitiveness, and social cohesion in compliance with European values. For the European social model to be sustainable, Europe needs to step up its efforts to create more economic growth, a higher level of employment and productivity while strengthening social inclusion and social protection in line with the objectives provided for in the Social Agenda." (Presidency Conclusions, European Council, 23–24 March 2006, paragraph 69)

"The Commission and the Council will inform each Spring European Council with the Joint Report on the progress in the area of social protection and social inclusion." (Presidency Conclusions, European Council, 23–24 March 2006, paragraph 70)

"The European Council reaffirms the objective of the Partnership for growth and jobs that steps have to be taken to make a decisive impact on the reduction of poverty and social exclusion by 2010." (Presidency Conclusions, European Council, 23–24 March 2006, paragraph 72).

ONE

Introduction

Social inclusion is one of the declared objectives of the European Union (EU). When, at the Lisbon Summit of March 2000, EU Heads of State and Government decided that the Union should adopt the strategic goal for the next decade of becoming "the most competitive and dynamic knowledge-based economy [...] with more and better jobs and greater social cohesion", it was important that the phrase "social cohesion" appeared in the same sentence as "most competitive economy". The interpretation became clear when common objectives in the fight against poverty and social exclusion were set at the December 2000 Nice European Council. Key social ambitions of the EU were subsequently embodied in a first set of indicators of social performance adopted by EU leaders at Laeken (Belgium) in 2001. The importance of social inclusion policy, which "should be pursued by the Union and the Member States", and of a "multifaceted approach", were confirmed at the European Councils in March 2005 and March 2006.[1]

The aim of this book is to describe the progress made since Lisbon with the EU Social Inclusion Process and to examine the challenges faced in taking forward the Process in new circumstances. Its central subject is the future implementation of the Social Inclusion Process. As explained in the Preface, this book is based on a report which was designed in the first instance to provide an input into the 2005 official *mid-term review* of the Lisbon Agenda, and specifically into the evaluation by the Commission and the Member States of the operation of the *Open Method of Coordination* (OMC) in the field of social policy. (This evaluation resulted in the revised objectives and new working arrangements for a streamlined OMC on social protection and social inclusion that were subsequently adopted at the European Council in March 2006, as we will see below.)

If the EU is to make significant progress towards reducing the number of people at risk of poverty or social exclusion, then we need to know much more about "what actually works" in terms of social inclusion strategies. The need for "effective monitoring and evaluation provisions" in social policy was emphasised in one of the *key messages* to EU Heads of State and Government adopted in March 2005 by the *Employment, Social Policy, Health and Consumer Affairs* (EPSCO) formation of the EU Council of Ministers: "The forthcoming evaluation process [...] should focus on strengthening the delivery of objectives, in line with the overall thrust of the mid-term review of Lisbon. The Member States and the Commission should particularly assess how national strategies can be made more effective by the use of targets, benchmarks and indicators, better links with economic and employment policies, effective monitoring and evaluation provisions" (Council, 2005). This was stressed again a year later in the 2006 Joint

Report on Social Protection and Social Inclusion (European Commission, 2006a), which exposes the *gap* between what Member States commit to in the common European objectives and the policy effort to implement them: "the process should move beyond identifying broad principles to focus on the effectiveness of policies" and "monitoring and evaluation of social policies should be strengthened" (2006a, pages 2 and 15).

This introductory Chapter describes the context within which the book has been written. It outlines the contents of each Chapter and seeks to set the European debate in a wider global context. Since 2000, there has been significant progress in the EU approach to social inclusion. This progress has been made at a time when the EU itself has been changing dramatically, with the Enlargement from 15 to 25 Member States in May 2004. In addition, the evolution of the EU has taken place at a time when concerns about poverty and social exclusion have been growing in the world as a whole, notably on account of the adoption of the Millennium Development Goals in September 2000. Within the EU, even during the period we worked on the original report and subsequent book, the environment has changed, especially with regard to some important aspects of EU governance.

1.1 Setting the scene: persistent problems and new challenges

The Social Inclusion Process started from concerns about poverty and social exclusion in the EU that were far from new. Thirty years ago, the European Communities adopted the first European Action Programme to combat poverty (see Chapter 2 for a short review of the *Poverty* programmes). The Commission, in its Interim Report of 1989, estimated that in 1975 there were some 38 million poor people in the 12 countries that constituted the Community in 1989 (European Commission, 1989). Under Jacques Delors, the social dimension received more attention, based on a foundation of scientific research on poverty. The Final Report on the Second Programme, taking expenditure rather than income as the indicator of resources, reached the estimate for 1985 of 50 million poor people (see O'Higgins and Jenkins, 1990), based on the study carried out by the late Aldi Hagenaars, together with Klaas de Vos and Asghar Zaidi (1994).

At the same time there was increasing debate (see, for example, Room, 1995; Silver, 1995; Nolan and Whelan, 1996) about the underlying concepts. What is meant by the phrase, now used widely by the EU, "poverty and social exclusion"? In what sense is "social inclusion" the reversal of "social exclusion"? Do we mean poverty or "risk of poverty"? These issues go to the heart of our societal objectives, and it is not surprising that they are not yet fully resolved. Moreover, the debate has been widened by the 2004 Enlargement. How far, for example, are notions like social inclusion and social cohesion differently interpreted in the "new" Member States that previously had communist regimes? We cannot provide here an extensive discussion, but there are certain essential elements:

- The long-standing *social inclusion* objective of the EU is concerned that all EU citizens participate in the benefits of economic integration and economic growth, with appropriate account being taken of Europe's responsibilities in the world as a whole. The EU cannot be successful if significant groups are left behind as prosperity rises.

- The definition of *poverty* has therefore been based on the notion of *participation*. The EU Council of Ministers (hereafter the Council) in 1975 defined the poor as "individuals or families whose resources are so small as to exclude them from the minimum acceptable way of life of the Member State in which they live", with "resources" being defined as "goods, cash income plus services from public and private sources" (Council, 1975). In this sense, it is a relative definition.

- The move to "poverty and social exclusion" reflected a growing acceptance that *deprivation* is a multi-dimensional concept, and that, while financial poverty remains a major preoccupation, our concerns have to be broader. The European Commission, in its 1992 submission on "Intensifying the Fight Against Social Exclusion", argued that the term "social exclusion" is more encompassing than the term "poverty". The Commission suggested that social exclusion captures more adequately the "multi-dimensional nature of the mechanisms whereby individuals and groups are excluded from taking part in the social exchanges, from the component practices and rights of social integration" (European Commission, 1992, page 8).

- With this broader focus came an emphasis on *dynamics*. People are excluded not just because they are currently without a job or income, but also because they have little prospects for the future or for their children's future. "When poverty predominantly occurs in long spells [...] the poor have virtually no chance of escaping from poverty and, therefore, little allegiance to the wider community" (Walker, 1995, page 103). Just as poorer Member States aspire to converge on the EU average, so poorer EU citizens aspire to better individual prospects.

- The concept of exclusion introduces the element of *agency*. When René Lenoir coined the phrase "les exclus" in 1974, he was concerned with those who were excluded from the French welfare state. In all countries, the design of social protection, and way in which it is administered, exclude certain citizens. The State is a major actor, but it is not the only actor.

- Recognition of the limitations of an income measure has led to the EU adopting the term "at risk of poverty" to denote people living in households with incomes below the specified threshold.

- Finally, this book is mainly concerned with those social indicators that are to be used in the EU Social Inclusion Process; or, put differently, in the social inclusion dimensions of the *streamlined* EU Social Protection and Social Inclusion Process (on the concept of "streamlining", see Sections 2.3 and 6.1). We often refer to them as indicators for "social inclusion" (i.e. indicators for use in the Social Inclusion Process) even though they all are obviously indicators for "poverty and social exclusion". Sometimes, we also simply use the terms "social indicators". All these expressions are thus used interchangeably and refer to the same indicators.

Over time, there have been great improvements in the data available to implement the different concepts. The most recent EU situation is summarised in the 2006 Joint Report on Social Protection and Social Inclusion (European Commission, 2006a and 2006b). Overall this shows that the number of people affected by poverty and social exclusion remains sizeable, though there is considerable diversity among Member States.[2] 16% of the EU-25 population were living at risk of (financial) poverty in 2003; that is 73 million people. Some groups are particularly at risk, such as single parents (34%), large families (27%) and the unemployed (42%). It is not just a matter of income. Poverty and material deprivation are often deepened by an inability to participate fully in social life, as a result of inadequate access to employment, education and training, housing, transport or health services. As rightly emphasised in the Technical Annex to the 2006 Joint Report, "particular concerns are raised when children are growing up in a jobless household, as the absence of a working adult as a role model could be a factor affecting the educational and future labour market achievement of children" (European Commission, 2006b, page 18). In 2005, the proportion of children living in jobless households was 9.6% for the EU-25 as a whole, ranging from 2.7% in Slovenia to 16.5% in the United Kingdom. More details on the data on poverty and social exclusion can be found in Chapter 3.

Given the continuing high levels of poverty and social exclusion there is, as the 2005 Joint Report on Social Protection and Social Inclusion concluded, a need for "both perseverance and ambition". Perseverance is essential, as the EU has yet to make substantial progress in reducing the extent of poverty and social exclusion. We are still talking of tens of millions of people at risk. Ambition is justified "because the process of collective action by all stakeholders across the EU is now firmly anchored" (European Commission, 2005b, page 16). The machinery has been put in place, and expectations have been raised.

To the long-standing concerns about the overall extent of poverty and social exclusion are now added new policy preoccupations. We are observing changes in the composition of the excluded population. Traditional priorities were with the elderly, lacking adequate pensions, and with unemployed breadwinners. A generation ago, awareness grew of the problems of single parent families, and of the disabled. Today we are witnessing renewed concerns about people who are working but who live in a household at-risk-of-poverty, and about children living at-risk-of-poverty, issues that are interconnected. We return to the issue of child poverty in Section 1.2 and in Chapters 3, 4 and 5.

Enlargement

The 2004 Joint Report on Social Inclusion noted, "with Enlargement, the Union will have to face new and comparatively greater challenges in promoting social inclusion" (European Commission, 2004b, page 12). Before accession, the Commission engaged in a bilateral cooperation process, which led to each new Member State drafting a *Joint Inclusion Memorandum* (JIM, see Section 2.2), with the aim of identifying the key social issues and the major policies in place or planned. In July 2004, the 10 new Member States submitted their first National Action Plans on social inclusion (NAPs/inclusion, see Section 2.2). From the information contained in the NAPs/inclusion and in the EU analyses by the Commission and Member States, taking the form of *Joint Reports* and *Commission Staff Working Papers* (see Section 2.2), one obtains a picture of poverty and social exclusion in the EU and how it has been affected by Enlargement. In Chapter 3 we examine this in detail, showing how the impact of Enlargement differs across different dimensions of social exclusion.

At the same time, Enlargement, and the prospect of further new Member States, raises a number of issues. Just as the new Member States have had to adapt dynamically to the evolution of EU policy, such as the Lisbon Agenda, so the Union has to adapt to its augmented composition. There is now a considerably wider range of per capita incomes across Member States. How does this affect the way in which we conceive and measure poverty and social exclusion? Do we need to reconsider the role of relative poverty risk and absolute deprivation? Enlargement has brought into the EU new societies with different histories and cultures, which are reflected in differences in social institutions. How do these affect the measurement of exclusion and the implications for policy? Policy learning can now draw on a richer variety of sources. Enlargement has also increased the concentration of Member States by size: the smallest third of countries in fact have fewer than 5% of the total EU population, whereas the largest third of countries have 80% of the population. Increased population concentration is going to raise more sharply the question as to whether we should give any additional weight to smaller countries when calculating EU averages.

Global poverty

This book is about Europe and the European Union. It is important, however, to bear in mind that issues of social exclusion present themselves to an even greater degree on a global scale. It was for this reason that, at the Millennium Summit in September 2000, the states of the United Nations set out a vision of a global partnership for development, directed at the achievement of certain targets. Specifically, 189 countries signed up to the Millennium Development Goals (MDGs). The concrete goals include the halving by 2015 of the proportion of people living in extreme poverty, halving the proportion hungry, and halving the proportion lacking access to safe drinking water. The objectives include the achievement of universal primary education and gender equality in education, the achievement by 2015 of a three-quarters decline in maternal mortality and a two-thirds decline in mortality among children under five. They include halting and reversing the spread of HIV/AIDS and providing special assistance to AIDS orphans. There is an evident parallel with the social indicators agreed by the EU at Laeken.

Achievement of these goals depends critically on the actions of the developing countries, but it also depends on the policies of rich countries. The European Union has a particular responsibility in this regard. Fears that the establishment of a customs union diverts trade, at the expense of third parties, have been expressed since the founding of the European Economic Community. James Meade (1962), for example, argued that the key test for the United Kingdom in deciding whether or not to join should be the treatment of Commonwealth countries. The Common Agricultural Policy is important, but the impact on manufactured goods is also significant, with quantitative restrictions limiting the opportunities for the Newly Industrialising Countries (NICs). To this have been added concerns about the impact of domestic policy, such as subsidies, regional assistance and public procurement. In its enthusiasm to drive forward the European project, the Union has often emphasised the advantages to Europe's citizens and downplayed the external impact.

Given the ambition of the EU to be an outward-looking, not a purely inward-looking community, it is therefore essential that its policy choices should be seen in a global context. The MDGs provide not only a point of reference but also a reminder that our concerns extend beyond the boundaries of Europe. As it is put in the Communication from the Commission on the 2005 Review of the EU Sustainable Development Strategy, "Europe's future can only be seen in this global context" (European Commission, 2005g, page 3; see also below, Section 2.5).

1.2 The relaunched Lisbon Strategy and the Social Agenda 2005–2010

This book on the development of the Social Inclusion Process is written at a time when the European debate is dominated by the economic challenges faced by the EU. The Lisbon aspiration that Europe will become "a dynamic knowledge-based economy with more and better jobs" does not seem closer to realisation than six years ago. If anything, the challenge posed by globalisation seems greater. Job creation has proved elusive, and Member States are more and more concerned about the failure of their growth rates to match those of the United States. In November 2004 a High-Level Group chaired by Wim Kok reported on progress towards the Lisbon objectives and recommended that overriding priority be given to economic and employment growth policies (European Communities, 2004). The *Kok Report* argued that fulfilment of the social objectives would result from progress in these two areas: primacy should therefore be given to job creation.

The change in direction advocated by the Kok Group was reflected in the Spring Report prepared by the Commission for the March 2005 meeting of EU Heads of State and Government (European Commission, 2005a and 2005e). The March 2005 European Council in turn concluded that "it is essential to relaunch the Lisbon Strategy without delay and re-focus priorities on growth and employment. Europe must renew the basis of its competitiveness, increase its growth potential and its productivity and strengthen social cohesion, placing the main emphasis on knowledge, innovation and the optimisation of human capital" (paragraph 5). At the same time, however, the European Council made it clear that the other dimensions of the Strategy were to be retained. As may be seen from paragraph 36, with which we headed this book, the March 2005 Presidency Conclusions contained explicit references to the pursuit of the social inclusion objective. The motto adopted by the Commission for the second phase of the Social Agenda 2005–2010 underlines "jobs and opportunities for all" but also calls for a "social Europe". The Social Agenda says that the Commission will "put forward the idea of a European Year of combating poverty and social exclusion in 2010" (European Commission, 2005d, page 10). This approach was reinforced in the Conclusions of the March 2006 European Council. In paragraph 69 the Conclusions stressed that:

> The new strategy for jobs and growth provides a framework where economic, employment and social policy mutually reinforce each other, ensuring that parallel progress is made on employment creation, competitiveness, and social cohesion in compliance with European values. For the European social model to be sustainable, Europe needs to step up its efforts to create more economic growth, a higher level of employment and productivity while strengthening social inclusion and social protection in line with the objectives provided for in the Social Agenda.

Furthermore, in paragraph 72 of the Conclusions, the European Council reaffirmed "the objective of the Partnership for growth and jobs that steps have to be taken to make a decisive impact on the reduction of poverty and social exclusion by 2010".

Here we seek to examine how the Social Inclusion Process can be advanced in the new context set by the March 2005 and March 2006 Presidency Conclusions and the Social Agenda 2005–2010. In this context, social policy has two roles. First, it contributes to combating poverty and promoting social inclusion, which remains an important objective of national but also EU policy. While giving priority to employment and growth, the Presidency Conclusions safeguarded the social dimension of the Lisbon Strategy. As it was put by Luxembourg Prime Minister Jean-Claude Juncker in a speech to the European

Parliament in January 2005, "when we draw up the mid-term review of our strategy, we must keep its three dimensions together: economic, social, and environmental" (Luxembourg Presidency website). He went on "I say yes to competitiveness; I say no to abandoning our social and ecological goals". As set out by the Commission in the Social Agenda 2005–2010, modernised social protection is a key component of the Lisbon mid-term review: "Member States have already sought to make their national minimum income schemes more effective. However, many people are still in considerable difficulties and are obtaining neither employment nor the national minimum income protection" (European Commission, 2005d, page 10).

The second role is that social policy, if properly designed, can contribute to employment and economic growth. One of the unique selling points of Europe is that European social protection, in its diverse forms, allows structural change to be achieved without an unacceptable human cost. It is no accident that the European Communities had their origins, at least in part, in the need to restructure the basic (coal and steel) industries of Europe. This does not mean that the system of social protection devised for the 1950s and 1960s is appropriate today. Europe needs constantly to reform and renew its welfare state, but at the heart is a partnership, not an antagonism, between economic and social policies. This is recognised clearly in the subtitle of the 2005 publication by OECD, *How Active Social Policy Can Benefit Us All*. As the OECD report says, "while traditional social policy continues to be needed [...] this is not enough – it is also essential to emphasise an active approach that focuses on investing in people's productive potential" (OECD, 2005, page 39).

The approach that has been emphasised in the 24 "*Integrated guidelines for economic and employment policies (2005–2008)*" (see Section 2.3), proposed by the European Commission (European Commission, 2005h) and formally adopted by the Council on 12 July 2005 (after a few amendments and following political endorsement by the June 2005 European Council), is that of seeking synergies. For instance: "Implement employment policies aiming at achieving full employment, improving quality and productivity at work, and strengthening social and territorial cohesion" (Integrated Guideline for Growth and Jobs No. 17, Annex 2 to the Presidency Conclusions of the June 2005 European Council).

Children mainstreaming

The two roles of social policy are well illustrated by the explicit reference to child poverty in the EU Presidency Conclusions of March 2005 (in paragraph 36) and March 2006 (in paragraph 72). In the 2006 Conclusions the European Council specifically asked the Member States "to take necessary measures to rapidly and significantly reduce child poverty, giving all children equal opportunities, regardless of their social background". More generally, both European Councils stressed the need for investment in the youth of Europe. The 2005 European Council specifically adopted the European Pact for Youth, and the 2006 European Council urged its implementation. The Pact – see Box 1.1 – calls upon Member States to give priority under their national social inclusion policy "to improving the situation of the most vulnerable young people, particularly those in poverty, and to initiatives to prevent educational failure" (see Annex 1 to March 2005 Presidency Conclusions).

Box 1.1: The European Pact for Youth (Summary from March 2005 EU Presidency Conclusions)

"The Youth Pact aims to improve the education, training, mobility, vocational integration and social inclusion of young Europeans, while facilitating the reconciliation of working life and family life."

"The European Council calls on the Union and Member States, each within the limits of its own powers and in particular under the European employment strategy and under the social inclusion strategy, to draw upon the following lines of action:

- Employment, integration and social advancement
- Education, training and mobility
- Reconciliation of working life and family life."

The emergence of child poverty as an EU issue is a good example of the dynamics of policy making in the Union. When the first NAPs/inclusion were drawn up in 2001, only a few Member States highlighted the issue of children living in households at risk of poverty. The United Kingdom stood out for having adopted in 1999 a high-profile commitment to eradicating child poverty in 20 years and halving it in 10 years (Blair, 1999). But there was increasing recognition of the problem in other Member States in the next few years. As was observed in the 2004 Joint Report on Social Inclusion, "in most countries children experience levels of income poverty that are higher than those for adults" (European Commission, 2004b, page 17). The Joint Report notes the vulnerability of children in households where no one is in employment, but also draws attention to increasing concerns about in-work poverty.[3] Against this background, the European Commission commissioned a thematic study to analyse policies that are effective in reducing and preventing child poverty (Hoelscher, 2004).

The risks of poverty and social exclusion among children are important in their own right, but they also have implications for the future. Investment in children today is crucial, as children experiencing poverty and social exclusion "face the risk of losing choices" (Kutsar, 2005). Indeed, as noted by the *Conseil de l'Emploi, des Revenus et de la Cohésion sociale* (CERC) in their June 2005 Report, "poverty affects not only children's well-being at the moment when resources are insufficient, but also children's *well-becoming* [*'bien-devenir'*]. It hinders their capacity to develop, to build the required capabilities, including knowledge capital, cultural capital, social capital, health capital" (2005, page 6).

The essential nature of an investment in children has been emphasised by the Commission: "Material deprivation among children must be a matter of serious concern, as it is generally recognised to affect their development and future opportunities" (European Commission, 2004b, page 17). This led the 2004 Joint Report to call for action to end "poverty and social exclusion among children as a key step to combat the intergenerational inheritance of poverty with a particular focus on early intervention and early education initiatives which identify and support children and poor families" (European Commission, 2004b, page 35). This also led the EPSCO Council to emphasise in their *"Key Messages"* to the March 2005 meeting of Heads of State and Government, that "priorities for action [in the area of social inclusion] include preventing child poverty" (Council, 2005).

In France, the 2004 Report by the CERC noted that addressing child poverty was vital for two reasons:

> Most theories of social justice agree upon the duty for a society to compensate for the inequalities suffered by people who are in no way responsible for the situation they are in. This applies to children more than for any other persons. The second reason is that poverty suffered in one's childhood increases the risk of being poor as an adult. (CERC, 2004, page 5)

Or, put differently, children experiencing poverty are "at risk of entering a trans-generational cycle of poverty" (Hoelscher, 2004, page 110). The 2004 CERC Report concluded "social justice goes hand in hand with efficiency when emphasising the importance of the fight against child poverty" (page 5).

A focus on children may appear to be ignoring the very real needs of other key groups, notably older people, who still face serious problems of poverty and social exclusion in a number of Member States. It is for this reason important to think in terms of the *life-course as a whole*. The interests of the old and the young are bound together, by macro–economics as well as by family ties. This led the High-Level Group on the future of social policy in an enlarged European Union to put forward a "new intergenerational pact" based on a "positive perception of the future and a new intergenerational balance" (European Commission, 2004e, page 7). The policies proposed by the Group included a basic income for children, delivered by Member States, and measures to "allow young couples to have the number of children they desire". The intergenerational approach has been highlighted by the European Commission in the Social Agenda 2005–2010, which proposes a Green Paper on the intergenerational dimension, to analyse "the future challenges in the relations between the generations and in the position of families" (European Commission, 2005d, page 4). It was picked up in the first line of the Annex to the March 2005 EU Presidency Conclusions describing the European Pact for Youth, which referred to the "background of Europe's ageing population". The 24 "Integrated guidelines for growth and jobs (2005–2008)" agreed in July 2005 include as Guideline 18 "Promote a lifecycle approach to work" (Annex 2 to the Presidency Conclusions of the June 2005 European Council). The Commission Green Paper "Confronting demographic change: a new solidarity between the generations" calls for a global approach to the "working life cycle" (European Commission, 2005j, page 8).

It is essential to emphasise that policy measures for fighting child "poverty" have to be *multi-dimensional*. They need to cover the various dimensions of social exclusion and should therefore not focus solely on families' financial resources:

> It is not only money that matters, but rather a complex interplay of different factors [...] The reduction of child poverty [...] is not just a by-product of general anti-poverty strategies but demands for an explicit and integrated strategy of child, family and women-friendly policies that
> • first of all make children and families in general and child poverty in particular a political priority,
> • secure and increase the financial resources of families,
> • enhance child development and well-being,
> • include the most vulnerable. (Hoelscher, 2004, page 110)

Therefore, "no single policy alone can be successful in the fight against child poverty. Necessary are a comprehensive and integrated approach and the implementation of a policy mix that meets the complexity of children's life situations" (Hoelscher, 2004, page iv).

The key role – for today's living standards and for tomorrow's productivity and social cohesion – leads us to take investment in children as the recurring case study of our book. Chapters 3 to 5 cover a wide range of topics, but in each case a thread that runs through them is that of "children mainstreaming". We have used the word "mainstreaming" advisedly, rather than the words "target groups" that appear in the Presidency Conclusions. Our purpose is not to single out a particular priority group; poverty and social exclusion are unacceptable for all groups in society. Rather, our aim is to suggest, as with gender mainstreaming,[4] a perspective to approaching the general problem of poverty and social exclusion. For us "children mainstreaming" involves viewing social inclusion from a child's perspective and implies integrating a concern with the well-being and social inclusion of children into all areas of policy making.

1.3 Contents of the book

The next Chapter (Chapter 2) provides the social policy background to the book. It presents a brief historical account of the development of EU cooperation in social policy from the Treaty of Rome to the re-focused Lisbon Strategy post-March 2005.[5] It describes what led up to the EU *social processes* that were launched following the Lisbon Strategy, and more particularly the *Social Inclusion Process* and the *Open Method of Coordination* in the social field. It takes account of the 2004 Enlargement and the challenges faced by new Member States as a result of the developments that have taken place between the Copenhagen criteria of EU accession adopted in 1993 and the adoption of the Lisbon Strategy. It discusses the role of indicators in terms of the Social Inclusion Process and presents the set of common indicators for poverty and social exclusion agreed to date and the wider *Structural Indicators*. It highlights the changes arising from the 2005 *mid-term review* of the Lisbon Strategy leading to the adoption, by the March 2006 European Council, of new working arrangements and revised objectives for the streamlined Open Method of Coordination on Social Protection and Social Inclusion. In each case, it seeks to flag the key issues for future consideration.

The book then consists of four main Chapters:

• Exploring statistics on poverty and social exclusion in the EU (Chapter 3),
• Strengthening policy analysis (Chapter 4),
• EU indicators for poverty and social exclusion (Chapter 5),
• Taking forward the EU Social Inclusion Process (Chapter 6).

As indicated above, the risks of poverty and social exclusion remain core problems for the EU. Development of an effective strategy for fighting these problems requires a firm understanding of the underlying mechanisms. At the level of individual Member States, considerable efforts have been made to analyse the causes of poverty and social exclusion, and the findings are reflected, to varying degrees, in their National Action Plans. As part of the Social Inclusion Process, the EU has assembled a rich body of information about the different dimensions of social exclusion. The potential value of this information is well illustrated by the very informative Technical Annex to the 2006 Joint Report on Social Protection and Social Inclusion (European Commission, 2006b). In Chapter 3, we explore how the social indicators can be used to "tell a story" about differences across Member States, about the impact of Enlargement, and about the relation between different dimensions of social exclusion. Even restricting ourselves to the body of aggregated information now represented by the EU social indicators, we suggest that a lot can be learned.

One conclusion from Chapter 3 is that we need to strengthen policy analysis. This applies in the case of the risk of poverty but also to other dimensions of social exclusion. In Chapter 4, we begin by examining the treatment of policy analysis presented in the NAPs/inclusion prepared in 2003 by EU-15 countries and in 2004 by the new Member States as well as the EU analysis of these national reports in Joint Report and Commission Report (European Commission, 2004b and 2004d). We ask how far this gives answers to the central questions. How far will the announced policies go towards achieving Europe's social objectives? Are there realistic policies that could achieve these objectives?

Chapter 4 sets out two main types of policy analysis: modelling the impact on representative families, and using household survey and/or administrative data to simulate the impact of policy changes. It argues that, by careful consideration of the institutional structure of social protection in each Member State, coupled with representative data for their populations, it is possible to provide a common analytical framework for policy analysis, to complement the common indicators. In this way, a real step forward can be taken in EU comparative policy analysis.

Social indicators play a key role in the policy analysis. In Chapter 2 we describe the social indicators agreed at Laeken in 2001 and summarise the outcome of the subsequent refinements and extensions. The development of indicators is a dynamic procedure, and in Chapter 5 we consider some of the ways in which it could usefully be taken further. Our objective is not to provide a full history of the evolution of the social indicators that have been commonly agreed at EU level, but to take the current indicators as our starting point and to look to the future. In the light of experience with the use of the common indicators, and in particular following on the accession to the EU of 10 new Member States with relatively low average living standards, it is timely to revisit certain aspects of the content and use of the set of indicators to see whether improvements can be suggested, whether they can be further enriched and made more policy-relevant. Moreover, the new EU data source (*Community Statistics on Income and Living Conditions* (EU-SILC)), which is to become the EU reference source for income, poverty and social exclusion as from the 2007 Joint Report on Social Protection and Social Inclusion, raises some new issues regarding the common indicators already in use especially with regard to the income concept(s) to be used for calculating the income-based common indicators. Chapter 5 discusses the need to balance the development of indicators to cover several areas not adequately covered by the currently available set against the dilution that might ensue if there were to be a proliferation of indicators. We also briefly discuss comparisons with non-EU industrialised countries.

In Chapter 6 we turn to the implications for carrying forward the EU Social Inclusion Process. How can the Social Inclusion Process – now that it has been streamlined with the other social processes – be carried forward without losing the post-Lisbon momentum? The Chapter examines the potential role of target setting. Targeting was already in use at the EU level in the case of employment, and the March 2002 Barcelona European Council urged Member States to set national targets for social inclusion. Chapter 6 examines the use of targets at the national level in the NAPs/inclusion of Member States and what is involved in moving from indicators to targets at the EU level. A necessary condition to guarantee a credible and meaningful Social Inclusion Process is to truly embed it in domestic policy making. Chapter 6 goes on to consider how progress could be made towards better anchoring the Process in domestic policies, and towards better integrating social inclusion, employment and economic policies at the national and sub-national (regional and/or local) levels. In this context, the Chapter underlines the pivotal role that the *restructured* NAPs/inclusion can play as a key strand of the streamlined OMC on social protection and social inclusion. It makes practical suggestions regarding the way Member States could in future re-focus and reorganise their NAPs/inclusion into actual "action plans" (i.e. strategic planning documents). Following on from this, the Chapter emphasises the need for *joined-up Government*, committed political and administrative leadership, and parliamentary scrutiny to guarantee a credible and meaningful Social Inclusion Process. It also discusses the need to establish a scheme of (*ex ante* and *ex post*) systematic policy assessments, as well as the importance of raising the awareness of the EU Social Inclusion Process and of further mobilising the different actors involved in the fight against poverty and social exclusion at the sub-national, national and EU levels.

Finally, Chapter 7 summarises our assessment and views about the way forward. We hope that these conclusions will be of value to the European Commission, to Member States, to NGOs, to the social science research community, and to the individual citizens of Europe. We should indeed emphasise the fact that this book has several target audiences. It is for this reason that we cover in Chapter 2 the history of EU cooperation in social policy. While this material may be known to those who are actively engaged in the EU social processes, there are many who are unaware of, and yet interested in, the background. One of the limitations of the Social Inclusion Process to date is the low level of awareness. The adoption of the Social Agenda 2005–2010, for example, has not been widely reported in the press. We have therefore sought to make the book accessible to those not already engaged in these processes, and to those who are specialists in one, but not all, of the different dimensions. There is at present too little communication between specialists, and it is not easy to keep up with a rapidly changing field. Material that is familiar to one group is new to another. We also believe that it is important that the debate should not be limited to technical specialists. Many of the questions may appear largely technical, but behind such questions often lie fundamental matters of judgement. To give just one example, it may be thought that we can leave to statisticians the choice of the equivalence scale: the method by which incomes are adjusted to allow for differences in the composition of households. Yet the choice of scale affects both the level and composition of poverty, and may therefore affect our view as to whether child poverty, or poverty among older people, should be our priority. A diverse readership is what we are *deliberately* seeking. We have therefore erred in the direction of inclusion, and apologise to those readers who have everything at their finger-tips.

Notes

[1] The European Council, which brings together the EU Heads of State and Government and the President of the European Commission, defines the general political guidelines of the EU. The decisions taken at the European Council meetings (or "Summits") are summarised in "Presidency Conclusions" available from the website of the EU Council of Ministers: http://www.consilium.europa.eu/showPage.ASP?lang=en. All Presidency

websites can also be found at this address. Since the March 2000 Lisbon Summit, the European Council holds every spring a meeting that is more particularly devoted to economic and social questions – the "Spring European Council".

[2] Updated national figures, as they become available, can be downloaded free of charge from the website of Eurostat, the statistical office of the European Communities: http://epp.eurostat.cec.eu.int/portal/page?_pageid=1090,30070682,1090_30298591&_dad=portal&_schema=PORTAL.

[3] The European Parliament in a 2005 Report on social inclusion in the new Member States called on new Member States' Governments to devote particular attention to eliminating child poverty. (European Parliament, 2005, page 5).

[4] On gender mainstreaming in the EU process, see, among others, Booth (2002), Atkinson and Meulders (2004), and Van der Molen and Novikova (2005).

[5] For direct access to EU law (including Treaties, international agreements, etc.), see EUR-Lex EU website: http://eur-lex.europa.eu.

TWO

The EU Social Inclusion Process
and the key issues

Even though the founding fathers of the EU had expected social progress to evolve naturally from the economic progress generated by the Common Market, for many years the Single European Market and the European Monetary Union largely eclipsed the social dimension of the EU. It is only since March 2000, when EU Heads of State and Government adopted the *Lisbon Strategy*, that social policy has truly become a specific focus of attention for EU cooperation. In this Chapter, the main emphasis is on the Lisbon Strategy and the EU *social processes* that were launched in this context, and more particularly the *Social Inclusion Process*, but the Chapter begins in 1957 with the Treaty of Rome. We believe that it is important to understand the origins of EU cooperation in social policy, and the extent to which the current processes have roots in the past. Such a long-run historical perspective reduces the danger of being over-influenced by today's immediate political pressures.

2.1 The long road towards EU cooperation in social policy

In March 1957, when signing the Treaty of Rome establishing the European Economic Community, the then six EU Heads of State and Government resolved to ensure both the economic and the social progress of their countries by developing a Common Market, in the optimistic belief that the economic progress resulting from economic integration would automatically translate into social progress.

In the early days of the European Communities, social policy received little attention, and the Community institutions were provided with very limited powers in the social field. Social policy was, to a large extent, a means towards achieving other objectives. The restructuring of the coal and steel industries, through the European Coal and Steel Community, involved social measures in aid of training and to finance adjustment. There was concern with removing barriers to labour mobility and ensuring that differences in the costs of social protection did not prevent competition in the supply of goods. But in January 1974, the EU Council of Ministers (hereafter the Council) adopted its "Resolution concerning a social action programme" (Council, 1974). Since the adoption of this text, the Council has established various programmes to combat poverty and social exclusion.

The Poverty Programmes

First, the Council adopted its Decision of July 1975 concerning a programme of pilot schemes and studies to combat poverty, amended in 1980 by a Decision on a supplementary programme to combat poverty (Council, 1975 and 1980); this programme, which covered the period from December 1975 to November 1981, is better known as the *Poverty 1 Programme*.[1] This was followed by the *Poverty 2 Programme* (Council, 1985), providing for specific Community action to combat poverty, covering the period from January 1985 to December 1988, and by the *Poverty 3 Programme* (Council, 1989b), establishing a medium-term Community action programme concerning the economic and social integration of the economically and socially less privileged groups in society, for the period from July 1989 to June 1994. In order to continue and extend the actions undertaken under Poverty 3, the European Commission submitted in September 1993 a proposal for a Council Decision establishing a medium-term action programme to combat exclusion and promote solidarity.[2] This *Poverty 4* proposal, which envisaged a programme to be implemented between July 1994 and December 1999, was not adopted by the Council because of opposition from Germany and the United Kingdom, whose objections were based on the *subsidiarity principle* and the lack of proof of the programme's effectiveness (the adoption required a unanimous vote in the Council).

The Poverty Programmes 1–3 allowed considerable progress to be made in the description, quantification and understanding of poverty and social exclusion. However, it is only from the end of the 1990s, and even more so from March 2000 when the Lisbon Strategy was launched, that social protection and inclusion have become *specific policy areas* for EU cooperation. In order to understand better the policy dynamic that has progressively led to this cooperation, it is worth looking at six "EU texts" that have played a particularly important role in this shift. The six key texts are set out in Appendix 2a.

Six key EU texts on social protection and social inclusion

The first such text is a Council Resolution on "Combating Social Exclusion" (Council, 1989a) adopted in September 1989, that is a couple of months after the launch of the Poverty 3 Programme. In this Resolution, the Council emphasised that "combating social exclusion may be regarded as an important part of the social dimension of the internal market" and points to "the effectiveness of *coordinated, coherent development policies* based on active participation by local and national bodies and by the people involved". It highlighted the need for action at the then European Economic Community (EEC) level, as well as by Member States, undertaking "to continue and, as necessary, to step up the efforts undertaken *in common* as well as those made by each Member State, and to pool their knowledge and assessments of the phenomena of exclusion". We see therefore, 17 years ago, two elements were already important: (i) the linking of social policies and economic policies (at that time, the completion of the internal market); and (ii) a role for the Community as well as the Member States in the social sphere. This was followed up in the Council Recommendation of June 1992 (the second text in Appendix 2a) on "Common criteria concerning sufficient resources and social assistance in social protection systems", which urged EU Member States to recognise the "basic right of a person to sufficient resources and social assistance to live in a manner compatible with human dignity as a part of a comprehensive and consistent drive to combat social exclusion".

The form to be taken by Community involvement became clearer in a third text adopted one month later, in July 1992: a Council Recommendation on the "Convergence of social protection objectives and policies". Arguing that "comparable trends in most of the Member States may lead to common problems (in particular the ageing of the population, changing family situations, a persistently high level of unemployment and the spread of poverty and forms of poverty)", the Council recommended that this "de facto convergence" should be further promoted by establishing what was termed a "*convergence strategy*" and which consists basically of the identification of "*common objectives*". The Recommendation suggests that these "*fundamental objectives of the Community*" should act as guiding principles in the development of national social protection systems, while stressing that Member States remain free to determine how their systems should be financed and organised. In other words, the Council acknowledged that Member States' systems are based on common values and objectives (see the third text in Appendix 2a). This laid the basis for the social policy dimension to be developed under subsidiarity.[3]

As we have seen from the rejection of the Poverty 4 Programme proposal, this approach did not immediately take root. This is an important lesson of EU history. While there is a strong line of continuity running through the development of EU cooperation in social policy, movement has not always been in one direction. This led the Commission to advance the argument, in the fourth text on "Modernising and Improving Social Protection in the European Union" (European Commission, 1997), that social protection systems, far from being an economic burden, can act as a *productive factor* that can contribute to economic and political stability and that can help EU economies to perform better. The EU debate on the economic relevance of social protection had been launched a few months before the publication of this important Commission Communication, at the conference on Social policy and economic performance" organised under the Dutch Presidency (Amsterdam, 23–25 January 1997). As stated a few months later by A.P.W. Melkert, the then Minister of Social Affairs and Employment of the Netherlands:

> By maintaining stability, social policy can actually contribute
> considerably to improving economic performance. New economic
> developments such as globalisation, may call for a certain amount of
> flexibility, but in no way should this lead to a dismantling of social

protection. The maintenance of the fundamental principles of social cohesion and solidarity is not only a major social objective, but also an important productive factor. Social policies may have to be readjusted to economic developments, but at the same time they should maintain a high level of protection. Achieving such an even-handed policy is, in my view, the challenge of the new European social dimension for the next decade. (Melkert, 1997; see also Begg *et al*, 2004; European Commission, 2004g; Fouarge, 2003)

These arguments undoubtedly contributed to the acceptance of the new legal base for the fight against social exclusion incorporated in the Treaty of Amsterdam signed in October 1997 (see fifth text in Appendix 2a). Quoting again from Melkert:

With the Amsterdam Treaty the EU shall be more properly equipped to deal with social issues. The EU [...] will be an organisation able to stand upright when facing its task in the 21st Century. The resulting new social dimension should not only benefit European citizens, but also prove to be an asset for our economic performance. (Melkert, 1997)

A concrete implementation of this new legal base (the sixth text in Appendix 2a) was the July 1999 Communication by the European Commission on "A concerted strategy for modernising social protection" (European Commission, 1999). In its Conclusions of 17 December 1999, the Council endorsed the four broad objectives identified by the Commission: to make work pay and to provide secure income, to make pensions safe and pensions systems sustainable, to promote social inclusion and to ensure high quality and sustainable health care. The Council welcomed the Commission's proposal to establish a new "high-level group"; a group that subsequently became the EU *Social Protection Committee* (SPC). This Committee is comprised of high-level officials from the relevant ministries in each Member State and reports to the EU Ministers in charge of social policy: the EPSCO Council of Ministers. The Council recalled that "social protection which guarantees an adequate safety net for all citizens is also an *investment* in balanced economic development and a significant competitive advantage in a globalising economy and recognised that the aspects relating to finance are common to all the (above) objectives of social protection".

With its December 1999 Conclusions, the Council launched EU cooperation in the modernisation of social protection on the basis of "a structured and permanent dialogue, follow-up and *exchange of information, experience and good practice* between the Member States, concerning social protection", while respecting the subsidiarity principle and in particular the Member States' competence for the organisation and financing of their social protection systems. Equally important, the Council emphasised that "the aim of the European Union should be to ensure a link between economic and social development". It is worth noting that the Council supported the Commission's suggestion to "associate the European Parliament with this process", an association which has not yet been truly realised; we return to this "democratic deficit" in Chapter 6.

Conclusions

From this brief historical account, we can see that there has been quite strong continuity in the basic ideas underlying the development of EU cooperation in social policy: the setting of common objectives, with Member States free to determine how they are achieved, and an integrated view of economic and social policy making, seeking to emphasise the positive ways in which social policy can contribute to economic performance. The fact that progress has been made unevenly should not be allowed to obscure the underlying continuity.

2.2 The EU social processes and the Open Method of Coordination

A major reason why, as from December 1999, Member States started cooperating at EU level in the field of social protection and inclusion policy, is the growing acknowledgment that national social protection systems face common challenges demanding reforms and modernisation – for instance, concerning the need to fight poverty and social exclusion, and to ensure financially sustainable and socially adequate pensions and health care systems for an ageing population.

With the Amsterdam Treaty and then, one step further, with the Nice Treaty (signed in February 2001 and in force since February 2003), EU level cooperation and coordination processes have progressively developed to "support and complement" Member States' activities in various fields relevant to social policy, which include "social security and social protection of workers", "combating of social exclusion" and "modernisation of social protection systems". For those fields, the Council, while taking into account "the diverse forms of national practices" under subsidiarity, is entitled to "adopt measures designed to encourage cooperation between Member States through initiatives aimed at improving knowledge, developing exchanges of information and best practices, promoting innovative approaches and evaluating experiences" (Nice Treaty, Articles 136 and 137).

As we have seen in the previous section, the links between the economic and social spheres were increasingly considered as being of central importance and as complementary. This was underlined in the aforementioned strategic goal adopted at the March 2000 Lisbon European Council that the EU should become by the next decade "the most competitive and dynamic knowledge-based economy in the world capable of sustainable economic growth with more and better jobs and greater social cohesion". A part of the reasoning behind this core target is that the social dimension is expected to make an essential contribution to overall socio-economic policy. In June 2001, the Gothenburg European Council agreed on a strategy for *sustainable development* by adding the environmental dimension to the original three pillars of the Lisbon Strategy.

As emphasised in the Joint Report on Social Protection and Social Inclusion adopted by the Council in March 2005:

> At its heart, the Lisbon Strategy promotes the idea of a positive interaction between economic, employment and social policies. It aims at promoting a model of sustainable development for the Union which raises the standard of living of all European citizens by combining economic growth with a strong emphasis on social cohesion and the preservation of the environment. In so doing, it stresses the need to improve EU level coordination mechanisms in order to foster consistent and mutually reinforcing policies in the economic, employment and social areas. (European Commission, 2005b, page 2)

Recent Commission thinking on social protection and social inclusion are reflected in the *Social Agenda* (European Commission, 2005d) and the *EU Sustainable Development Strategy* (European Commission, 2005f and 2005g). Furthermore, the December 2005 Commission's Communication "On the Review of the Sustainable Development Strategy" (European Commission, 2005k) reinforces the importance of social inclusion objectives (see Section 2.5).

Open Method of Coordination (OMC)

The EU social processes that have been launched since the March 2000 Lisbon European Council are, in chronological order, the *Social Inclusion Process*, the *Pensions Process* and the *Health Care and Long-Term Care Process*. EU cooperation in the field of *Making Work Pay* is also under way, even if this cooperation cannot be considered as a "policy process" *per se* and if various aspects of this issue have already been, and will continue to be, addressed in the context of the Broad Economic Policy Guidelines and the Employment Guidelines. To date, EU cooperation in the social field therefore covers all four policy domains that the Council had retained back in December 1999, following on from the Commission's recommendations (see Section 2.1 above).

To take account of the diversity of national social protection systems, the Lisbon European Council, when introducing social policy as a distinct focus of attention for EU cooperation, agreed that the process should be advanced through an *Open Method of Coordination*, building on the experience with the Employment Strategy (see below). This OMC is a mutual feedback process of planning, monitoring, examination, comparison and adjustment of national (and sub-national) policies, all of this on the basis of common objectives agreed for the EU as a whole. Through this *peer review exercise* (which involves the Commission and all Member States), and thus the sharing of experience and good practices, all the countries can learn from one another and are therefore all in a position to improve their policies. With this approach, the EU has found "a way that implies a credible commitment to a social Europe" which, provided certain conditions are met, "can *effectively* lead to social progress" (Vandenbroucke, 2002a).

In its most developed form, open coordination is quite similar to the *European Employment Strategy* initiated in 1997 under the Luxembourg Presidency of the EU, whereby the European Council endorses each year a set of *Employment Guidelines* (proposed by the Commission) for the Member States, and monitors progress towards achieving the agreed objectives through reviews of *National Action Plans* for employment (NAPs/employment). A *Joint Employment Report* is then prepared jointly by the Commission and the Council on the basis of the national Plans. The European Employment Strategy has served to demonstrate how coordination at EU level, with agreed common objectives and monitoring procedures, can play a central role in the field of social policy.[4]

Since Lisbon, open coordination is applied to the *fight against poverty and social exclusion*, with the first common objectives in this area set a few months later by the December 2000 Nice European Council. The detailed content of the Nice objectives and related implementation arrangements were confirmed by the EPSCO Council at their December 2002 meeting (Council, 2002), with a few amendments stressing the importance of setting quantitative targets in National Action Plans on social inclusion (see Chapter 6), the need to strengthen the gender perspective in those Plans (in the analysis of social exclusion and in assessing policy impact), and the risks of poverty and social exclusion faced by immigrants. The Social Inclusion Process is supported by a *Programme of community action to encourage cooperation between Member States to combat social exclusion*, which was launched on 1 January 2002 to last for a period of five years. This programme aims at promoting policy analysis and the collection of statistics (e.g. the new *Community Statistics on Income and Living Conditions instrument* (EU-SILC); see Chapters 3 and 5), the exchange of good practice, and the networking across Europe of NGOs and regional and local authorities active in combating the risks of poverty and social exclusion.[5]

During the summer of 2001, the then 15 Member States submitted to the Commission their first NAPs/inclusion, covering the period 2001–3. Drawing extensively from these Plans and their *peer review*, the first *Joint Inclusion Report* was then "jointly adopted" by the Commission and the EPSCO Council, and subsequently endorsed by the Laeken European Council of December 2001 (European Commission, 2002b). The second set of Plans (for the period 2003–5) was submitted two years later, during the summer of 2003, with the resulting Joint Report adopted by the EPSCO Council in March 2004 (European Commission, 2004b). The third round of NAPs/inclusion took place in July 2004, when all 10 new Member States submitted their first Plans for the period 2004–6. These NAPs/inclusion, the analysis of which was presented in a *Commission Staff Working Paper* (European Commission, 2005c), built on the work begun in 2002 when the then accession countries and the Commission started preparing *Joint Memoranda on Social Inclusion* (JIM). For each country, the JIM outlined the situation and the key policy challenges with regard to poverty and social exclusion and described the main policies and institutions in place. The 10 JIM were all signed in December 2003 and were subsequently summarised in a Commission Staff Working Paper issued in June 2004 (European Commission, 2004d). Subsequently in 2005, JIM were also signed with Bulgaria and Romania and work has started on preparing JIM with Turkey and Croatia. In 2005, EU-15 countries prepared "Implementation Reports" on their 2003–5 NAPs/inclusion. These led to the preparation of a Commission Staff Working Document, "Social Inclusion in Europe 2006" (European Commission, 2006c), the key messages from which informed the preparation of the 2006 *Joint Report on Social Protection and Social Inclusion* (European Commission, 2006a and 2006b). Following the streamlining of the Social Protection and Social Inclusion Process (see Sections 2.3 and 6.1), all 25 Member States are to draw up new NAPs/inclusion for the period 2006–8, as part of the *National Reports for Strategies on Social Protection and Social Inclusion*, to be submitted to the Commission for the first time in September 2006.[6] (This paragraph has referred to several different types of EU documents; Box 2.1 explains the recent changes in the status of different EU reports.)

Box 2.1: Status of EU Reports post-Enlargement

As a result of the May 2004 Enlargement (and the related increase in the number of EU official languages), a large number of former *Joint Reports* (i.e. Reports adopted by both the Council and the Commission, and translated into all official languages) will be replaced by *Commission Staff Working Papers/Documents*. Even though their drafting will closely involve the Member States (in this specific case, *inter alia* through the Social Protection Committee), these documents will no longer be formal "joint" reports: it is only the Commission that will adopt them and they will not be translated into all EU official languages. As to the Joint Reports, they will have to be very short but will go on being translated into all official languages and will still be formally adopted by both the Council and the Commission.

Open coordination was later launched in the field of *pensions*, with the agreement by the Laeken European Council on a first set of 11 common objectives. In the EU cooperation under the pensions' process, there are no national *Action Plans* but rather *Strategy Reports on pensions*, in which Member States present in detail how they expect to meet the common objectives. This slight difference in wording is justified by the fact that action in the field of pensions is expected to stretch over a much longer time frame (various calculations, including projections of public expenditure on pensions, are done at least up to the year 2050) and the strategic aspect is paramount. The first Strategy Reports were submitted in September 2002 by EU-15 countries, and the results of their examination (including *peer review*) by the Commission and the Council were summarised in a Joint Report endorsed by the 2003 Spring European Council. (In the case of pensions, both the EPSCO and ECOFIN Council's formations have to adopt the Joint Report, which is essential in view of the nature of the three dimensions covered by the pensions' common objectives: safeguarding the capacity of systems to meet their social objectives, maintaining their financial sustainability and meeting changing societal needs.[7]) A first set of common indicators for pensions has been developed by the Indicators Sub-Group of the Social Protection Committee (SPC) and should contribute to strengthening the pensions' process by providing objective criteria against which to assess progress of Member States. Strategy Reports, making use of some of these indicators, were submitted in July 2005 by all 25 Member States of the enlarged EU. Following a peer review (by both the Social Protection Committee and the Economic Policy Committee) in September 2005, a Commission Staff Working Document, *Synthesis Report on adequate and sustainable pensions* (European Commission, 2005d) was adopted in February 2006.

More recently, a looser form of EU policy cooperation on *health care and long-term care* was launched by the EPSCO Council of 4 October 2004 following on from the recommendations contained in the April 2004 Commission's Communication on *Modernising social protection for the development of high-quality, accessible and sustainable health care and long-term care: Support for the national strategies using the Open Method of Coordination* (European Commission, 2004a). The first Reports are short "Preliminary Policy Statements", rather than reports *per se*, submitted in the second quarter of 2005 by all 25 EU countries. In these "statements", countries were asked to set out their views on what constitute the key challenges and the most important directions for the reform of health and long-term care systems, and to do so by reference to the three broad principles put forward in the Commissions' Communication – accessibility (based on the principles of universal access, fairness and solidarity), quality and long-term financial sustainability. With a view to contributing to the discussion on common indicators which are being developed in this area by the Indicators Sub-Group of the SPC, countries were also invited to provide information on key indicators that are used in the monitoring and steering of health and long-term care systems. The Commission prepared a note, *Review of Preliminary National Policy Statements on Health and Long-term Care*, which was discussed at the July 2005 meeting of the SPC. This note and discussion at the SPC together with the work on pensions described in the previous paragraph informed the preparation of the 2006 *Joint Report on Social Protection and Social Inclusion* and the preparation of the Commission's Communication in December 2005 on the future working arrangements and objectives of the streamlined Open Method of Coordination on social protection and social inclusion (European Commission, 2005l). Finally, the SPC is working on the question of *making work pay* in order to identify the specific contribution which social protection systems can bring to this overall objective (e.g. regarding the incentive structures of benefit systems) – see European Commission (2003a).

The modalities of the future implementation of the OMC in the social area, including the role of the European Parliament in this context, are defined in the *Treaty establishing a Constitution for Europe*,[8] which was signed on 29 October 2004 by the 25 EU Heads of State and Government. Under this as-yet-unadopted Treaty, for social policy, including "social security and social protection of workers", "the combating of social exclusion" and "the modernisation of social protection systems" (see Part III, Articles III-209 up to III-219), as well as for public health (see Article III-278), the Commission is expected to encourage cooperation between the Member States within the strict limits of subsidiarity. If the OMC is not referred to by name, it is however exactly this procedure that is suggested in this context. The Commission is indeed encouraged to take "initiatives aiming at the establishment of guidelines and *indicators*, the organisation of exchange of best practice, and the preparation of the necessary elements for periodic *monitoring* and *evaluation*". The Commission expressed the view, in its May 2003 Communication (see below: European Commission, 2003c), that in creating a streamlined process in the social policy field, methods to involve the European Parliament as appropriate and practical should be seriously explored. It is therefore worth stressing that the Treaty explicitly mentions that "the European Parliament shall be kept fully *informed*" of those Union's initiatives, without further specifications; this could be a first step towards addressing the real problem of the democratic deficit involved by the current method. The Treaty, if ratified, by promoting intergovernmental cooperation in the social protection and inclusion areas, will *de facto* provide legitimacy to intergovernmental rather than Community actions. Therefore, notwithstanding the vagueness of its wording, the importance of the new Article I-15 on "the coordination of economic and employment policies" (Part 1 of the Treaty) should not be undervalued as it opens the way to coordination (rather than intergovernmental cooperation) in the social field by specifying that "the Union may take initiatives to ensure coordination of Member States' social policies".

Conclusions

EU cooperation in the field of social policy is thus under way in four different domains, with a significant difference in the degree and nature of cooperation from one domain to the other.

2.3 From individual EU policy processes to a "Streamlined Strategy"

We have described above the four elements of the present social processes, which operate alongside the policies for economic policy and employment: the Broad

Economic Policy Guidelines and the Employment Guidelines respectively. The reader can doubtless understand a desire for "streamlining".

In December 2002, the Council approved the European Commission's proposal to establish three-year cycles for the policy coordination and synchronisation of two of the three main pillars of the Lisbon Strategy: the annual economic and employment policy coordination strategies. The policy coordination and synchronisation of these two Treaty-based strategies, or their "streamlining", was expected to translate into a *mutual feedback* between the streamlined components, allowing them to reinforce and complement each other and therefore to improve their effectiveness. At their June 2003 meeting in Thessaloniki, EU Heads of State and Government were presented for the first time with the two sets of Guidelines under the new streamlined procedure, covering the period 2003–5 (European Commission, 2002a).

Based on the same logic, and with the objectives of strengthening the social dimension of the Lisbon Strategy and enhancing the quality and coherence of the overall socio-economic governance of the EU, the Commission issued a Communication in May 2003 (European Commission, 2003c) proposing that the various *social policy processes at EU level* launched as a follow-up of Lisbon (described in the previous section) should be streamlined as from 2006. In October 2003, the Council endorsed the general approach suggested by the Commission under the condition that an agreement could be found between the Member States and the Commission on the concrete implementation of the suggested streamlining, which includes: the future nature of the individual social processes, the concrete steps towards streamlining and their respective timing (see Social Protection Committee, 2003a). The timetable for policy coordination on social issues and that for the Treaty-based Macro-economic and Employment Strategies was to be synchronised from 2006 onwards, that is, once the second round of the streamlined employment/economic strategies is launched (for the period 2006–8). This streamlining posited:

1. a *synchronisation* of the timetable for the various EU social processes, with that of the streamlined employment and macro-economic strategies; and
2. a *rationalisation* of EU cooperation in the field of social policy.

We were therefore to have had a "double streamlining": on the one hand, the streamlining of the EU social processes, and on the other hand, the synchronisation of the "streamlined social processes" with the "streamlined macro-economic and employment strategies".

Since then, however, the situation has altered. As already mentioned, the Council adopted in July 2005, 24 "*Integrated guidelines for economic and employment policies (2005–2008)*", bringing together, after some amendments, the Commission's recommendation for the Broad Economic Policy Guidelines and its proposal for the Employment Guidelines in a single coherent text. As suggested by the Commission at the March 2005 European Council (European Commission,

2005i, page 2),"a new cycle of governance" started in 2005 and is to be renewed in 2008. On the basis of the Integrated Guidelines, Member States tabled their first "National Reform Programmes" in autumn 2005. The Guidelines asked Member States to develop programmes which "respond to their needs and specific situations, and which reflect this integrated and consistent approach involving macro-economic policies, micro-economic policies, and employment" (Presidency Conclusions of the June 2005 European Council, paragraph 11). These Programmes cover a three-year period but can be reviewed in case of major changes in domestic politics. At the end of January 2006, the Commission presented its first Annual Progress Report on Growth and Jobs, "*Time to Move Up A Gear*" (European Commission, 2006f). In autumn 2006 and autumn 2007, Member States will submit to the Commission a single report on progress in implementing these programmes. EU Heads of State and Government will review progress each spring and consider any necessary adjustment of the Guidelines on the basis of analysis presented by the Commission. A Lisbon Community Programme has also been adopted, covering all actions to be undertaken at EU level in support of the goals of growth and employment, in parallel with the preparation of the Integrated Guidelines setting out action at country and EU levels. At country level, in order to improve coordination, delivery and awareness of the on-going reforms, Member States have designated a coordinator (see European Commission, 2005h and 2005i).

Alongside the new Lisbon governance cycle launched in 2005, there will be a simplification and streamlining of the reporting mechanisms under the OMC. Separate reporting will continue as part of the OMC on social protection and social inclusion. The annual Joint Report on Social Protection and Social Inclusion will remain a separate document, not be integrated into the "renewed" Lisbon Strategy, either in the Member States annual reporting to the Commission or in the Commission's reports to the Spring European Council. The OMC in the social field will continue in full, but the information relevant to the Lisbon Strategy goals will also be expected to be reflected in the National Reform Programmes. Those elements that create synergies for growth and jobs (for example, bringing more people into the labour market, modernisation of social protection systems or education and lifelong learning) can be picked up by the Commission's Annual Progress Report since they are an essential element of the renewed Lisbon Strategy (see European Commission, 2005i).

The Social Protection Committee and the European Commission have agreed detailed recommendations in relation to the new reporting and monitoring framework encompassing the social inclusion, pensions and health care areas (Social Protection Committee, 2006; Indicators Sub-Group, 2006b). The Report on Social Protection and Social Inclusion drafted by the Commission for joint adoption by the Commission and the Council prior to each Spring European Council is to comprise: i) a short main report summarising key issues and trends and assessing progress in reaching the common streamlined objectives; ii) a set of more detailed country *fiches* (covering all individual Member States); and iii) a supporting and more lengthy Commission document treating the issues in more depth. The Report will also review how social protection and social inclusion policies are contributing to the Lisbon goals of employment and growth and assess how progress towards those goals is impacting on social cohesion. The assessment will draw on the *National Reports on Strategies for Social Protection and Social Inclusion* as well as any other relevant national and EU information, and the analysis will be largely based on the newly adopted set of commonly agreed indicators covering the revised objectives for the streamlined OMC on Social Protection and Social Inclusion (see below).

Given the new structure of the overall Lisbon Strategy, it is clearly important that the expected *mutual, reinforcing feedback* be monitored closely. In particular this should involve monitoring the feedback between the Broad Economic Policy Guidelines and the Employment Guidelines, on the one hand, and the OMC in the social field (including the Social Inclusion Process, which "should be pursued by the Union and by Member States, with its multifaceted approach"; 2005 and 2006 Spring European Councils), on the other hand. The OMC in the social field should contribute to achieving the goals of growth and jobs of the re-focused Lisbon Strategy; and, at the same time, policies to promote growth and jobs should contribute to promoting social cohesion and social inclusion, which remains a key objective of the re-focused Lisbon Strategy. Following the suggestion by the EU Employment Committee and the EU Social Protection Committee in their *Joint Opinion* on the 2005–8 Integrated Guidelines for Growth and Jobs, this has been clarified in the final text of the Council Decision on the Employment Guidelines thanks to a useful addition to recital (3): "*The strengthening of social cohesion constitutes also a key element for success of the Lisbon Strategy. Conversely, as set out in the Social Agenda, the success of the European Employment Strategy will contribute to the achievement of greater social cohesion*" (Employment Committee and Social Protection Committee, 2005). In the same vein, the European Parliament in its recent Report on social inclusion in the new Member States urged their Governments "in formulating their policies, to treat social inclusion as a social problem falling under the Lisbon Strategy" (European Parliament, 2005, page 5).

However, the evidence from the first round of National Reform Programmes (NRPs) in 2005 was disappointing in that they showed that there was only limited interaction with the social processes. This was in spite of the fact that, at the country level, a lot of work took place in 2005 in the context of the OMC in the social field: the national "Preliminary Policy Statements on health and long-term care" and the "National Strategy Reports on pensions" (see Section 2.2), but also the Implementation Reports on the NAPs/inclusion (see above and see Section 2.5). Most countries did not appear to reflect on best ways to ensure that all this national material *fed into* and indeed *influenced* the formulation of their 2005 National Reform Programmes. As the 2006 *Joint Report on Social Protection and Social Inclusion* points out, the "links between the OMC and the NRPs are not always clearly drawn" (European Commission, 2006a, page 7). However, the Joint Report did identify ways in which the social processes contribute to the growth and jobs agendas. This was then reflected in the *key messages* sent from the EPSCO Council to the 2006 Spring European Council, which stressed the mutually reinforcing nature of economic, employment and social policy. They emphasised that "The challenge of ensuring that the Open Method of Coordination and the revised Lisbon process are mutually reinforcing is vital in light of the contribution that well designed social protection policies can bring to the objectives of growth and jobs" (Council, 2006a). Furthermore it was encouraging that the 2006 Joint Report on Social Protection and Social Inclusion formed part of the annual re-focused strategy "package" submitted to the Spring Summit in 2006, as had already been the case in March 2005, together with the *key messages* contained in the Joint Report as summarised by the EPSCO Council. This will hopefully continue to be the case in the future in the light of the Conclusions of the Spring 2006 European Council, which stated that "The Commission and the Council will inform *each* Spring European Council with the Joint Report on the progress in the area of social protection and social inclusion" (paragraph 70).

Looking ahead, there are some grounds for cautious optimism that the mutual interaction between the two processes will be strengthened in future. The second overarching objective of the new streamlined objectives (see Appendix 2b and Section 2.5) for the OMC on social protection and social inclusion emphasises the "effective and mutual interaction between the Lisbon objectives of greater economic growth, more and better jobs and greater social cohesion, and with the EU's Sustainable Development Strategy". This is then reinforced in the Guidelines that have been agreed between the Commission and Member States for preparing the 2006–8 National Reports on Strategies for Social Protection and Social Inclusion (Social Protection Committee, 2006). Furthermore, the new Social Protection and Social Inclusion Process is being rationalised with the "new cycle of governance" for the re-focused Lisbon Strategy and the new National Reports on Strategies for Social Protection and Social Inclusion; and within the National Reports the new NAPs/inclusion will cover the period 2006–8. Then, by 2008, there should be *full* synchronisation with the second round of the "new cycle".

However, to achieve a real interaction between the two processes a true *mainstreaming of social inclusion* in domestic policy making, at national and sub-national levels, will have to be implemented through establishing a scheme of systematic policy assessments (both *ex ante* and *ex post*). To this end, the impact of specific employment, economic and sustainable development policies on social inclusion should also be systematically monitored, so as to identify possible ways of adjusting such policies to strengthen their contribution to promoting social inclusion (see Section 6.7).[9] Mainstreaming social inclusion should in fact also be implemented at EU level: as emphasised by the European Commissioner in charge of Employment, Social Affairs and Equal Opportunities, "We must integrate the social inclusion objective in all Community policies" (Špidla, 2005).

Conclusions

In this book, we concentrate on the continuing social processes, and particularly on the Social Inclusion Process, but taking account of the synergies for growth and jobs.

2.4 Enlargement

In June 1993, the Copenhagen European Council took a decisive step towards Enlargement, by agreeing that "the associated countries in Central and Eastern Europe that so desire shall become members of the European Union" and that "accession will take place as soon as an associated country is able to assume the obligations of membership by satisfying the economic and political conditions required". It also defined the membership criteria (often referred to as the "Copenhagen criteria"), namely:

> Membership requires that the candidate country has achieved stability of institutions guaranteeing democracy, the rule of law, human rights and respect for and protection of minorities, the existence of a functioning market economy as well as the capacity to cope with competitive pressure and market forces within the Union. Membership presupposes the candidate's ability to take on the obligations of membership including adherence to the aims of political, economic and monetary union. (Presidency Conclusions)

It is on this basis that, between 31 March 1994 and 10 June 1996, in chronological order, Hungary, Poland, Romania, Slovakia, Latvia, Estonia, Lithuania, Bulgaria, the Czech Republic and finally Slovenia submitted their applications for EU membership; Cyprus and Malta had already applied in July 1990, and Turkey in April 1987. Since then Croatia (February 2003) and the Former Yugoslav Republic of Macedonia (March 2004) have also submitted their applications. In December 2002, negotiations were concluded with the 10 countries that joined the EU in May 2004. On 25 April 2005, Bulgaria and Romania became "acceding" countries. Croatia, the Former Yugoslav Republic of Macedonia and Turkey have the intermediate status of "candidate" countries. In December 2005, the Council adopted a revised Accession Partnership for Turkey; and one month later, it adopted Council Decision No 2006/35/EC on the "principles, priorities and conditions contained in the Accession Partnership with Turkey".

   In the context of our book, it is important to bear in mind that the EU that the new Members joined in May 2004 was very different from the one of 1993. This is especially true of the field of social policy (for discussion, in the case of the Czech Republic, see Potůček, 2004). In Tables 2.1a and 2.1b (see Appendix 1), we set out some of the main developments since 1993 (most of which have been described earlier in the Chapter). Those moves form an integral part of the *EU acquis*, that is, the detailed laws and rules adopted on the basis of the EU founding treaties that candidate countries have to accept and fulfil before actually joining the EU. This acquis includes of course the "soft" Open Method of Coordination, which was launched in Lisbon and has quite quickly developed over the last years as emphasised in previous Sections. It has been a huge challenge for the 10 new Member States to board a (fast) moving train; and it will be even more challenging for the acceding/candidate and future applicant countries.

2.5 The mid-term review of the Lisbon Strategy

In 2005, Member States and the European Commission carried out a *mid-term review* of the Lisbon Strategy. In this context, a major assessment of the Open Method of Coordination in the fields of pensions and social inclusion was launched at the beginning of 2005, in order to inform the decision to be taken by the Council in early 2006 concerning the implementation of a streamlined social process (i.e. covering the various EU social processes introduced above, in Section 2.2). Following an extensive process involving all the relevant actors (i.e. the different levels of Government in Member States, EU institutions, EU and national social partners, and EU and national civil society stakeholders), the Commission adopted a Communication in December 2005 setting out its proposals for new working arrangements and revised objectives for a streamlined Open Method of Coordination on social protection and social inclusion. This Communication (European Commission, 2005l), drew on a number of inputs:

1. The replies to a questionnaire that was sent to Member States and to the Social Partner and NGO organisations at European level at the beginning of 2005 and aimed at assessing how effectively the Social Inclusion Process and the Pensions' Process had been conducted since they were launched, that is, how these have impacted on their policies. Drafted by the Commission and finalised together with the SPC, this questionnaire addressed the following issues: the added value of the Open Method of Coordination in the areas of social inclusion and pensions; the appropriateness of the present common objectives (see Section 2.2) in view of past experience and taking account of the 2004 Enlargement; the suitability of the existing commonly agreed indicators to identify problems and challenges, to measure progress towards the common objectives and to serve as a basis for setting targets; the working methods used so far at both the EU and national/sub-national levels; and an assessment of the future development of open coordination in the social field. The Commission analysed the questionnaires after they were returned at the end of June 2005 and a synthesis of the replies is to be found in a Commission Staff Working Document (European Commission, 2006e).
2. The analyses of Member States' Implementation Reports on the 2003–5 NAPs/ inclusion (European Commission, 2006c) and of their National Strategy

Reports on Pensions (European Commission, 2006d) were also important sources.

3. The conclusions from international expert workshops and conferences that took place in the course of 2005, particularly the Luxembourg Presidency Conference on *Taking Forward the EU Social Inclusion Process*, the *Fourth Meeting of People Experiencing Poverty* and the UK Presidency *Round Table Conference on Poverty and Social Exclusion*, as well as other relevant academic work were important inputs.

4. An evaluation of the aforementioned Community Action Programme on social exclusion was also taken into account (see Section 2.2).

A number of themes emerge strongly from the different inputs. There is a general recognition that the OMC on social protection and social inclusion has had a positive impact on policy making and, in particular, that the social inclusion objectives have provided a useful framework at country and EU levels. The emphasis on a multi-dimensional approach and on both prevention and alleviation has been reinforced. However, particularly in relation to the Social Inclusion Process, there is a feeling that there has been an implementation gap and that the NAPs/inclusion need to become more focused and strategic, with a stronger focus as of 2006 on the implementation of goals, the delivery of policy reforms, and the monitoring and evaluation of results. A key role is played here by the analysis of policy, on which we concentrate in Chapter 4. The need for greater visibility for the social processes emerges strongly. It is frequently stressed that streamlining should not undermine the distinctive identity of the different processes nor reduce the scope for an in-depth focus on each policy field. The importance attached to the exchange of learning and good practices as an integral part of the OMC is highlighted as is the need to link this better with the work of reporting and monitoring. The need to strengthen interaction with the renewed Lisbon Strategy on growth and jobs and to strengthen the mainstreaming of social inclusion objectives is reinforced. The promotion of good governance and in particular the involvement of all relevant actors emerges as one of the successes of the Social Inclusion Process that should be further developed in the future.

Following the publication of the Commission's Communication (2005l), a period of intensive discussion took place on the Commission's proposals. This involved Member States but also other stakeholders, particularly NGOs and the social partners. This culminated in the endorsement at the March 2006 meeting of the EPSCO Council of a Joint Social Protection Committee and Economic Policy Committee Opinion on the Communication (Social Protection Committee and Economic Policy Committee, 2006). This opinion outlined various amendments to be made to the Commission's original proposals on the new objectives and working arrangements for a streamlined OMC on social protection and social inclusion. These amendments were adopted by the Council and the agreed objectives and working arrangements, as provided in Appendix 2b, were then endorsed at the Spring 2006 European Council. As indicated above, an important result of this decision is that there will be in future *National Reports on Strategies for Social Protection and Social Inclusion*, one "strand" of which will be National Action Plans on social inclusion. The first National Reports are on a two-yearly basis (2006–8), starting in September 2006. They will then subsequently be on a three-yearly cycle to bring them into line with the revised Lisbon process on jobs and growth (see Section 2.3).

The new common objectives (see Appendix 2b) commence with three overarching objectives. These cover, first, the need for "adequate, accessible, financially sustainable, adaptable and efficient social protection systems and social inclusion policies"; secondly, the importance of "effective and mutual interaction between the Lisbon objectives of greater economic growth, more and better jobs and greater social cohesion, and with the EU's Sustainable Development Strategy"; and, thirdly, the need for "good governance, transparency and the involvement of stakeholders in the design, implementation and monitoring of policy" (Social Protection Committee and Economic Policy Committee, 2006). These are then followed by three objectives for each of the three strands of social inclusion, pensions and health care and long-term care. The three social inclusion objectives are more or less consistent with the original social inclusion objectives agreed at Nice in 2000 but are more generalised in style as they do not detail the different policy areas nor do they specify the different vulnerable groups. The first restates the importance of ensuring "access for all to the resources, rights and services needed for participation in society, preventing and addressing exclusion, and fighting all forms of discrimination leading to exclusion". The second stresses the importance of "the active social inclusion of all, both by promoting participation in the labour market and by fighting poverty and exclusion". The third is very similar to the original fourth social inclusion objective on mobilising all stakeholders and stresses aspects of good governance such as better coordination, the involvement of relevant actors and the mainstreaming of social inclusion goals into national policy making. Significantly, the three objectives are preceded by an overarching aim of making a *decisive impact on the eradication of poverty and social exclusion*.

It is our view that these new objectives and arrangements, particularly when read in conjunction with the *Guidelines for Preparing National Reports on Strategies for Social Protection and Social Inclusion* (Social Protection Committee, 2006) agreed by the Member States and the Commission at the March 2006 meeting of the Social Protection Committee, satisfactorily address many of the concerns we raised in our original report for the Luxembourg Presidency Conference. They provide a strong basis for the future development of the EU efforts to promote greater social inclusion and for reinforcing the struggle against poverty and social exclusion. These new objectives and arrangements are assessed in more detail in Chapter 6.

The Social Agenda 2005–2010

Complementing the mid-term review of the Lisbon Strategy is the Social Agenda 2005–2010, a Communication from the Commission in February 2005 (European Commission, 2005d). The accompanying European Commission Press Release described the Social Agenda as "the social policy dimension of the refocused Lisbon growth and jobs strategy". The Press Release goes on to stress that "social policy has not been downgraded in importance. [...] we are more, not less, ambitious, about ensuring high social standards, good healthcare and a proper social net". In its Communication, the Commission states clearly that "the added value of the Social Agenda is beyond doubt. The Agenda makes it possible to facilitate the modernisation of national systems against a background of far-reaching economic and social changes. It supports the harmonious operation of the single market while ensuring respect for fundamental rights and common values" (European Commission, 2005d, page 2).

The Social Agenda, which drew on the Report of the "High-Level Group on the future of social policy in an enlarged European Union" (European Commission, 2004c) and the Kok Report on *Facing the Challenge* (European Communities, 2004), develops a two-pronged strategy. The first element is concerned with building the confidence of EU citizens. Here it emphasises an intergenerational approach, reflected in the European Pact for Youth, to which reference has already been made in Chapter 1, and the social dimension of globalisation, citing the ILO World Commission on the Social Dimension of Globalisation, the commitments of the Copenhagen World Social Summit, and the Millennium Development Goals. The second element presents key measures under two main headings: employment, and equal opportunities and inclusion. The first of these refers both to the revamped cycle of the European Employment Strategy and to synergies with other instruments, notably the European Social Fund, which will provide support to the Employment Strategy. The second refers to the modernisation of social protection, the Open Method of Coordination for health and long-term care, a Community initiative on minimum income schemes and the integration of people excluded from the labour market, the designation of 2010 as the "European Year of combating poverty and social exclusion", promoting diversity and non-discrimination, the establishment of a European Gender Institute, and a clarification of the role of social services of general interest. (On the complex issue of the social services of general interest in the EU, see *inter alia* European Commission, 2006g.)

Sustainable Development Strategy (SDS)

Sustainable development is about ensuring that the needs of the present generation are met without compromising the ability of future generations to meet their own needs. It is an overarching objective of the EU, which is set out in Article 2 of the Nice Treaty and should govern all the Union's policies and activities. At their June 2005 meeting, EU Heads of State and Government approved a "Declaration on the guiding principles for sustainable development", based on four key objectives: environmental protection, social equity and cohesion,[10] economic prosperity and meeting our international responsibilities. This Declaration provided the renewed Strategy with a conceptual framework, which should serve as a basis for renewing the Sustainable Development Strategy (SDS) agreed upon by the June 2001 Gothenburg European Council (see Section 2.2).

The Commission then adopted, in December 2005, a Communication *On the Review of the Sustainable Development Strategy: A Platform for Action* (European Commission, 2005k; see also Employment Committee and Social Protection Committee, 2006). This stresses the need to give urgent attention to the fight against poverty and social exclusion, and especially to childhood poverty. Its section on operational objectives and targets includes "to pursue the setting of specific EU targets for reducing the number of people at risk of poverty by 2010 with special focus on the need to reduce child poverty, in the context of the OMC" (European Commission, 2005k, page 28).

Given the horizontal nature of Sustainable Development, a "Friends of the Presidency Group on the Review of the Sustainable Development Strategy" was set up to help the Austrian Presidency of the EU (during the first half of 2006) conduct a comprehensive review between February and May 2006. The resulting renewed SDS, based on the aforementioned four key objectives and endorsed by EU leaders at their June 2006 meeting, focuses on 7 priority areas for action, which include: "public health", "social inclusion, demography and migration"[11] and "global poverty and sustainable development challenges". It also addresses key cross-cutting policy issues such as education and training, research and development, and financial and economic instruments. The aim of ensuring public ownership of the Strategy is reflected in a section on communication and mobilisation of all actors concerned. Furthermore, the renewed SDS provides for effective follow-up and monitoring of progress and seeks to clarify how the EU SDS and the EU Lisbon Strategy on growth and jobs are expected to "complement each other" (Council, 2006b).

The renewed SDS emphasises the need for "better policy making":

1. "The EU SDS sets out an approach to better policy making based on better regulation and on the principle that sustainable development is to be integrated into policy making at all levels. This requires all levels of Government to support, and to cooperate with, each other, taking into account the different institutional settings, cultures and specific circumstances in Member States.
2. In this respect all EU institutions should ensure that major policy decisions are based on proposals that have undergone high quality Impact Assessment (IA), assessing in a balanced way the social, environmental and economic dimensions of sustainable development and taking into account the external dimension of sustainable development and the costs of inaction. Other tools for better policy

making include ex-post-assessment of policy impacts and public and stakeholders' participation. Member States should make wider use of these tools, in particular IA, when allocating public funds and developing strategies, programmes and projects.

3. All EU institutions should ensure that proposals for targets, objectives and measures are feasible and, where needed, accompanied by the necessary instruments at EU level." (Council, 2006b)

In the light of these developments, the renewed Strategy could prove a useful reinforcement of the Social Inclusion Process. In particular the emphasis in the Strategy on impact assessments when developing policies and the encouragement of wider use of evaluation to assess the *ex-post* impact of policies can reinforce this important aspect of the Social Inclusion Process (we come back to these issues below).

Creating the (new) dynamic between the OMC in the social field, and the Broad Economic Policy and Employment Guidelines, as we described in Section 2.3, is in fact directly linked to this key issue of sustainable development. Such a dynamic is indeed "vital if real synergies are to be achieved between social, economic, employment and environmental policies so that they are mutually reinforcing and ensure really *sustainable development in all fields* – something that has been somewhat lacking to date" (Frazer, 2005). Happily the new objectives for the Social Protection and Social Inclusion Process recognise these inter-linkages, but much remains to be done. As put by the Council:

> Research into sustainable development [...] has to promote inter- and trans-disciplinary approaches involving social and natural sciences and bridge the gap between science, policy making and implementation. [...] There is still a strong need for further research in the interplay between social, economic and ecological systems, and in methodologies and instruments for risk analysis, back- and forecasting and prevention systems. (Council, 2006b)

The implementation of the renewed Strategy "will be closely monitored and followed up by the European Council on a regular basis" (Presidency Conclusions of the June 2006 European Council).

Conclusions

The Social Agenda 2005–2010 and the renewed Sustainable Development Strategy provide the strategic context within which we can consider the elements of the Social Inclusion Process, such as the commonly agreed social indicators, to which we now turn.

2.6 Commonly agreed Social Inclusion ("Laeken") Indicators: achievements to date

To help the Member States and the Commission with the monitoring of national and EU progress towards the EU common objectives in the area of social inclusion (see above), the December 2001 Laeken European Council endorsed a *first set* of 18 common indicators for social inclusion. The indicators, generally referred to as the *Laeken indicators*, were expected to be used by all the Member States in their NAPs/inclusion from the 2003 round of NAPs/inclusion and in the EU reporting on social inclusion.

The design of these indicators drew on a history of social science research dating back over 30 years. In the United States, this was represented by the official publication *Toward a Social Report* (US Department of Health, Education, and Welfare, 1969). For Europe, reference should be made to Delors (1971). In Scandinavia, the desire to move beyond purely monetary indicators of well-being led to a broader concept of social welfare (see Johansson, 1973, and Erikson and Uusitalo, 1987). More recently, work has been undertaken on *The Social Quality of Europe* as part of an initiative during the Netherlands Presidency, reported by Beck, Van der Maesen and Walker (1997); and by the EuReporting Project, coordinated by ZUMA at Mannheim, concerned with the conceptual basis for social reporting (see, for example, Berger-Schmitt, 2000). Berger-Schmitt and Noll (2000) provide a very clear account of the relationship with concepts of quality of life, social cohesion, social capital, and social exclusion.

In the development of the common indicators, the key role has been played by the Indicators Sub-Group (ISG) of the Social Protection Committee, in conjunction with the Commission, notably Directorate-General "Employment, Social Affairs and Equal Opportunities" (DG EMPL) and the Statistical Office of the European Communities (Eurostat), and other bodies, in particular the OECD. The ISG consists of national delegations of experts, with a secretariat that is the responsibility of the Commission (DG EMPL). The ISG examines the technical issues and submits recommendations to the SPC. These cover not only the Social Inclusion Process, but also the OMC on pensions, the OMC on health care and long-term care, as well as the studies of making work pay. The SPC "Report on indicators in the field of poverty and social exclusion" (Social Protection Committee, 2001), prepared in 2001 by the ISG and adopted in Laeken in December 2001, set out the first methodological principles underlying the construction of the common social indicators, and proposed the first set of common Laeken indicators.

The ISG has since then continued to work on these common social inclusion indicators with a view to refining and consolidating the original set as well as extending it. It has also been very much involved in the review of the 2003 and 2004 NAPs/inclusion as far as indicators, data and monitoring issues are concerned. A great deal of ground has been covered in developing the indicators. We refer to some areas of work below, but do not attempt a comprehensive evaluation of all the many areas investigated in the field of social inclusion (which include housing, homelessness, deprivation measures, access to health care, premature mortality, and migration). Nor do we consider the work of the ISG with regard to the other processes (pensions, health care and long-term care, and making work pay). Given the importance of the work of the ISG, the Commission may consider an independent analysis of its operation. We only make three points here. The first is that it would be very valuable if the key working documents of the ISG, including the minutes of meetings, could be made publicly accessible, along with the reports made to the Social Protection Committee when endorsed. The publication of the original report in 2001 has demonstrated the value of such transparency. Secondly, in view of the extent of inter-connections between different fields, in terms of topics covered (income, employment, health, housing and homelessness, education, and so on) but also methodology and data sources, it is important that there be close liaison between ISG delegates and the national experts involved with other bodies, in particular EU (Council bodies, Eurostat Task Forces, and so on) and OECD bodies, UN and other groups concerned with social statistics. Thirdly, it would be very helpful to have a further development of the information already provided, in the form of an ISG statistical/ methodological document providing a sort of an "ID card" for each commonly agreed indicator. For each indicator, one could have:

- name of indicator, exact definition;
- data source;
- algorithm used for its calculation;
- "quality profile" (a user-oriented summary of the main quality features, strengths/weaknesses of the indicator [...] for which the starting point could be the quality profile Eurostat has developed for assessing Structural Indicators[12]);
- the most up-to-date figures with perhaps a brief comment.

These indicator ID cards should be made widely publicly accessible. They would provide extremely useful information to people in charge of using these indicators within the Commission and within countries' ministries (at national and sub-national levels), to all researchers interested in using these unique comparative tools, and to the wider public.

Monitoring framework prior to the 2006 streamlining

Social indicators are, of course, used for a variety of purposes. It is essential to stress that here the focus is on their use in one *very specific context*, namely as part of the Open Method of Coordination – that is, with the purpose of facilitating international comparisons of *actual performances* achieved by national and sub-national social policies, and hence improving mutual learning and exchange of good (and bad) practices among countries. For this reason, the first set of selected EU indicators focused solely on social outcomes rather than the means by which they are achieved (for example, the level of education attained rather than the total spending on schools). Member States, while agreeing on the indicators by which performance is to be judged, are left free to choose the methods by which these objectives are realised (under the *subsidiarity* principle). One country may achieve low poverty rates by active labour market policy; another may place more reliance on social transfers. In one country transfers may be provided by the state; in another country transfers may be private. In one country, training may be associated with apprenticeships; in another, training may be part of the school system. Of course the distinction is not a rigid one, but in general the aim of the EU indicators is to measure social outcomes. There is however, as we discuss later, a role for indicators relating to policy inputs (e.g. expenditure on social transfers). Input indicators have an obvious value when reporting on policy. But the common indicators are (and should go on being) primarily concerned with outcomes.

The specific nature of EU (performance/outcome) indicators to be used in the Social Inclusion Process is reflected in the nine methodological principles set out in the Report, cited earlier, of the Social Protection Committee (2001) endorsed in Laeken. Of these principles, six refer to individual indicators (1–6) and three to the portfolio as a whole (7–9):[13]

1. An indicator should capture the essence of the problem and have a clear and accepted normative interpretation.
2. An indicator should be robust and statistically validated.
3. An indicator should be responsive to policy interventions but not subject to manipulation.
4. An indicator should be measurable in a sufficiently comparable way across Member States, and comparable as far as practicable with the standards applied internationally.
5. An indicator should be timely and susceptible to revision.
6. The measurement of an indicator should not impose too large a burden on Member States, on enterprises, nor on the Union's citizens.
7. The portfolio of indicators should be balanced across different dimensions.
8. The indicators should be mutually consistent and the weight of single indicators in the portfolio should be proportionate.
9. The portfolio of indicators should be as transparent and accessible as possible to EU citizens.

The agreement reached in Laeken contributed to making the OMC in the field of social inclusion operational, by providing policy makers with a common basis on which the starting positions and progress over time in the different Member States in terms of key areas of social concern can be reliably compared. While evaluating the contribution of specific policy initiatives on the evolution of indicators will always be difficult (see Chapter 4), common performance indicators significantly enhance the scope for policy learning – even if the potential has not yet been fully realised. Concentrating on outcomes means that Member States, in reporting on policy, are encouraged to relate those interventions to the desired/planned impact on outcomes, rather than simply present a catalogue of policy measures. Policy interventions can then play their appropriate role, as means to an end, rather than as they are so often presented, as if they were ends in themselves.

This being said, it is worth emphasising that in order to highlight national specificities in particular areas, and to help interpret the common indicators, Member States are expected to include *nationally defined indicators* in their NAPs/inclusion[14] (Social Protection Committee, 2001). It should also be highlighted that the "performance" information conveyed by the indicators commonly agreed at EU level needs to be supplemented with other information, which allows a better linkage between policies and social outcomes (see Chapter 4), and thus also a better assessment of policies' efficiency; this matters not only at the national and sub-national levels but also at the international level (in the context of the *peer reviews* and the identification of good and bad practices). We therefore very much support the approach followed in the new integrated monitoring framework that the ISG prepared for use in the streamlined *National Reports for Strategies on Social Protection and Social Inclusion* and related EU reporting and analyses (Indicators Sub-Group, 2006b), to which we now turn.

The new integrated monitoring framework resulting from the 2006 streamlining

Since December 2001, when the Laeken European Council endorsed a *first set* of 18 common indicators for social inclusion, the SPC Indicators Sub-Group has refined, consolidated and extended the original set. It has also (see Section 2.2) worked on the development of indicators in the fields of pensions and health care and long-term care. In the first half of 2006, in line with the new objectives for the streamlined OMC on social protection and social inclusion, it undertook a comprehensive review and reorganisation of all these indicators. This has resulted in an agreement in May 2006 between the Member States and the European Commission on a new, integrated monitoring framework for the streamlined OMC (Indicators Sub-Group, 2006b) and, in particular, a portfolio for each of the three individual "strands" of the streamlined OMC (social inclusion, pensions, health) and an "overarching" portfolio. This framework is expected to be used by Member States in the National Reports to be submitted to the Commission for the first time in September 2006, and by the Commission in its reporting and independent assessment of countries' performances.

The new framework follows the structure of the new common objectives for the OMC on social protection and social inclusion (see Appendix 2b), and consists of four sets of indicators: a set of commonly agreed indicators appropriate to the overarching objectives and one appropriate to each strand of the streamlined process. Even though it largely builds on the methodological principles agreed for the original set of Laeken indicators (see above), the new framework significantly departs from the original one in two respects. Firstly, in an attempt to better reflect the action and impact of policies, the choice of indicators is no longer strictly limited to outcome indicators (even though outcome indicators still form the vast majority of the streamlined portfolios). Secondly, some "flexibility" has been introduced in the way the Laeken principles are to be applied, notably allowing for the inclusion in the list of "commonly agreed *national* indicators". These indicators are based on commonly agreed definitions and assumptions but, contrary to "commonly agreed *EU* indicators", they do not satisfactorily fulfil all the criteria for the selection of EU indicators (especially the comparability and/or normative value); this is, for instance, the case of the new social inclusion indicator on the employment gap of immigrants (see below).[15]

The very slightly revised methodological framework for the selection of commonly agreed indicators consists of eight criteria, with five of them referring to individual indicators (criteria 1–5, which in the case of "commonly agreed national indicators" are not all satisfactorily met) and three to each individual indicators portfolio (criteria 6–8):

1. An indicator should capture the essence of the problem and have a clear and accepted normative interpretation. (This means that there must be agreement among countries that a movement in a particular direction or within a certain range is a positive outcome, which is to be assessed against past performances; this is particularly important when we turn to the issue of setting targets – see Chapter 6.)
2. An indicator should be robust and statistically validated.
3. An indicator should be responsive to policy interventions but not subject to manipulation.
4. An indicator should provide a sufficient level of cross-countries comparability, as far as practicable with the use of internationally applied definitions and data collection standards.
5. An indicator should be built on available underlying data, and be timely and susceptible to revision.
6. Each of the four indicators portfolios should be comprehensive and cover all key dimensions of the common objectives.
7. Each of the four indicators portfolios should be balanced across the different dimensions.
8. Each of the four indicators portfolios should enable a synthetic and transparent assessment of a country's situation in relation to the common objectives.

For the overarching part, a set of 14 commonly agreed (national and EU) indicators has been endorsed to monitor the first two broad objectives (the third objective, related to governance, is currently not covered by common indicators). These indicators cover social inclusion, pensions, health care and long-term care, as well as more "overarching" issues (such as the in-work poverty risk, i.e. the "working poor" indicator). The EU overarching indicators can play a valuable role in linking across the different social policy processes as well as between the EU social, economic and employment processes – with the working poor as an important example. They are to be analysed in the light of commonly agreed key contextual information; where possible and meaningful, the analysis is also expected to review past and future trends. The list of 12 background statistics provided for (Indicators Sub-Group, 2006b) is of course only indicative and leaves room for any other contextual information that would be relevant to better frame and understand the national socio-economic context. (See Tables 2.2a and 2.2b in Appendix 1.)

In the sets of indicators to be used for monitoring policies developed in the individual strands, the distinction between *Primary* and *Secondary Indicators* agreed upon in Laeken is maintained. Accordingly, a reduced number of Primary (EU and national) Indicators provides a "synthetic set of lead indicators" covering all key dimensions of the defined objectives and/or highlighting the social situation of key sub-populations; whereas Secondary (EU and national) Indicators support these lead indicators by describing in greater detail the nature of the problem or by describing other dimensions of the problem. There is also a set of supporting commonly agreed contextual information, which is meant to assist Member States in interpreting the indicators. As indicated by the Sub-Group, each strand list has been built with a view to constitute "a commonly agreed synthetic and comprehensive monitoring tool of a country's social situation with regards to the common objectives in each strand" (Indicators Sub-Group, 2006b). It is therefore to be hoped that Member States will assess their situation using *inter alia* the various overarching indicators as well as all Primary Indicators included in the strand portfolios. This assessment, supported by relevant commonly agreed Secondary Indicators and contextual information as well as relevant national level information, should provide a powerful tool to identify priority objectives in their national plans/strategies for social protection and social inclusion. On this basis, Member States are expected to specify which indicators (common and national) they will use for monitoring progress towards these objectives. We come back to this in Chapter 6 (see Figure 6.1).

The streamlined social inclusion indicators are now to comprise 11 *Primary Indicators* covering the broad fields that have been considered the most important elements in leading to poverty and social exclusion, and three *Secondary Indicators* intended to support the lead indicators and describe other important dimensions of the phenomena. In addition, a further set of 11 statistics has been specified for the social inclusion portfolio as providing "context" information to help in interpreting trends in the Primary and Secondary Indicators. Table 2.3a shows the Primary Indicators, Table 2.3b the Secondary Indicators, and Table 2.3c the "Context Information" (see Appendix 1).[16]

The Primary Indicators for social inclusion encompass poverty risk (Indicators 1, 2 and 3), unemployment and joblessness (Indicators 4 and 5), low educational qualifications (Indicator 6) and the employment situation of migrants (Indicator 7). They also include indicators relating to material deprivation, housing,[17] access to health care and child well-being (Indicators 8, 9, 10 and 11 respectively) that are currently being developed. Although certain key dimensions are still under development, the (planned) set of indicators can be said to be multi–dimensional in its scope (we will come back to these important dimensions in Chapter 5). A gender breakdown of each of the Primary Indicators, and a breakdown of most by broad age group, is also presented.

The Secondary Indicators then comprise more detailed disaggregations of income poverty risk by smaller age groups, household type, household work intensity, labour force status, and tenure status, as well as with alternative income thresholds (Indicator 1 together with 1a-1e breakdowns). The other two Secondary Indicators relate to adults with low educational attainment and 15-year-olds with poor literacy levels (Indicators 2 and 3 respectively).

The "Context Information" relates to income inequality (the S80/S20 income quintile ratio and the Gini coefficient[18]), regional disparities in employment rates, life expectancy, the at-risk-of-poverty rate with the income threshold anchored at a moment in time, the at-risk-of-poverty rate before social cash transfers (other than pensions),[19] the distribution of jobless households by main household types, in-work poverty risk (separately for full-time and part-time workers), some measures of work incentives ("making work pay" measures), a measure of the relationship between social assistance and the at-risk-of-poverty threshold (for three types of jobless households), and self-reported limitations in daily activities by income level.

This represents a considerable change from the set of indicators originally endorsed in 2001, in terms of both the precise indicators and the way they are organised and expected to be used. The main changes are as follows:

1. New indicators have been introduced in the Primary and Secondary lists: new indicators on employment gap of migrants and low reading literacy performance of pupils (based on the OECD *Programme for International Student Assessment* (PISA)), as well as indicators explicitly foreseen in the Primary list but yet to be developed on material deprivation, housing, access to health care and child well-being.
2. A new breakdown of the at-risk-of-poverty rate has been added in the Secondary list: the breakdown by the *work intensity of households* (WI), which usefully completes the information provided by the "working poor" indicator included in the list of overarching indicators (and in the social inclusion "context statistics", where it is usefully broken down for full-time and part-time workers; we come back to this in Chapter 5). WI is calculated only for households with at least one working-age person, whereas households composed solely of students are excluded from the calculation.[20] Poverty risks can then be calculated for the total population in different work intensity categories as well as for broad household types in different work intensity categories.
3. Other refinements to the precise definition of existing indicators (especially on the indicator of *jobless households*) and breakdowns (especially on the

calculation of the *most frequent activity status*, which is used in particular for calculating the WI of households and the "working poor" indicator) have also been made. The "most frequent activity status" is now defined as the status that a person declares to have occupied for more than half the total number of months for which information on any status is available during the period concerned – that is at least seven months, not necessarily in a row, where the person has provided information on his/her activity status over the entire calendar year (i.e. the income reference year). The "children" age group has been harmonised in all four portfolios; except if stated otherwise, it now systematically refers to people aged below 18.

4. On the key dimension of health, the Laeken indicator of "self-perceived health status by income level" has been dropped from the social inclusion portfolio and is expected to be replaced by a yet-to-be-developed indicator on access to health care. It is important that an agreement on this new indicator be reached in time for its inclusion in the 2007 Joint Report on Social Protection and Social Inclusion, which should be greatly facilitated by the fact that the required data (from EU-SILC) will become available for all 25 Member States by the end of 2006 (see Chapter 5). In the meantime, for the 2006–8 National Reports on Strategies for Social Protection and Social Inclusion, the only commonly agreed statistic covering the health dimension will be the *context statistics* (i.e. currently not an "indicator" *per se*) on "self-reported limitations in daily activities by income quintile"; a situation that is clearly not satisfactory but will hopefully be only temporary.

5. Finally, the presentation has been considerably amended, with the major change being a significant pruning of the Primary set of indicators to avoid losing focus in a profusion of indicators, in line with the strong plea we had made in our original report. Various indicators have now been moved from the Primary or Secondary set to the "context" set, some rearrangement of Primary versus Secondary Indicators has been applied and a few original indicators have been dropped from the portfolio as a whole (apart from "self-perceived health status by income level", this is the case for: the persistent at-risk-of-poverty calculated with a 50% income threshold, the long-term unemployment share and the very long-term unemployment rate).

Structural Indicators and Commission's Reports to Spring European Councils

As part of the Lisbon Strategy, the European Commission has been required to produce each year since 2001 a *Spring Report* to the Spring European Council (see, for instance: European Commission, 2005a). Those reports draw from the implementation reports of the annual economic and employment policy coordination strategies, that is, the Broad Economic Policy Guidelines and the Employment Guidelines[21] as well as from the so-called *Structural Indicators*. The latter are proposed by the Commission and agreed upon by the Council, with the aim of allowing for an objective assessment of Member States' progress towards the Lisbon European Council objectives; they were expanded at Gothenburg and refined by subsequent European Councils. Structural Indicators cover six domains: general economic background, employment, innovation and research, economic reform, social cohesion and environment.

In its October 2003 Communication on Structural Indicators, the Commission suggested a radically different approach to Structural Indicators compared with earlier years (see European Commission, 2003b); an approach that was broadly endorsed by the Council (Council, 2003) and was therefore applied to the 2004 and 2005 Spring Reports. With a view to creating greater clarity in the annual assessment of progress being achieved by Member States, the Commission now concentrates *primarily* on a shortlist of only 14 Structural Indicators (see Table 2.4 in Appendix 1), instead of the 42 indicators used in the 2002 and 2003 Reports.

We have already emphasised that the multi-dimensional nature of social inclusion requires a broad range of indicators, more than the three indicators retained for this domain in the shortlist (at-risk-of-poverty rate, long-term unemployment rate and regional cohesion). The need to supplement the shortlist in order to better monitor structural reforms also applies to the other domains to be covered by the Structural Indicators. For this reason, the Commission maintains, in parallel to the shortlist, a publicly accessible database containing a larger number of indicators. To date, as far as "social cohesion" is concerned, this longer list contains the seven indicators shown in Table 2.5 (see Appendix 1), which are a subset of the revised Laeken portfolio presented in Tables 2.3a, 2.3b and 2.3c (see Appendix 1). Where necessary, the more detailed indicators used in the individual policy processes (i.e. the Laeken indicators in the case of social inclusion) can obviously also complete the Commission's analysis.[22] This list is likely to be amended in the second half of 2006.

2.7 Commonly agreed Social Inclusion ("Laeken") Indicators: issues

A number of issues relating to agreed indicators and their use need to be addressed. The first issue is that of coverage. There are recognised gaps in the agreed indicators for social inclusion, with those relating to material deprivation, housing, access to health care, and child well-being explicitly flagged in the Primary set but still being developed. (Indicators of socio-economic inequalities in health are to be developed under the health portfolio; we come back to this in Section 5.3 when addressing the gaps in the agreed social inclusion indicators, as such indicators are also highly relevant from a social inclusion perspective.)

The second need is for the refinement of existing indicators. The necessity for further work on common indicators reflects the fact that, in arriving at the current set, many significant choices had to be made, and while indicators should have a reasonable degree of stability in order to fulfil their monitoring function, the process of development is necessarily a dynamic one. A good example is provided by the EU definition of the risk of financial poverty, based on relative rather than absolute or fixed thresholds. In the context of an enlarged Union, however, we need to take account of the larger differences across countries in average living standards, which is why it is so important to keep in mind the values of the national thresholds when doing comparative analysis of the at-risk-of-poverty rate at the EU level. It is to be hoped that the indicator being developed by the SPC Indicators Sub-Group to reflect material deprivation will go some way towards filling this need.

As can be seen from Tables 2.3a, 2.3b and 2.3c (see Appendix 1), *children* and the *elderly population* are now given a special focus within the EU indicators of social inclusion. It has been agreed that it is especially important not to base the examination of child poverty risk and social exclusion on a single at-risk-of-poverty indicator. This explains why a standard breakdown by broad age groups is now applied to most of the Laeken indicators. At the same time, as we discuss in Chapter 5 and as is now explicitly recognised in the new integrated EU monitoring framework (Indicators Sub-Group, 2006b), children mainstreaming may lead us to propose moving outside the existing set of indicators and developing one or several specific child-focused indicators rather than simply rely on age breakdowns.

A *gender breakdown* is now also more systematically applied to the EU indicators, i.e. again each time where relevant, meaningful and statistically possible. It should be noted here that gender is important in terms of disaggregation, but also in the definition of indicators. The definitions chosen may not be "gender neutral". For instance, the measurement of the poverty risk assumes that financial resources are equally divided among all those living in a household. All are poor or all are non-poor. In reality, household income may be unequally divided among household members. There may well be households, recorded as being above the risk of poverty threshold, where the women members are sufficiently disadvantaged relative to the men members that the women are in fact at risk of poverty although in a non-poor household.

Apart from the need to re-examine the indicators in an enlarged Union, there are other reasons why the choice of indicators should not be regarded as fixed in stone. These include the need to refine their definition but also their implementation on the basis of the concrete experience gained in employing them. For instance (see Chapter 4), the common indicators agreed at EU level, which focus primarily, though no longer exclusively, on performance (i.e. outcome) indicators for the reasons explained above, need to be complemented with other information (indicators/statistics), that allow a better linkage between policies and outcomes. This has been addressed to some extent in the framing of "context" indicators, but more work may be necessary to improve that linkage, and to respond to new issues and challenges generated by the constantly changing socio-economic situation, as well as reflecting the views of all relevant actors (social partners, Non-Governmental Organisations, persons experiencing poverty or social exclusion, academics). Finally, the data at our disposal are also changing over time (e.g. the newly launched EU-SILC instrument, see Chapters 3 and 5), and progress in filling gaps in the social indicators depends crucially on the statistical infrastructure. As the Social Protection Committee (2003b) noted, "the use of indicators to monitor progress depends to a great extent on the availability of relevant and timely data. Thus [...] Member States may wish to identify gaps in existing data and to stress the need to develop further their statistical infrastructure". Put differently, and this aspect is too often underestimated, improved *statistical capacity* – in terms of coverage, reliability and timeliness – is a necessary condition for the process to achieve its aims. As we will see in subsequent Chapters, apart from filling the gaps in available *data*, this also calls for the building of specific *analytical expertise* at sub-national, national as well as EU levels (including expertise in our understanding of the determinants of social well-being); the commitment of resources by the Member States and the Commission will thus be indispensable.

For all these reasons, the composition of the set of EU social indicators will have to be regularly reconsidered, which means that new indicators may be added but also that existing ones will have to be amended or dropped since the number of common indicators should be kept limited (see Hills, 2002).

Use of the indicators

The single most important issue surrounding the common social indicators is their use – or, more accurately, their lack of use. As was recognised in the 2004 Joint Inclusion Report, the indicators have yet to be "used to full advantage to assess performance in practice" (European Commission, 2004b, page 135). To date, the indicators have still not penetrated sufficiently either at the level of the EU or within Member States. Despite the efforts made in the NAPs/inclusion and in their EU analyses by the Commission and Member States (Joint Reports and Commission Staff Working Papers), the potential of the social indicators has yet to be fully exploited. The common indicators can play a number of key roles in the Social Inclusion monitoring framework, as we have tried to illustrate in Figure 2.1.

To be more concrete, we can identify four respects in which the social indicators could be used more intensively. The first is the use of the indicators in a forensic manner to identify possible explanations of differences in Member State performance. The Commission has begun to make such analyses. One example is the interesting graph showing the correlation between risk of poverty and per capita social expenditure in 2000 (European Commission, 2004b, Figure 13). Two more examples are given by the Technical Annex to the 2006 Joint Report on Social Protection and Social Inclusion (European Commission, 2006b). This Annex provides a very helpful overview of social protection expenditure (distinguishing between the various functions involved) and receipts in the 25 EU Member States, on the basis of data compiled by Eurostat in the *European System of Integrated Social Protection Statistics* (ESSPROS) system of accounts. It also provides a very useful analysis of the financial incentives to work from a social inclusion

Figure 2.1: The social inclusion monitoring framework

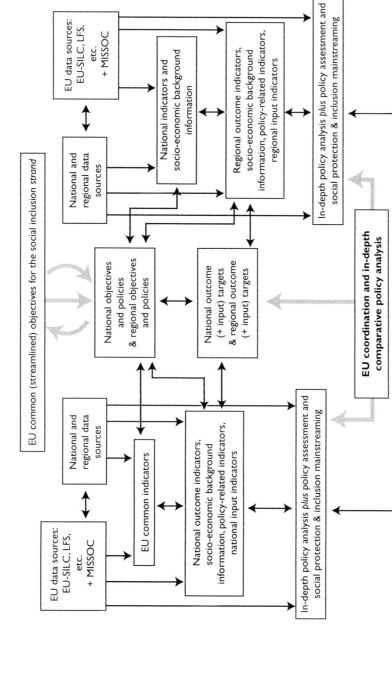

Notes: MISSOC = Mutual Information System on Social Protection, LFS = Labour Force Survey

perspective. There is considerable scope to develop such systematic cross-country analysis, bearing in mind the potential pitfalls, well known from the social science literature, some of which we consider in Chapter 3.

The second application is in the individual NAPs/inclusion. EU-15 countries (in the 2003–5 round of NAPs/inclusion) and EU-10 countries (2004–6 round) were requested to make use of the commonly agreed indicators. They were to be used not only to provide a description of the state of affairs with regard to poverty and social exclusion but also to underpin the analyses of the prevailing social situation and to measure any progress made in respect of the agreed common objectives. Member States did so to quite varying degrees, with some of them making extensive use of the Laeken indicators and others, for different reasons, only limited use. Among the reasons for limited use are that the social indicators are not sufficiently closely related to national policy measures, such as the national minimum income level, and that the Laeken outcome indicators are subject to other influences, notably the economic cycle. We understand these concerns, but believe that they can be overcome by the greater use of background information and by a systematic analysis of the underlying determinants. As indicated in Figure 2.1, national input indicators also need to be brought into the picture.

A fuller embedding of the social indicators within the NAPs/inclusion requires also that the EU indicators be related back to the national indicators used by Member States. It is clearly important that the results given at EU-level can be reconciled with those obtainable from national sources where the latter are available, and that differences in definition be addressed. Put more concretely, people need to know how to relate the EU indicators, such as those in the Annexes to the Joint Report on Social Inclusion (European Commission, 2004b) and the Joint Reports on Social Protection and Social Inclusion (European Commission, 2005b and 2006b), to the "headline" national figures from national sources.

A number of Member States have made such reconciliation in their NAPs/ inclusion. In the case of Italy, the Statistical Annex identifies three sources of difference (Government of Italy, 2003). The first lies in the use of a different source in the national estimates: the Survey of Household Budgets carried out by the Italian statistical institute (ISTAT). The second is the use of consumption, rather than income. The Annex argues that "conceptually speaking, consumption is perhaps a better measure" (page 17), on the grounds that it is more stable with respect to income fluctuations and is less subject to under-reporting. It notes that, "where there is a high rate of submerged employment [...] there may be much reticence in declaring the real household income" (page 17). They expect to find that the measured poverty rate is lower using consumption expenditure, although the difference is not in fact particularly marked. The third difference lies in the definition of the poverty threshold and the equivalence scale (Carbonaro scale).[23] The differences in equivalence scale mean, for instance, that a family with two children under 14 years of age is treated as equivalent to 2.1 single adults under the modified OECD scale used at EU level, and as 2.7 single adults under the Italian Carbonaro scale.

The Dutch NAP/inclusion similarly examines the relation between the national minimum income, taken as a performance standard, and the common indicator (Government of the Netherlands, 2003). It identifies (page viii) the following differences:

- The national minimum is below 60% of the median.
- Students are not included as households with a minimum income in the Netherlands but they are incorporated in the EU definition.
- The EU definition is based on equivalised income, which treats families with children in a different way from the definition of the minimum income.
- The minimum income is defined excluding housing benefit, whereas the EU definition includes as income any housing benefit received.

The consequences of these differences are considerable: more than half (53%) of those below the EU 60% median norm in the Netherlands are not designated as people who must get by on a minimum income. Conversely, a quarter (27%) of those on minimum incomes in the Netherlands do not fall under the EU 60% median threshold. As is noted in the NAP/inclusion, this has consequences for the population composition. The EU definition identifies as at risk of poverty more working people, more youths (students) and more families with children.

We believe that the systematic examination of the relationship between the commonly agreed indicators and the national indicators should, as far as possible, be conducted for all dimensions, and that this will facilitate the wider application of the commonly agreed EU indicators. The two-way arrows on the left-hand side of Figure 2.1 are important.

The third application is to increase the degree of "joined-up Government". The multi-dimensioned nature of the EU indicators for social inclusion not only reflects the fact that exclusion is a multi-dimensional concept, but also serves to underline the need for cooperation between different agencies of Government as well as, in some countries, between different agencies belonging to different levels of Government. The overlap between NAPs/employment and NAPs/inclusion is an obvious example. Policies to reduce long-term unemployment and joblessness require *inter alia* joint action by the ministries of employment and social affairs. Indeed, all the indicators potentially involve joint action by different agencies, and one of the latent functions of the OMC is to promote coordination not just across countries but also within countries. *Joined-up Government* will become even more important if, as should be a key priority, NAPs/inclusion are integrated more clearly with policy formation (see Chapter 6). The EU choice to focus on social outcomes rather than the means by which they are achieved may help encourage joined-up Government; it may foster a cooperative attitude between the different (national, regional, local) bodies that have competence in these areas, whereas as far as inputs are concerned these bodies could be more inclined to see competition for resources as a zero-sum game.

The fourth application is to target setting (see the centre of Figure 2.1). In the first round of NAPs/inclusion, submitted in 2001, only a minority of the then 15 Member States had outcome targets. Furthermore, not all these targets were systematically linked to indicators to be used for monitoring progress towards achieving them. A few did have high-level national targets, notably Ireland which already had such a target at the core of its National Anti-Poverty Strategy, framed in terms of a domestically developed measure of "consistent poverty", which combines being at risk of poverty with experiencing basic deprivation. Overall, though, the setting of targets for key outcomes was rare and their coverage extremely patchy. The impetus for an enhanced role for targets in the next round of NAPs/inclusion came from the March 2002 Barcelona European Council: "The European Council stresses the importance of the fight against poverty and social exclusion. Member States are invited to set targets, in their National Action Plans, for significantly reducing the number of people at risk of poverty and social exclusion by 2010" (Presidency Conclusions, para 24).

The thinking behind this, and a detailed elaboration of how Member States might approach target setting, was contained in the Common Outline for the 2003–5 NAPs/inclusion agreed upon between the SPC and the Commission (Social Protection Committee, 2003b). It was clear from the Common Outline that these statements of objectives and priorities were intended to go beyond the general and aspirational. It spelt out that quantified targets should be set for reducing the number of people at risk of poverty and social exclusion. These should draw as appropriate on the commonly agreed indicators. In Chapter 6, we examine how Member States responded to this request. Here we note that the setting of targets at either national or EU level represents a potentially important use for the commonly agreed indicators.

In line with the Common Outline for the 2003–5 NAPs/inclusion, the Guidelines agreed by the Member States and the Commission for the preparation of the 2006–8 *National Reports on Strategies for Social Protection and Social Inclusion* suggest the following:

> Member States are invited to set clear specific quantified targets for the reduction of poverty and social exclusion by 2010, with, as appropriate, interim targets for the period covered by the plan. These could draw as appropriate on the work of the Social Protection Committee on commonly agreed indicators and on the discussion on indicators and targets in the Report commissioned by the Luxembourg Presidency on Taking Forward the EU Social Inclusion Process. They could also draw on national or sub-national data when this better reflects those aspects of poverty and social exclusion that are a priority for a Member State. Member States are encouraged to disaggregate targets by age and sex whenever data is available and this

is relevant. [See Appendix 2 on target setting.] Member States may also want to supplement overall national targets with targets at sub-regional level where appropriate. (Social Protection Committee, 2006)

It is to be hoped that the recently adopted common objectives for the streamlined OMC on social protection and social inclusion, the new integrated monitoring framework presented above and the expertise that has been built in the setting of targets as a result of previous rounds of NAPs/inclusion will allow countries to better respond to this key challenge in their 2006–8 National Reports.

Figure 2.1 summarises some of the ways in which national and EU data, indicators and targets might be used in a complementary and integrated way to monitor progress and help take forward the EU Social Inclusion Process. It refers in addition to some of the methods of policy analysis examined in Chapter 4. As brought out in the detailed discussion in Chapter 6 below, the aim is not a rigid common monitoring framework; instead, Member States should develop their own social inclusion monitoring framework, responding to their national specificities and including targets and indicators based on reliable and timely data, but with clear links made to the common indicators and the EU methodological framework.

2.8 Concluding comments

We began this Chapter with history. This has demonstrated the strong continuity in basic ideas underlying the development of EU cooperation in social policy: the setting of common objectives, with Member States free to determine how they are achieved, and an integrated view of economic and social policy making, seeking to emphasise the positive ways in which social policy can contribute to economic performance. The fact that progress has been made unevenly should not be allowed to obscure the underlying continuity.

Since 2000, three EU social "processes" have been launched: in chronological order, the *Social Inclusion Process*, the *Pensions Process,* and the *Health Care and Long-Term Care Process*. (EU cooperation in the field of *Making Work Pay* is also under way, even if this cooperation cannot be considered as a "policy process" *per se* and if various aspects of this issue have already been, and will continue to be, addressed in the context of the Broad Economic Policy Guidelines and the Employment Guidelines.) These three processes have been taken forward via the OMC. As far as the Social Inclusion Process – our main focus here – is concerned, this has involved objectives set at the EU level, embodied in the common objectives for the streamlined OMC on social protection and social inclusion and the commonly agreed social indicators, the preparation of NAPs/inclusion by Member States, and the EU analyses by the Commission and Member States.

The aim of this book is to contribute to taking forward the Social Inclusion Process. We seek to do so in four main respects:

1. Demonstration of the potential for a systematic comparative analysis of the performance of Member States, using commonly agreed indicators (Chapter 3).
2. Investigation as to how policy analysis can be strengthened (Chapter 4).
3. Development of the social indicators to fill gaps, refine existing indicators, respond to Enlargement, and widen their use (Chapter 5).
4. Examine how the Social Inclusion Process can be taken forward in the new streamlined context, considering the role of target setting, and embedding the Process more firmly in domestic policies (Chapter 6).

Notes

[1] The results were analysed by the Commission in a report issued in 1981 (European Commission, 1981).

[2] European Commission, 1993b, not published in the Official Journal of the European Communities.

[3] For an extensive discussion of the development of the principle of subsidiarity in the EU, see *inter alia* Fouarge (2004).

[4] The NAPs/employment, which Members States submit annually to the Commission since 1998, as well as the resulting Joint Employment Reports, can be downloaded from the website of the European Commission's Directorate-General "Employment, Social Affairs and Equal Opportunities" (DG EMPL): http://www.europa.eu.int/comm/employment_social/index_en.html.

[5] There are currently four Community Action Programmes that provide financial support to the EU Social Policy Agenda. These programmes, which will run until the end of 2006, cover the fight against social exclusion, anti-discrimination, gender equality, and employment incentive measures. As part of the discussions on the new Community financial perspectives for the period 2007–13, the Commission proposed (in 2004) to merge these programmes together to form the integrated Community Programme for Employment and Social Solidarity (PROGRESS). This single programme will also support the improvement of the working environment and conditions, including health and safety at work and reconciling work and family life. It will complement the European Social Fund as well as the financial support provided for social dialogue, free movement of workers and social studies. Discussions with the European Parliament and the Council are on-going. If everything goes according to plan, the European Parliament and the Council should jointly adopt the new programme by the end of 2006. PROGRESS should then be up and running by 1 January 2007. For more information, see http://www.europa.eu.int/comm/employment_social/index_en.html. (See also European Commission, 2005m.)

[6] The NAPs/inclusion as well as the resulting Joint Reports or Commission Staff Working Papers can be downloaded from http://www.europa.eu.int/comm/employment_social/index_en.html. The same applies to the Joint Report on Social Protection and Social Inclusion and their statistical and methodological annexes.

[7] The 2002 National Strategy Reports as well as the related Joint Report can be downloaded from http://www.europa.eu.int/comm/employment_social/index_en.html

[8] The full text of the Treaty is available from the Official Journal of the European Union, 16 December 2004, C310.

[9] The debate on mainstreaming has recently been advanced with the publication of a report, *Better Policies Better Outcomes: Promoting the Mainstreaming of Social Inclusion* (Combat Poverty Agency, 2006), which is based on a "transnational exchange" project funded under the Community action programme on social exclusion.

[10] "Promote a democratic, socially inclusive, cohesive, healthy, safe and just society with respect for fundamental rights and cultural diversity that creates equal opportunities and combats discrimination in all its forms" (Annex 1 to the Presidency Conclusions of the June 2005 European Council).

[11] The overall objective of this priority area is "to create a socially inclusive society by taking into account solidarity between and within generations and to secure and increase the quality of life of citizens as a precondition for lasting individual well-being" (Council, 2006b).

[12] See: http://epp.eurostat.cec.eu.int/portal/page?_pageid=1133,47800773,1133_47805778&_dad=portal&_schema=PORTAL.

[13] The methodological approach taken in the 2001 Committee's Report was consistent with the broad thrust of recommendations contained in the study on EU indicators for social inclusion by Atkinson, Cantillon, Marlier and Nolan (2002) commissioned by the Belgian Presidency of the EU, though differing in some details. Readers interested in a detailed discussion of the nine principles can refer to this study, where they were originally proposed. For more information on the technical and political details of the process that lead to this agreement, see *inter alia* Atkinson, Marlier and Nolan (2004), Marlier (2003) and Politica Economica (2002).

[14] These *nationally defined indicators* are often referred to as "level 3" indicators, as opposed to "level 1" indicators (Primary Indicators) and "level 2" indicators (Secondary Indicators).

[15] Commonly agreed *national* indicators "provide key information to assess the progress of Member States in relation to certain objectives, while not allowing for a direct cross-country comparison and not necessarily having a clear normative interpretation"; they

"should be interpreted jointly with the relevant background information (exact definition, assumptions, representativeness)" (Indicators Sub-Group, 2006b). In Tables 2.2a, 2.3a and 2.3b (see Appendix 1), "NAT" refers to commonly agreed *national* indicators whereas "EU" refers to commonly agreed *EU* indicators.

[16] For detailed definitions, see Indicators Sub-Group, 2006b. Updated national and EU figures for all commonly agreed indicators and context statistics (for all four portfolios), as they become available, can be downloaded free of charge from the website of Eurostat, the statistical office of the European Communities: http://epp.eurostat.cec.eu.int/portal/page?_pageid=1090,30070682,1090_30298591&_dad=portal&_schema=PORTAL.

[17] Even though there is no agreement yet on common indicators on housing, an important decision was made in Laeken on a common approach to be followed for this key area: since the 2003 round of NAPs/inclusion, Member States are expected to report on housing quality, housing costs, and homelessness and other precarious housing. This housing element is also part of the SPC Report endorsed by EU Heads of State and Government in December 2001. In practice, however, the absence of a common indicator in the field of housing has meant that most NAPs/inclusion do not satisfactorily (if at all) address this essential dimension of social inclusion. The importance of this housing element has been usefully recalled in Indicators Sub-Group (2006b).

[18] Measures of income inequality were included in the original Laeken set but are now in the portfolio of overarching indicators rather than the social inclusion portfolio *per se* (where they have been put in the list of "context" information), because they have been considered to relate to social cohesion rather than social inclusion.

[19] "This indicator is meant to compare the observed risk of poverty with an hypothetical measure of a risk of poverty in absence of all social transfers (other than pensions) all things being kept equal. In particular, household and labour market structure are kept unchanged. This measure does not take into account other types of transfers that have an impact on household disposable income such as transfers in kind and tax rebates" (Indicators Sub-Group, 2006b). For a discussion of this indicator, see *inter alia* Atkinson, Cantillon, Marlier and Nolan (2002).

[20] WI is obtained by dividing the number of months that all working-age household members have actually worked during the income reference year, by the total number of months that they could theoretically have worked during that period of time (i.e. the number of months spent in any activity status by all the working age members of the household). Working age persons are persons aged 18–64 years with the exception of individuals aged 18-24 years who are both economically inactive *and* living with at least one of their parents (these individuals are considered "dependent children"). Individuals are classified into work intensity categories ranging from WI=0 (no one in employment, which is very close though not identical to the definition of the (amended) Laeken *jobless households* indicator) to WI=1 (full work intensity).

[21] As indicated in Section 2.3, a new governance cycle covering the period 2005–8 was launched to follow the implementation of the Lisbon Strategy re-focused on growth and jobs. The first Commission Annual *Progress Report* produced in this context was adopted in January 2006 (European Commission, 2006f). Progress Reports have taken over the role of previous *Spring Reports*, i.e. to prepare discussions of the Spring European Council concerning the implementation of the Lisbon Strategy.

[22] Comprehensive information on Structural Indicators including definitions and available national figures (for all Member States as well as candidate/acceding countries) can be downloaded from: http://europa.eu.int/comm/eurostat/structuralindicators.

[23] The national methodology applies the criterion that the poverty line for a childless couple is equal to the mean consumption per capita. The thresholds for other types of household are obtained by applying the equivalence scale estimated by Carbonaro. In contrast, the EU definition is 60% of the median equivalised income, using the modified OECD scale.

THREE

Exploring statistics on poverty and social exclusion in the EU

Member States have so far made use of the commonly agreed indicators to quite varying degrees. While many countries did use indicators to provide a description of the state of affairs with regard to poverty and social exclusion, these descriptions were not, on the whole, integrated into the central part of the NAPs/inclusion, which deals with the strategic approach to combating poverty and social exclusion. One of the reasons for the limited framing of policies in relation to the common indicators in the NAPs/inclusion is that the social indicators have not to date been very fully exploited for analytical purposes. As pointed out in Chapter 1, the social indicators have not yet been used to "tell a story" about differences across Member States and about the relation between different dimensions of social exclusion, or about the impact of Enlargement.

The aim of this Chapter is to explore how much one can learn about these key questions just by restricting ourselves to the body of aggregate information now represented by the common indicators. It should be emphasised that we do not, in general, attempt to consider other sources of empirical evidence, be it aggregate information or individual micro-data. Nor do we attempt to provide an overall explanation of poverty and social exclusion. Clearly, a proper account and understanding of the complex phenomena at stake would require a differentiated examination of the causes of poverty and social exclusion, based on a detailed and multi-dimensional analysis of the underlying micro-data on households and individuals, and drawing on a variety of sources and the extensive research literature available for individual countries. Such a (very valuable) enterprise would be well beyond the scope of the present Chapter. Instead, by deliberately limiting our analysis to the published common indicators, our aim is to bring out how their potential can be *more* fully exploited – and also the limits to such an analysis of aggregate information. The expectation is of course not that countries would rely solely on these common indicators in monitoring, analysing and reporting on social inclusion; rather, it is that the national indicators they develop and use for these purposes, together with in-depth multi-dimensional analysis of the underlying micro-data, should be *linked back* to the common indicators as far as possible, in order to facilitate mutual learning.

In Sections 3.2 and 3.3, we examine the "baseline" situation with respect to poverty and social exclusion in the EU. This goes beyond the EU analyses in two ways. First, we explicitly compare EU-15 and EU-25, asking how Enlargement has changed the pattern of poverty and social exclusion. This is an important question, which the published common indicators are well designed to answer. A second departure here is to investigate correlation in the performance of countries across different dimensions of poverty and social exclusion. How far, for example, is poverty risk correlated with performance in terms of education? (Note that this is not the same as looking at the effect of education on poverty risk for an individual – such a "causality analysis" would require analysis of individual-level data not country-level statistics.) After presenting the evidence, we consider what conclusions, if any, can be drawn from the observed cross-country differences (Section 3.4). Finally, as already explained in Chapter 1, we seek to draw together the discussion on children mainstreaming in Section 3.5. Before seeking to interpret the evidence from the commonly agreed indicators, however, we briefly discuss the data sources from which many of the indicators are produced in Section 3.1.

3.1 EU data on poverty and social exclusion

As a result of the work of the Social Protection Committee and its Indicators Sub-Group, in conjunction with Eurostat, DG EMPL and Member States, the EU has assembled a valuable dataset about poverty and social exclusion in the EU-25. There are other important sources of internationally comparable data, but here we concentrate on what can be learned from the EU sources. The key reference is:

• The Technical Annex to the 2006 Joint Report on Social Protection and Social Inclusion (European Commission, 2006b), covering EU-25, the latest income data relating to the year 2003.

In some cases, we also draw on data from the following EU sources:

• The Statistical Annex to the 2004 Joint Inclusion Report (European Commission, 2004b), covering EU-15, the latest income data relating to the year 2000.
• The Annexes to the Commission Staff Working Paper *Report on Social Inclusion 2004* (European Commission, 2005c), covering the 10 new Member States.
• The Technical Annex to the 2005 Joint Report on Social Protection and Social Inclusion (European Commission, 2005b) covering EU-25 for non-income-based indicators.

Compared with 10 years ago, we now have a rich body of statistical information for the EU-25, assembled with the intention of being, as far as possible, comparable across countries and across time. Although the limitations of the data are clearly signalled, and there has been less experience to date with the new Member States, the degree of comparability is high by international standards. Yet these data have not been very fully exploited. While the Joint Reports have used the common indicators to considerable effect to demonstrate the scale of poverty and social exclusion, there have been relatively few attempts to explore the relationships between the different dimensions of deprivation – the *multifaceted* nature of exclusion highlighted in the Presidency Conclusions of the March 2005 and March 2006 European Councils.

In some documents, the common indicators have simply been included as an annex, with little reference being made in the main text. The data appear as simply an appendage. This is particularly the case with the "Structural Indicators" (see Section 2.6). In the case of the Kok Report (European Communities, 2004), for example, the Annexes show the relative performance of Member States (EU-25) according to the shortlist of Structural Indicators, and the relative improvement 1999–2003 (or the closest available period) for the EU-25 and the US. In the absence of any analysis in the text, readers may be tempted to make their own use of the data. Suppose, for example, that the reader were to take the employment rate, of central concern in the Kok Report, and the at-risk-of-poverty rate, of particular interest here, and to plot the latter against the former. What, if anything, could be concluded from such a bi-variate analysis? Are there not other forces at work? Suppose that the reader considers instead the *relative improvement*, in terms of the average annual percentage point change, in the two Structural Indicators. Does this neutralise the cross-country differences caused by other factors? Or do differences in the timing of the observations for the two variables (income relates to 2003, employment to 2004) vitiate the comparison? In the absence of an explicit analysis, readers are left in the dark as to what, if anything, can be concluded.

One important reason for caution is concern for data quality. The main data source for the employment-related and education common indicators is the EU Labour Force Survey (LFS). For the income-related indicators, at the time of the first and second (EU-15) rounds of NAPs/inclusion (in 2001 and 2003 respectively) the European Community Household Panel survey (ECHP), coordinated by Eurostat, was the sole harmonised EU data source.[1] As we describe below, the ECHP has been replaced by the newly launched *Community Statistics on Income and Living Conditions (EU-SILC)*, which has become the EU reference source for the level and composition of poverty and social exclusion. EU-SILC is coordinated by Eurostat and covers *inter alia* all 25 Member States of the EU. In the Technical Annex to the 2006 Joint Report on Social Protection and Social Inclusion, the income data for the year 2003 are presented.[2] In the case of 12 countries (Belgium, Denmark, Greece, Spain, France, Ireland, Italy, Luxembourg, Austria, Portugal, Finland and Sweden), the reference source is EU-SILC. The income data for the other countries are from national sources that have been harmonised *ex-post* for maximum consistency with EU-SILC methodology. However, the data cannot be considered fully comparable (European Commission, 2006b: Technical Annex 1b; see also Chapter 5).

It is essential to bear in mind that the vast majority of social indicators are estimated from sample survey data, rather than comprehensive censuses or administrative sources with comprehensive national coverage. The point estimates have been carefully constructed to approximate closely the true population values but there remains sampling error. No estimates of sampling error are at present given in conjunction with the EU indicators. Such estimates would be a valuable addition, and Eurostat is working on the calculations as part of the EU-SILC annual quality assessment report (see Section 5.1).[3] In the meantime, caution needs to be exercised, and small differences in the indicators between countries, or over time in one country, should not be given too much emphasis.

Statistics on income and living conditions

The ECHP was an EU harmonised cross-national longitudinal[4] survey focusing on household income and living conditions in their multi-dimensionality, which ran from 1994 to 2001 (2002 in some Member States). In the first wave a sample of some 60,500 households, containing approximately 130,000 adults aged 16 years and over, were interviewed across the then 12 Member States. In 1995 and 1996 respectively, Austria and Finland joined the ECHP. From 1997, Sweden provided cross-sectional data derivable from its National Survey on Living Conditions so as to ensure a complete coverage of EU-15. In most countries the surveys were carried out using a harmonised questionnaire.

Three particularly valuable features of the ECHP were:

1. The multi-dimensional nature of the topics covered – providing micro-data (i.e. data on individual persons and households) on a wide range of socio-economic topics, which include: income, demographics, education, employment, housing conditions, health, social life, etc.
2. The longitudinal nature of the survey – individuals who were members of a household in the first wave were followed over time allowing one to examine how their circumstances change over time.
3. The cross-national comparability of the data, with general implementation of common procedures at all stages – from the design of a harmonised questionnaire, harmonised definitions and sampling requirements.[5]

The ECHP was discontinued from 2001 (or 2002) and its replacement by EU-SILC marks an important stage in the evolution of the Social Inclusion Process. EU-SILC was launched in 2003 on a gentleman's agreement basis in six Member States (Belgium, Denmark, Greece, Ireland, Luxembourg and Austria) and Norway. By 2005, EU-SILC was operating in all EU-25 countries as well as Turkey (pilot survey), Iceland and Norway. EU-SILC, like the ECHP, aims at producing cross-sectional and longitudinal micro-data that are multi-dimensional in terms of the topics covered and are comparable across participating countries, but it uses a different approach. It establishes a common framework for the systematic production of Community statistics on income and living conditions, rather than a common survey – both surveys and administrative registers can be used, provided they are "linkable" at the micro-level, and while there is a longitudinal element it is confined in most Member States to a rotational design in which an individual is followed only for four years. A priority is to provide timely data, leaving Member States a fair degree of autonomy in the areas of sampling design, questionnaire editing and data compilation while harmonised definitions and minimum methodological requirements aim to permit valid comparisons between countries. (EU–SILC and its measurement of income in particular are discussed in more detail in Chapter 5.)

Consistency with national sources

In this Chapter, we focus on the evidence provided by the published commonly agreed indicators. It is however important that these results be compared with those obtained directly from national sources. Twenty years ago, there was a dearth of information on poverty and social exclusion. In various Member States this has now been replaced by several sources, and we need to understand the relation between them. How do the figures cited here compare with the "headline" figures appearing in national newspapers? Do they tell the same story about trends over time? Eurostat has recognised this issue clearly and has initiated a number of studies. Callan and Nolan (1997), for example, compared the ECHP data relating to 1993 with those from other sources. In order to test the external validity of the ECHP, a questionnaire on national measurement of the risk of poverty was sent to national statistical institutes (Eurostat, 2000). We do not go into this question of consistency here, but wish to signal its importance.

In this respect, one significant point concerns the availability of the evidence about the common indicators. The fact that the Commission has published Statistical Annexes containing all the values, and that information is readily available on the Eurostat website, means that Europe's citizens have access to information about this key feature of their society. Moreover, the availability to researchers of the underlying EU micro-datasets (if as expected it materialises, at reasonable pricing conditions, for EU–SILC, but also for the Labour Force Surveys and the Household Budget Surveys) would mean that one could probe the published indicators and carry out other analyses including multi-dimensional analyses. All of this contributes to a more informed public debate, and allows campaigning groups access to information that in a different set of circumstances might have been confined to Government ministries. This is a little recognised, but important, contribution to mobilising the relevant actors.

3.2 Establishing the baseline: EU citizens at risk of poverty

The common indicators of today are the direct descendants of the statistics on poverty in Europe that Jacques Delors used to quote widely, and the first role of the indicators is to establish the current extent of poverty and social exclusion. The statistics serve both as a measure of the seriousness of the social challenge and as a baseline to judge progress.

Figure 3.1 shows the at-risk-of-poverty rate for the 25 Member States, using data for the income year 2003 (except the Czech Republic where it is 2002 and Malta where it is 2000). The data for the Netherlands and Slovakia are provisional.[6] We do not comment here on the comparability of the statistics, taking them at face value. The location of the new Member States is marked with * in Figure 3.1 (as in other graphs).

The EU overall percentage at-risk-of-poverty, defined as having an equivalised disposable income below 60% of the national median, is 16%. With the EU-25 population at 455 million, this suggests that a total of 73 million EU citizens are at risk of poverty. The countries in Figure 3.1 are ranked in ascending order of the at-risk-of-poverty percentage. Countries where a high proportion of the population is below the threshold are Slovakia, Portugal, Ireland, Spain and Greece, where the poverty risk is around 20%. Countries between 17% and 19% are Italy, the United Kingdom, Estonia and Poland. Germany and Latvia are at the EU-25 average. Then come Malta, Lithuania, Cyprus, Belgium, France and Austria with rates of 13–15%. Finally, the best performing countries, with a risk of poverty around 10%, are the Netherlands, Hungary, Sweden, Finland, Luxembourg, Denmark, Slovenia and the Czech Republic.

Figure 3.1: At-risk-of-poverty rates for EU-25 (2003)

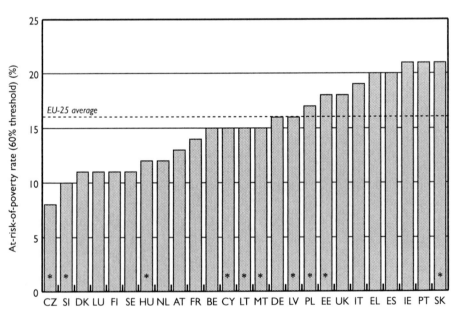

* New Member States

Source: European Commission (2006b) – Annex 1c. Statistical Tables

Notes: At-risk-of-poverty rates income reference year: 2003, except for CZ (income year 2002) and MT (2000); CZ, DE, EE, CY, LV, LT, HU, MT, NL, PL, SI, SK, UK: national source harmonised *ex-post* for maximum consistency with EU-SILC methodology; NL, SK: provisional

The ranking of countries may look surprising if compared to rankings of countries based on the widely used indicator of Gross Domestic Product (GDP) per capita – in particular, if one looks at the performance of some of the new Member States. In fact it is important to remember that the poverty risk indicators are measures of "relative (financial) poverty". This means that we look at the proportion of the population falling below a threshold defined with reference to the income distribution *in the country*. Relative poverty indicators must therefore be understood as indicators of inequality rather than measures of deprivation or living standard in any absolute sense. The national threshold being defined with reference to the national median income, it varies substantially across the EU-25. Comparative analysis of national poverty risks therefore always needs to be carried out in the light of related national poverty risk thresholds, especially when the analysis focuses on countries with large differences in living standards as is the case for EU-25 Member States. We investigate differences in the poverty threshold later in this Section.

For the previous EU-15 the rankings of at-risk-of-poverty rates are generally similar to earlier ones based on figures drawn from the ECHP, although Germany now has a rather higher risk than previously. A recent OECD study by Förster and d'Ercole (2005) presenting figures for 16 Member States (and other non-EU OECD countries) for about 1999–2002 also shows a similar picture, except that Greece did not have as high an at-risk-of-poverty rate as in Figure 3.1. It is also worth noting that the value of goods for own consumption is taken into account in estimating income for the new Member States, unlike the EU-15.[7]

In Figure 3.1 we are treating all Member States individually; in forming the EU-wide at-risk-of-poverty rate, the countries are weighted by their population size. This is important in view of the large differences in population sizes and also of the choice that was made by the SPC, and which we fully support, to focus on *relative* rather than *absolute* poverty risk. The EU-wide figure of 73 million is then dominated by the five biggest Member States (Germany, Italy, the UK, France and Spain). This is illustrated in Figure 3.2, where countries are ranked in increasing order of the absolute number of people estimated to be at risk of poverty, beginning with Luxembourg that contributes the smallest number (54,000 people) because its population is small and its risk-of-poverty rate is low. The graph highlights the degree of concentration. Only 10 million of the 73 million are to be found in the first 16 Member States. If one contemplates the risk of poverty in the EU, one tends to think of the Iberian Member States and Greece, and of the new Member States, but over half (some 40 million) of those at risk live in Germany, Italy, the UK and France. Again, remember that this relates to country-specific relative income thresholds; one should not infer from this any conclusion about the distribution of absolute living standards in the EU population.

How far do the conclusions drawn depend on the level at which the poverty threshold is drawn? Förster and d'Ercole (2005, page 22) note that the population tends to be "clustered", so that the results can be sensitive to the precise choice of cut-off. Using the much stricter 40% of the median threshold, the overall

Figure 3.2: Concentration of those at-risk-of-poverty for EU-25 (2003)

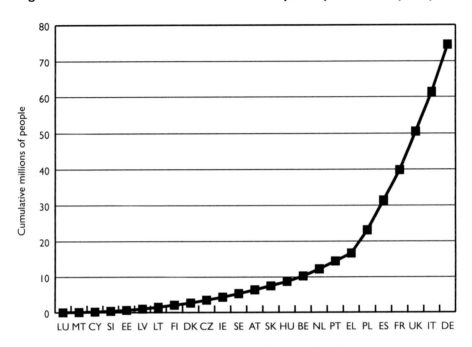

Cumulative millions of people at-risk-of-poverty (below the poverty threshold (60%) of their respective countries)
Source and notes: See Figure 3.1 for at-risk-of-poverty rates. Population figures from Eurostat, on 1 January 2003

percentage is some 5% or 23 million people at risk of poverty. The ranking of the Member States for which data are available differs somewhat according to the poverty threshold that is used, although most of the worse-than-average countries in Figure 3.1 remain in that position with the 40% threshold. The major changes are that France and Ireland improve their ranking. Again, the 23 million are concentrated in the larger Member States, with six out of 10 in Germany, Spain, France, and Italy.

The ranking of Member States by the (relative) median at-risk-of-poverty gap is very similar to the poverty risk ranking with the 40% threshold. This poverty gap measure is the difference between the median equivalised income of people living below the 60% at-risk-of-poverty threshold and the value of that threshold (expressed as a percentage of the threshold). It adds a valuable additional dimension, indicating "how poor the poor are" and therefore aiding understanding of the position in individual Member States. The 2003 Luxembourg NAP/inclusion, for example, notes that the low value of this indicator for Luxembourg indicates that the risk of poverty is less intense: "a great part of the people below the line of risk of poverty have a disposable equivalent income relatively close to the threshold" (Government of Luxembourg, 2003, page 7), an observation that is reconfirmed by the income data relating to 2003. For the EU-25, the median poverty gap in 2003 was 23%, meaning that half of those at risk of poverty were at least 23% below the relevant at–risk–of–poverty threshold. Put differently, they had to live on an equivalised income of at most 46% of the median equivalised income in their country ((100-23)=77% of the 60% of median threshold).

Diversity of EU performance

The EU at–risk–of–poverty statistics are, in one sense, well-known. The overall total receives considerable newspaper coverage. But the variation across Member States merits closer attention.

First, there is the impact of Enlargement on poverty risk, measured according to the common indicator. It is interesting to observe that Enlargement has not appreciably increased the range of rates of poverty risk. The Czech Republic at 8% and Slovenia at 10% have the lowest at–risk–of–poverty figure, lower than any of the EU–15 countries, but Finland and Sweden both recorded figures that low in 1997 (European Commission, 2004b, Table 1). At the other end of the spectrum Slovakia is on the highest rate with 21% but shares that position with Ireland and Portugal.

It is perhaps surprising that Enlargement has not led to greater diversity of outcome. Figure 3.3 plots the at–risk–of–poverty rates against the at–risk–of–poverty threshold, which as we have seen above is the national reference income below which one is considered at risk of poverty and is determined by the overall living standards in the country (being a proportion of national median income).[8] The threshold is here expressed in Purchasing Power Standards (PPS), which – on the basis of Purchasing Power Parities (PPP) – converts amounts expressed in a national currency to an artificial common currency that equalises the purchasing power of different national currencies (including those countries that share a common currency). In other words, PPS is both a price deflator and a currency converter; it eliminates the differences in price levels between countries. The EU–15 countries are shown by shaded boxes; the new Member States by solid boxes. As is clear from Figure 3.3, there is a distinct tendency among the EU–15 countries for the poverty risk to fall as we move from poorer countries to richer EU members. There are departures from a straight line (the graph shows the linear regression fitted to predict poverty risk for the EU–15 as a function of the median income), and it has been noted (see for example Morley, Ward and Watt, 2004, page 43) that countries with a more narrow income distribution, such as Denmark, Finland and Sweden, tend to lie below the line, and countries with greater income dispersion, such as Ireland and the UK, tend to lie above the line.

On this purely statistical basis, the at–risk–of–poverty rates in the new Member States could be expected to be comparable to, or higher than, those in the poorer EU–15 countries. In fact, this is only true for Slovakia. All other new Member States have typically lower at–risk–of–poverty rates than would be predicted simply from their level of income, as may be seen from observations marked by solid boxes in Figure 3.3. Indeed, the Czech Republic[9] and Slovenia have a lower rate

**Figure 3.3: Poverty risk plotted against poverty risk threshold (in PPS) for
EU-25 (2003)**

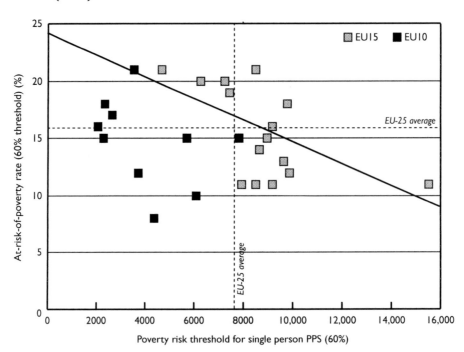

Source: European Commission (2006b) – Annex 1c. Statistical Tables

Notes: (1) The threshold is here expressed in Purchasing Power Standards (PPS), which – on the basis of Purchasing
Power Parities (PPP) – converts amounts expressed in a national currency to an artificial common currency that
equalises the purchasing power of different national currencies (including those countries that share a common
currency). In other words, PPP is both a price deflator and a currency converter. (2) Regression line fitted by ordinary
least squares to EU-15 observations. (3) Reference year: see Figure 3.1.

than the best performer among the EU-15. On this basis, Enlargement has added
little to the diversity of the EU.

The main conclusion to be drawn is that there was already considerable diversity
within the EU-15. The difference in the at-risk-of-poverty rate between the
best EU-15 performers (the Scandinavian Member States and Luxembourg) and
the worst (Ireland and Portugal) is a factor of almost 2 to 1. (Similar diversity is
exhibited by the degree of income inequality, measured by the ratio of the income
share of the top 20% to that of the bottom 20%, one of the social inclusion
"context" indicators mentioned in Chapter 2.)

A classification of countries can be made from Figure 3.3 (for some "borderline"
cases, namely Cyprus, Latvia and Germany, reference was made also to the S80/
S20 ratio when determining the classification):

1. countries with a below-average poverty risk and above-average purchasing
   power (Austria, Belgium, Cyprus, Denmark, Finland, France, Germany,
   Luxembourg, the Netherlands, and Sweden);

2. countries with a below-average poverty risk, but below-average purchasing power (the Czech Republic, Hungary, Lithuania, Malta and Slovenia);
3. countries with an above-average poverty risk and an above-average purchasing power (Ireland and the UK);
4. countries with an above-average poverty risk and a below-average purchasing power (Estonia, Greece, Italy, Latvia, Poland, Portugal, Slovakia and Spain).

43% of European citizens live in group 1 countries, 6% and 14% live in the second and third groups respectively, and 37% of Europeans live in countries in the high poverty risk/low purchasing power group 4. This is indicative of the great diversity that exists in Europe in terms of income and income distribution.

How do differences within the EU compare with those in the United States? In order to allow comparison with poverty risks at State level in the US calculated by Jesuit *et al* (2002), using a threshold set at 50% of median income in the State in question and shown in Figure 3.4, we use for the EU-25 in Figure 3.5 a threshold set at 50% of the Member State median. For the "old" Member States, we draw on the ECHP, with income reference year 2000, whereas for the New Member States, we draw on data from the Joint Memoranda on Social Inclusion, with income reference year 2002.[10] Europe, as a whole, does significantly better than the US. Using the 50% threshold at State level, the median across Member States for the EU-25 amounts to 9%, compared to 16.5% across states for the US. The figure for the best-performing EU Member States (the Czech Republic and Denmark) is 4%, compared to 11% for the best-performing US State (Hawaii). Seventeen of the EU-25 countries have a lower risk of poverty than the best-performing US State. Likewise, if one compares the scores of the worst performers, Europe comes out on top: the poverty risk in Slovakia is 16%, compared to 22% in Washington DC. However, not unimportantly, the dispersion within the EU-25 (and especially within the EU-15) is much greater than within the US: the standard deviations are respectively 3.5 and 3.6 for the EU-25 and the EU-15, compared to 2.5 for the US. Other measures of dispersion are shown in Box 3.1. It is of course the case that there is greater dispersion in GDP per capita within the EU-25 than across states within the United States.

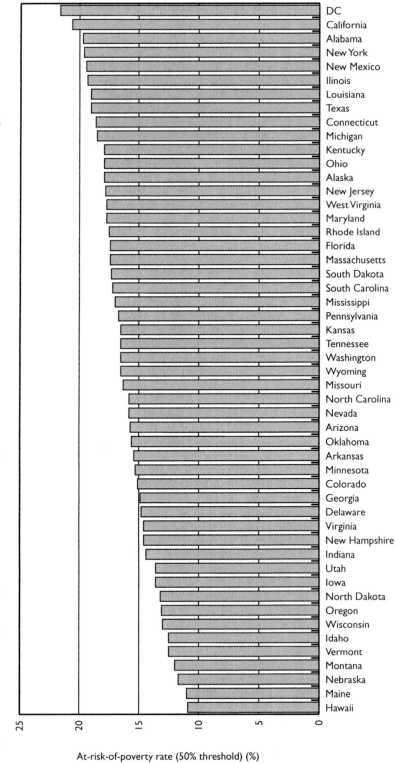

Figure 3.4: At-risk-of-poverty rates for US states (threshold set at 50% of median income for each state), mid 1990s

At-risk-of-poverty rate (50% threshold) (%)

DC
California
Alabama
New York
New Mexico
Ilinois
Louisiana
Texas
Connecticut
Michigan
Kentucky
Ohio
Alaska
New Jersey
West Virginia
Maryland
Rhode Island
Florida
Massachusetts
South Dakota
South Carolina
Mississippi
Pennsylvania
Kansas
Tennessee
Washington
Wyoming
Missouri
North Carolina
Nevada
Arizona
Oklahoma
Arkansas
Minnesota
Colorado
Georgia
Delaware
Virginia
New Hampshire
Indiana
Utah
Iowa
North Dakota
Oregon
Wisconsin
Idaho
Vermont
Montana
Nebraska
Maine
Hawaii

Source: Jesuit, Rainwater and Smeeding (2002)

Figure 3.5: At-risk-of-poverty rates for EU-25 (threshold set at 50% of median income for each state), around 2000

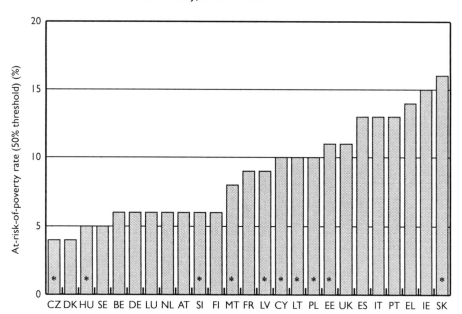

* New Member States

Sources: European Commission (2004b), Table 8 for EU-15; and European Commission, 2005c, Table 8a for EU-10
Notes: Reference year: EU-15 = 2001 figures, income reference year 2000; EU-10 = income reference year 2002 except for CY (1997) and MT (2000): see European Commission (2005c), page 173

Box 3.1: Dispersion indicators for at-risk-of-poverty rates (share of persons living in households with an equivalised income below 50% of state-level (US) or national (EU) median income)

	Standard deviation	Minimum	Maximum	Median	Interquartile ratio	Inter-quartile distance
US	2.5	10.9	21.6	16.5	1.2	3.3
EU-25	3.5	4.0	16.0	9.0	2.0	6.0
EU-15	3.6	6.0	15.0	7.0	2.2	7.0
EU-10	3.5	4.0	16.0	10.3	1.8	4.5

Sources: US: Jesuit, Rainwater and Smeeding (2002); EU-15: Statistical Annex to European Commission (2004b); EU-10: European Commission (2005c)

Persistent at-risk-of-poverty

The longer people remain on a low income, the greater their risk of becoming permanently excluded. The persistent at-risk-of-poverty Laeken indicator, defined as the share of persons with an equivalised disposable income below the at-risk-of-poverty threshold in the current year and at least two of the preceding three years, is very important for that reason. Data from EU-SILC for this indicator will not be available for some time, as we discuss in more detail in Chapter 5, but ECHP data for the EU-15 show that long-term income poverty is typically 40% below poverty risk measured at a point in time. We would expect them to be associated, but the cross-country comparison shows a surprisingly high correlation between poverty risk and persistent poverty risk. Luxembourg has a higher persistent poverty rate than could be expected given its rate of poverty risk and Spain a lower one, but in the other EU-15 countries there is a close relationship between the values of the two indicators. As far as the EU-15 is concerned, this confirms previous insights regarding the relationship between inequalities and poverty on the one hand and mobility on the other. Contrary to what sometimes is suggested, greater relative income poverty in a country does not appear to be compensated for by greater income mobility.

Summary

To summarise, the evidence from the at-risk-of-poverty indicators for the EU-25 suggests that:

- 16% of the EU population are living at-risk-of-poverty.
- In the EU-25, half of those living at-risk-of-poverty had incomes of no more than 77% of the relevant threshold.
- Enlargement has increased only marginally the degree of diversity of rates of poverty risk in the EU.
- But there was (in EU-15), and remains (in EU-25), considerable diversity in rates of poverty risk within the EU, and scope for Member States to improve their performance.
- The rate of persistent risk of poverty is closely associated across countries with the at-risk-of-poverty rate in any one year.

The evidence presented above must be interpreted carefully, taking account of the limitations of the methods and sources. International comparison of overall risks and depth of poverty is not an easy task. Besides the common problems relating to the measurement of household income, cross-national differences in socio-economic and demographic structures make comparisons difficult. These may systematically affect the conclusions drawn. It has been argued that poverty risk in the Southern European countries may be relatively overstated. The Cyprus and Greek NAPs/inclusion pointed out that, compared to other countries, owner-occupation in their country is high, particularly among the population at high risk of poverty. Taking the benefits from owner-occupation into account when the disposable income variable is computed would therefore reduce the overall rate of poverty in these countries more than elsewhere in Europe. Secondly, different NAPs/inclusion refer to the importance in the South of family solidarity in improving the subjective and objective situation of those living with an income below the poverty threshold. Third: the underestimation of the incomes of farmers and small businessmen is more of a problem in the Southern European countries. Fourth: the number of old people living in institutions rather than private households is larger in Northern Europe than in the Mediterranean, so the fact that these are generally omitted from the figures means that old-age poverty rates may be understated there. (We return to some of these issues, including imputed rent, in Chapter 5.)

Poverty-risk figures pertaining to the former socialist countries pose additional problems. There are difficulties in capturing information about income from the hidden economy, which arguably is more of a problem in the new Member States. Issues also arise from the definition of the common indicator. As is mentioned by the European Commission (2005c, page 21) and by different new Member States, a major limitation of the Laeken indicators in relation to these new Member States is the absence of an indicator regarding the very poor, which would provide insight into the degree of deprivation in these countries. Finally, a number of the new Member States questioned in their NAPs/inclusion the relevance of the standard equivalence scales (used to take account of the differing needs of households of different size and composition), when applied to their situation; this is again an issue to which we return in Chapter 5.

3.3 Establishing the baseline: the multifaceted nature of social exclusion

The 2005 *Spring Summit* Presidency Conclusions emphasised the multifaceted nature of social exclusion. In this Section, we examine the common indicators that are not income-related. Analysis of social exclusion is often criticised for focusing too exclusively on income. We now examine the baseline for other dimensions and, in particular, ask how far they change the picture with regard to the relative performance of different Member States and with regard to the impact of Enlargement. Do the same countries perform well on non-income indicators? We briefly take up the issue of multiple deprivation at the individual- or household-level (i.e. the accumulation of disadvantage) in Chapter 5. Here the country is the unit of analysis, not the individual person or household.

The Technical Annex to the 2006 Joint Report on Social Protection and Social Inclusion (European Commission, 2006b) contains a number of non-income-related common indicators for the EU–25, and this is the source on which we draw here – we only consider indicators available for the whole EU–25. As in the previous Section, we do not consider the comparability of the data, taking them at face value. The indicators that we consider are drawn from the long list of Structural Indicators for social cohesion (discussed in Chapter 2), together with life expectancy (although there are reasons to question whether that can be regarded as an indicator of social exclusion – see Atkinson, Cantillon,

Marlier and Nolan, 2002, page 151) and an index of material deprivation from the Eurobarometer surveys.

Long-term unemployment

There has long been concern about the long-term unemployed, defined in the common indicators as being unemployed for at least 12 months on the ILO definition, expressed as a proportion of the total active population aged 15 years or more. Figure 3.6 shows the EU-25 ranked according to their rates of long-term unemployment (males and females combined). The United Kingdom has the lowest rate, at 1%, while Slovakia approaches 12%. It may be noted that 17 of the 25 Member States have rates below the EU-25 average of just over 4%.

The new Member States, marked with *, constitute six of the eight countries with above-average rates of long-term unemployment. In contrast to the risk of poverty indicator, the accession of the 10 new Member States widened considerably the range of EU performance. Among the EU-15, the range is from 1.0% (the United Kingdom) to 5.6% (Greece); this now extends to 11.8% in Slovakia. The standard deviation has increased from 1.6 to 2.7.

Figure 3.6: Long-term unemployment rates for EU-25 (2004)

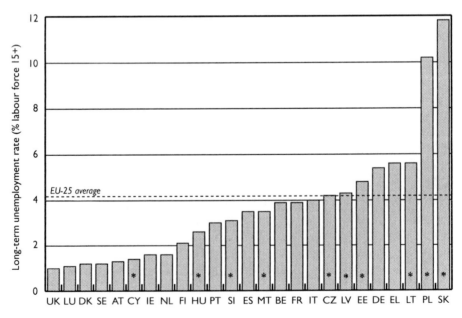

* New Member States
Source: European Commission (2006b) – Annex 1c. Statistical Tables
Notes: Long-term unemployment is unemployment for at least 12 months on the ILO definition, expressed as a proportion of the total active population aged 15 years and over

People living in jobless households

A second important indicator of possible labour market exclusion is provided by the indicator of people living in jobless households. Here we concentrate on prime-age adults, examining the position of children in Section 3.5.

Figure 3.7 shows the proportion of adults aged 18–59 living in jobless households[11] (the data in general relate to 2004, but the figures for Denmark and Luxembourg relate to 2003 and data for Sweden are not available). The first immediately apparent feature is that the ranking of countries differs from that on long-term unemployment. It is true that Luxembourg appears among the best performers and Poland among the least well-performing on both, but Belgium and Hungary were previously below the EU-25 average but are now second- and third-highest scoring countries. The UK moves from having the lowest rate of long-term unemployment to an above-average rate of adults living in jobless households. It is possible that these differences are due to definitional issues, or to data issues, but it is quite probable that the two indicators are identifying different dimensions of labour market exclusion.

Equally it is interesting to observe the position of the new Member States. Poland again extends the range, but Cyprus is now the best-performing on this indicator, and new Member States make up four of the best-performing eight

Figure 3.7: Prime-age adults living in jobless households for EU-25 (2004)

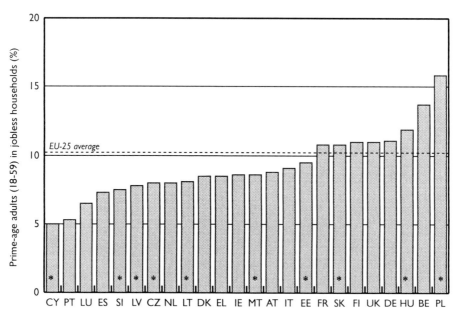

* New Member States
Source: European Commission (2006b) – Annex Ic. Statistical Tables
Notes: Proportion of the population aged 18-59 that lives in a household where none of the members is in paid employment. DK and LU refer to 2003. SE not included

countries. The standard deviation is increased by Enlargement, but only from 2.3 to 2.5.

Early school leaving

One of the Laeken indicators is the share of persons aged 18–24 who have only lower secondary education and have not received education or training in the previous four weeks. Figure 3.8 reveals yet another pattern for this indicator. Three of the four best-performing countries with respect to adults living in jobless households (Cyprus, Portugal and Spain) are now to be found with above-average proportions of early school leavers. Poland has the lowest rate of early school leavers. In this case, Enlargement has increased the spread, compared with EU-15, but primarily by adding three top-performing countries (Poland, the Czech Republic, Slovakia).

For the EU as a whole, the situation set out in Figure 3.8 should be a matter for concern, given the emphasis in the 2005 *Spring Summit* Presidency Conclusions on human capital investment. For 16 of the Member States, including all the larger ones, more than one person in 10 aged 18–24 has only a low level of educational qualification and is not currently in education or training.

Figure 3.8: Early school leavers not in education or training for EU-25 (2004)

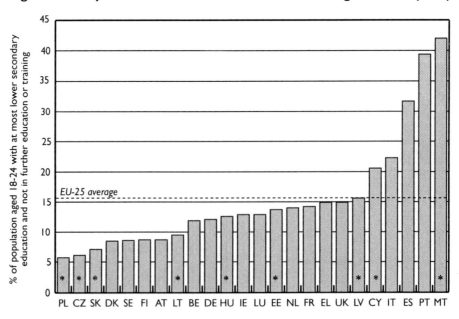

* New Member States

Source: European Commission (2006b) – Annex 1c. Statistical Tables

Notes: Proportion of the total population aged 18-24 who have at most lower secondary education and are not in further education or training. SI not included. In CY, the reference population (denominator) excludes students abroad. In DE participation in personal interest courses is excluded

Life expectancy

The life expectancies for males and females in 2002 are plotted in Figure 3.9, where countries are ranked according to the life expectancy of women, although it should be noted that the variation, at least since Enlargement, is greater for men. The diagram brings out how greatly the life-chances of Europeans differ across Member States. An average Latvian man lives 65 years, 13 years less than a Swedish man. In all former socialist countries, life expectancy is below the EU average (81 for women, 75 for men). In the EU-15, life expectancies are much more homogeneous, ranging from 74 for Portuguese men to 78 for Swedish men (and from 80 for Danish women to 84 for Spanish women).

In the previous Section, we plotted (in Figure 3.3) the at-risk-of-poverty rate against the risk of poverty threshold, taking the latter as a measure of the overall living standards, expressed in a common Purchasing Power Standard (PPS). This showed a distinct tendency for the poverty risk, measured by the EU 60% median indicator, to fall as we move towards countries with higher living standards. The new Member States did not, however, fit the EU-15 regression line. In contrast, life expectancies in the EU-15 are not obviously related to median country incomes, whereas in the new Member States there is a stronger association if we

Figure 3.9: Life expectancy (LE) at birth by gender for EU-25 (2002)

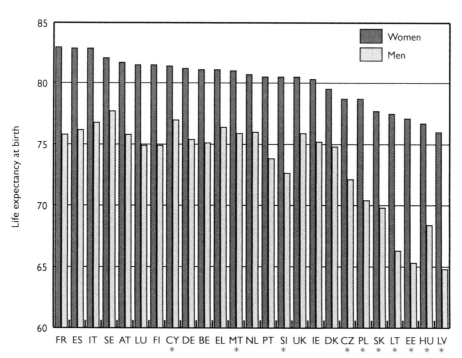

* New Member States

Source: European Commission (2006b) – Annex Ic. Statistical Tables

plot the life expectancies of men or women against the risk of poverty threshold expressed in PPS. This is another example of a difference between the income-related and non-income-related indicators.

Material deprivation

The final non-income indicator considered here is not an indicator commonly agreed at EU level, but is drawn from the *Quality of Life in Europe* series, *Perceptions of living conditions in an enlarged Europe* (European Commission, 2004f, Table 3). Deprivation is measured in Figure 3.10 in terms of the lack of consumer goods, namely television, video recorder, telephone, dishwasher, microwave, car or van, and PC. The rationale for such an indicator is considered in Chapter 5. The level of the bars shows the average score on the seven-item scale for the EU-25 (apart from Sweden, not covered in the data).[12] We see that Malta, Cyprus, Slovenia and the Czech Republic score relatively well, but that, otherwise, the new Member States (all former socialist states) constitute a group with a relatively high degree of material deprivation. Only Portugal of the EU-15 is comparable for its extent of deprivation, measured in this way. Greece, Spain and Ireland come next, but Enlargement has clearly widened the EU range for this non-income indicator.

Figure 3.10: Level of deprivation on a 7-item scale (1996-2002)

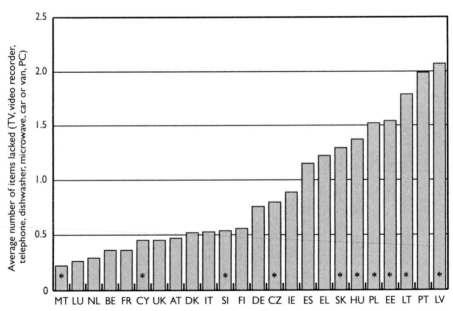

* New Member States
Source: European Commission (2004f), Table 3
Notes: Eurobarometer EU-10 (2002); ECHP (1996). SE not included

Inter-relation between indicators

From our consideration of the different non–income common indicators, it is clear that they do indeed tell a different story about the relative social performance of the different EU-25 Member States. They also differ among themselves with respect to the ranking of countries. We now take four of the indicators and explore their interaction more explicitly: the at–risk–of–poverty rate, long–term unemployment, adults living in jobless households, and early school leavers.

Figure 3.11 and Box 3.2 show the rankings of the EU-25 on the four common indicators listed above. There is considerable movement up and down the ranking as we move from one indicator to another. When the common indicators were

Figure 3.11: Rankings of EU-25 countries (2003-2004) (rank from top)

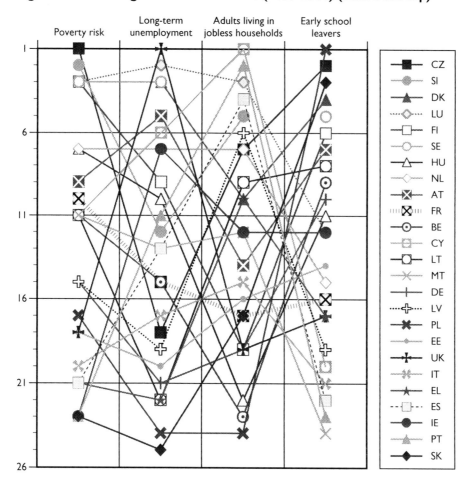

Source: See Figures 3.1, 3.6, 3.7 and 3.8
Notes: Reference year: (1) Poverty risk: income reference year 2003, except CZ (2002) and MT (2000); see Figure 3.1. (2) Long-term unemployment: 2004. (3) Prime-age adults living in jobless households: 2004, except DK and LU (both 2003). SE not included. (4) Early school leavers, 2004; SI not included

Box 3.2: Ranking of EU-25 Member States on four dimensions (2003-2004)

	At-risk-of-poverty rate	Long-term unemployment	Adults in jobless households	Early school leavers
CZ	1	18	7	2
SI	2	12	5	:
DK	3	3	10	4
LU	3	2	3	12
FI	3	9	19	6
SE	3	3	:	5
HU	7	10	22	11
NL	7	7	7	15
AT	9	5	14	7
FR	10	15	17	16
BE	11	15	23	9
CY	11	6	1	20
LT	11	22	9	8
MT	11	13	12	24
DE	15	21	19	10
LV	15	19	6	19
PL	17	24	24	1
EE	18	20	16	14
UK	18	1	19	17
IT	20	17	15	21
EL	21	22	10	17
ES	21	13	4	22
IE	23	7	12	12
PT	23	11	2	23
SK	23	25	17	3

Source: European Commission, (2006b) – Annex 1c. Statistical Tables

Notes: Countries with equal rates are assigned equal rankings.
Reference year: (1) Poverty risk: income reference year 2003, except CZ (2002) and MT (2000). NL and SK are provisional; see Figure 3.1. (2) Long-term unemployment: reference year 2004. (3) Prime-age adults living in jobless households: reference year 2004, except DK and LU (both 2003). SE not included. (4) Early school leavers: reference year 2004. SI not included

first mooted, there was general agreement that they should be multi-dimensional. This view was held largely on *a priori* grounds: that it was right in principle. Now that we have the experience of values being given to the indicators, enriched by Enlargement, we can see that the multi-dimensional approach is indeed crucial. On the four dimensions shown in Figure 3.11 and Box 3.2, Member States find themselves rising and falling in the ranking. The best performers on poverty risk have a strong tendency to be ranked lower on long-term unemployment and/or the proportion of adults living in jobless households (with Luxembourg as a notable exception). Eleven countries – the Czech Republic, Cyprus, Denmark, Finland, Luxembourg, Poland, Portugal, Slovakia, Slovenia, Sweden, and the

United Kingdom – feature in the top three countries for one of the four indicators shown in Figure 3.11. Thus nearly half of the EU Member States can claim to be in the "top three".

Rankings may be misleading, since, where observations are bunched, a country may lose several places on account of a tiny difference. An alternative is provided by the correlations of the indicator values. If the different indicators are highly correlated across countries, then this suggests that there is little value added from considering additional dimensions, at least in determining their relative performance. It should be re-emphasised that we are considering here countries as the unit of analysis. We learn nothing from these correlations about the extent to which risks are correlated at the individual level within any country. The at-risk-of-poverty rate may be much higher in countries with high rates of early school leavers, but this does not imply that individual early school leavers in country A are at high risk of poverty. In order to explore the latter correlation, we would have to go back to the micro-data, that is, the observations on individual persons and households.

If we look first at the EU-15, then we see that the at-risk-of-poverty rate is positively correlated across the 15 Member States with the proportion of early school leavers, the correlation coefficient being 0.682 – see Box 3.3. This positive association is quite high (compared, for example, to the correlation of the heights of fathers and sons, which is about 0.5). But it falls a long way short of a perfect correlation (1.00), and shows that the early school-leaving indicator conveys definite additional information. Nor is early school leaving correlated with long-term unemployment: the correlation for the EU-15 is only 0.283 and with the proportion of adults living in jobless households, it is minus 0.562. The negative correlation means that countries with a high rate of early school leaving tend to have a lower proportion of adults living in jobless households. This confirms what is shown on the right-hand side of Figure 3.11, where there are many

Box 3.3: Correlation coefficients between different indicators

	EU-15			EU-25		
	Long-term unemployment	Adults living in jobless households	Early school leavers	Long-term unemployment	Adults living in jobless households	Early school leavers
At-risk-of-poverty rate	0.475	-0.210	0.682	0.415	0.032	0.406
Long-term unemployment	–	0.252	0.283	–	0.475	-0.183
Adults living in jobless households	–	–	-0.562	–	–	-0.467

Source: European Commission, (2006b) – Annex 1c. Statistical Tables

Notes: (1) Poverty risk: income reference year 2003, except CZ (2002) and MT (2000). NL and SK are provisional, see Figure 3.1. (2) Long-term unemployment: 2004. (3) Prime-age adults living in jobless households: 2004, except DK and LU (both 2003). SE not included. (4) Early school leavers: 2004. SI not included

crossings of the rankings. This may in part reflect the fact that young people entering work early still live at home, and hence reduce the incidence of jobless households, but, if so, this highlights the tension between different objectives.

How does the at-risk-of-poverty rate correlate with the labour market exclusion indicators? First, as we have already noted, the two labour market indicators are not themselves highly correlated, the coefficient being 0.252. So that, while there is a modest positive association between poverty risk and long-term unemployment (correlation 0.475), it is not perhaps surprising that we find a different relationship between poverty risk and the proportion of adults living in jobless households. There is in fact a negative, low correlation between poverty risk and the proportion in jobless households (correlation minus 0.210). This is illustrated in the scatter diagram shown in Figure 3.12, where the shaded boxes correspond to EU-15 countries (the solid boxes relate to the new Member States). If we highlight countries with a high level of joblessness, then there is some tendency to find different ones from those with a high risk of poverty.

The first of the correlations – between poverty risk and long-term unemployment – changes slightly (0.415) when we consider the whole EU-25. However, the correlation with adults living in jobless households becomes 0.032,

Figure 3.12: Joblessness (adults) (2004) and poverty risk (2003) for EU-25

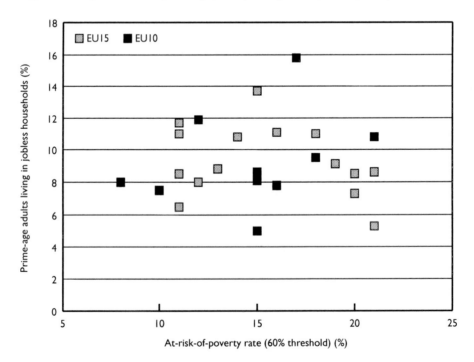

Source: European Commission (2006b) – Annex I c. Statistical Tables
Notes: (1) At-risk-of-poverty rates: income reference year 2003, except for CZ (income year 2002) and MT (2000); see Figure 3.1. (2) % Prime-age adults (18-59 years) living in jobless households: Spring results 2004 (except for DK, LU (2003) and FI: annual average)

which essentially means that there is no statistical relationship – see the full set of points in Figure 3.12. If we highlight countries with a high level of joblessness, then they are more or less a random drawing from countries ranked according to the risk of poverty. The relation between poverty risk and early school leaving is reduced when we consider the full EU-25 to 0.406, from 0.682 (see Box 3.3). The indicators become, in terms of direct correlations, less closely associated. In fact, 0.475 is the largest absolute value in the correlation matrix for the EU-25. With Enlargement, the importance of considering multiple dimensions of social exclusion appears to have perceptibly increased.

We earlier identified four groups of Member States according to their risk of poverty and their overall purchasing power (see Section 3.2). In Tables 3.1a and 3.1b (see Appendix 1) we show the countries in the four groups, with in each case the at-risk-of-poverty rate and the values of the non-income-related indicators, taking for this purpose a wider set, including the gender breakdowns, life expectancy, and material deprivation. For each indicator we take as the standard the median across countries, dividing them into quartiles. So those in the first quartile are marked "- -", the second "-", the third "+" and the fourth quartile "++". For most of the indicators, a high value represents poor performance: a country with ++ for the long-term unemployment rate is performing badly with respect to this dimension of the labour market. In contrast, for the life expectancy indicators, ++ and + represent good performance. In Table 3.1a the countries that are performing poorly relative to the median on the different indicators are highlighted. (This means values of + or ++ for all except the life expectancy indicators.) There are many different combinations, and no totally shaded columns. Quite a number of countries have shading for about half of the indicators. (In interpreting the results, it should be borne in mind that the different dimensions are represented by differing numbers of indicators.) At the same time, there is a denser concentration among the group of Member States on the right-hand side who have above average poverty risk and lower purchasing power. Some countries in the left-hand group stand out for their small number of shaded cells, notably Austria, Cyprus, Luxembourg, the Netherlands, and the Nordic Member States. In order to bring out more clearly these cases of good performance, Table 3.1b highlights those countries that are performing in the top quarter on the various indicators, which may be helpful in seeking to identify possible best practices. The same subset of the left-hand group again stands out. But all except four countries are in the top quarter for at least one indicator. If we can learn from the Nordic countries how best to avoid the risk of poverty, we can learn about reducing the extent of joblessness from countries such as Cyprus, Greece, Luxembourg, Slovenia, Spain and Portugal.

Summary

In this Section, we have seen the following:

- The importance of a multi-dimensional approach to social exclusion has been borne out by the outcome of the indicator process.
- The ranking of countries changes considerably as we move to non-income-related indicators, and within these indicators. Eleven of the 25 Member States are in the "top three" on one of the four indicators: poverty risk, long-term unemployment, joblessness, and early school leaving. Of these, five are new Member States.
- The impact of Enlargement differs across the different indicators. We saw in Section 3.2 that the new Member States had only slightly increased the diversity of at-risk-of-poverty rates. Enlargement has, however, increased substantially the range of labour market performance, notably with regard to long-term unemployment. It has also increased the differences in life expectancy, especially for men. In the case of early school leaving, in contrast, Enlargement has increased the range by adding a number of top performers.
- With Enlargement, the importance of considering multiple dimensions of social exclusion appears to have perceptibly increased.

3.4 What can we learn from cross-country comparisons?

What can be learned from this rich set of cross-country data about the causes of poverty and social exclusion, and about the impact of policy? For some people, the answer is that we can learn little. The individual countries of the EU-25 are so diverse in their history and institutions that observed differences in performance contain no lessons for other Member States. That such differences are important is clearly true; one has only to consider the history of the past 50 years. The question is however one of degree. Any conclusions may have to be qualified, but is there really *nothing* that can be said?

Suppose, for instance, that one observes countries with high and low risk of poverty, and divides them into countries with high and low levels of policy effort to eliminate the risk of poverty. Suppose, for example, we observe high poverty/low effort countries, low poverty/high effort countries, and high poverty/ high effort countries, but the remaining quadrant is empty – there are no low poverty/ low effort countries. Then we cannot advise the Government of a high poverty/low effort country that increasing policy effort will reduce the risk of poverty, but we can say that there is no precedent for supposing that a low poverty/ low effort outcome can be achieved. To seek this combination would be entering into uncharted territory.

The example just given is bi-variate (relating poverty to a single variable), whereas there can be little doubt that the explanation of poverty and social exclusion involves many variables. In the upper part of Table 3.2 (see Appendix 1), we have assembled a selection of the background variables contained in the Joint Reports on Social Inclusion. We have taken the four-fold grouping of Member States described earlier in Section 3.2, and highlighted countries below the EU median (in the upper part of the Table). Here we ask how far the "++"

etc. are associated when we read down the Table. For instance, three countries out of six in the lower quartile for the employment rate among the population aged 15–64 (i.e. the "- -", that is those with lowest employment rates) are also in the higher quartile for the at-risk-of-poverty rate (highest poverty risks): Greece, Slovakia and Italy. By considering such "likely candidate" variables, we can explore some of the possible linkages. However, while some cross-country econometric research proceeds by such a heuristic approach, there are good reasons for starting from the *a priori* mechanisms that one believes may be in operation and working through how it can be expected to affect the risk of poverty (or other outcome indicators). In this way, it is more probable that we identify the full range of factors in operation. This approach is illustrated by the study of Tsakloglou and Papadopoulos (2002). The basis for their econometric analysis of social exclusion is, on the one hand, the capability theory of Sen (1985), and, on the other hand, the theory of welfare regimes of Esping-Andersen (1990), Leibfried (1992) and Ferrera (1996). Tsakloglou and Papadopoulos (2002), using ECHP data for 12 EU Member States, find the extent of social exclusion to be related both to individual characteristics and to the nature of the welfare state regime.

The lower part of Table 3.2 illustrates a second approach, which seeks to explore the underlying causes via disaggregation. Here we compare the poverty risks of a number of at-risk-of-poverty groups *with the average risks in the country in which they live*. This way, we gain insight into the at-risk groups per country. If the subgroup is at greater risk than the national average, then the subgroup is marked "+" for that country; if the subgroup's risk is smaller, then it is marked "–". If the group's situation deviates substantially from the national average, i.e. a poverty risk that is 25% lower or higher, then that subgroup is marked "- -"or "++" respectively. If the group's poverty risk is at least 75% higher (or lower) than the national average, then that subgroup is marked '+++' (or "- - -"). Despite the variety in the average poverty risk throughout the countries of the EU, the same high-risk groups appear in many Member States. Women, children, young people (16- to 24-year-olds) and those aged 65 and above, the unemployed and pensioners, as well as lone-parent households, households with three or more children, and single persons are all at a higher-than-average poverty risk in most countries. Of these subgroups, the unemployed and single parent families are at particularly high risk in all countries. In 22 countries the unemployed face an at-risk-of-poverty rate that is 75% higher than the national average; in the case of single parents, the at-risk-of-poverty rate is in 18 countries at least 75% higher than the national average. Single women also face a very high poverty risk in most countries: in 11 countries their poverty risk is at least 25% higher than the national average, in another 11 countries their poverty risk is 75% higher than the national average poverty risk. These are examples of groups that appear as particularly vulnerable to the risk of poverty across the EU-25.

If we look at the position of couples with three children, then we find that in 10 countries there are double plus signs and in nine countries triple plus signs. The poverty risk is below the average only in Slovenia. Overall, child poverty is in most countries higher than the national average. At the same time, this is not universally true. It is not the case in Denmark, France, Cyprus, Finland, Sweden, Slovenia and Greece. While the national contexts, such as traditional attitudes to the family, differ considerably across countries, policies towards households with children in these Member States may be of particular interest when it comes to establishing potential best practices. Similarly, in contrast to the majority of Member States where pensioners and single persons aged 65 and above have a strongly increased poverty risk, we find a below-average poverty risk for older people in a substantial minority of countries. This is the case in Luxembourg, the Netherlands, Germany, the Czech Republic, Hungary, Lithuania, Estonia, Italy, Poland, Latvia and Slovakia.

Both of these elements – specifying a full set of candidate explanatory variables and disaggregation – have a role to play in developing an analysis of poverty and social exclusion. At the same time, there will be certain variables on which we wish to focus. Here we consider two such variables – social protection expenditure and employment – in relation to the at-risk-of-poverty rate.

Focusing on social protection?

There are good reasons to expect the level and effectiveness of social protection to influence, along with other factors, the risk-of-poverty rate. Arithmetically, for any given pre-transfer rate of poverty risk, social protection expenditure can be expected, depending on how well it is targeted, to reduce the post-transfer rate of poverty risk. (We return later to the issue of targeting, and to the fact that the pre-transfer risk may be affected by the extent of social protection.) The 2004 Joint Report on Social Inclusion contained a graph for the EU–15 relating the risk of poverty to social expenditure per capita (measured in PPS). For the EU–15, the Joint Report concluded that "the relationship between the level of expenditure in social protection and the risk of poverty is reasonably established on empirical grounds. [...] Member States with higher than average per capita social expenditure tend to show relatively lower risk of poverty, and vice versa" (European Commission, 2004b, page 51).[12]

A similar graph is shown in Figure 3.13 expressing social protection expenditure as a percentage of GDP for the EU–25. The EU–15 countries are again shown by shaded boxes; the new Member States by solid boxes. The solid line shows a linear regression fitted to the observations for EU–15. Although the various countries are scattered around the diagram, no country below the first quartile in terms of social expenditures (shown by the vertical dotted line) falls below the first quartile in terms of the at-risk-of-poverty rate (shown by the horizontal dotted line). No EU–15 country has total social protection expenditure of 19% or below and at the same time achieves a risk-of-poverty rate below 12%. We are in the situation described hypothetically at the start of this Section. If it is possible to attain low or moderate poverty rates without significant social spending, then it has yet to be demonstrated by any EU country.

Figure 3.13: Social protection expenditure (2001) and poverty risk (2003) for EU-25

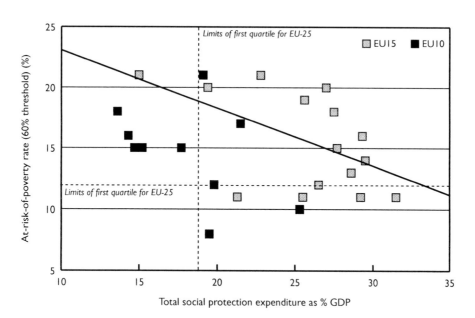

Total social protection expenditure as % GDP

Source: European Commission (2006b) – Annex 1c. Statistical Tables
Notes: (1) At-risk-of-poverty rates: income reference year 2003, except for CZ (income year 2002) and MT (2000); see Figure 3.1. (2) Total social protection expenditure as % of GDP reference year 2001. (3) Linear regression line restricted to EU-15

Has the extension to EU–25 changed the picture? It is true that the lower left-hand quadrant (low spending/low poverty risk) remains empty, although the Czech Republic achieves the lowest at-risk-of-poverty rate with spending of only 20% of GDP. At the same time, it is clear that, with one exception (Slovakia), the new Member States, shown by solid boxes, lie below the fitted line for EU–15 countries. If we fit a separate relation for the EU–10, it proves to be parallel to that shown, some five percentage points lower. What are we to conclude from the fact that, other things equal, the same level of social protection expenditure (as % GDP) is associated with a risk of poverty that is five percentage points lower? Why should the new Member States be on a different relationship?

In seeking to answer these questions, we need to introduce other variables that can explain cross-country differences in poverty risk. After making the statement quoted above, the 2004 Joint Report goes on immediately to warn:

> This simple correlation should not be taken as the only guide for policy action. A number of other equally relevant factors are at play in determining the share of the population falling below the poverty threshold, such as the extent to which the tax system responds to social equity objectives, the way in which the benefit system is

structured by major branches, the targeting of welfare provision, the efficiency of services delivery, the age structure of the population, the business cycle, and the general pattern of income distribution and overall economic prosperity. (European Commission, 2004b, page 51)

All of these considerations rightly point to the need for a more textured investigation of the relation between poverty risks and overall social expenditures. The analysis needs to be (i) disaggregated by different categories of household, (ii) accompanied by institutional details of different social protection schemes, and (iii) accompanied by a range of other explanatory variables. Here we simply highlight three points.

First, we should stress the importance of the institutional structure of social protection expenditure, including the degree to which it is targeted to particular categories of recipient and to particular income groups. Welfare states differ in more respects than the size of total expenditures. If this were the only important characteristic, the policy recommendation might be simple: increase expenditure. However, things are not that straightforward; the degree of targeting and the method of financing are both important. As Oxley *et al* (2001) have argued, some countries achieve better "efficiency" in terms of child poverty risk reduction (i.e. poverty is reduced more for each Euro spent) by targeting more on low-income groups. The importance of institutional details is brought out in the comparative study of social assistance in Europe by Saraceno and colleagues (Saraceno, 2002). A simulation by Van den Bosch (2002) using Luxembourg Income Study data suggested that expanding welfare state expenditures within the existing social transfer systems will not always have a strong impact on risk-of-poverty rates.[14] The simulation did confirm the general intuition that more social spending generates less poverty risk. Nevertheless, the response of risk-of-poverty statistics to increased social expenditures was smaller than expected, indicating that in most countries poverty risks are far less sensitive to increases in social transfers than the cross-country pattern would suggest. This is due to various institutional factors. In Italy for instance – where poverty risk was found to actually increase with higher social spending – a large part of the social budget is devoted to pensions. In this country, increasing pensions has only a marginal impact on old age poverty risk whereas more households of active age are at greater risk of poverty on account of the increase in taxes and social security contributions. A comparative study by Callan *et al* (2004), focusing on why Ireland has such a high proportion falling below relative income thresholds, highlighted the role of social protection, but differences in both levels and structures compared with countries such as Denmark and the Netherlands with much lower numbers below such thresholds were seen to be important. The difference between levels and structure of spending is particularly important in post-communist Member States that have seen a major redesign of social protection.

The second point to be stressed is that differences in the levels of social protection expenditure cannot be regarded as a final explanation; these levels themselves have to be explained. This has to be borne in mind when interpreting the aggregate relationship. It is not necessarily chance that has led some Member States to spend more. There may be third variables that lead, for example, to poverty risk being low and spending high, so that we cannot draw conclusions about the strength of the causal connection between spending and poverty from graphs such as Figure 3.13. The same may apply to the *structure* of social protection spending. The degree of targeting is a political choice, just as is the level of spending. Policy "effort" (how much money is spent) and the degree of "targeting" may be related as a result of the underlying political factors. As has been noted by Jeandidier and Reinstadler (2002), this may make it difficult to separate their effects in any empirical cross-country analysis.

The third point we want to highlight concerns the relation between social spending and the at-risk-of-poverty rate before transfers.[15] As can be seen from Figure 3.14, there is in fact little sign either that countries with high social spending have high pre-transfer poverty risk, or – interpreting the relation the other way round – that countries with high pre-transfer poverty risk have high social spending. It is striking that 21 of the 25 Member States have pre-transfer risk-of-poverty rates between 35% and 45%. Maître *et al* (2005) conclude in a study of 13 members of the EU-15 that the pre-transfer risk of poverty is quite

Figure 3.14: Social protection expenditure (2001) and pre-transfer poverty risk (2003) for EU-25

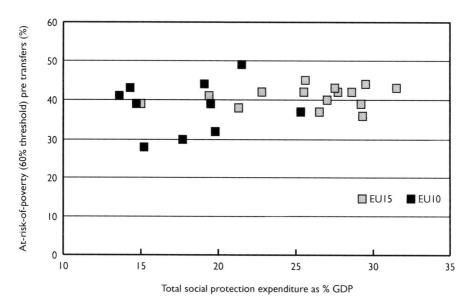

Total social protection expenditure as % GDP

Source: European Commission (2006b) – Annex Ic. Statistical Tables
Notes: (1) At-risk-of-poverty rates before social transfers: income reference year 2003, except for CZ (income year 2002) and MT (2000); see Figure 3.1. (2) Total social protection expenditure as % of GDP reference year 2001

similar across welfare state regimes: social-democratic, liberal, corporatist and Southern.

The status of pensions is, however, rather different from that of other transfers, not least because of the role played by private pension schemes in certain Member States. Figure 3.15 shows therefore the relation between the risk–of–poverty rate before transfers but *after pensions* and the post-transfer risk. The diagonal line shows where the two rates would be equal. Figure 3.15 suggests there is within the EU-25 some, but not very strong, relationship between pre-transfer and post-transfer poverty risk. Ireland, the UK, Slovakia and Portugal have distinctively high pre-transfer risk-of-poverty rates and stay above-average post-transfer, while Slovenia and Hungary are low pre-transfer and stay low. On the other hand, Denmark, Sweden and Finland succeed in neutralising a high pre-transfer poverty risk by means of social redistribution to arrive at a relatively low poverty risk, while the Czech Republic succeeds in considerably reducing an already low pre-transfer at-risk-of-poverty rate. Most other countries fall in a rather narrow range on pre-transfer risk of poverty but they diverge strongly post-transfer. For example, Luxembourg, Austria, the Netherlands, France, Latvia, Spain, Lithuania and Italy all are on 22–26% pre-transfer but end up on a range from 11% all the way up to 20% (see also Marlier and Cohen-Solal, 2000).

Figure 3.15: Poverty risk pre- and post-social transfers for EU-25 (2003)

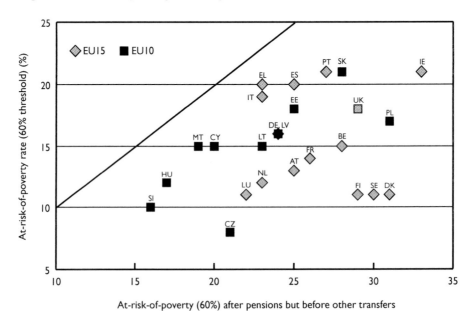

At-risk-of-poverty (60%) after pensions but before other transfers

Source: European Commission (2006b) – Annex 1c. Statistical Tables
Notes: (1) At-risk-of-poverty rates and at-risk-of-poverty rates after pensions but before other transfers: income reference year 2003, except for CZ (income year 2002) and MT (2000); see Figure 3.1. (2) The line shows where the values of the national poverty risks pre- and post-social transfers are the same

Focusing on employment?

As noted at the beginning of this Chapter, a reader of the Kok Report (European Communities, 2004) may be tempted to take the employment rate, of central concern there, and the at-risk-of-poverty rate, of particular interest here, and plot the latter against the former. Figure 3.16 shows the results of such an exercise using data from the Statistical Annex to the 2004 Joint Inclusion Report (European Commission, 2004b), covering EU-15 countries, the latest income data relating to the year 2000, and the Annexes to the Commission Staff Working Paper, Report on Social Inclusion 2004 (European Commission, 2005c), covering the 10 new Member States, the income data mostly relating to 2002. It should be noted that, rather than taking the employment rate data for the most recent available year, we have sought to match as far as possible the employment rate to the date on which the risk of poverty was observed.

For the EU-15, shown by shaded boxes in Figure 3.16, there is a modest negative association between the employment rate and the at-risk-of-poverty rate: the solid line shows the linear regression. For the EU-25, the association is weaker as the deviations around the fitted line are larger. The dashed lines divide countries into those with above-average and those with below-average values. Although the greatest number of countries is found either in the quadrant indicating "below-average employment – above-average poverty risk" or in that indicating

Figure 3.16: Employment rate (2004) and poverty risk (2003) for EU-25

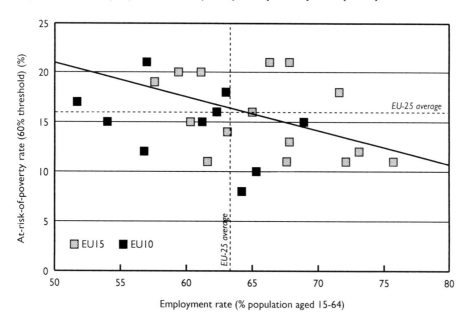

Employment rate (% population aged 15-64)

Source: European Commission (2006b) – Annex 1c. Statistical Tables
Notes: (1) At-risk-of-poverty rates: income reference year 2003, except for CZ (income year 2002) and MT (2000); see Figure 3.1 (2) Employment rate (% population aged 15-64) annual average 2004. (3) Linear regression line restricted to EU-15

"above-average employment – below-average poverty risk", there are also countries (e.g. Belgium, Hungary, Malta and Luxembourg) that combine low employment with a below-average risk of poverty. Ireland, Portugal and the UK, on the other hand, combine above-average risk-of-poverty rates with high employment.

In seeking to understand this cross-country pattern, it may be helpful to make explicit the different steps in the argument linking employment and the combating of the risk of poverty. Within any country, it is certainly true that the risk of poverty among those in paid work is far lower than among those who are not in paid work, certainly if one considers only the non-elderly. We cannot however assume that an increase in the employment rate would necessarily reduce the overall proportion at risk of poverty by an amount equal to that observed difference. The actual outcome may depart from this amount for several reasons. First, considering the person on their own, the outcome depends on the wage and in-work benefits received, relative to the replacement income currently paid. Here we have to confront the problem of in-work poverty. In its recent report, *Extending Opportunities*, the OECD argued that poverty and social exclusion reflect more than lack of jobs:

> Many of the jobs available may not pay enough to lift households out of poverty, or may not provide career prospects to the workers who hold them. While the risk of falling into poverty is much higher for households with no adult in employment than for those where someone works, households with one or more workers represent a very substantial proportion of the income-poor in all OECD countries. [...] The fact that many of the "poor" hold jobs, at least for some part of the year, goes a long way towards explaining the lack of a significant cross-country association between relative poverty [and] employment rates. (OECD, 2005, page 128)

In their recent study of in-work poverty in the EU, Bardone and Guio note:

> By adopting a common indicator of in-work poverty, Member States have finally acknowledged the importance of the problem of in-work poverty and are prepared to measure the extent to which participation in employment is not sufficient to escape income poverty. This certainly represents progress in the policy debate about the fight against poverty, where inactivity and in particular unemployment have long been the predominant labour market-related factors used to explain poverty. (2005, page 8)

On an individual basis, they find that in the EU-15 around a quarter of the persons aged 16 and over at risk of poverty are in employment, or around 11 million workers (Bardone and Guio, 2005, page 3).

Secondly, we have to consider the household context: it depends on whether or not the newly employed person lives in a household at risk of poverty. Job growth does not always benefit jobless households. In Ireland the proportion in workless households fell quite sharply when employment levels rose, as Table 17 of the 2004 Joint Report on Social Inclusion Statistical Annex shows (European Commission, 2004b). The same Table also shows the Netherlands having some decline – from 11% to 8% of working-age adults – in the most recent period. However, in a number of countries, employment growth over the past decades has not been to the benefit of workless households. According to Gregg and Wadsworth (1996), the rise in the UK employment rate during the 1980s and 1990s masked a polarisation between what they called work-rich and workless households. The proportion of working-age individuals in work had risen in the UK, but so had also the proportion of households with no one in work. Job growth had mainly benefited households with already one person in work. De Beer (2001) has documented a similar dynamic in more detail for the Netherlands in the mid-1990s. Employment growth may therefore add to the incomes of households above the poverty threshold, rather than those at risk of poverty. (See also Iacovou (2003) for a 14 European countries analysis of "work-rich and work-poor couples".) To further complicate the picture, increasing employment income levels may well feed into an increase in the at-risk-of-poverty threshold, making it more difficult to "escape" above it.

Finally, we should note that many workers face also a "low wage trap", which means that there may be limited financial gain to increasing working hours (say, from part time to full time) or work effort. The Technical Annex to the Joint Report on Social Protection and Social Inclusion (European Commission, 2006b) has examined the benefit in 19 different Member States from increasing earnings from 33% to 67% of average production worker earnings. They calculate the "marginal effective tax rate" (METR), which is the percentage of the rise in gross earnings that is taken away in the form of higher tax and social security charges and lower welfare benefits. In 2004, for a two-earner couple with two children, the METR ranged from 12% in Portugal to 59% in Belgium. In six countries the METR was 50% or higher. For a lone parent, the METR was 50% or higher in 11 of the 19 countries. As noted in the Technical Annex, these high METR can arise on account of policy measures taken to deal with other "traps": "measures aimed at reducing one trap (e.g. through widespread use of in-work benefits) could cause another type of trap to arise at a higher income level" (European Commission, 2006b, page 67).

Growth and changes over time

Drawing inferences from cross-country comparisons is subject, as we have seen, to the general objection that there are underlying differences between the countries. Observing country A with an at-risk-of-poverty rate of 10% and an employment rate of 70% (or social protection spending of 30% GDP) does not mean that country B can achieve the same poverty rate by increasing its employment rate to 70% (or its social spending to 30%). This has led to the study of changes over time across countries, or "panels of countries". To the extent that the unobserved country differences are constant over time, we can neutralise them by focusing on the changes over time. We can ask how far *growth* in employment has contributed to social inclusion in the EU.

With such a panel of countries approach, we are seeking to learn from the directions of movement. In a single country context, Burgess, Gardiner and Propper (2001) studied the relation between poverty risk and recorded unemployment in the UK in the years since 1971. As updated by Hills (2004, page 85), this shows that unemployment in the UK rose from 2% in 1973 to 10% in 1983 with virtually no change in the rate of poverty. The UK poverty rate then rose sharply in the next 10 years, whereas the unemployment rate in 1993 was again around 10%. Between 1993 and 2001, the unemployment rate fell back to the levels at which it started in the 1970s, but the poverty rate remained little changed. Hills concludes that, in the UK, "the relationship between unemployment and poverty just for those of working age is fairly weak" (2004, page 85).

The Annex to the Kok Report shows the changes in the common indicators for the EU-15, but not for comparable periods in the cases of poverty risk and employment, since the poverty data lag those for employment. We need to match up the time periods. Figure 3.17a shows the changes in the at-risk-of-poverty rate between 1994 (1997 for Finland and Sweden) and 2000, and in the employment rate. The arrows mark in each case the direction of movement. The

Figure 3.17a: Changes in employment rate and risk of poverty 1994-2000 for EU-15

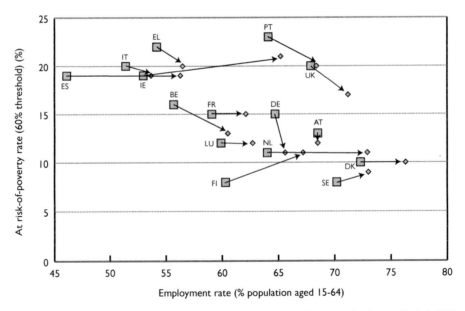

Source: European Commission, 2004b, Table 1; employment rate from European Commission, Employment Outlook 2005
Notes: Reference period for FI and SE: 1997-2000

employment rate rose in every case except for Austria, where it was already above the EU average. In six EU–15 countries, the employment rate rose and the at-risk-of-poverty rate fell: Belgium, Greece, Germany, Italy, Portugal and the UK. The slopes range from steep (Germany) to quite flat (Italy). They are counter-balanced by a further five countries where the employment rates rose but the at-risk-of-poverty rate was unchanged over the six-year period: Denmark, Spain, France, Luxembourg and the Netherlands. And the at-risk-of-poverty rate rose in Ireland, Finland, and Sweden, where the employment rates rose at the same time. (The upward trend in poverty risk in Finland and Ireland is confirmed by the OECD figures used by Förster and d'Ercole (2005).) The picture is a mixed one.

The use of changes over time offers a potential solution to some of the methodological problems; at the same time, it introduces problems of its own. As has been noted in the panel data literature, the approach risks making the estimates more subject to measurement error (see, for example, Freeman, 1984). By weakening the signal, we are raising the noise-to-signal ratio. The estimates of the at-risk-of-poverty rate ·in any one year are subject to sampling error. As indicated at the beginning of this Chapter, no estimates of sampling error are at present given in conjunction with the common indicators (and Eurostat is planning to introduce them), but we may ask about the significance to be attached to a one percentage point change in the at-risk-of-poverty rate, as in Austria or Italy. In a panel study, this is even more complicated given that the representativeness of the sample may be sensitive to attrition from the panel.

More concretely, in the present application we have to confront the issue that, as previously emphasised, with a relative income threshold, policies to raise employment will affect not only the incomes of those at risk of poverty but also the median household income used to judge the risk of poverty. (The relative nature of the poverty line also complicates any use of the concept of the "poverty elasticity of growth" – see Bourguignon (2003).) As has been emphasised in the Irish context (Nolan, 1999), where there is strong overall income growth, relative poverty rates may rise even where those on low incomes are enjoying rising standards of living. This illustrates the limit of focusing only on relative poverty to assess the success of policies. It may be the case that the income of *all* citizens is on the rise and at the same time that poverty risk increases. One may want to repeat the analysis taking a threshold anchored in real terms (i.e. only uprated by inflation) at a moment in time (which is one of the overarching indicators; see Table 2.2a in Appendix 1). This is shown in Figure 3.17b, which has to be based on the shorter period 1997–2000 for which the anchored indicator is given by the European Commission (2004b, Table 11). We now have a predominance of downward arrows to the right. In all countries anchored poverty risk declined, except in the Netherlands and Finland, where employment was on the rise but there was no change in the poverty risk. In this case, the picture is much more uniform. The debate about the "trickle down" benefits from employment growth

Figure 3.17b: Changes in employment rate and anchored risk of poverty 1997-2000 for EU-15

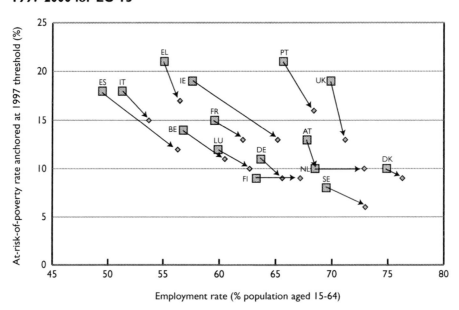

Source: European Commission, 2004b, Table 11; employment rate from European Commission, Employment Outlook 2005

may therefore depend in part on whether the poverty threshold is anchored in real terms or is increased in line with rising real incomes.

Changes over time may provide insights into the impact of social protection expenditure, discussed above. Most Member States have expanded their social protection programmes over the post-war period, and have seen over the same period considerable falls in their poverty rates. The expansion and maturing of pension schemes, for example, have meant that many more older people enjoy financial independence. But again there are other factors at work. There has been a large increase in the size of the older population. A sizeable part of the increased social spending has been due to an expansion of scale rather than improvement in individual benefits. The proportion in poverty may have been changing for other reasons. Increased private savings and private pensions may have generated a reduction in poverty. There may be interdependencies. The expansion of social protection may have caused people to save less, and raised the pre-transfer poverty rate. All of this points once more to the need to understand the mechanisms in operation. The aggregate relation between social indicators and levels of spending, or other policy variables, is a "black box". We need to look inside the box if we are to be confident in drawing conclusions about the implications of pulling different policy levers.

Conclusions

To respond to the question posed in the title of this Section, we believe that it is both necessary and possible to steer a course between two extreme positions. One extreme is to draw definite policy conclusions from simple correlations; the other extreme is to reject all statistical analysis of the common indicators. Here we have argued for a more textured approach. For example, we have suggested that one can learn by comparing the relationships found for the EU-15 with those for the full EU-25; we have explored some of the consequences of comparing, not levels, but changes over time. There is no doubt that the process is complex, multivariate and needs to be disaggregated. We need to base any empirical conclusions on a theoretical framework linking the different mechanisms in operation.

3.5 Children mainstreaming

To help draw together the threads of our analysis, and to respond to the stress laid on child poverty in the 2005 and 2006 Spring Summits Presidency Conclusions, we end this Chapter by considering *children mainstreaming*. As already explained in Chapter 1, our purpose is not to single out children as a priority group, but to explore the general issues of poverty and social exclusion from the perspective of children.

Child poverty

The seriousness of the issue of child poverty has come increasingly to be recognised in OECD countries (see, for example, Cornia and Danziger, 1997; Bradbury and Jäntti, 2001; Vleminckx and Smeeding, 2001). It received a great deal of international attention as a result of the UNICEF Report Card, Child Poverty in Rich Countries 2005 (UNICEF, 2005a – see also UNICEF, forthcoming). As summarised by Corak:

> Child poverty rates vary by more than a factor of ten across the OECD, from less than three percent to over 20 and almost 30%. These countries fall into four main groups, those with child poverty rates less than 5%, those with higher rates but still less than 10%, those with rates higher than 10% and as high as 20%, and finally two countries with more than one-in-five children being poor. Such variation creates at least the presumption that there is nothing inevitable about the level of child poverty in a given country. All OECD countries operate broadly similar free-market economic systems, and their widely differing child poverty rates reflect different policies interacting with labour market and social institutions. Indeed, poverty rates based upon disposable (after tax – after transfer) incomes vary much more than those

calculated from solely market incomes. Second, in the strong majority of countries for which reliable data are available child poverty rates, far from progressively declining, have actually gone up since the early 1990s when the Convention on the Rights of the Child first came into force. In 16 of 24 OECD countries the child poverty rate at the end of the 1990s was higher than at the beginning, and in only three countries has it declined to a measurable degree. (2005, pages 44–5)

It should be noted that Corak is using a poverty threshold set at 50% of the median (rather than 60% as used as a Primary EU indicator). The two countries with child poverty rates in excess of 20% are the US and Mexico, but the UK, Portugal, Ireland and Italy are above 15%. The OECD study by Förster and d'Ercole (2005) found that relative poverty rates (with 50% median threshold) are higher for children than for the overall population in most OECD countries, although with much variation across countries. In a study produced as part of a Nordic Research Council project, Ritakallio and Bradshaw (2005) have used the data from the European Community Household Panel (ECHP) to examine levels and changes in child poverty in the EU-15 countries from 1994 to 2000. The UK had the highest child poverty rate (defined using a 60% threshold) in 1994 but it had fallen by 2000, below the rates in Italy, Spain, Ireland and Portugal. The overall rate was lowest in the Nordic countries, but increases over the period are shown in the cases of Finland and Sweden, as well as in the Netherlands, France and Luxembourg. Ritakallio and Bradshaw (2005) go on to consider non-income-related indicators (see below). For a study on children and disability that covers a number of the new Member States, see UNICEF (2005b).

We begin by considering the evidence about child poverty using the breakdowns in the 2006 Joint Report (European Commission, 2006b). We are interested both in the risk of children living in poverty, and in the relationship between this risk and that of adults. As we discuss in Chapter 5, it must be remembered that the measurement of child poverty, and particularly the comparison with the adult rate, may be influenced by the choice of equivalence scale. The statement that children are at less risk than adults in country A may be reversed if we adopt an equivalence scale giving different weight to children. This is no theoretical curiosity. Foidart, Génicot and Pestieau (1997) showed using Belgian data that the effectiveness of family allowances in reducing poverty is sensitive to the choice of equivalence scale. Ritakallio (2002) has shown that moving from using the OECD equivalence scale to using the modified OECD scale (as in the indicators commonly agreed at EU level) has the effect, in most countries, of reducing the proportion of children at risk of poverty.

Figure 3.18 shows the proportion of children living in households at risk of poverty. It brings together the evidence for the EU-15 with that for the new Member States, seven of which did not feature in the UNICEF study. The risk of poverty threshold is set here at 60% of the median. In all except Denmark, Finland and Slovenia, the proportion of children at risk is in excess of 10%. In

Figure 3.18: Child poverty risk rate and median poverty risk gap for EU-25 (2003)

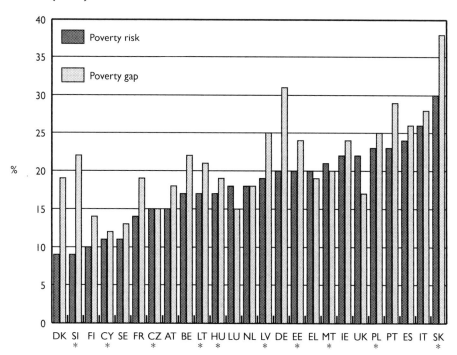

* New Member States

Source: European Commission (2006b) – Annex 1c. Statistical Tables

Notes: (1) At-risk-of-poverty rates (60%) of children aged 0-15 years and relative median at-risk-of-poverty gap (60%) for children 0-15 years, income reference year 2003, except for CZ: income year 2002; Data for MT refer to income year 2000; see Figure 3.1. (2) The relative median at-risk-of-poverty gap is the difference between the median equivalised income of persons below the at-risk-of-poverty threshold and the threshold itself, expressed as a percentage of the at-risk-of-poverty threshold

eight Member States, the rate exceeds 20%, including the UK (at that date), Italy and Spain. As is noted by Corak, Lietz and Sutherland (2005), the severity of poverty differs from the incidence across countries. In Figure 3.18, we also show the median at–risk–of–poverty gap alongside the child poverty risk. This gives a somewhat different impression. The severity of income shortfall is not very different in the Nordic countries from that in Luxembourg, the UK and Austria. The child poverty risk is less in Greece than in the UK, but the median income shortfall is, if anything, larger in Greece.

In order to understand the specific circumstances of children in each Member State, we need to view the child poverty risk in relation to the overall poverty risk. Figure 3.19 shows that the relative risk is greater for children in the majority of Member States; indeed in nine of the 25 the rate is at least 25% higher. This includes certain countries with a low overall rate of poverty risk, such as the Czech Republic, Luxembourg and the Netherlands. The 2003 Luxembourg NAP/inclusion notes that the "risk–of–poverty of people aged less than 25 years

Figure 3.19: National child poverty risk relative to national overall poverty risk for EU-25 (2003)

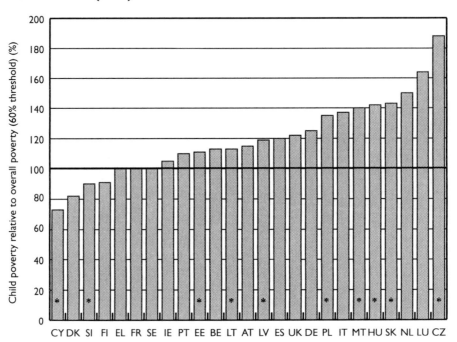

* New Member States

Source: European Commission (2006b) – Annex Ic. Statistical Tables

Notes: At-risk-of-poverty rates of children aged 0-15 years and overall at-risk-of-poverty rates (by age and gender), income reference year 2003, except for CZ: income year 2002; data for MT refer to income year 2000; see Figure 3.1

is higher than for the whole of the population" (Government of Luxembourg, 2003, page 6). We are justifiably concerned about the position of children.

Other dimensions of social exclusion

Relative child income poverty alone is however not a sufficient indicator of children's economic situation. Children mainly depend on their parents' decisions as to how family income is spent, and these can either favour or disadvantage children (see Hoelscher, 2003). Furthermore, children's economic situation is only one, albeit important, dimension of their well-being. It is crucial to understand the complexity of children's lives, the links between their well-being today and their well-becoming in the future (highlighted in the UN Convention on the Rights of the Child). We have made clear that the logic of the focus on children relates not just to income poverty but also to other aspects of social exclusion; once again one needs to think in multi-dimensional terms. However, despite the aim to give as many breakdowns as possible, the EU data on which we have focused in this Chapter only provide information about one non-income-related social inclusion indicator that relates directly to children: the proportion of children aged 17 and under living in jobless households. (The Secondary Indicator on literacy of pupils, which has usefully been added to the original Laeken set, also relates to children but is not included in those sources; see Table 2.3b in Appendix 1.) Figure 3.20 shows that, in contrast to the income-based measure, children are less likely to be living in jobless households than prime-age adults. In only the UK and Ireland does the rate for children exceed that for adults by more than 20%.

The importance of looking at other dimensions has been recognised in many national studies, including the measures of child poverty developed by the Department for Work and Pensions in the United Kingdom. In a comparative study of the EU-15 countries, Ritakallio and Bradshaw (2005) make use of the subjective questions in the European Community Household Panel (ECHP), and of the ECHP material deprivation measures (which differ from those considered in Figure 3.10[16]). They show, for instance, that the percentage of children living in households lacking on one or more of the criteria ranged from 39% in the Netherlands to 89% in Greece and 90% in Portugal. The proportion lacking three or more items ranged from 9% in Denmark to 53% in Greece. Ritakallio and Bradshaw (2005, page 10) suggest that in order to derive a measure of child poverty that is more reliable than purely income, we should consider those children who are classified as poor on two of the three dimensions: income, subjective poverty,

Figure 3.20: Children living in jobless households relative to adult rate for EU-25 (2004)

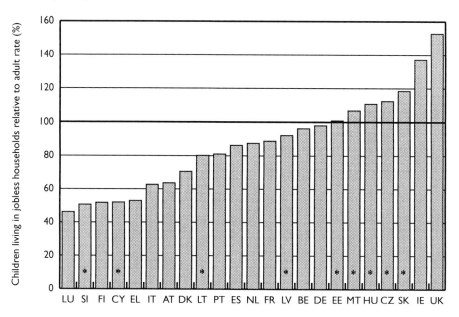

* New Member States
Source: European Commission (2006b) – Annex 1c. Statistical Tables
Notes: People living in jobless households: children (0-17 years) and prime-age adults (18-59 years), Spring results 2004 (except DK, LU (2003) and FI: annual average), SE and PL excluded

and deprivation (three or more items on the nine-item scale). This does not greatly change the ranking of countries, with Denmark having the lowest score and Portugal the highest among the 12 EU countries covered, but it gives a quite different impression of the direction of movement. Their measure shows that child deprivation fell between 1996 and 2001 in all of the 12 countries except Denmark and Portugal. Composite child-specific indicators in multi-dimensional terms are also employed to make comparisons across the EU-25 by Bradshaw *et al* (2006, forthcoming), which we discuss in Chapter 5.

Conclusions

In suggesting a children mainstreaming, we have been following in the footsteps of the Social Protection Committee and its Indicators Sub-Group, which have agreed to give children and the older population a "special focus" (European Commission, 2004b, page 6), and have provided breakdowns by age wherever relevant and meaningful. This has been essential in highlighting the extent to which EU children are living at risk of poverty; and in stressing that "in most countries children experience levels of income poverty that are higher than those for adults" (European Commission, 2004b, page 18). Figure 3.19 shows that in 18 of the 25 EU Member States, child poverty risk is higher than overall poverty risk.

At the same time, the main conclusion from this "case study" is that the present common indicators are of limited assistance, and tell us little about the non-income dimensions. As we have seen, examination of non-income indicators may change our assessment. This suggests that, as far as the common indicators are concerned, we need to approach the issue from the opposite direction: to start from the perspective of children and then consider the selection of indicators. This is particularly pertinent since it has recently been agreed that an indicator of "child well-being" is to be incorporated into the set of Primary Indicators for social inclusion (see Table 2.3a in Appendix 1), with the specifics of that indicator to be developed. We return to this in Chapter 5.

3.6 Concluding comment

In this Chapter we have deliberately limited our horizons, both theoretically and empirically. We have not attempted to give a structured account of the basic causes of poverty and social exclusion. We have not attempted a comprehensive review of the statistical evidence about poverty and social exclusion in the EU. We have not sought to compare the evidence available from EU sources with that available from national sources (although we agree that consistency with national sources is very important and needs to be studied). We have limited ourselves (with a few exceptions) to the indicators commonly agreed at EU level (and widely publicly available), and have asked what we can learn directly from this source about the EU-25 countries. The Commission and the Member

States have invested in the production of these data, and we have sought to exploit them more fully.

Even within this narrow compass, the common indicators are a rich source of information about poverty and social exclusion in the EU-25. Although the data have to be used and interpreted with care, we have tried to show how they can be used to provide a baseline against which to judge progress, and to begin to explore the underlying mechanisms. In our analysis, the main conclusions of which have been summarised at the end of each Section, we have explored the impact of Enlargement, contrasting the EU-15 and the EU-25, and have emphasised the multi-dimensional nature of social exclusion.

Notes

[1] More information on the *ECHP, EU-SILC* as well as the *EU LFS* and other EU harmonised surveys can be found on the Eurostat website: http://forum.europa.eu.int/Public/irc/dsis/Home/main.

[2] Income data for the Czech Republic refer to 2002; and data for Malta refer to the income year 2000. The income data for the Netherlands and Slovakia are provisional.

[3] Guio (2005a) has already presented illustrative figures for a few countries – showing the confidence intervals for the at-risk-of-poverty rate, the poverty gap, the Gini coefficient and the S80/S20 ratio. On this issue, see also Osier and Museux (2006).

[4] As a reminder to readers, cross-sectional data are data pertaining to a given time or a certain time period, whereas longitudinal (panel) data are data pertaining to individual-level changes over time, observed periodically over a certain duration.

[5] Eurostat has prepared a number of detailed documents on the ECHP: "blueprint" ECHP questionnaires, methodological documents, agenda and minutes of ECHP meetings, etc. For more information, see: http://forum.europa.eu.int/Public/irc/dsis/Home/main.

[6] See Figure 1.1 in the Technical Annex to the 2006 Joint Report on Social Inclusion (European Commission, 2006b), which covers the EU-25 except Malta.

[7] This component will be included in EU-SILC from 2007 (see Chapter 5). However, for new Member States as well as acceding and candidate countries, income in kind is in part included in the total income definition, as it is considered to be a more substantial component of the disposable income for these countries than is the case of EU-15 Member States, meaning that its exclusion would significantly underestimate the actual situation. Income in kind covers, when available in the national data sources, goods produced directly by the household through either a private or a professional activity (e.g. own production of food by farming households or a household whose leisure activity is connected with agriculture; products from hunting or fishing; withdrawals

from stocks by tradespeople, and so on). Services obtained free of charge as part of a professional activity are also classified as 'benefits in kind' (e.g. provision of housing, company vehicle, crèche facilities, free meals at work, etc.).

[8] The relation between the median and the mean, more usually taken as a measure of overall living standards, depends on the shape of the distribution.

[9] It may be noted that the study by Večerník (2004), using the same source shows a similar at-risk-of-poverty rate for earlier years in the 1990s.

[10] The US figures given by Jesuit *et al* (2002) are for the mid-1990s for which data for the EU-25 are not available, and they relate to a threshold set at 50% of median income for which figures were published in these sources but not in European Commission (2006b).

[11] It should be noted that students aged 18–24 years who live in households composed solely of students are counted in neither numerator nor denominator.

[12] It has to be emphasised that figures for EU-15 countries are from 1996 (and may have changed since then), whereas figures for the new Member States are from 2002. As a result of the implementation of EU-SILC, it will be possible to compute various deprivation measures for all 25 EU countries and a few non-EU countries from a harmonised dataset as from the end of 2006 (see Chapter 5). For an exploratory study of deprivation based on the first EU-SILC results, available only for 13 EU countries and Norway, see Indicators Sub-Group (2006a).

[13] On this relation, see also the studies by Beblo and Knaus (2001); Bradbury and Jäntti (2001); Cantillon *et al* (1997); Oxley *et al,* (2001); Jeandidier and Reinstadler (2002); and Förster (2004).

[14] This simulation was conducted as follows. In each country, the social transfers received by working-age households were increased by the same proportion, such that they constituted 22% of aggregate income of all working-age households. (This is slightly more than the actual percentage of the best-performing EU Member State in the analysis, viz. Finland. Sweden was excluded from the simulation as its 29% transfer score would be too far off for the other countries.) At the same time, all income other than transfers was also adjusted proportionally, but in the opposite direction, so that average and aggregate total household income remained constant. Next, poverty rates were recalculated from the micro-data. This simulation is equivalent to an across-the-board and proportional increase in all social transfers, paid for by a proportional tax or contribution (bonus) on all other sources of income.

[15] We have to remember that the pre-transfer poverty risk is not an independent variable, because it is itself influenced by the level of redistribution. The level of poverty risk one would observe in the absence of the transfers in question almost certainly does not

coincide with the level of poverty risk measured simply by subtracting transfers from disposable income – if benefits did not exist, then people would change their behaviour, including decisions about household formation and labour force participation.

[16] In Ritakallio and Bradshaw (2005), the nine criteria are adequate heating, annual holiday away from home, replacing worn-out furniture, afford new clothes, afford meat/fish, ask friends home, rent arrears, mortgage arrears, and savings.

FOUR

Strengthening policy analysis

The commonly agreed indicators for social inclusion that we described in Chapter 3 are in general outcome indicators aiming to measure the extent of progress towards the common objectives of promoting social inclusion. To bring about a substantial improvement in the reported indicators requires long-term and structural policy efforts in the fields of economic growth, social protection, minimum wages and employment. It has, moreover, to be recognised that the outcomes measured by the indicators depend partially on developments outside the control of Governments (such as trends in family formation and dissolution). This is the reason why most Member States highlighted in their NAPs/inclusion lists of policy measures and policy-related indicators, which can be more easily integrated within the development of a policy strategy, such as the number of unemployed or long-term unemployed persons who are assisted by some labour market measure, the number of available social housing units and the amount of minimum income benefits. What we need to do, however, is to link policy and outcomes. Crucial to the EU Social Inclusion Process is a better understanding of this relationship. The purpose of this Chapter is to consider how this analysis can be strengthened. What are the key elements in establishing the relationship between policy measures, as listed in the NAPs/inclusion and their EU analyses by the Commission and Member States (Joint Reports on Social Inclusion, Joint Reports on Social Protection and Social Inclusion and Commission Staff Working Papers), and outcomes, as measured by the commonly agreed indicators? What are the strong and weak points of different types of analysis? How can they be applied at Member State and EU level?

We begin in Section 4.1 with a brief survey of the policy analysis presented in the NAPs/inclusion prepared in 2003 by EU–15 countries and in 2004 by the new Member States as well as the EU analysis of these national reports in Joint Report and Commission Report (European Commission, 2004b and 2004d), identifying some of the directions in which it could be developed. For this purpose, it is necessary to make use of modern tools of policy analysis, and in Section 4.2 we examine two types of approach: model families analysis and micro-simulation models. The ground covered will be familiar to many readers, but, as stressed in Chapter 1, we would like to make the book accessible to those who have not been engaged in the technical debates. In each case, we are trying to bring out the strengths and weaknesses of the different approaches. Here one is able to learn from other bodies with long experience of cross-country comparisons of policy, notably the OECD, with whom the European Commission is working jointly on policy analysis. In Section 4.3, we examine how the two methods can be applied to the EU Social Inclusion Process. Three types of application are considered: mapping the relation between Member State policies and the common indicators, projecting at a national level the future impact of policy reforms, and examining policy at the EU level. We describe how the analytical tools can be employed to develop a EU *common analysis*, so that we have a commonly agreed and defined analytical approach, alongside the agreed common indicators. To this point, the discussion is largely methodological, rather than dealing with substantive problems. In the final Section 4.5, we therefore take a particular problem – children at risk of poverty and social exclusion- and use this as a case study to help draw together the different threads of our earlier discussion.

4.1 Policy analysis in the NAPs/inclusion and at the EU level

Central components of the Social Inclusion Process are the NAPs/inclusion of individual Member States, now including the new Member States, and their EU analyses by the Commission and Member States.[1] The first round of NAPs/inclusion had to be produced to a tight timetable, and with no precedent to guide their authors. The first Joint Inclusion Report of the Council and the Commission (European Commission, 2002b) was a substantial 226-page document, which represented a landmark in the history of the EU. As noted in the Executive Summary, "it is the first time that the European Union endorses a policy document on poverty and social exclusion" (European Commission, 2002b, page 9). The second round of NAPs/inclusion submitted in July 2003 maintained the momentum. They are certainly weighty documents: the NAP/inclusion for Denmark is (in English) 60 pages long; for Finland 68 pages; for Portugal 116 pages. Germany, whose first plan was a rather slender document, has a NAP/inclusion 2003–5 that extends to 109 pages. The 2003 NAPs/inclusion for the EU-15 were reviewed in the Joint Report on Social Inclusion 2004 (European Commission, 2004b). In July 2004, the 10 new Member States submitted their first National Action Plans. They are, like those for the existing Member States, extensive in their coverage. The NAP/inclusion for Estonia, for example, at 57 pages (in English) is one of the shortest; the NAP/inclusion for Hungary consists of 63 pages plus an appendix of 31 pages. The NAPs/inclusion for the 10 new Member States were analysed by the Commission in a Commission Staff Working Paper *Report on Social Inclusion 2004* (European Commission, 2005c).

The NAPs/inclusion and their EU analyses have been an important first step in advancing the Social Inclusion Process. At the same time, they can be further developed, particularly in the analysis of the relation between policy and outcome. Without in any way seeking to devalue the achievements of the NAPs/inclusion and their EU analyses, we can identify the following limitations:

- The concrete implications of policy actions are not typically assessed in terms of outcomes, and, specifically, in terms of improved performance according to the commonly agreed Laeken indicators.
- We lack adequate accounts of the baseline policy situations from which the extent of policy departures can be assessed; it is hard to separate new from existing policies.
- The total effects of policies on social exclusion are not investigated, so that we cannot understand the interactions between different policies and the impact on poverty and social exclusion of policies that do not have social inclusion as their central focus.
- Member States have not sufficiently examined in their NAPs/inclusion how their social performance could be improved by the adoption of policies and institutional processes (see Chapter 6) employed in other Member States.
- EU analyses have included quantitative analysis, as we have discussed in Chapter 3, but such analysis could be extended to an assessment of the likely impact of the policy choices of different Member States.

In identifying these missing elements, we are not asserting that they are completely absent from all the NAPs/inclusion and their EU analyses; rather we are suggesting that the analysis is in need of further development.

Outcome analysis

The NAPs/inclusion follow the framework laid down by the Social Protection Committee (see Social Protection Committee, 2003b). Section 3 of the Plans describes the strategic approach. In the case of Luxembourg, for example, the Government explains in its 2003 NAP/inclusion that it seeks "An active social state which does not provide all but which operates in a spirit of responsible solidarity in an open and participatory society which does not exclude anyone" (Government of Luxembourg, 2003, page 14). It goes on to explain that the Social Inclusion strategy is based on three pillars: education, active labour market policy and social protection. In the case of Sweden, to take another illustration, the strategic section refers to "full employment and universal social insurance", "an ultimate safety net", and "integration".

Section 4 of the Plans typically refers to "policy" (some Member States refer to "political") measures. In the case of Sweden, for example, reference is made to (i) alteration to the rules concerning unemployment insurance; (ii) a ceiling on childcare fees and increased parental leave; (iii) the Equal Community initiative to combat discrimination in and exclusion from the labour market; (iv) a reformed old-age pension system; (v) the introduction of an extended health care guarantee; (vi) a programme for improving health at work; (vii) tightening of sickness benefits and transfer of part of the cost to the employer; (viii) expansion of the pre-school programme; (ix) actions to strengthen the protection of children at risk;

(x) establishment of shelters for girls at risk from honour-related violence; and (xi) support for the efforts of local authorities to combat homelessness.

As illustrated by the Swedish list, policy measures differ a great deal in their scale and specificity. The measures to improve access to health care were allocated a total of SEK3.75 billion over the period 2002–4. The measures to encourage and support the work of local authorities on homelessness were allocated SEK30 million. The 2003 NAP/inclusion for Ireland refers to the €14.2 billion Employment and Human Resources Operational Programme over the period 2000–6, and to the €65 million allocated since 1997 to Local Drugs Task Forces. In Germany, the 2003 NAP/inclusion refers to the fact that the Federal Government is allocating €4 billion over 2003–7 to the establishment of all-day schools, and that it is spending €91 million a year on additional training places in the new Länder. Some measures are reckoned in billions; others are counted in millions.

We are not questioning these relative allocations; rather we are pointing to the problem of analysing policy initiatives that are very different in scale. Our central interest is in the link between the policies and the outcomes. How much, for example, will this policy reduce the number at risk of poverty? How do the costs of policy initiatives compare with the measured poverty gap? The scale is clearly a relevant consideration. One would not expect a measure directed at a small group of the population necessarily to have effects that show up in indicators for the population as a whole. One would be looking for its impact in terms of, say, the composition of the excluded population. Even here the impact may be hard to discern, perhaps because the relevant groups, such as the homeless, are not covered by the statistics to hand. It is quite possible therefore that some of the specific measures listed in the NAPs/inclusion cannot be analysed other than on a separate basis, without reference to the common indicators.

The example of financial poverty risk reduction corresponds to one of the Laeken indicators. However, one major limitation of the NAPs/inclusion is that a number do not relate policy analysis to the Laeken indicators in any systematic way. Some Member States do make such comparisons. But such systematic use of the Laeken indicators is rare. The Dutch report, for example, bases its examination of poverty risk largely on the number of people who are dependent on the national minimum income and the development of that income. They say clearly "these indicators link best with the national policy surrounding the minimum income" (Government of the Netherlands, 2003, page vii). They recognise in the appendix that "in an EU context other indicators have been developed to compare the performance of the various countries", referring to the 60% of median (and 40%, 50% and 70%) indicator, but argue that "the choice of a specific threshold is comparatively arbitrary" (Government of the Netherlands 2003, page vii). In other cases, there is a disjuncture, where one part of the Plan deals with policies and a second part, often in an appendix, presents the social indicators. The indicators are not really embedded in the policy process. More specifically, we need to ask: will the announced policies lead to significant improvement in social indicators? In the case of the Hungarian NAP/inclusion, for example, there is reference to the extension of the eligibility of lone parents for the regular child protection benefit, and to the expected rise in the number of children receiving this benefit, described as "the most significant cash assistance to families" (Government of Hungary, 2004, page 50). But we need to know how much this can be expected to contribute to the elimination of the child poverty risk. Or, to turn the question round, to which of the outcome indicators is a policy directed? Is a measure intended, for example, to reduce the extent of poverty or its depth?

Policy baseline

In examining the policy proposals as a whole, we want to know how they are going to improve social performance. In making such an assessment, we need first to establish a baseline for policies. Reading the NAPs/inclusion, it is often difficult to discern just how far the policies represent departures relative to the status quo. For understandable reasons, Member States take up quite a large part of their NAPs/inclusion with a rehearsal of their existing policies. As the 2003 NAP/inclusion for Luxembourg notes, the two-yearly NAPs/inclusion periodicity should not get in the way of long-term strategic planning; as a result a number of the measures presented are a continuation of those covered in the 2001 NAP/inclusion (Government of Luxembourg, 2003, page 10). Separating new policies from existing policies is not therefore always easy. Moreover, the policy objectives of the Government may be embodied in legal regulations that should be analysed even if they are not reported in the NAPs/inclusion.

The NAPs/inclusion are not always transparent on the policy baseline. The announcement of a "Programme for 2003-2005" does not always make clear whether this is the renewal of a programme in force or a totally new initiative. If we are asking how the NAP/inclusion can be expected to reduce, say, the proportion of families living at risk of poverty, then it is not always easy to list the precise measures that constitute the "policy change" from the baseline. The same applies to the timing. Policies are announced in advance of their enactment, and may be "re-announced" in the period before they come into force. It may not be easy to relate policy announcements to their starting dates; yet this is clearly relevant to determining their impact in terms of outcomes. The policy baseline has moreover to be dynamic. As has been brought out by Callan (2005), where wages and prices are rising, a neutral tax-benefit policy may be defined as one that indexes benefit levels, tax thresholds, and tax bands in line with rising incomes. This is then the benchmark against which policy change is to be assessed. The dynamic nature of the calculation is particularly important given the delay with which data on outcomes become available. Even with improvements in the timeliness of data (as a result *inter alia* of the replacement of the ECHP by EU-SILC), this will always be a problem.

The next difficulty concerns the counterfactual for the outcomes. A Government may have set in train measures that will reduce the risk of poverty by two percentage points, but the underlying trend may be upwards. If, in the absence of the new measures, we could have expected the risk-of-poverty rate to rise by two percentage points, then the policy will only succeed in holding the line. If there is a target, say, to reduce the risk-of-poverty rate, then it will not be achieved. As has been noted in the UK (see Brewer *et al*, 2005), measures to help low-income families with children may have been successful, but have been working against a negative trend. In such a situation, the success of the policy would be found in the fact that child poverty did not become worse. This would not be detected by simply tracking changes in the outcome indicator. In other cases, the underlying trend may be favourable. The NAP/inclusion for Cyprus, for instance, notes that developments in the area of employment since 1997 "will have positively influenced matters – in the direction of lower risk of poverty" (Government of Cyprus, 2004, Annex, page 7).

Total effect of policies

It is evidently important to look at the total range of policies that impact on the problems of social exclusion. There is, first of all, a political risk that the NAPs/inclusion of national Governments will be selective in coverage, favouring those policy domains where their record is best. "Even as reports, the NAPs/inclusion are limited by the lack of balance. Most Governments have simply used them to 'showcase' their strongest anti-poverty policies" (European Anti-Poverty Network, 2003, page 9).

A full coverage is equally necessary because of the inter-relatedness of different policies. Measures to improve access to jobs for single parents, for example, may raise their employment rate, but the impact on their income depends on the interaction with social transfers, housing benefits, educational grants, etc. The UK NAP/inclusion describes how the new Child Tax Credit introduced in April 2003 "provides a single seamless system of support for families with children" (Government of the United Kingdom, 2003, page 35). It certainly clarifies the situation where people move in and out of the labour market, but it remains the case that the income of the family will depend on other Government policies, such as those with regard to the minimum wage, housing benefit, and the availability of childcare. It was also the case that the new Child Tax Credit replaced several other benefits, and it is the *net* effect of the change that is relevant.

A full picture needs to encompass measures that form part of the NAPs/inclusion and those that form part of the NAPs/employment. As is made clear in the 2004 Joint Report on Social Inclusion (European Commission, 2004b), we need to ask how the employment generation process will impact on the Laeken social indicators. For understandable reasons, Member States have sought to keep separate their employment and social inclusion measures. The 2003 Danish NAP/inclusion, for example, states that the action plan avoids "any overlaps with the corresponding action plan on employment" (Government of Denmark, 2003, page 3). However, an analysis of the social inclusion proposals cannot leave out of account the impact, positive or negative, of employment measures on the social inclusion indicators. The 2004 Joint Report points out that "both plans should be read together to get a fuller picture of the measures being taken to combat social exclusion through participation in the labour market" (European Commission, 2004b, page 44). As we have seen in the previous Chapter, nothing can be presumed in advance about the complex relationship between job creation and reductions in poverty and social exclusion. As is noted in the 2003 NAP/inclusion of Luxembourg, a challenge for the future is to develop the synergies between the NAP/inclusion and the NAP/employment (Government of Luxembourg, 2003, page 16).

Learning from others and comparative analysis

The peer review process is designed to encourage mutual learning as part of the Social Inclusion Process. At present, there are few signs that this is being actively pursued in a systematic way. We appreciate that national specificities, and indeed differences within Member States, with regard to policy institutions mean that it is difficult to apply one country's policies directly to another Member State. One cannot simply "lift" a particular policy structure or intervention from one country and apply it in another, since the broader institutional context in which it is set may be critical to understanding why it is effective. At the same time, countries can learn from each other. To begin with, one would expect Member States to identify the dimensions of social exclusion on which their performance is relatively less satisfactory, and to concentrate on these. One can then ask why performance is relatively less good. In part, the reasons can be found within the Member State, particularly where there are identifiable geographic differences within the country. But in part they may be identified by looking outside. The EU process provides a context with which they can ask why another Member State performs better on certain indicators. One would expect Member States to ask how far other countries had encountered similar problems and to examine their resolution of these problems.

   The common indicators agreed at EU level furnish a starting point for such a comparative analysis within the EU. As we have seen in Chapter 3, not all countries perform equally well or badly on all social indicators. It is true that Sweden, for example, is commonly among the top four countries for income-related indicators, and that Portugal is typically near the bottom. But, when we look at prime-age adults living in jobless households, we see that Sweden falls and Portugal rises to second place. Comparative analysis of how policy affects these outcomes is a central ingredient in learning from each other. However, it has to be done in a way that does not isolate particular policies from their broad context, but instead seeks to understand how specific policies work within the broader system in which they are set.

   Such learning by national Governments need not, of course, be limited to the EU-15 or EU-25. The OECD provides a forum where EU members can learn from, for example, the US, Canada, Japan, Australia, and New Zealand. In so far as the US has been in the lead in the globalisation of its economy and the development of Information and Communication Technologies (ICT), there is good reason to examine its experience, albeit in the context of different social priorities. The comparison with the US has indeed been explicit in the development of the Lisbon Agenda. The EU Structural Indicators (updated Annex to the 2005 Report from the Commission to the Spring European Council; see European Commission, 2005e) include columns for Japan and the US. For 10 of the 15 Structural Indicators, values are given for these two countries in addition to EU-25 and acceding/candidate countries. These include long-term unemployment, and the three environmental indicators, but not, unfortunately, the at-risk-of-poverty rate. It would be helpful if the full set of Structural Indicators could be given (as a minimum) for Japan and the US, and if consideration could be given to developing values for the US for the long list of Structural Indicators for social cohesion. We return to this proposal in Chapter 5.

Policy analysis

A valuable feature of the 2001 and 2004 Joint Reports on Social Inclusion has been their use of the common social indicators to make comparisons between Member States of their social performance, and to identify key trends and emerging challenges. The 2004 Joint Report, for example, referred to fears about the impact of the current economic slowdown (European Commission, 2004b, page 29). It identified as major factors: structural changes in the labour market, the impact of ICT, the ageing of the population, increased migration and growing ethnic diversity, family dissolution and the growing numbers of lone-parent families, and higher labour market participation by women.

The NAPs/inclusion have, in many cases, identified vulnerable groups. Just to take one example, the Austrian NAP/inclusion lists children, women, families, people with disabilities, people requiring long-term care, asylum seekers, migrants, people with excessive debts, homeless people, and people who have committed criminal offences (Government of Austria, 2003, page 2). The significance of the different groups may vary from Member State to Member State, but this is one point of departure for policy analysis. We can imagine a matrix where these categories form the rows, and the columns constitute the policy actions affecting these groups – see Box 4.1 for an illustration. In each cell there would be an assessment of the impact of the policy in column i on the group identified in row j: for example, the extent to which the long-term unemployed benefit from family cash transfers. From such a matrix, we can see the totality of the policies affecting particular groups. The groups may, of course, overlap: children may live with a father who is long-term unemployed. We should also bear in mind that there are two ways of approaching the subject: from the direction of the policies and from the direction of the groups affected. As we stress in this book, children mainstreaming means not necessarily giving children priority, but approaching

Box 4.1: Illustrative matrix of policy interventions and vulnerable groups				
	Family benefits	Labour market activation	Personal social services	...
Children				
Long-term unemployed				
Elderly				
Disabled				
...				

issues from their perspective: that is, reading across the matrix not down. The same equally applies to gender mainstreaming.

The key policy actions are manifold. One of the most important, but not the only, is social protection. Both the 2004 Joint Inclusion Report and the 2006 Joint Report on Social Protection and Social Inclusion (European Commission, 2004b, 2006a and 2006b) discuss the relationship between the level of expenditure on social protection and the risk of poverty, which – together with its qualifications – we have considered in Chapter 3 (see in particular Figures 3.13–3.15). In order to probe this correlation more deeply (as the Joint Reports make clear is necessary), we have to examine the underlying policy institutions. A good example is provided by benefits in and out of work. The 2004 Joint Report refers to the increasing popularity of in-work benefits. Noting that the UK and Ireland have a long tradition of such benefits, the Report (European Commission, 2004b, page 56) goes on to describe developments in the Netherlands (increased tax credits), Belgium (bonus "crédit d'emploi"), France ("prime pour l'emploi"), Finland (earned income disregard) and Luxembourg. In the Technical Annex to the 2006 Joint Report, an extensive analysis is made of incomes in and out of work, using the results of a joint EC-OECD project. This finds that "countries differ substantially in terms of the minimum safety nets they provide to workless households" but that "only a few countries provide workless households with a minimum income and related (i.e. housing) benefits that are sufficient to lift them close to or above the 60% of median income threshold" (European Commission, 2006b, page 68). The Annex goes on to note that "on the other hand, even employment is not sufficient to lift families out of poverty risk if it pays a low wage. In all countries except Poland and the United Kingdom, the net income of a one-earner family with two children remains below the 60% threshold if the only worker holds a full-time job paying the minimum wage" (page 69).

This question may be asked in the direction we have just discussed: policies to outcomes. What is the effectiveness of specified policies in achieving improved social performance as measured by the social indicators? In the NAPs/inclusion, Member States have set out their current policies and their proposals for policy reform. What will be the impact of policies, for instance, on the poverty risk or the number of working poor or the proportion of jobless households? These questions consider the relation between

$$\text{Policies} \longrightarrow \text{Indicators ?}$$

But it is also important to reverse the process and ask what changes in policy are necessary to achieve a specified reduction in different social indicators:

$$\text{? Policies} \longleftarrow \text{Indicators}$$

As discussed in more detail in Chapter 6, the Commission has in the past recommended the setting of targets. Three years ago, in its Communication to the Spring European Council in Barcelona, the European Commission proposed that the European Council should set the target of halving the at-risk-of-poverty rate from 18% to 9% by 2010 (European Commission, 2002c, page 16). This proposal was not accepted by the European Council, but it was evidently regarded as realistic by the Commission at that time. Part of the background research should therefore have been to ask – what measures need to be taken to achieve a halving of the risk-of-poverty rate? These measures may be indirect. Success in reaching the employment target is likely to reduce the proportion of jobless households. Where the jobs created are "good jobs", then higher employment rates may bring with them success in reducing the risk of poverty. But will this reduction be sufficient to halve the risk-of-poverty rate? If the answer is "no", then we also have to consider direct measures. We need to ask how these can be best designed and what scale of programme is necessary.

Input indicators

There may here be an important role for *input indicators*: that is, indicators of policy effort. Valid and comparable input indicators would obviously be of great value for the evaluation, comparison and analysis of social and economic policies. Recent developments at the EU level have enhanced the relevance of input indicators in the field of social protection significantly (see Cantillon *et al*, 2004). It is important that such indicators should be measurable in a *sufficiently comparable way across Member States*. Full comparability is an ideal that cannot normally be attained, since, even where data are harmonised across Member States, variations in institutional and social structure mean that there may (have to) be differences in the interpretation of the data. The extent of variations has been increased by the 2004 Enlargement: "the inclusion of new Member States will make the pension landscape, for example, more diversified than […] in the EU-15"

(Schmähl, 2004, page 8). Indicators that are over-sensitive to these structural differences or raise specific problems of interpretation for particular Member States should be avoided. The aim should be an acceptable standard of comparability.

In considering input indicators, we have to take account of the fact that household incomes are always income packages, implying that mostly they are the result of not one but several welfare state arrangements (e.g. minimum wages, social security transfers, childcare subsidies, tax credits and reductions). More precisely, they need to take account of interactions between parts of the social protection system: changes in one arrangement may lead to changes in the entitlements in other programs (e.g. an increase in the minimum wage may mean a reduction in housing benefits). Secondly, the link between input indicators and relevant outcomes must be established (Atkinson, 2000). For example, a rise in the level of, say, minimum income protection in social assistance should be shown to lead to a meaningful reduction in poverty. This could be done in several ways, as we discuss below.

Conclusions

The NAPs/inclusion and their EU analysis (Joint Reports on Social Inclusion, Joint Reports on Social Protection and Social Inclusion and Commission Staff Working Papers) have contributed a great deal to advancing the Social Inclusion Process, but the policy analysis needs to be further developed. It lacks an adequate analysis of the baseline policy situation and a counterfactual for the outcome indicators; the total effects of policies on poverty and social exclusion need to be investigated, as well as the contribution of each individual policy; the policy analysis is insufficiently comparative, and individual policies need to be studied within their broader institutional setting. To help think further, we have suggested a matrix with vulnerable groups along one dimension and policy interventions along a second dimension.

4.2 Tools for policy analysis: model families analysis and micro-simulation models

We turn now to the explicit analysis of the impact of *policy change*. If a Member State announces a policy change, designed to combat poverty, how can we investigate its potential impact? In this Section, we describe two types of analysis widely used at a country level to examine the impact of policy on financial circumstances: model families analysis and micro-simulation models. They are presented separately, but we suggest below that they are best seen as complementary and that the best way forward may be through an integrated modelling framework (Sutherland, 2005).

Model families analysis

An individual, when presented with a policy proposal, is likely to examine how he or she, and their immediate family, are affected. Suppose that the Government proposes an income tax credit for workers with children, and earning less than a specified amount, with a tapered withdrawal for a range of earnings above this amount. The person will ask – am I eligible? If so, how much will I get? If I am eligible, how will this affect my decisions about choice of job? For example, the new proposal may affect whether or not I accept the promotion offered. If I am not eligible, then can I change my behaviour to qualify? The same questions, writ large, concern the policy analyst. The Government Minister will no doubt want to know the impact of the proposal on "model" individuals, chosen to be representative of the population. Suppose that we consider the impact on child poverty. The Minister will want to see calculations for representative families with children who are currently below the poverty line. How much will they benefit? Will the proposal be sufficiently generous to lift them above the poverty threshold?

The model families approach basically involves calculating the financial consequences of fiscal and social policies for a set of hypothetical families. The calculations allow one to see the effect of policy variations; they allow one to examine the effects of changes in household circumstances, such as an increase in gross income (and hence calculate marginal tax rates). This technique starts with defining specific family types, making assumptions about the number of persons in the household, their age, their marital status, their status on the labour market, their gross earnings, their housing situation, etc. For these family types the amount of taxes and social insurance contributions is computed, as well as the amount of fiscal and social benefits, given existing welfare state arrangements. This way the net disposable income for each family type can be determined. The analysis may be conducted in terms that allow one or more variables to vary continuously, such as gross income, the results then being presented as functions of income (for example in the form of a graph depicting net disposable income as a function of gross income). Model families results thus reveal the level of social protection provided to households in various situations. The policy parameters may be the same for each household, or they may vary: for example, by geographical location (see below).

The usefulness of model families for comparative research on social policy is evident from the frequent use of this technique (e.g. Bradshaw *et al*, 1993). The OECD has been using the method for many years for several purposes such as calculating tax burdens (OECD, 2003), replacement rates for the short-term and the long-term unemployed (OECD, 2004), and support for families (OECD, 2005). As they say, "the results from the tax benefit models allow policy makers to see in detail how their policies might affect one family. This can be a powerful tool, in that aggregation can sometimes erase details important to the individual" (communication to the authors from OECD). By calculating net disposable incomes and by comparing them to income poverty lines and minimum and average wages, model families results can give a clear indication of the level of (minimum) income protection, and also the financial incentive to take up work associated with a package of fiscal and social measures. Therefore they are related to the main objectives of social protection: minimum income protection, maintenance of the acquired standard of living and promoting social participation, in particular labour market participation.

One strength of this approach is that model families calculations can bring together different elements of Government policy. The calculations of net disposable incomes take into account gross benefits and wages, income taxes, social contributions and local taxes as well as child benefits and housing benefits. So family models compute the financial consequences of a *package* of social protection measures, taking into account the interaction between various fiscal and social protection measures. The analysis given in the Technical Annex to the 2006 Joint Report (European Commission, 2006b), for instance, takes account of social assistance, unemployment benefit, housing benefits, family benefits, and in-work benefits. The impact of a policy initiative to increase the employment rate of single parents, for example, will increase the earnings of the household by an amount that depends on the wage earned, which may be influenced by the minimum wage. The policy initiative will have consequences for the entitlement of income-tested transfers. Entry into employment may make the household eligible for in-work benefits. Figure 4.1 illustrates some of the different elements that may enter the calculation of net disposable income. They can take account of the fact that household incomes are income packages, combining incomes from different sources, accruing to different members of the household, and affected by several welfare state arrangements.

Figure 4.1: Schematic outline of the determinants of household income

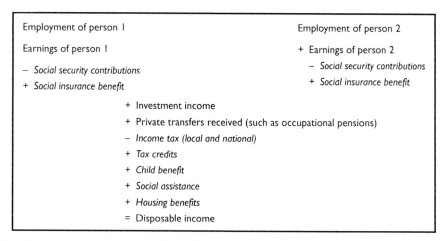

Note: The items shown in normal type are the specified characteristics of the household; the variables shown in italics are calculated as functions of these characteristics and the parameters of the tax and benefits systems

Taking a broad view of policy instruments is especially important in comparative analysis, because what households have to pay for out of their after-tax income varies markedly across countries. There are significant cross-country differences in the cost of housing, health care, childcare, etc. Several studies indicate for instance that results differ significantly according to the treatment of housing costs (e.g. Kuivalainen, 2003). In their international comparison of child benefit packages, Bradshaw and Finch (2002) calculate – by means of the model families approach – net disposable incomes not only after taxes and social contributions but also after the benefits and costs for housing, health care, education and childcare.

In making these calculations, a number of key assumptions have to be made, and these need to be borne in mind when considering the results. Firstly, the *eligibility rules* can exclude certain categories from income protection. Working-age people refusing a job or training, for example, sometimes receive a reduced benefit or are suspended. Secondly, family models assume that all families claim and receive the benefits for which they are eligible. In other words, family models do not take into account the *administrative operation* of social protection measures and related *non-take-up rates*. Several studies indicate that non-take-up rates for social assistance benefits can amount to 20% and more (Van Oorschot, 1995; Hernanz *et al*, 2004). Experience with means-tested benefits has shown that a significant proportion of those entitled to these benefits may not claim their entitlement. "The evidence reviewed in this paper suggests that low take-up of welfare benefits occurs across both countries and programmes. Estimates typically span a range of between 40% and 80% in the case of social assistance and housing programmes, and between 60% and 80% for unemployment compensation" (Hernanz *et al*, 2004, page 4). Non-claiming can reflect lack of information; it may reflect the compliance costs, notably time; in some situations receipt of means-tested benefits may be perceived as stigmatising. Thirdly, in several countries, benefit levels are not set by the national Government but differ across the regions or even municipalities. There are several options to deal with cross-regional variations in social assistance benefits and/or housing benefits. Benefit levels can (i) be based on the national average; (ii) be based on a representative case; or (iii) not be simulated. Finally, there are important benefits, notably those from collective services, which are typically omitted altogether. (These may also be expected to vary geographically.)

These considerations underline the twin problems of this approach: the selection of hypothetical family types and their aggregation to reach overall conclusions. Model families studies do not always make explicit their criteria for choosing family types. This can generate concern that they are tailored to the policy interventions under investigation, with the attendant risk that the analysis will neglect other vulnerable groups. In a comparison across countries, there is the possibility that the choice of hypothetical family types will be biased inadvertently in the direction of families that are more represented in one country than in another. Countries differ, for instance, in the share of families with one, two and three children and the share of lone parents.

So far two main ways have been used to synthesise the results of model families simulations into a few numbers. The first is to weight equally: for example, Kuivalainen (2003) and Nelson (2003) calculated the average benefit level for all model family types. There seems little rationale for equal weights *per se*, and it seems preferable to use survey or administrative data to weight the different types. This then raises the issue of the choice of basis. The ranking of countries in terms of the child benefit packages, for example, may change significantly when weights for (say) Belgium, rather than weights derived from (say) UK data, are used. If the model families findings were highly correlated across types of household, then this would not be so much of a problem. But this is not the case. Even within a single branch, such as social assistance, countries occupy substantially different positions, depending on the type of household. Social assistance regimes (in conjunction with family allowances and housing benefits) differ significantly in the way they treat families with children relative to childless families (see Bradshaw and Finch, 2002). Moreover, we have to consider variation not just with household composition, but also with labour market status, and other circumstances. We may want to make calculations for the unemployed out of work for less than 12 months, at least 12 months, and at least 24 months. We may want to distinguish between the jobless and pensioners. We may want to treat owner–occupiers separately from tenants.

These qualifications should be borne firmly in mind when using model families analysis. Nevertheless, this approach is clearly illuminating. Moreover, one major reason why the model families approach is frequently used in comparative research on social policy is that these models are relatively *easy to develop and to maintain*. Such models only consist of some carefully chosen fiscal and social regulations for a limited set of family types. The model families approach requires a minimum of empirical data (e.g. average earnings or average rent). Therefore it is fairly simple to keep model families results up-to-date and to construct time series. This is of particular significance when one considers their use by campaigning groups, often short of resources, and journalists. This last advantage is not shared by the second approach considered in this Section: micro-simulation modelling.

Micro-simulation modelling

We now consider the potential contribution of tax-benefit micro-simulation models designed to investigate the impact of changes in taxes and benefits on disposable household income for a representative sample of the population. In contrast to the model families approach, the model starts from information about actual households, obtained from sample surveys or (anonymous) administrative records or a combination of the two sources. In other words, the elements shown in normal type in Figure 4.1 correspond to the situation of actual people, rather than being hypothetical. We start from the actual earnings, investment income, and private transfers. Obtaining this information is not necessarily straightforward, and micro-simulation is much more resource-heavy than the model families approach. To just give one example, the income information recorded in the European Community Household Panel (ECHP) was in a number of countries net of income tax and social security contributions. Methods were therefore necessary to work back to gross income (see Immervoll and O'Donoghue, 2001).

Starting from the observed situation, we model the effect of changes in policy. From knowledge of the tax and benefit legislation, and administrative practice, we can calculate how the disposable income of a given household would be changed by a policy proposal. Take, for example, an income tax credit for workers, with children, earning less than a specified amount, with a tapered withdrawal for a range of earnings above this amount. The micro-simulation model allows us to identify the families eligible for this benefit and calculate the amount of benefit to which they would be entitled. The calculations then have exactly the same form as with model families analysis, following a schema like that set out in Figure 4.1. As with the model families analysis, the calculations can take account of the interactions between different elements of the tax and transfer systems. Not only can such a model calculate the level of fiscal and social costs and benefits for each individual, it can also provide information on the *coverage* of a certain measure. (For further discussion of this type of micro-simulation model, see *inter alia* Atkinson and Sutherland, 1988; Verbist, 2002 and 2005; Legendre *et al*, 2003; Immervoll *et al*, 2005; Bourguignon and Spadaro, 2006.) Over the last two decades many such models have been developed in various European countries. (Sutherland, 1998, gives an overview of national models in the EU in the first half of the nineties.)

As a micro-simulation model operates on a representative sample of the population, it is not necessary to make all of the *assumptions* required to define model families. The number of household members, their demographic and socio-economic characteristics etc. are provided by the source data. No assumptions have to be made regarding regional and local variations, provided the respondent's place of residence is available from the data. Actual benefit receipt provides some evidence about take-up. At the aggregate level, the source includes the weights for the different persons and households, so that we do not have to confront the weighting issue described above. Moreover, the use of actual survey or administrative data forces the analyst to confront the diversity of household circumstances, which may be missed if we start by enumerating model families in abstract. An important example is that of multi-family households. There may be people living in the household, other than the family for whom the model calculation is made. The risk of poverty in the EU indicators is measured over whole households that may contain grown-up children, older parents, adult siblings, and unrelated adults. The presence of these other household members may heighten or lessen the risk of poverty. This is particularly important in that the extent, and form, of multi-family households varies across EU Member States; in Section 4.4, we cite the evidence regarding children given by Corak *et al* (2005).

The extent to which micro-simulation models enjoy an advantage over model families analysis depends, of course, crucially on the quality and timeliness of the underlying data. The representativeness of the findings from micro-simulation may be open to question if there is not a sufficiently large sample, or if there is serious differential non-response. We may be able to get more accurate aggregate figures from model families weighted by results from administrative records than from a micro-simulation based on a highly unrepresentative sample survey. The accuracy of the calculations for individual households depends on there being adequate information about the relevant socio-economic characteristics. For example, the geographical information may not be sufficiently detailed to pinpoint the precise administrative authority. In some cases, due to the limitations of the input data, it is not possible to model particular transfers, such as survivor pensions and disability benefits. Policy initiatives may have attached conditions that cannot be verified with the available data or the policy may be restricted to groups of the population that cannot be identified. An example would be where the child tax credit is conditional on school attendance, as in Greece. This means that there are certain classes of policy change that cannot be simulated.

The accuracy of the simulation results depends also on the household responses being provided without serious error. This is one reason why it may not be possible to re-create the observed taxes paid and benefits received: the taxes and benefits calculated by applying the rules may not be equal to the amounts recorded. It is not the only reason for such a departure. In reality, the administration of taxes and benefits may not follow the formal rules. There may be mistakes in the calculations; the family may make an incorrect statement to the authorities of its income or other circumstances. Where it is not possible to reproduce in the simulation model the current levels of taxes and transfers, we have to take as the basis for the simulation the calculated figure; otherwise the results will confound errors and policy changes. The total cost of a policy proposal, for example, has to be calculated using the differences in the simulated figures before and after the policy change.

We should not exaggerate the differences between model families analysis and micro-simulation modelling. It may be possible to infer something about the propensity to claim benefits from observed receipt, but the simulation of take-up still involves assumptions. Assumptions have to be made in both cases about the extent of tax evasion and benefit fraud. Also, using the distributional data one can estimate the approximate percentages of the population represented by different family types, which can then be used to weight model families results. In this way, they may be seen as part of an integrated modelling framework.

In both cases — model families analysis and micro-simulation models — the calculations usually cover a wide range of benefits, and much of the direct tax structure, but they typically omit an important class of taxes (indirect taxes) and an important class of benefits (those provided by public services). The picture is to this degree a partial one. We may be missing important policy interventions that aid those faced with poverty and social exclusion; we may be overlooking the burden of indirect taxation on the same families. (To deal with the latter, the micro-simulation model would need to be extended to include data on expenditure patterns as collected in the Household Budget Surveys (HBS).)

Behavioural change

In the model families analysis and the micro-simulation models just described, labour market behaviour is assumed fixed, which means that the models cannot allow for the effects of policy that operate via behavioural change. If a new working tax credit induces a lone parent to enter the labour force, then the resulting income gain is not recorded. Nor can the model be used to predict changes in the Laeken labour market indicators (see Tables 2.3a and 2.3b in Appendix 1). For this reason, they are sometimes described as "static", and are criticised for not casting light on the behavioural changes with which policy makers are concerned.

This criticism is too severe in that both kinds of analysis can provide a valuable *input* into the analysis of behavioural change. One product of model families analysis can be calculations of the impact of policy change on the incentives faced by the family. For different possible variations in labour supply, or in savings behaviour, we can see how the policy change affects the return to extra effort or to extra savings. This is the *marginal tax rate*: the amount taken away from €1 extra gross income as a result of the operation of the tax and benefit system. It should be noted that the deductions may arise either from taxation or from the withdrawal of income-tested benefits. If a family earns €1 more, then its working families' tax credit may be reduced by, say, €0.30. If, in addition, there is a social security and income tax of 20%, then the marginal tax rate is 50%. (Or, if the working credit is assessed on income net of tax, it is 44%.) In the same way, we can calculate the impact of the policy change on the replacement rate: the relationship between income out of work and income in work. The introduction of a working family tax credit, for example, raises incomes in work, and hence reduces the replacement rate. The same calculations can be made using micro-simulation models, so that we can obtain distributions of marginal tax rates. We can see how many people face a marginal tax rate of 50% or higher and whether these rates are to be found at the bottom of the earnings distribution, where people are in receipt of one or more means-tested benefits, or at the top of the earnings distribution, among those facing the top rates of income tax.

These calculations cast light on the implications for work incentives. They also allow us to highlight the many different dimensions of labour supply. A person can increase labour supply by working more hours, or by taking a job that requires more effort. These may both increase earnings, but the implications may be different. For example, if benefits are paid subject to an hours' condition, then a person may become eligible by increasing working hours. A couple can increase its labour supply via an increase in the hours of the man or the woman. Again the implications may be different: for example, where husbands and wives are taxed independently. In the same way, savings can take different forms. A savings bank may offer both taxable and non-taxable accounts. A person can invest in shares that generate capital growth rather than dividends. A person can invest in extending their house rather than in financial instruments. The marginal tax rate may be different in all cases. For example, where transfers are subject to an assets test, certain classes of asset (such as owner-occupied houses) may be excluded.

The marginal tax rate calculations, however, take us only part of the way. They do not tell us what is predicted to happen to labour supply or savings as a result of the policy change. We cannot say that unemployment will fall by x%. We cannot say that there will be a y% reduction in the proportion of the population living in jobless households. For this we require a model of behavioural response.

In the case of labour supply, the literature is very extensive: the survey in the *Handbook of Labor Economics* by Blundell and MaCurdy (1999) has some 150 pages, and contains around 160 references in the bibliography. This econometric research has exploited the vastly improved micro-data from sample surveys and administrative sources. At the same time, there are several reasons why it is not straightforward to incorporate into micro-simulation models the findings of this literature:

1. Many of the estimates relate to a subset of the population.
2. The estimates cover only certain dimensions of labour supply; it is easier to study variables like hours of work than variables like effort;
3. Econometric models predict behaviour up to a stochastic disturbance term, and we need to consider how it is to be interpreted (a transitory variation, a fixed taste difference, a "mistake");
4. Households make multiple decisions and these are inter-related (for example the decision to return to work and to claim working tax credits);
5. It is not easy to explain to the users of the results the basis for the predictions.

It should be stressed that these are reasons, not for rejecting the approach, but for developing the research. They are a challenge. And models of labour supply have been fruitfully used to examine specific policy proposals, such as the study by Blundell (2001) of the UK working families tax credit. This shows that, by focusing on the groups targeted by the policy change (single parents and couples with children), the models may incorporate the behavioural reactions of particular interest to policy makers. (There remains, of course, the risk that other, unexpected, responses will be overlooked.) In France, the study by Laroque and Salanié (2002) treats the labour force participation decision of women, who are assumed to work full time or not at all, for women aged between 25 and 49 years old. This is a decision of particular interest to policy makers in view of the EU employment targets. They model both labour supply and labour demand, taking account of the minimum wage, in a way that provides a rich framework for analysis of income maintenance schemes (Laroque, 2005).

In seeking to incorporate empirically estimated behavioural responses into the analysis of the Social Inclusion Process, the first necessary step is an agreement on the most important responses to be included. There is here a clear link with the EU employment and growth objectives. We have referred earlier to the EU employment targets, and these indicate that labour force participation is the key variable. In just the same way as we suggested in Section 4.1 that one could work back from poverty risk targets to the policies required to deliver these targets, so too we can imagine using a behavioural micro-simulation model to work back to the policy initiatives that could achieve a 70% employment rate in Member States currently below this level. (At the very least, it could help establish whether or not the employment increase is feasible.) Such a study may also cast light on the effect of such policies on the working hours of those already participating in the labour force, although, as noted above, labour supply has many dimensions, and it may be more difficult to capture the impact on key variables such as decisions about education and skill acquisition.

Gender and income sharing

The tools of analysis described above are, in our view, extremely valuable. At the same time, we should not lose sight of the fact that they embody a set of assumptions about our values and objectives. A good example of such an assumption is that about income sharing within the household, which is very relevant to the gender dimension of poverty and social exclusion. The European Commission, in its discussion of social indicators, has stressed the gender dimension. As it was put by the Social Protection Committee in its submission to the Council Meeting of 3 December 2002, Member States are asked to "underline the importance of mainstreaming equality between men and women in all actions [...] by taking into account the gender perspective in the identification of challenges, the design, implementation and assessment of policies and measures, the selection of indicators and targets and the involvement of stakeholders" (Council, 2002). On the revised Laeken indicator list, the majority of indicators are broken down by gender.

Yet the policy analysis does not take the gender dimension fully into account. Analyses based on survey data typically treat the household as a unit, assuming an equal sharing of financial resources within households. There are two important aspects here. The first is empirical: the actual distribution of resources within the household. The assumption of equal sharing does not necessarily reflect reality. The second issue is one of judgement: should individuals be dependent on the sharing of resources within the household? The answer to this second question may depend on whether we are concerned with *standards of living* or with *rights*. Sharing may ensure that women have a comparable standard of living, and the observed differences in money income may be the result of a mutual agreement, but it remains the case that people do not have the same entitlement as where the income comes to them directly. We may therefore, on a rights basis, be concerned with the share of income that they receive as of right.

There is therefore a case for complementing the existing indicators by a calculation that replaces the income-sharing assumption by one that seeks to allocate income to its recipient. For some income sources, such as joint savings accounts, there may be no obviously superior alternative to assuming equal division, but for other sources there is a clearly identified recipient. Indeed in some countries, entitlement to benefits, such as child benefit, is legislated in such a way as to influence the within-household distribution of income. (One purpose of the proposed calculation is that it would allow us to examine the impact of such provisions.) In the UK, calculations have been made by Sutherland (1997), where the individually identified incomes include earnings, self-employment income, maternity and sick pay, occupational and private pensions, social insurance benefits, maintenance payments, and student grants. The results demonstrate that the gender dimension of income distribution matters. In the UK in 1995–6, the gender composition is remarkably equal when incomes are calculated on a household basis, but on an individual basis there is a clear gender gradient. Women account for some 80% of those in the bottom income groups, and about 20% of those in the top income groups. This suggests that it would be valuable to study more closely the individual share of income by adults in a household.

Conclusions

Both of the approaches described in this Section are important tools in the armoury of policy analysis. They are complementary, both having strengths and weaknesses. Micro-simulation modelling is richer in that it incorporates evidence about the distribution of household characteristics; and it automatically allows aggregates to be derived using distributional weights. The construction of such a micro-simulation model is, however, resource-intensive, and the validity of its results may depend crucially on the timeliness and accuracy of the underlying data. The strongest selling points of the model families approach are clearly its simplicity and limited data requirements. Results can be produced and made up-to-date very quickly and without a sophisticated statistical apparatus. At the same time, they cannot fully reflect the variety of household circumstances; and there is no satisfactory method for aggregation unless recourse is had to distributional data. Rather than seeing the two types as alternatives, therefore, we should treat them as part of a unified approach to modelling, with different elements being stressed for different applications.

In developing such a unified modelling framework, the main shortcoming is that the techniques do not yet exist for behavioural responses to be introduced on a routine basis. In this case, there is a need for further research, a need that could be supported by the Community action programme to combat social exclusion (and, from 2007, its replacement PROGRESS; see Section 2.2) and that should be taken into account in the design of the seventh and subsequent EU RTD Framework Programmes. Finally, we have highlighted the gender dimension of the analysis, and proposed complementing the existing indicators by a calculation that replaces the assumption of income sharing within the household by one that seeks to allocate income to its recipient.

4.3 Applying policy analysis to the EU Social Inclusion Process

In this Section, we consider how far the analytical methods described in Section 4.2 can be applied to the EU Social Inclusion Process. We appreciate that there are other approaches that could be adopted, but our aim is to show that the analysis can be deepened, not to cover all methods exhaustively. We consider three types of application: (i) mapping the relation between Member State policies and the common indicators agreed at EU level; (ii) projecting at a national level the future impact of existing and announced policies; and (iii) examining policy at the EU level. In each case, we ask how the analysis can best be designed to inform the Social Inclusion Process, where we have in mind both the specification by the SPC and the Commission of the structure of the NAPs/inclusion to be submitted in the future by Member States (see our proposals in Chapter 6) and the analysis to be applied by the Commission and the Member States in the Joint Reports and in Commission Staff Working Papers.

We earlier described a matrix linking two of the key elements of the Social Inclusion Process: policy actions and vulnerable groups (see Box 4.1). To this two-way classification, we should add a third dimension: the measurement of performance on the common indicators. We shall be particularly concerned with the three-way linkage: policy, vulnerable groups, and indicators – see Figure 4.2.

Figure 4.2: Policies, vulnerable groups and common indicators

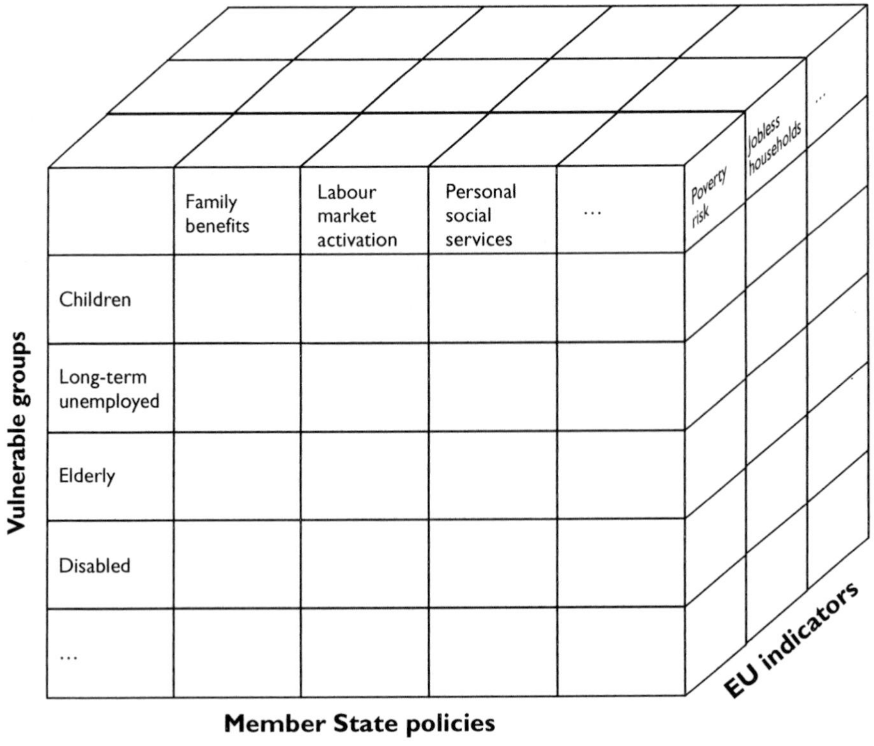

Member State policies

The three-dimensional box is – literally – vacuous, and this is a key point. At the moment we tend to approach issues either from the perspective of policies, or from the perspective of vulnerable groups, or from the perspective of indicators. But the intersection – the contents of the cells – is only just beginning to be filled out.

Mapping the relationship between Member State policies and common indicators

We have stressed the need to examine the totality of policies that impact on individuals and families. As explained in the previous Section, there are inevitably policy variables that cannot readily be incorporated, but the aim is to be as comprehensive as possible. This means taking account of the full range of social transfers and taxes, and of the interaction between them: for example, that an increase in the minimum pension may reduce the amount of housing benefit to which a pensioner is entitled, or it may so reduce the entitlement that the person considers it no longer worth claiming. The OECD tax-benefit models summarised in the annual publication *Benefits and Wages* have the following objectives:

> [They] are designed primarily to examine the rules underlying each
> country's system of taxes and benefits for the working-age population.
> [They] try to include *all* rules in a country which involve a monetary
> transfer, either from a wage earner to the Government or vice versa,
> as well as any other monetary exchanges which might be usual, such
> as required contributions to private funds. (Communication to the
> authors from OECD)

The ambition of covering all policy instruments is not, of course, always easy to realise. In seeking to apply the analysis as part of the Social Inclusion Process, we have to recognise that there will be limits to the policy variables that can be included. In order to ensure comparability, this will require the specification by the SPC of the policy scope. In the case of model families analysis, this can draw on the experience with the OECD/European Commission tax-benefit model to specify the range of policy interventions covered in the common analysis. In the case of micro-simulation modelling, the coordination of national modelling exercises is more complex. In seeking comparability, it will be necessary to consider the limits imposed by national data availability on the extent to which individual variation in taxes and benefits can be calculated. It will be necessary to consider the procedures to be applied where the calculated and recorded values for taxes and benefits do not coincide. It will be necessary to consider the assumptions made about tax compliance and about benefit claiming.

On the second dimension – vulnerable groups – the two methods have rather different implications. For model families analysis, this raises the question as to how the model families are defined. As we have seen, model families are defined by a large number of assumptions: the number of persons in the household, their age, their marital status, their willingness and capacity to work, their income (from work, capital, etc.), their housing situation (home-owner or tenant, the size of the house, etc.), whether or not they claim benefits and pay taxes. The rationale for the choices is often not made explicit, and we can in fact distinguish two different, if complementary, ways of approaching the issue of definition. The first is to seek to understand how policy instruments work. This has been well described by the OECD in the case of *Benefits and Wages*:

> The family models chosen are not meant to be representative: instead, by looking at identical household situations across countries, it is possible to focus on the *mechanics* of tax-benefit systems. The use of "typical" family models allows many of the determinants of tax and benefit amounts to be held constant while changing one household characteristic at a time. (Communication to the authors from OECD)

A key aspect in this case is the comparison of the results for different model families.

A second approach is to choose model families that are representative, not perhaps of the population, but of the groups with which policy makers are especially concerned. The model families are chosen to bring out the range of policy impacts on vulnerable/targeted groups. In this case, the categorisations given in the NAP/inclusion provides a natural starting point. Or, put the other way round, a list such as that cited from the Austrian NAP/inclusion (see Section 4.1) furnishes a checklist against which the choice of model families can be assessed. On this basis, children, families and women are typically well represented. Other groups, such as asylum seekers or people with excessive debts, are less commonly taken as cases studied in model families analysis. There is, moreover, the issue that the appropriateness of a particular specification of model families may vary across countries. One Member State may have a high incidence of people requiring long-term care; another, with a younger population, may not regard this group as of high priority.

If model families analysis is to be useful in the Social Inclusion Process, then it will require agreement on the range of family types. The SPC Indicators Sub-Group has already made a start in this direction with its specification of household types: households with no dependent children (single under and over 65, two adults, etc.) and households with dependent children (single parent family, two adults with differing numbers of children). But we need to specify the amount and sources of income (one-earner versus two-earner households, etc.), the housing status and housing costs, the ages of the children, the region, etc. In seeking to reach agreement among the EU-25 Member States on a set of model families, we suggest that both of the considerations outlined above – understanding the mechanics of policy, and the impact on vulnerable groups – are relevant. While the former can be considered on *a priori* grounds, agreement on the latter will depend crucially on consultation with Member States and with representatives of the groups concerned. This is a clear illustration of a case where the Social Inclusion Process can be made more participatory.

The position of a micro-simulation model is different. Indeed the data on which such a model is typically based provide a third way of identifying the model families that should be considered. Alternatively, it provides a check on the identification by Governments of vulnerable groups. Famously, one of the main contributions of the 1965 UK study by Abel-Smith and Townsend, *The Poor and the Poorest*, was to use survey evidence to highlight groups whose poverty had escaped public attention. The reverse is however also true. The list of vulnerable groups may help identify groups in the population of particular concern where it is necessary to over-sample in order to be able to study properly their individual circumstances. Reading the NAPs/inclusion, one sees that Governments are often concerned with groups for whom the typical sample survey would generate insufficient observations to yield reliable results. This is becoming of even greater importance as policy interventions become more targeted. Over-sampling is a technique that has often been employed, frequently in conjunction with the use of administrative data.

The third dimension concerns the common indicators. Here we can simply observe that the methods described above for analysing policy are directed at the income-related indicators. In this respect, they are limited. They tell us directly nothing about the employment, health, or education dimensions. As discussed under the heading of "behavioural change", they can tell us about the effect on work incentives, which may indirectly lead to changes in unemployment or joblessness, but any more definite application depends on future research.

We are not arguing that the analytical tools are a panacea. They cannot contribute directly to the understanding of the non-income dimensions of social exclusion; nor are they straightforward to apply across the EU-25. At the same time, the tools offer possibilities for deepening the analysis of current policies and their relationship with the common indicators of social performance. Even with a relatively narrowly defined set of model families, we can learn about how individual households are affected by taxation and social transfers. This is a direct application of the OECD/EU analysis. Even if national micro-simulation models are not fully comparable, it would be a valuable exercise to set in parallel analyses of the impact of varying different components of the existing policy set. In this way, we can learn about the mechanics of policy impact.

Projecting future policy impact

The analytical tools can be used, not only to investigate current policy effects, but also to project the impact of new or proposed policies. They treat policies parametrically, so that these parameters can be varied. We can compare the situation before and after a policy change. This comparison can be made at the individual level or, in the case of the micro-simulation model, at the level of the aggregate population. It is possible, in the latter case, to project the effect on the income-related common indicators. If, for instance, a country's NAP/inclusion includes proposals for a new in-work benefit for families, directed at both employment and social inclusion objectives, then it would be reasonable to expect that this account would be accompanied by the results of a micro-simulation exercise identifying (i) the number of potential recipients; (ii) the impact on their disposable incomes, and hence on the at-risk-of-poverty indicators; and (iii) the effect on incentives to leave unemployment or to work longer hours. Such an exercise is likely to have been undertaken already within the national Government.

From the standpoint of the Commission, the Social Agenda 2005–2010 envisages that 2010 will be declared the European year of combating poverty and social exclusion. What are likely to be the prospects for poverty and social exclusion by that year? To answer this question, an exercise needs to be undertaken to project the evolution of EU social performance over the period up to 2010. In the first instance, this could concentrate on the overall risk-of-poverty indicator, although it would be very desirable to consider breakdowns of this total. This projection should take account of the present policies of Member States, and of the new policies embodied in the NAPs/inclusion. It should be interpreted using the results from studies of model families, chosen on a consistent basis across Member States. Such a projection will inform policy makers about the extent to which existing policies promise to generate significant progress towards reducing poverty and social exclusion. It should of course be noted that we are talking about the contribution of policy change; the actual evolution will also depend on economic forces and on demographic developments. Forecasting is a more ambitious undertaking, although it can yield valuable insights.

The projection can make use of national simulation models, which will allow testing of progress towards the targets set by individual countries. For example, in the case of Spain, the stated aim was to reduce the number of people with a level of income below 60% of the average by two percentage points during the period of the plan. For Greece, the aim was that by 2010 the percentage of individuals at risk would be down to the EU-15 average. For Portugal, the aim was that the risk-of-poverty rate would be brought down by three percentage points by 2005.

The NAPs/inclusion stress learning from "good practice" as a means of developing future policies, and this could be further developed using the tools described here. In an informal way, learning from other countries has long been practised, as is well illustrated by the history of the diffusion of social insurance. More recently, a number of European countries have been influenced by the Earned Income Tax Credit of the United States. Here we have in mind a more formal process, where the parameters of the scheme of country A are translated to the context of country B. A good example is provided by the study by Callan *et al* (2004) of *Why is Relative Poverty so High in Ireland?* They consider the implications of introducing in Ireland a welfare system closer to that of Denmark, a country that has a low risk-of-poverty rate. In the same way, the study by Levy (2003) of Spain compares the child-targeted reforms in that country with the policies of Denmark, France, Germany and the UK. In the context of today's EU, it could be interesting to make similar comparisons of countries with different policies, and countries with different social performance.

This kind of analysis can be conducted in terms of model families, which can be valuable in identifying some of the complexities. Suppose, for example, that we introduce in country B the higher child benefit found in country A. In country A, however, child benefit is taken into account in the assessment of income-tested housing benefit, whereas it is exempt in country B. Should we take account of the increase in assessing housing benefit in country B? Then there is the issue of revenue-neutrality. The higher child benefit has to be financed. We need then to model the increase using a micro-simulation model, in order to establish the net cost, allowing for any reduction in income-tested transfers or any increase in income tax revenue. For an equal cost comparison, an adjustment has to be made in some other policy variables, such as tax rates. The "policy swap" has to be precisely specified. It should also be noted that the comparison would not necessarily be the same as that obtained from the reverse operation. The reduction in risk of poverty in country A from applying B's policies is not equal to the increase in poverty in country B from applying A's policies. The impact of the policies depends on the distribution of the population, as does the cost. Once again, it must be emphasised that specific policies and their impacts can only be properly understood in the context of the broad institutional setting – in terms of for example labour market regulation and collective bargaining arrangements – in which they operate; some may therefore be more easily transferred across countries than others, so system-wide analysis is also required.

EU-wide analysis and common analytical framework

The EU social indicators published as part of the Joint Reports and Commission Staff Working Papers typically include the EU-25 or EU-15 average, calculated as a population-weighted average of the available national values. During his Presidency of the European Commission, Jacques Delors frequently talked about 50 million people in Europe being in poverty. In many other domains, the EU considers the Union as a whole, for example in the setting of the employment targets. In the economic sphere, Europe is moving to the construction of aggregate statistics: for example, total GDP for the Euro-zone. In the social field, too, there are good reasons to carry out analyses at the EU level, asking how the combined actions planned by Member States will affect the total situation of the EU. Most importantly, it would bring together the Social Inclusion Process and the EU social cohesion policy, concerned with convergence of Member States. The whole thrust of cohesion policy is to see the Union as a whole.

Such an EU-wide perspective involves aggregating across the different national systems, and cannot readily be obtained alone by model families analysis, although such analysis could form one of the building blocks. Instead, we have to consider the case for constructing a micro-simulation model covering the EU as a whole.

The feasibility of constructing such an EU-25 model has been demonstrated by the European micro-simulation model EUROMOD, developed for the 15 countries that were members of the EU prior to 2004 (Immervoll *et al*, 2000 and 2004; and Sutherland, 2001). The project, which was funded by the European Commission's Targeted Socio-Economic Research (TSER) programme, involved:

- establishing a micro-database for each country, in a number of cases drawn from the European Community Household Panel, containing the input variables necessary for tax-benefit calculations, together with variables to be used in analysis of model output;
- collection, coding and parameterisation of policy rules for the various tax-benefit systems;
- design of the model framework identifying common features applicable to all 15 Member States, allowing results to be produced for all countries or for a subset of countries;
- testing and validation of simulated outputs from the model (for example, comparison of income distribution and risk-of-poverty statistics with other sources, including national statistical series);
- documentation of the work done, by country.

The main output from an EU-wide micro-simulation model of this type would be a measure of household disposable income for each household in the sample for each country, with different tax and benefit parameters. It would allow the user to examine the effect on household disposable incomes of changes in policy, whether in one Member State alone or in all Member States. As such, it would provide an important tool for exploring the impacts of social and fiscal policies, and reforms to existing policies, on the risk of poverty, on the correlation of the risk of poverty with other variables, and on income inequality. This includes analyses of proposed changes in social and fiscal policies with reference to targets set by Member States for the reduction in poverty and social exclusion (discussed in detail in Chapter 6). In addition, it is possible to explore the relative effectiveness of policies across countries, facilitating Member States in learning from the experience of other countries.

Of course, micro-simulation models have inherent *limitations*, as we have seen in Sections 4.2 and 4.3. Some of these become particularly significant when we consider the ambitious enterprise of constructing an EU-wide model. An important limitation is the cost involved in constructing and maintaining such a model for the EU. Developing a tax-benefit model requires time and money, and the cost has increased with the addition of ten new countries as a result of the May 2004 Enlargement. Therefore, one will need to make certain choices (regarding the extent of the model, a static or a dynamic model, inclusion or not of behavioural reactions, etc.). In this respect the model families approach is far less demanding in terms of construction and maintenance costs, and can therefore be kept more easily up to date. Since a model families analysis can be seen as forming one element in the construction of a micro-simulation model, it would be a natural first step, building on the work already underway.

In developing this type of analysis, it would be highly unproductive for individual countries and the Commission to all proceed in different directions using different models and specifications of the key input and output parameters. It may thus be useful to think in terms of a *common framework* for policy analysis. The possible architecture of such a common framework is illustrated in Figure 4.3. This envisages that the Commission would work closely with the Member States to arrive at both an agreed set of key policy parameters, and a set of categories by which households should be distinguished in examining policy impact (for example household composition, gender and age of household members). Bringing together this harmonised input and output framework with data (in time from EU-SILC) on a representative sample of households in each country, one can investigate the impact of alternative policies on different family types and on aggregate indicators for the sample as a whole, and compare these across countries. Specific policy options may be of higher interest and relevance to some countries than others, and it will not always be sensible to analyse a given policy across all countries, but a common framework will facilitate policy learning.

Crucially, the common framework would help build the link to the effects on the common indicators, in addition to indicators that are of national concern. Given the nature of the analytical tools at present available the output will initially refer to the income-based indicators only. But over time, the framework can be developed. In particular, the inter-related challenges of seeking to incorporate behavioural responses and extend the scope to include non-income-based indicators could probably best be addressed within such a common framework.

Figure 4.3: Possible architecture for a common framework for policy analysis

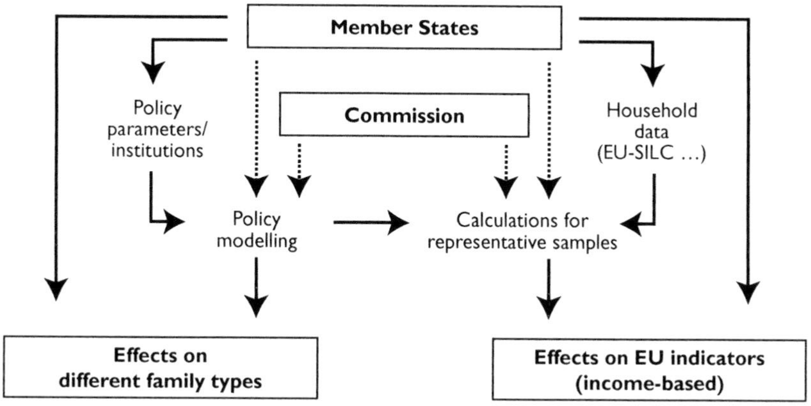

As Figure 4.4 illustrates, the starting point is the specification of changes in the key policy parameters of interest – for example tax or benefit rates or structures. The modelling methods described above can be used to derive estimates for a

Figure 4.4: The challenge of behavioural responses

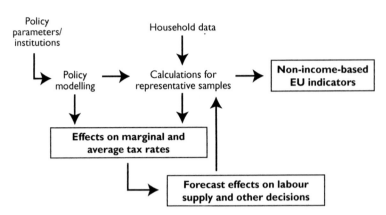

representative sample of the population of the impact these changes would have on marginal and average tax rates (including the withdrawal of benefit as income rises). These in turn, combined with available estimates of the responsiveness of, for example, labour supply of people in different circumstances, can be used to forecast the extent of changes in key aspects of behaviour, again for a representative sample of the population. Those changes can then be incorporated into the estimation of the overall impact of the policy change(s) on household income. Much needs to be done to enhance our understanding of the scale and nature of those behavioural responses – and extending beyond labour supply to, for example, family and household formation – and how they vary across different institutional settings, but there is a base of research on which to build.

Extending that analysis to the impact of policy changes on indicators of social exclusion going beyond income – such as deprivation levels, education and access to health services – is equally challenging, but a shared understanding of the nature of the exercise and a common framework within which it can be approached, by policy makers and researchers at national and EU levels, would help in making progress. As already emphasised, such a common framework will have to recognise the differences in institutional setting across countries. These differences will no doubt mean that specific policies will have different impacts, but the suggested approach will serve to make explicit the need to consider the social and economic system as a whole.

The weighting issue

EU-wide social indicators complement, but do not replace, the indicators for individual Member States. EU-wide measures are, after all, dominated by the large Member States. In an EU with more than 450 million citizens, the performance of countries with populations of 10 million or less is not going to change greatly the overall rate. If 10% of the Swedish population were suddenly to fall below the risk-of-poverty threshold – a dramatic development for Sweden – the EU risk-of-poverty rate would rise by less than 0.2 percentage points. (For Luxembourg, with a population one-twentieth of that of Sweden, the effect would be only 0.01 percentage point.) In contrast, if the UK were to reduce its risk-of-poverty rate to that experienced in the 1970s, then the overall EU rate would fall by some 1.5 percentage points.

This consideration is becoming more serious for the EU in view of the increasing concentration of the population of the EU with successive Enlargements. If we were to take the original EU-6, then a third of the countries (the two largest countries) have 63% of the total population. In the EU-25, the largest third of countries have 80% of the population, whereas the smallest third of countries have fewer than 5% of the total EU population. The increase in the number of Member States may generate a natural tendency to focus on the EU aggregates, but the increased population concentration means that it is even more important to continue to monitor the performance of individual Member States. Otherwise, the experience of the smaller countries will be almost completely submerged in the aggregate measures.

In sum, we need figures both for individual Member States and totals for the EU as a whole.

Conclusions

Starting from a three-way linkage of policy, vulnerable groups, and indicators, we have seen that the purchase of the two analytical tools – model families analysis and micro-simulation modelling – on the common indicators is limited, at least in direct terms, to the income-related measures. With this qualification, the tools do nonetheless offer a way forward in developing the analysis. As part of a unified approach to policy modelling, they can provide a basis for incorporating a range of policies and their interactions, allowing us to learn about the mechanics and (potential) impact of policy. The design of model families can reflect the vulnerable groups identified in the NAPs/inclusion, and the micro-simulation models can throw light on their quantitative significance.

More concretely:

• The systematic use of model families analysis by Member States in their NAPs/inclusion could be facilitated by agreement on the range of family types, building on the start already made by the ISG with its specification of household types, and on the experience with the OECD/European Commission tax benefit model.
• Member States should be encouraged to present the results of micro-simulation modelling of policy initiatives, and an attempt made to coordinate national micro-simulation modelling exercises in the EU-25.
• Consideration should be given to the construction of an EU-wide micro-simulation model for all 25 Member States, which – building on the experience

with common model families analyses – would provide an important tool for the assessment of the NAPs/inclusion and analysis of the likely impact of proposed changes in social and fiscal policies in achieving a significant reduction in the risk of poverty by 2010.

• These developments should form part of a unified approach to policy modelling, and we have proposed that the EU move towards a common framework for policy analysis.

In this way, we can move towards adding an *EU common analysis* to the common indicators.

4.4 Children mainstreaming: an application

The 2004 Joint Inclusion Report noted the "particular concern in several countries (e.g. UK, IE, DE, IT, LU, PT, SE) over the situation of children growing up in families on low incomes" (European Commission, 2004b, page 31). That Joint Report went on to call for a Key Priority to be "A focus on ending child poverty as a key step to combat the intergenerational inheritance of poverty with a particular focus on early intervention and early education initiatives which identify and support children and poor families" (European Commission, 2004b, page 36). As we have seen, the analytical methods discussed here are not well suited to examine the impact of early intervention and early education initiatives, but they can usefully be applied to the risk of child financial poverty. The Technical Annex to the 2006 Joint Report on Social Protection and Social Inclusion also refers to the fact that children are a particularly vulnerable group with an at-risk-of-poverty rate higher than for any other age group, and pointed to the proportion living in jobless households as of particular concern (European Commission 2006b, page 18). In its March 2006 Conclusions the European Council specifically asked the Member States "to take necessary measures to rapidly and significantly reduce child poverty, giving all children equal opportunities, regardless of their social background" (Presidency Conclusions). More generally, both European Councils stressed the need for investment in the youth of Europe.

Mapping from policies to outcomes

"Governments have come under increasing pressure to make explicit and indeed to quantify the impact their budgetary decisions have on particular groups in society" is the opening sentence of the study by Corak, Lietz and Sutherland (2005) of the impact of tax and transfer systems on children in the EU-15. As the authors bring out, such calculations are not straightforward. In terms of the policy/group matrix, we cannot simply label some policies as "family benefits" and measure their size. Obviously, it is not simply a question of adding up spending on child cash and in-kind benefits and the cost of child tax allowances. One has to consider the child element of other transfers, such as housing benefit. One has to allow for the fact that some child benefits are taxed under income tax, and that some are taken into account in assessing income-tested benefits.

It is for this reason that the broad reach of policy models is essential. The comparison made, for example, by Bradshaw and Mayhew (2005) of the tax benefit package in eight European countries (six from the EU-15) takes account of tax benefits, income-tested cash benefits, non-income-tested cash benefits, social insurance contributions, rent/housing benefits, local taxes and benefits, childcare costs and benefits, social assistance, and guaranteed child support. Their model families calculations are based on a selection of family types (including, for comparison, a childless married couple) with a variety of earnings, related to the national average. The findings suggest that, when this range of policies is taken into account in each country, the differences in child benefit packages as a percentage of average earnings differ by a factor of about 2 to 1.

As we have noted, the selection of model family types can be informed by survey or administrative data covering the whole population. Corak, Lietz and Sutherland (2005) note that a significant proportion of children live in households where there are adults other than their parents. Such a household composition is not typically taken into account in model families analysis. The additional adult may be a sibling, a grandparent, or may be unrelated. In Spain and Portugal, for example, only 63% of children live in a household where there are no adults other than their parents (Corak, Lietz and Sutherland, 2005, Table 2). They go on to use the European micro-simulation model, EUROMOD, described above, to examine the child-contingent components in the tax transfer system. This involves recalculating the household disposable income as though there were no children present. The results show that the per capita spending per child, as a proportion of per capita household disposable income, was highest in Luxembourg, at 23%, followed by Austria and Belgium, and then a large group of countries (Ireland, the UK, France, Germany, Denmark and Finland) with spending around 15%. In Greece and Spain, spending is less than 5%. Their results show the importance of including tax concessions and the tax treatment of transfers.

Analysing policy reform

The calculations above refer to the current situation. Policy analysis is particularly concerned with possible reforms. Here we take two concrete examples as to how the analysis could be applied to policy changes directed at child poverty.

In the previous Section, we suggested the use of "policy swapping". What we have in mind is well illustrated by the study of Jeandidier *et al* (1995). This study takes the family benefit systems of five EU-15 countries (Belgium, Germany, France, Luxembourg, and Ireland) and compares their impact. The study uses a range of methods, including both model families analysis and micro-simulation based on a sample of French families. As the title of the article by Jeandidier (1997a) indicates, the results "arouse one's curiosity"; his study shows how the different methods can yield different insights into the impact of a policy issue, in this case the targeting of benefits in favour of single parent families. The study by Jeandidier (1997b) uses a sample of French households to simulate the impact of the child benefit systems of Belgium, France, Ireland and Luxembourg. Immervoll *et al* (2001) use the micro-simulation model EUROMOD to contrast the child benefit systems of the Netherlands and the UK, in each case applying to data for one country the other country's system on a revenue-neutral basis. Family transfers in Southern Europe are studied by Matsaganis *et al* (2004).

Taking now a EU-wide perspective, suppose that the EU wished to halve the number of children in the EU living at risk of poverty, and that there was a political commitment to bring this about by requiring each Member State to provide a minimum income for children. This could be achieved under subsidiarity, with each state free to choose the method. The amount of the minimum would take account of the circumstances of each Member State, particularly the lower per capita incomes of the new Member States. It could be defined as a common percentage of the Member State median equivalised income for each child (and possibly age-related). (For a valuable discussion of the setting of targets for reducing child poverty and related issues, see Corak, 2005.)

Implementation would be left to Member States, and different Member States would make different choices. By considering a range of model families with children, Member States could determine the possible combinations of changes in policy parameters that would guarantee a minimum income for each child in their country. Tax allowances for children can be increased, or introduced; they can be accompanied by tax credits for those not subject to income tax. Child benefit, a universal cash benefit, is the most direct form of cash transfer. Child credits, income tested, may appear a more targeted mechanism, although such credits in practice suffer from incomplete take-up. Targeting may also be achieved by concentrating increased benefits on families already in receipt of social insurance or social assistance.

The choice between different possible policy combinations would undoubtedly be influenced by considerations of cost and of effectiveness. Using a micro-simulation model, it is possible to make estimates of the cost of different proposals. The net effect on the Government budget depends on the interaction between different elements: for example, an increase in child benefit may be partly offset by reduced social assistance payments. An integrated tax-benefit model is necessary to take account of these feedback effects. The same model can be used to calculate the impact of different policy choices on the risk-of-poverty rate among children. It would be possible to plot the EU-wide risk-of-poverty rate as a function of the different levels at which the (common) child minimum income, as a (common) percentage of the Member State median, could be set; this would give a first-round measure of the policy change necessary to achieve a specified reduction in the risk of child poverty.

4.5 Concluding comment

Strengthening policy analysis is essential for individual Member States and for the EU as a whole. Member States, responsible for the implementation of the EU Social Protection and Social Inclusion Process, are centrally concerned with the effectiveness of policy measures. They need to know what works. They need to be able to learn from other Member States. For them a deeper understanding is required of the link between policy measures and outcomes. For the EU as a whole, policy analysis is essential to understand whether there are realistic policy options to achieve the EU social objectives. The Commission needs to be able to work back from the desired outcomes – such as reduced risk of poverty, or reduced proportions of jobless households – to the policies that can bring them about.

The aim of this Chapter was not to answer these questions, but to show some of the ways in which they can be (partially) answered, drawing on social science research. This has not yet fully penetrated the NAPs/inclusion and their EU analyses, which need to be developed further. For the most part one does not get a clear sense of exactly how the stated goals are to be achieved: broad approaches and detailed policies are often described, but the linkage between those and the achievement of quantitative outcome targets is not addressed. We lack an adequate specification of the baseline situation; the total effects of policies on poverty and social exclusion need to be investigated; the policy analysis is insufficiently comparative.

Note

[1] The reviews by national experts of their country's NAPs/inclusion are an important element of the process, on which we do not comment here. Only a limited number of these have been placed in the public domain, and it is hard to make a systematic analysis; this would, however, be potentially of considerable interest. In this context, it is worth mentioning the European Commission "network of non-governmental experts" which supports the Directorate-General for Employment, Social Affairs and Equal Opportunities (DG EMPL) in its task of assessing independently the implementation of the Social Inclusion Process. The network currently consists of 28 independent experts, one for each Member State plus one each for Bulgaria, Romania and Turkey. For accessing the experts' reports and for more information on the network (including the list of members), see: http://ec.europa.eu/employment_social/social_inclusion/index_en.htm. See also: http://www.peer-review-social-inclusion.net/peer/en/general_information.

FIVE

EU indicators for poverty and social exclusion

The set of outcome indicators adopted formally by the European Council at Laeken in December 2001, and developed substantially since that date, is intended to play a central role in monitoring the performance of Member States in promoting social inclusion. The purpose of these indicators is to allow the Member States and the European Commission to monitor national and EU progress towards key EU objectives in the area of social inclusion (see Chapter 2), and to support mutual learning and identification of good (and bad) practices in terms of policies and institutional processes (see Chapter 6). This represents a major step forward in the development of EU cooperation in social policy, and has the potential to transform the framework within which Member States develop their national (and sub-national) policies to tackle poverty and social exclusion. The value of having regular and publicly available data on these indicators, allowing for an independent assessment of the performance of Member States, must be emphasised.

The development of indicators is a dynamic process, in which the Indicators Sub-Group of the EU Social Protection Committee has performed a very important role since it was set up in February 2001 (see Chapter 2). The work of the national delegations of experts, who make up the Sub-Group, and the secretariat provided by the European Commission Directorate-General on "Employment, Social Affairs and Equal Opportunities" (in close cooperation with Eurostat), has allowed the set of indicators (and breakdowns of these) to be considerably enriched. A prime example is provided by the progress made on capturing the relationship between poverty and work (see Lelièvre, Marlier and Pétour, 2004; Bardone and Guio, 2005); progress has also been made towards developing indicators relating to material deprivation, housing and access to health care.

Our objective here is not to provide a full history of the evolution of the commonly agreed social indicators, but to revisit certain aspects of the content and use of the set of indicators to see whether improvements can be suggested, whether they can be further enriched and made more policy-relevant. This is timely in the light of experience with the use of the common indicators, of changes in data availability, and in particular following on the accession to the EU of 10 new Member States with relatively low average living standards. Moreover, the recently launched EU data source *EU-SILC* ("Community Statistics on Income and Living Conditions", already introduced in Chapter 3) raises some new issues regarding the common indicators already in use.

It should be stressed that we have not attempted to provide a comprehensive review of the common indicators for social inclusion; rather our aim is to highlight a number of key issues. The principles and considerations on which the selection of the current set of indicators was based have been discussed in Chapter 2, and apply in seeking to move forward. Since statistical capacity impinges directly on the indicators, we focus first in Section 5.1 on the switch from the European Community Household Panel (ECHP) to EU-SILC and its implications for the common indicators. The implications of Enlargement of the EU for the choice and use of indicators are then addressed in Section 5.2. Enlargement has meant a much wider spread in terms of average income levels across the Member States, giving even greater significance to the convergence of average living standards. In addition, historic and institutional differences between the "old" 15 and the "new" 10 may have implications for the approach they would wish to take in framing social inclusion indicators. As we have seen in Chapter 3, extending the common indicators to the new Member States has led to a number of interesting changes in how we view poverty and social exclusion in the EU.

The move to EU-SILC, and Enlargement, provide the context for our examination in Section 5.3 of possible refinements of the social indicators and how best to fill some widely acknowledged gaps in the coverage of the original set. The latter are in important areas where there were either no common indicators or those available were particularly limited, notably housing, health, and non-monetary deprivation indicators. In Section 5.4, we turn to the use of the set of common indicators, highlighting the hazards of allowing a proliferation of indicators. We also briefly discuss how cross-cutting indicators can be used to build links between the different EU policy processes, and comparisons with non-EU industrialised countries. Section 5.5 considers the specific issue as to how indicators can contribute to children mainstreaming.

5.1 EU-SILC and income measures

Reliable and timely indicators, reflecting the multi-dimensionality of poverty and social exclusion, are indispensable for monitoring Member States' performance in promoting social inclusion as well as for mutual policy learning and identification of good (and bad) practices. This means that having the required statistical infrastructure and capacity in place at the national and EU levels is a necessary condition for the Social Inclusion Process to achieve its aims. The commitment by the Member States and the Commission of the resources required to build and analyse that capacity is indispensable.

As discussed in Chapter 3, the ECHP, which ran in 14 of the then 15 Member States (generally) from 1994 to 2001, served as the source for many of the commonly agreed social inclusion indicators as the OMC gathered pace. The ECHP was crucial for the first two rounds of EU-15 NAPs/inclusion (2001 and 2003), despite the fact that the reliability of its data for several countries was questioned, the results were available only after a substantial lag and were therefore criticised as out of date, and in most countries it was not satisfactorily integrated with the national statistical systems. With the aim of solving these problems, of conforming to the internationally agreed definition of income (Expert Group on Household Income Statistics (The Canberra Group), 2001) and of extending the data collection to the enlarged EU (and beyond), the decision was taken to stop the ECHP and launch EU-SILC.

Community Statistics on Income and Living Conditions (EU-SILC)

EU-SILC is a major statistical development, even though it will obviously not fill in all the statistical data gaps faced in constructing the required national and EU indicators for the Social Protection and Social Inclusion Process (see below). The investment made by all those concerned will transform the basis for social reporting in the EU. Indeed, its impact extends beyond the EU, since it will in time cover, in addition to all 25 Member States, a number of non-EU countries (including acceding and candidate countries). EU-SILC was launched in 2003 on a gentleman's agreement basis in six Member States (Belgium, Denmark, Greece, Ireland, Luxembourg and Austria) as well as in Norway. Eurostat, in close cooperation with Member States national statistical institutes, used this data to evaluate the full process of data collection and the computation of cross-sectional indicators. They have carried out methodological investigations focusing on survey quality, data cleaning and on the impact of the changes of source and (mainly income) definitions on the cross-sectional income-based Laeken indicators. In 2004, under a framework Regulation of the European Parliament and the Council,[1] EU-SILC was implemented in 12 EU-15 countries (exceptions being Germany, the Netherlands and the UK) as well as in Estonia, Iceland and Norway. By 2005, EU-SILC was operating in all EU-25 countries as well as Turkey (pilot survey), Iceland and Norway. Bulgaria and Romania have launched EU-SILC in 2006, and Switzerland is expected to do so in 2007; subsequently EU-SILC should also be launched in the Former Yugoslav Republic of Macedonia and in Croatia.

The first cross-sectional EU-SILC indicators for 12 "old" Member States, for Estonia as well as for Norway, were released publicly by the end of 2005; and data for all 25 Member States of the current EU, Norway and Iceland should be available by the end of 2006. The first four-year longitudinal data required for the persistent at-risk-of-poverty indicator will only be available by the beginning of 2010, although some "interim variants" of that indicator could be computed on the basis of two or three waves only (but would then need to be aligned across countries and carefully labelled – e.g. "persistence over two years" – to avoid confusion with the commonly agreed indicator). This significant data gap at EU-25 level as well as, for several EU-15 Member States (who relied solely or primarily on the ECHP), at national level is therefore progressively being filled in. It is worth mentioning that for the interim period, EU-15 Member States who did not launch EU-SILC in 2003 agreed to compute the cross-sectional income-based Laeken indicators on the basis of national data sources. The new Member States, with methodological help from Eurostat, also supplied comparable indicators derived from national sources (often Household Budget Surveys). Thanks to these EU and (sub-)national efforts, and despite the inevitable discontinuities and comparability problems caused by this mix of sources (and definitions), information on most common cross-sectional indicators has already been made available for the 25 Member States and used in reports on social inclusion (see European Commission, 2005b, 2005c, 2006a, 2006b, 2006d).

EU-SILC is now becoming the EU reference source for information on the level and composition of income, poverty and social exclusion, and hence for a large number of common indicators for social inclusion. As with the ECHP and in fact most household surveys, it covers only people living in *private households*, which needs to be kept in mind when carrying out statistical analyses and when interpreting indicators within a given country as well as between countries. For instance, the impact of the exclusion from the samples of older people living in institutions may be very different from one country to the next. Some vulnerable groups living in private households may also be underrepresented because they are not easy to reach. It is therefore important that statistical efforts be made at the sub-national, national and EU levels to collect (better) statistical socio-economic information on these groups, which include people living in institutions, vulnerable groups including the homeless (see Section 5.3), ethnic minorities and migrants (see Section 5.3; see also European Commission, 2006h), people with disabilities, those with addiction problems, etc.

In view of its central role in the monitoring of the Social Inclusion Process, it is important to bring out at this stage some issues that arise from the switch from the ECHP to EU-SILC. EU-SILC shares many of the same objectives as the ECHP, aiming at producing cross-sectional and longitudinal micro-data which are multi-dimensional in terms of the topics covered and are comparable across participating countries, but it uses a different approach to producing data across countries in terms of data harmonisation. As explained earlier, unlike the ECHP, EU-SILC is organised under a framework Regulation and is thus compulsory for all Member States. It is based on the idea of a common "framework", rather than a common "survey" as was the case for the ECHP. Member States are allowed to use both survey(s) and administrative registers, provided that all the cross-sectional data (and, separately, all the longitudinal data) are "linkable" at the micro-level. They are, however, allowed to separate the cross-sectional element from the longitudinal element if they prefer, so the cross-sectional micro-dataset and the longitudinal micro-dataset may not necessarily be linked at the micro-level. Whereas the ECHP had to be a full panel survey, Eurostat recommends for EU-SILC a rotational design in which an individual is followed only for four years (the minimum requirement) – though a full panel is still an option if a country prefers.

The priority of EU-SILC is to provide high-quality and timely *cross-sectional* information for the enlarged EU and the acceding/candidate countries (and certain other European countries); it is this priority together with the willingness to anchor EU-SILC nationally (see below) that have determined its format and the resulting loss in the longitudinal data-sets compared with the ECHP. On timeliness, the Regulation describes in particular the dates by which cross-sectional and longitudinal data are to be delivered to Eurostat. As to the quality, the Regulation fixes a minimum effective sample size, and the obligation for countries to provide a detailed annual quality assessment report. Computation of systematic standard errors for the cross-sectional income-based Laeken indicators is part of this assessment.

A new concept of income

A key objective of EU-SILC is to deliver robust and comparable data on total disposable household income, total disposable household income before transfers (both with and without old-age and survivors' benefits), total gross income, and gross income at component level, whereas only net income (components and total) was required for the ECHP. In this context, it was decided that EU-SILC should adhere as closely as possible to the recommendations of the international Canberra Group (Expert Group on Household Income Statistics, 2001) on the definition of household income.

This objective has led to significant changes compared with the income concept used in the ECHP. Most important shifts in the income concept include the following:

1. As from the launch of EU-SILC:
   - Inter-household transfers: not only are the regular private transfers received from other households taken into account (they are included in the income, as was already the case in the ECHP) but also, which is new, the private transfers paid to other households have to be deducted from the income of the donor household. While this has attractions in avoiding double-counting, it may produce some misleading results in terms of poverty risk – a household making a substantial transfer may appear to be at risk, even when on a high cash income and making a discretionary transfer. For this reason, EU-SILC is rightly taking account solely of *regular* inter-household transfers paid and received (such as alimony and child maintenance). Ensuring that this regularity criterion is strictly respected is important.
   - Lump sum tax adjustments: they are deducted from/included in the household income.
   - Company cars available for private use: they are valued, and this amount is added to the income from work under gross non-cash employee income.
   - Reporting negative incomes (for the self-employed) is now possible, whereas negative self-employment incomes were put at zero in the ECHP.

2. As from 2007:
- Imputed rent: another significant change from the ECHP is that the net value of imputed rents (i.e. the money that one saves on full (market) rent by living in one's own accommodation or in an accommodation rented at a price that is lower than the market rent or rent-free) has to be estimated, and is to be included in household income from 2007.
- Self-consumption: the value of home consumption and of employer-provided benefits (on top of company cars) has to be included.
- Interest paid on mortgages has to enter the computation of the net imputed rent to be used for calculating total household income.
- Gross employers' social insurance contribution should be included provided that results of feasibility studies are positive.

As noted above, a key priority for EU–SILC is close adherence to the recommendations of the Canberra Group (Expert Group on Household Income Statistics, 2001) on the definition of household income. At the same time, income is defined for a purpose, and the appropriate definition may vary with the purpose. This is in fact clearly recognised by the Canberra Group itself: "it is important to recognise at the outset that different measures of income may be the most appropriate or the best available for different analytical purposes" (Expert Group on Household Income Statistics, 2001, page 11). Close adherence does not imply slavishly following every aspect of the Canberra definitions. In three cases – negative incomes, self-employment income, and imputed rent on owner-occupied houses or accommodation rented at below market rent – we suggest that consideration be given to departing from the general recommendations of the Canberra Group when addressing the specific issue of measuring the *risk of poverty*:

- Total household incomes may be negative, either on account of negative individual components, or on account of the subtraction of inter-household transfers, or of taxes. While we welcome the richer data now available, there is good reason to pay particular attention to negative incomes and to consider their proper treatment in the analysis of poverty risk. If poverty risk is assessed in terms of standard of living, then it is not obvious what interpretation can be placed on negative values. It is after all not income itself that we are concerned to measure, but income as an *indicator of risk*. In our view, to use negative values would re-open the debate about "standard of living" interpretations of poverty versus "minimum rights" interpretations (see Atkinson, Cantillon, Marlier and Nolan, 2002, page 81). Calculations of the S80/S20 income quintile ratio would, in particular, be seriously affected. In any case, it would be useful if there were to be a report of the number of cases of negative incomes, but we would go further and suggest that there be a harmonised procedure setting a minimum value to incomes for the purpose of measuring poverty risk (on a standard of living basis).

- The negative income issue suggests that the (always complex) topic of the income of the self-employed could usefully benefit from a specific investigation. The Canberra Group refers to the "net operating profit or loss accruing to working owners of, or partners in, unincorporated enterprises" (page 118), which points to an accountancy logic. We understand that the current logic of data collection could usefully be extended, with only limited additional burden on those respondents concerned, to request first the accounts submitted for legal purposes, secondly tax declarations, and thirdly amounts that the self-employed draw regularly from the business. The last of these figures may come closer to "permanent income", and may be a better basis for measuring the risk of poverty.

- From the standpoint of measuring overall inequality, inclusion of estimates of imputed rent (as EU–SILC will seek to do from 2007) represents an attempt to capture the real differences in living standards between, for instance, a household paying rent and another in owner-occupied housing on which no debt is outstanding. Failure to take this into account can mislead as to the relative situation of, for example, older people (many of whom own their own homes in many countries) versus young families or single adults who are either renting or are in the early stages of house purchase.[2] At the same time, the rent imputed to the household is not in fact equivalent to cash income actually received, in that it cannot be used to meet other expenditure needs. From a social inclusion perspective, this means that focusing purely on income including imputed rent could mislead as to the capacity of the household to avoid deprivation and social exclusion. Income is in that instance being used as an *indicator* of poverty risk, not as a measure in its own right. The example of an older person on a low income but owning and living in a large house is instructive. The substantial rent that would be imputed because of the size of the house is not available to pay for food, clothing or heating.[3] On the other hand, the pensioner does clearly enjoy *some* benefit from her house, and is better placed than her neighbour who is a tenant.[4] It is for this reason that the United Kingdom has regularly published the Households Below Average Income series (UK Department for Work and Pensions, 2005) both before and after housing costs. In the latter case, the risk-of-poverty figure is calculated by subtracting housing outgoings. We conclude that while the at-risk-of-poverty indicators including imputed rent are of value to obtain a more comprehensive picture, consideration should be given to also producing those indicators without including imputed rent in the total income and/or after housing costs; although open to debate, we would give more prominence to the at-risk-of-poverty indicators excluding imputed rent. More work is clearly necessary in this area of imputed housing income and the burden of housing costs before reaching any final decisions, and Eurostat has such investigation under way.

- Methodological work is also on-going into the treatment of income from private (i.e. voluntary) pension schemes, and corresponding treatment of contribution payments.

We appreciate that adopting any one of our suggestions would mean using a different income definition for different indicators (notably poverty risk versus income inequality). However, not to do so might, we believe, expose the EU poverty risk indicators to unnecessary criticism. These issues will have to be debated within the Indicators Sub-Group and with the European Statistical System, both conceptually and in the light of EU-SILC results.

In view of the major definitional changes between the ECHP (or national series) and EU-SILC, aimed at improving the robustness and comparability of income data, methodological work will be required before a link can (possibly) be made, for the common indicators, between the existing ECHP (or national) time series and the new EU-SILC ones. Some countries may have a relatively seamless transition, but some sharp discontinuities are inevitable. In-depth methodological investigation focused on the common indicators is required comparing the existing ECHP time series and the new EU-SILC figures. Eurostat has already carried out some particularly valuable analysis of the continuity of indicators during the transition (Eurostat, 2005). If the new EU-SILC series differs from the previous ECHP due to factors that can for the most part be understood and quantified, it may be statistically possible to link the two (in the same way that macro-economic series such as unemployment or growth rates often have to be linked where there is a break in the series due to changes in methods). In other instances where substantial differences appear, no such robust statistical link may be possible – because it is not possible to say much more than that the figures are different. In effect, there may then be little alternative to simply taking the initial level shown by EU-SILC as the baseline against which progress is to be measured in the future. This also has implications for setting targets, discussed in Chapter 6: if targets are set based on national sources in the transition, the definitions of indicators should still follow those commonly agreed.

A flexible approach aimed at anchoring the instrument nationally

Because EU-SILC data can be collected from different sources, including administrative registers, data collection is not based on the use of a harmonised questionnaire across all the participating countries, but on harmonised *target variables* that all Member States have to provide, agreed between the Commission and the Member States and then stipulated in compulsory regulations. Data for *primary* target variables are to be collected on an annual basis, whereas for *secondary* target variables data are to be collected every four years (or less frequently) from thematic modules. (The first such module, for 2005, was on the intergenerational transmission of poverty, the 2006 module is on social participation, the 2007 module is on housing conditions, and the 2008 module should be on financial exclusion and over-indebtedness.) The objective of this major shift in data collection, which encourages full use of existing national data sources (and thus allows for national sample designs), is to "anchor" EU-SILC in the national statistical systems – which is closely connected with embedding the Social

Inclusion Process in domestic policies. This may indeed be the only way to ensure timeliness and quality/reliability of the data and hence acceptance of the figures (indicators) at national and sub-national levels, which is a *sine qua non* for further progress.

With such a flexible format, it is not difficult to see potential problems relating to harmonisation and non-comparability arising, which is why Eurostat and Member States are working together on common guidelines and procedures aimed at maximising comparability. They do this through the aforementioned Council and European Parliament framework Regulations, adopted in 2003 and 2005, and through a series of implementing Commission's Regulations adopted under this framework. Apart from primary and secondary target variables, the Commission's Regulations cover definitions, fieldwork aspects, imputation procedures, sampling and tracing rules, and quality reports. Continuous detailed examination by Eurostat and the countries of the quality of EU-SILC data is therefore of crucial importance. The scientific conference on "Comparative EU Statistics on Income and Living Conditions: Issues and Challenges" organised by Eurostat and Statistics Finland in Helsinki in November 2006 is reviewing various dimensions of the EU-SILC instrument: quality (including international comparability and comparability over time), content, methodology, implementation, access to micro-data, etc. In this context, it should examine important issues linked to the change from ECHP to EU-SILC, including the significant shift in data collection and the major changes in the income definition (notably the treatment of imputed rent and the valuing of own-consumption).

Directly linked to the issue of statistical capacity building is that of *data access arrangements*. The process of data being widely used by researchers, which requires in particular reasonable pricing conditions as well as appropriate documentation on survey and data processing, is an important route by which data are assessed and problems identified. Such use serves to raise the visibility and public acceptance of the data source. In this way, the data are embedded in national scientific communities. The access arrangements for EU-SILC, like those for other key EU statistical data sources such as the *Labour Force Surveys* (LFS), the *Household Budget Surveys* (HBS) and the *European Community Household Panel* (ECHP), should ensure its effective use by independent researchers. As highlighted by the Belgian Presidency in an information paper it submitted to the EPSCO Council of 8 October 2001: "Use of data by the scientific community leads indeed to significant improvement of the data and documentation; the data access issue is therefore also linked with data quality improvements". The 2004 EU-SILC micro-data have been made available for scientific purpose to researchers from mid 2006, and experience with take-up and use of the data merits careful monitoring to ensure its research potential is fully exploited. This could be taken further through the establishment of an *EU-SILC Users Group* at EU level, which would allow for the exchange of EU-SILC based research and also for cooperation with Eurostat on ensuring that the Union has a high-quality EU reference data source on income and living conditions.

Conclusions

The introduction of EU-SILC represents a major step forward in social statistics; the transition from ECHP (and national sources) will need to be taken carefully into account in the construction and use of EU-SILC-based social indicators. The efforts of Eurostat together with Member States to set in place appropriate data access arrangements for the scientific community are very important; they should be pursued further to ensure effective and wide use of EU-SILC micro-data (and other key EU statistical micro-data sources). This could be taken further through the establishment of an *EU-SILC Users Group* at EU level. When analysing EU-SILC data, and more generally data collected in most household surveys, it is essential to keep in mind that these data cover only people living in private households. Some vulnerable groups that are in fact living in these households may also be underrepresented because they are not easy to reach. Statistical efforts need to be made at the sub-national, national and EU levels to collect (better) statistical socio-economic information on these vulnerable groups and on people not living in private households. Focusing on the use of EU-SILC income data, we would argue that:

1. In dealing with negative incomes there should be a harmonised procedure setting a minimum value to incomes for the purpose of measuring poverty risk (on a standard of living basis).
2. The treatment of the income of the self-employed could usefully benefit from a specific investigation; when measuring risk of poverty we may wish to replace accounting income by sums withdrawn regularly from the business.
3. Care is needed in using income including imputed rent to measure the risk of poverty, and consideration should be given to producing the common poverty risk indicators without including imputed rent in total income, and/or using income after housing costs.

5.2 The implications of Enlargement

The issues raised by Enlargement relate most obviously to the income-based indicators. As we have seen, the main emphasis in those indicators has been placed on country-specific relative income thresholds rather than thresholds that are common across countries or over time. This emphasis may, however, need to be revisited in the context of an enlarged Union. In considering this, we need to take account of both the average living standards and the degree of income inequality in the accession countries. The 10 new Member States have average incomes that are much lower – in some cases very much lower – than the EU-15, but also, at least in some cases, relatively low levels of income inequality (see Chapter 3).

An EU income threshold?

One response would be to introduce an income-based background variable applying a common standard across the Member States rather than country-specific ones. Thus an income threshold could be set at, say, 60% of the median equivalised income across the European Union, expressed in Purchasing Power Standards (for the definition of PPS, see Section 3.2 above). The percentage in each country falling below that common threshold could be presented. It would also be possible to calculate an EU-wide poverty gap, being the shortfall from the common threshold, an indicator with a much more obvious interpretation than the present relative median poverty gap.

The adoption of a common EU threshold of course produces significantly different results from those reached with country-specific thresholds, with fewer falling below the common threshold in the richer Member States and a very substantial proportion falling below in the poorer of the new Member States. It would change the conclusions drawn in Chapter 3 regarding the concentration of poverty risk in large (but rich) Member States. In a study of the EU-12, using data from household budget surveys around 1988, de Vos and Zaidi (1998) showed the effect of moving from a country-specific risk of poverty threshold to a Union-wide threshold, taking in both cases 50% of the mean equivalised expenditures. They showed that the combined share of Germany, France and the UK in total persons at risk of poverty was 48% according to the country-specific criterion but fell to 33% with the EU-wide criterion. With the enlarged, and in living standards more diverse, EU-25, the effect can be expected to be larger. Förster *et al* (2003) showed the effect of using a common threshold for the EU-15 plus the Czech Republic, Hungary and Slovenia. Of the 74 million at risk of poverty on this basis in 1999, 13.5 million were to be found in the latter three countries. They went on to devise an "innovative" measure that combines a European-wide income threshold and country-specific deprivation thresholds (see Section 5.3 for a short discussion of this type of "consistent poverty" approach in an EU context).

How should such an EU-wide income threshold in fact be defined? First, should we take the EU mean or the EU median? At the national level, the Eurostat Task Force recommended the adoption of the median in place of the mean (see Atkinson *et al*, 2002, page 94), and that was rightly followed by the ISG for the Laeken definition of the poverty risk indicators. There are strong arguments for maintaining the same choice at the EU level. The relation between percentages of the median and percentages of the mean are likely to be different in the distribution among all EU citizens. In broad terms, in several Member States, 60% of the median approximates to 50% of the mean, but if the EU distribution is more skewed this will not carry over to the EU as a whole.

The second practical issue with an EU-wide threshold concerns Enlargement. The EU-wide risk-of-poverty statistic could be based on the median income in the EU-25 starting in 2005 (the first year when EU-SILC has covered all 25

Member States), but what happens if there is further Enlargement? Should the possible accession of Turkey lower the EU-wide at-risk-of-poverty threshold? In our view, the regular EU-wide indicator should be calculated with a poverty threshold based on a fixed set of Member States, but the set would be reviewed at periodic intervals to reflect Enlargement, this generating a discrete change in the statistics. The regular threshold would therefore evolve over time in line with the rise, or fall, in the income (expressed in purchasing power standards) of the median person in the fixed set of Member States. The location of the median would, of course, change depending on the growth of population in different Member States and on the evolution of national income distributions (we are not suggesting a move from a relative to a fixed indicator, and the envisaged EU-wide statistics would be related to the current EU-wide median income).

The third practical issue concerns the use of purchasing power standards (PPS). As has been emphasised in research on the monitoring of the poverty Millennium Development Goal, the relevant adjustment is one that relates to consumption, not national product in total, and one that is relevant to households at risk of poverty. As it is put by Deaton, "the consumption bundles of the poor are not the same as the average consumption bundle, and price movements in the latter can be different from price movements in the former, for example if the relative price of food increases." (2002, page 1.9). If we are going to place more reliance on the PPS adjustments, then their distributional salience needs to be addressed.

The 2005 EU-SILC data due to be available for all 25 Member States at the end of 2006 would allow the introduction of a new "2005 Lisbon mid-term social cohesion (or convergence) statistic", based on 60% of the EU-wide median (calculated on the basis of a merged EU-25 micro-data set), along the lines defined above. If found valuable, the statistic could be repeated, either with the threshold being updated each year in line with the EU-wide median or with the threshold anchored at its 2005 level. Should we go down this route? The response depends in part on the approach taken to poverty (see Atkinson *et al*, 2002, page 81). On the view that combating poverty is concerned with ensuring the social rights of individuals, it seems reasonable to suppose that people have rights as EU citizens, and that, viewing the EU as a social entity, we would apply a "poverty" standard based on the median for the Union as a whole. Arguments can be made for such a perspective, given the broader aims of the EU of promoting social cohesion within as well as across countries, and also in terms of the broadening of the range of comparisons or reference groups that people have in mind in evaluating their own situation. On the other hand, if combating poverty is seen as ensuring a minimum standard of living, then use of the same poverty standard in purchasing power terms in each Member State would miss differences in the significance of goods in social functioning. An EU-wide approach misses some people in richer countries who are experiencing genuine exclusion from their own society, while counting substantial numbers in the poorer countries who are not experiencing such exclusion. For instance, the requirements for job seekers may be different in a rich European country from those in a less rich country.

Another argument sometimes advanced for country-specific rather than common thresholds is that convergence across countries and regions in overall living standards is a matter for other parts of the Union's structures and processes, not for the Social Inclusion Process. This, however, seems to us a procedural, rather than a substantive, argument. Structures and processes can change, whereas we are concerned here with the fit between the underlying, very real phenomena of social inclusion/exclusion and the indicators employed to reflect them. This does not therefore appear to be a sound reason for rejecting an EU-wide approach. Indeed, an EU-wide income threshold would be a way of bringing together these separate EU processes.

Views are likely to differ about the desirability of applying an EU-wide threshold. In our view, the EU Social Inclusion Process should continue with its existing poverty risk indicators, based on country-specific thresholds, but the Commission should complement these indicators with a background variable (a "context statistic"), not having the status of a social inclusion "indicator", based on an EU-wide threshold, along the lines described above. This would *complement* the set of social inclusion indicators and would provide a useful background "2005 Lisbon mid-term social cohesion statistic".

Risk of poverty and absolute measures

A move towards an EU-wide threshold might be seen as reverting to an absolute notion of poverty. The reasons why the EU has not gone down this route have been set out in the 2004 Joint Report on Social Inclusion:

> An absolute notion is less relevant for the EU for two basic reasons. First, the key challenge for Europe is to make the whole population share the benefits of high average prosperity, and not reach basic standards of living, as in less developed parts of the world. Secondly, what is regarded as minimal acceptable living standards depends largely on the general level of social and economic development. (European Commission, 2004b, page 14)

Our suggested use of a common income threshold is intended to address the key issue of social cohesion/convergence across the Union rather than capturing "absolute" poverty. It is nonetheless important to understand the meaning of the relative at-risk-of-poverty thresholds in different Member States. A step in this direction has been taken with the decision to provide the at-risk-of-poverty rates together with the value of the relative threshold (see Table 2.3a in Appendix 1), which is obviously valuable contextual information in interpreting this indicator. Thus we see from the Primary Indicator that the 60% of median at-risk-of-poverty threshold in 2003 in Germany or Denmark, for example, was four times as high as the corresponding threshold in Latvia (in PPS).[5]

One could, however, go beyond this. Taking the value of the at-risk-of-poverty threshold (in this case in national currencies, not PPS), we can ask what this implies in terms of the actual standard of living achievable in each Member State. What can a family on 60% of the median income, adjusted for its household size, in each country actually consume? Contextual quantitative information on household budget expenditures could be provided to help understand the living standard achievable at the at-risk-of-poverty threshold in each Member State. It would also help investigate the potential problem with purchasing power adjustments identified above, supported by research focused directly on how much the appropriate Purchasing Power Parities (PPP; see Section 3.2) adjustment varies across the income distribution. If the price relativities were moving against the poor, then this would become apparent from the implied budgets. Moreover, this could valuably be supplemented by qualitative information on how people "at risk" actually live. Such an approach would make more meaningful the otherwise arcane statistical procedures on which the risk-of-poverty indicator is based. It would be a good means by which Governments could engage those experiencing poverty and social exclusion, the member organisations of the European Anti-Poverty Network, and other bodies. (See Section 6.8 below for a short presentation of the important *European Meetings of People Experiencing Poverty.*)

In the same context, it would be valuable to investigate in a systematic way the relationship between the level of the relative income thresholds (notably the 60% of median one) and the minimum income provided or implied in many national social security systems. The extent to which those falling below the 60% threshold are in fact on that minimum guaranteed income would also be very helpful. This is often not a straightforward matter since the minimum guaranteed income can be complex to define, with support coming from a variety of schemes and varying not only with household composition but also with tenure and housing costs and perhaps other features of the household's situation. It would however be very useful both in providing a benchmark against which the level of the relative income thresholds in different countries can be framed, and indeed understanding the varying proportion falling below those thresholds. (As can be seen from Table 2.3c in Appendix 1, the "Context Information" for the social inclusion portfolio, introduced by the new EU monitoring framework (Indicators Sub-Group, 2006b), includes information on the net income of social assistance expressed as a percentage of the at-risk-of-poverty threshold.)

Non-monetary indicators

A second route to addressing differences in living standards is via non-monetary indicators seeking to measure deprivation directly. Income, while a key influence on capacity to participate, does not tell us everything we need to know about the resources or living standards of households. Some households on low income may be doing very much worse than others for a variety of reasons relating to how both their resources and needs have evolved over time. This is evident from a variety of national studies (e.g. Nolan and Whelan, 1996) as well as from analysis of data for all the EU Member States participating in the ECHP. While looking at income over a number of years rather than at a single point in time is helpful, the use of deprivation indicators to supplement income-based measures represents a complementary strategy. Deprivation represents the inability to possess the goods and services and engage in the activities that are socially perceived as necessities in one's society. This approach attempts to assess enforced deprivation directly by collecting data on the extent to which households that would like to possess specific "basic" commodities, or to engage in certain "basic" activities, cannot do so because of financial pressures.

The fact that deprivation indicators can supplement information about income has become even more important in the context of the enlarged Union (see, for instance, Guio and Marlier, 2004). This was recognised in EU discussions. The Social Protection Committee (SPC) saw considerable value in the development of these measures at EU level, on the basis that they can augment income-based measures in identifying those at risk of poverty, they provide a better understanding of the living conditions of the poor, and they give information about those domains where income-based indicators are less helpful. The possibility of using these non-monetary deprivation indicators to produce one or more common indicators for use at EU level has been the subject of extensive discussions in the Indicators Sub-Group since Laeken (see in particular Indicators Sub-Group, 2005a and 2006a), and is in our view a feasible and valuable option.

This set of concerns leads us to examine in greater depth in Section 5.3 the scope for non-monetary indicators. Specifically, we propose "absolute" indicators of deprivation in relation to broad living standards and in relation to housing problems, with the same weight being given to each item across the Member States and over time. These would reflect both current differences across countries and trends over time in living standards and deprivation levels. They would be complemented by a deprivation indicator of broad living standards where weights vary across Member States and over time, a more "relative" perspective.

Subjective measures of financial pressure and broader satisfaction

In addition to subjective measures of how people feel about "making ends meet" or the adequacy of their income, which we briefly touch on below, there is a long-standing literature in psychology on subjective measurement of life satisfaction or "happiness".[6] Such measures have been receiving increasing attention from economists in particular in recent years (see for example Frey and Stutzer, 2002; Van Praag and Ferrer, 2004; Layard, 2005). The OECD has recently published a study of alternative measures of well-being (Boarini, Johansson and d'Ercole, 2006), which refers to, among other variables, survey-based data on happiness and life satisfaction. Indeed, Layard has gone so far as to argue that increasing happiness should be the main object of policy. Data has been available for some rich countries (notably the US) for 50 years or more, and two striking features of overall life satisfaction measures have been noted. The first is that within countries there is a positive relationship between subjective satisfaction or happiness and measures of socio-economic status such as income, education and social class. The second, though, is that average satisfaction levels have not generally risen over time despite increasing average income/GDP per capita.

The accession of new Member States, with differing living standards and expectations, serves to prompt some reconsideration of the role of such subjective measures of satisfaction. Studies based on recent surveys have shown remarkably low levels of subjective satisfaction with various aspects of life in some of the new Member States (Fahey *et al*, 2004; Fahey and Smyth, 2004, and the series of reports on the *Quality of Life in Europe* published by the European Foundation for the Improvement of Living and Work Conditions, in Dublin). It is critically important from both a national and EU perspective that the factors underlying these low levels of satisfaction be understood and where possible addressed. However, it may well be that issues relating to social inclusion are only a part of the story, and that these countries are going through a painful adjustment process which will take some time to work its way through, not only in economic terms but also in terms of attitudes and psychological well-being.

The crucial point about such expressions of satisfaction is that they reflect not only the person's objective situation but also the interaction between that situation and expectations. Since expectations may adapt (to an unknown extent) in response to the realities of one's life situation, satisfaction scores may reveal as much about expectations as external reality. (Hagerty *et al* (2001) note that expressions of high levels of subjective well-being can be found in environmental conditions that are in fact life-threatening.) As the long-established literature on reference groups and equity evaluation shows, people respond to their objective standards by comparing their actual situation with some reference point, which can be a past or anticipated position, their notion of what is fair or reasonable or their view of what is practical in the current circumstances. Subjective satisfaction measures clearly have value as "indicators" of a gap between expectations and realities; while the precise significance of such a gap is often difficult to interpret, it is nevertheless of interest to know that the gap is there. Measures of overall life satisfaction or happiness are clearly valuable in investigating quality of life and its determinants, but this does not mean that they would be satisfactory as guides for policy and in monitoring progress in promoting social inclusion – the linkages between subjective satisfaction, social inclusion, and policy are too diffuse and not sufficiently well understood.

For the Social Inclusion Process *per se*, then, subjective assessments focused specifically on the degree of financial pressure rather than life satisfaction more broadly may have more direct value. These could be incorporated into non-monetary deprivation indicators of the sort discussed above, and that would certainly be the simplest way to build them into the indicators process. However, the fact that a respondent feels the household is "having great difficulty making ends meet" evidently has to be interpreted carefully. Some high-income households may have extravagant tastes that they have difficulty affording, but that does not represent social exclusion. The poor may have limited requirements because they have adapted their expectations to a low standard of living. Rather than conflating different types of measures of "being poor" and "feeling poor", it may be more helpful to keep the two distinct. The subjective measure may be seen as a "cross-check" on the income-related indicators. Treating them separately and examining the inter-relationships between household income, direct measures of living standards and deprivation, and subjective assessments of financial pressure is, we think, a more informative approach.

Equivalence scales

The accession of new Member States has also led to a questioning of the way in which income is adjusted for the size and composition of the household. This is conventionally done using what are called "equivalence scales", and at present the same scale – known as the "modified OECD scale" – is employed for each country (see the note to Tables 2.2a–2.3c, in Appendix 1). This assigns a value of 1 to the first adult in the household, 0.5 to each other adult, and 0.3 to each child below the age of 14. Some such adjustment is clearly necessary – otherwise a single adult and a family of four on the same income would be treated as at the same risk of poverty – but the problem is to know precisely what adjustment to make. Economists and statisticians have studied this topic intensively for many years, but a consensus has not been reached on how best to construct equivalence scales. As a result, different scales are in use in different countries, often based more or less loosely on those implicit in the structure of social security support rates. Conventional practice in making comparisons across countries has been to employ one of a limited set of scales and apply these across the board; for a time the so-called "OECD scale" (where each additional adult in the household was given a value of 0.7 and each child 0.5) was widely used, but more recently the "modified OECD" scale has come to the fore at the EU level. In contrast, the historical practice of a number of Member States was to use equivalence scales that gave greater weight to larger households (see Atkinson and Micklewright, 1992, Section 7.3). As it was put by Veèerník, on the basis of his comparison of Czech scales with those found in the US, "children are not cheap in Czechoslovakia" (1991, page 7). This is not just a concern for the new Member States – as shown for example in the second report on poverty and wealth published by the German Government (Bundesregierung, 2005) – but has been highlighted by Enlargement.

Reliance on equivalisation using any one scale is potentially misleading. If the "correct" scale were in fact very different, then this could have serious implications for the level of median equivalised income and thus the 60% of median at-risk-of-poverty threshold itself (or other proportions). It would particularly affect the measured *composition* of the population at risk. The results of Becker and Hauser (2001) show that in Germany in 1998 when using the original OECD scale the poverty rate for a married couple with two children was similar to that for single persons, but that with the modified OECD scale the poverty rate for married couples with two children was under half the rate for single persons. This can be critical from a policy perspective, since the conclusion that for example children or older people (often in single-adult households) are at particularly high risk can have a major impact on the way policy is focused, but may be dependent on the equivalence scale employed. (Trends over time in the pattern of risk are generally less sensitive.)

The problem, of course, is that we do not know the correct scale – and there is no reason to think that it would be the same in every country. The appropriate equivalence scale might be expected to vary with the structure of prices, in particular with the relationship between the cost of housing and other "fixed costs" of a household versus other goods and services. Where fixed costs are relatively low, as may be the case in a number of new Member States, then it may make sense to treat a second adult as adding 0.7 to the cost of living of a single person, rather than the 0.5 of the modified OECD scale. The appropriate scale also depends on the extent of public versus market-based provision of housing, education, childcare and health services. The "cost of a child" is greater in countries where parents have to pay for education.

Academic studies often present results using different sets of scales, for example the "OECD" and "modified OECD" ones, but for cross-country comparisons almost always apply the same scale to each country. If, however, the equivalence scale is taken as varying with the composition of expenditure, as with a standard of living approach, then this implies in turn that we may expect the appropriate equivalence scale to vary with the average income level in the country. The share of food in total spending falls, according to Engel's Law, as countries become richer. To the extent that food is largely "individual", whereas recreational goods, say, are "shared", this may point to a scale that gives more weight to larger households at low levels of average income. We need to consider whether there is a robust basis on which to say that a particular set should be applied in one country and a different one in another country. Eurostat has carried out some useful exploratory work on this for new Member States and acceding/candidate countries (see Dennis and Guio, 2004). On this issue, see also Guio and Marlier (2004).

In these circumstances, it seems desirable that some account should be taken of the potential sensitivity of the income-based social inclusion indicators to the choice of the equivalence scale. One way forward is to produce as *background information* the figures that might be most sensitive with both the modified and original OECD scales. This includes in particular the at-risk-of-poverty rates for different age groups and different household types. This would certainly deepen the information base, though as addressed below we have serious concerns about the profusion of figures that has already taken place in the current set of common indicators and the possible loss of focus and impact. It is for this reason that we recommend that they be labelled "background information". A second option –

which could be pursued in combination with the first or on its own – is to put the onus on Member States that are particularly concerned about the relevance of the modified OECD scale in their own circumstances. Such countries could be encouraged and facilitated in producing alternative estimates of scales, and at-risk indicators based on those could be included as useful country-specific indicators. Given the weak foundation on which reliance on a single common scale is based, and the difference it could make to key conclusions about at-risk groups, this is certainly worth pursuing. (The separate issue as to whether or not it is appropriate to treat everyone in a given household as having the same equivalised income has already been discussed in Chapter 4.)

Conclusions

To summarise the main points from this discussion of the implications of Enlargement for the commonly agreed social inclusion indicators, we have argued that the EU Social Inclusion Process should continue with its existing poverty risk indicators based on country-specific poverty thresholds, but that the Commission should use EU-SILC for the EU-25 to complement them with a background "2005 Lisbon mid-term social cohesion statistic". This would be based on the median income in the EU-25 as a whole, and would not have the status of an indicator.

Contextual information, both quantitative and qualitative, would help in understanding the actual living standard achievable at the at-risk-of-poverty threshold in each Member State, building *inter alia* on research focused on how much the appropriate PPP adjustment varies across the income distribution, and on the concrete experience of people living in poverty and social exclusion. This would provide a *bridge* between the at-risk-of-poverty indicators based on relative income thresholds and "absolute" measures based on living standards or a fixed income threshold. Non-monetary deprivation indicators also have much to offer in this context. Account could be taken of the sensitivity of income-based indicators to the choice of equivalence scale by producing the figures that might be most sensitive with alternative scales as background information, notably the at-risk-of-poverty rates for different age groups and different household types.

5.3 Refining and extending the agreed indicators

The commonly agreed social indicators were described in Chapter 2 (see Tables 2.2a and 2.3a–b in Appendix 1), where we noted that they are not fixed in stone. Since the establishment of the indicators at Laeken in 2001, a great deal of work has been undertaken by the ISG, in conjunction with the Commission (especially DG "Employment, Social Affairs and Equal Opportunities" and Eurostat). The degree of progress achieved is an impressive tribute to European cooperation, and it is too extensive to be documented in full here. Instead, we point to some further refinements that should be considered in this context (without aiming to systematically review and assess the indicators in use), and to how best to fill major gaps in the coverage of the indicators.

Joblessness and the working poor

Reflecting the emphasis on employment in tackling social exclusion, a Primary Indicator measures the number of persons in "jobless households". As a result of the methodological work undertaken by Eurostat and the ISG, this indicator is based on a fundamentally improved definition compared with that originally agreed in Laeken. Jobless households are those where no one is working, that is all adults are either unemployed or inactive, as shown by the Labour Force Surveys carried out in Member States.[7] As a summary indicator of the phenomenon, this indicator is well framed and very useful; it is presented separately for children and persons of working age since the focus of concern is when such individuals (rather than those beyond normal retirement age) are in households without direct contact with the world of work. However, in-depth analysis is required to understand the range of rather different circumstances involved (relating to unemployment, illness, disability, caring in the home, as well as distribution of working-age persons by household types and employment "polarisation" among households – see, for instance, Iacovou, 2003). It is also essential to relate these to social exclusion and to income in particular, so including a breakdown by household position, vis-à-vis the at-risk-of-poverty thresholds, is particularly important. The breakdown of the at-risk-of-poverty rate by the *work intensity of households*, which usefully complements the information provided by the "overarching" working poor indicator already provides very useful information, even though the definition of "jobless households" and that of households with a work intensity equal to zero is not identical (though very close). (See definitions in Section 2.6 above; see also Tables 2.2a–2.3c in Appendix 1, as well as Indicators Sub-Group, 2006b.)

The commonly agreed working poor indicator simply looks at the position of those individuals who are in work and at risk of poverty – although whether they are at risk of poverty may of course depend on non-personal characteristics such as the labour force status of other adults in the household (if any) and on the number of dependants present in the household (if any). Being "in work" is defined in terms of number of months in work over the income reference year, with only those reporting work as their "most frequent activity status" (i.e. a status they have occupied for more than half the number of months in the year; see Section 2.6) being counted as working.[8] Those categorised as "in work" include both employees and the self-employed, and in each case the individual might have been working part time and/or for not much more than half the year in question. The breakdowns of the working poor indicator distinguish *inter alia* where the person is employed or self-employed, working the full year or less, and working part time versus full time.

This working poor indicator needs to be analysed in the context of the corresponding rates for those who are unemployed and those who are inactive. Indeed, we believe it would be valuable to complement this indicator with "Context Information" to be included in the social inclusion portfolio (Table 2.3c) on the at-risk-of-poverty rate for employees working full time for the *entire* year, together with the corresponding rate for those unemployed all year, and the rate for those inactive all year. (In order to ensure consistency between those three at-risk-of-poverty rates, these calculations should however be limited to the same age group, the 18–59-year-olds.) It may be objected that this comparison will simply bring out the value of working. This is precisely the issue: how far does work, in the "best possible" conditions of working full time and for the full year, guarantee escape from the risk of poverty?[9]

In this context it should be emphasised that low pay and working poverty are related but different concepts. A person may be low paid (according to a specified standard), but the household in which he or she lives may not be at risk of poverty; a person may not be low paid, but the equivalised total household income may leave the household below the at-risk-of-poverty threshold. It would then also be useful to include in the set of overarching indicators a measure of the extent of low pay. This is conventionally captured by the proportion of employees falling below pay thresholds derived as proportions of median earnings in the economy in question (e.g. two-thirds of median hourly earnings). This, it should be emphasised, would not be proposed as an indicator of poverty or social exclusion, but a statistic that – together with work intensity – would help in understanding in-work poverty and the links between "making work pay" and social inclusion. (On the linkages between in-work poverty and low pay, see Chapters 3 and 4 above; see also *inter alia* European Commission, 2006b; OECD work on this issue; and Cazenave, 2006.)

Education and literacy

The common indicators for social inclusion in the education area are: the share of 18–24-year-olds not currently attending education or training and having achieved lower secondary education or less, which is a Primary Indicator; the proportion of the population of working age with a low educational attainment (measured as no higher than level 2 according to the 1997 *International Standard Classification of Education* (ISCED-97)), which is a Secondary Indicator; and low reading literacy performance of pupils, based on the OECD's *Programme for International Student Assessment* (PISA),[10] which is also now a Secondary Indicator. The latter represents the share of 15-year-old pupils who are at level 1 or below on the PISA combined reading literacy scale. In the social inclusion context, literacy and numeracy are important because of their impact on both prospects in the labour market and ability to fully participate in society. An indicator providing a breakdown of this share by relevant socio-economic background would thus be even more valuable in the context of social inclusion, but there are serious doubts about the quality of the relevant information collected for some countries. It is hoped that this will be improved in the future, and in the meantime this indicator should be complemented with available recent national (level 3) indicators showing the link between poor literacy and social background. It should be noted that these indicators give more information about young people's future life chances than about their present well-being, and only indirectly provide information about the early stage of the education process (see Section 5.5 on "children mainstreaming").

More generally, it is also important that countries seek to link concretely in their background information low educational attainment/skills and social disadvantage, so that the strength of the relationships can be identified and policies framed in response. It is worth mentioning that when adopting the low reading literacy indicator, the Indicators Sub-Group (rightly) accompanied it "with a note of caution concerning the presentation and interpretation of results that should clearly indicate dispersion measures" (2005b). This calls for the building of statistical capacity in this important area of poverty and social exclusion, notably by Member States and the OECD working together to improve the information coming from harmonised surveys.

Measuring literacy only for the current school-age population is obviously very important given that they are the adults of tomorrow. However, it is too narrow, and comparable indicators on literacy for the adult population (especially the working-age population) would also be highly relevant in the context of social inclusion, as was also highlighted by the ISG. Country experience with measuring literacy (and numeracy) among the adult population could usefully be exchanged, notably by Member States and the OECD working together to improve the information coming from harmonised surveys.[11] This measure is indeed complex. As discussed in Atkinson *et al* (2002), some important conceptual issues need attention. One major issue in terms of social exclusion is the unit of analysis: not only an individual's own literacy level but also those of other household members may affect their social functioning. Other issues include how literacy standards are to evolve over time as societies become more complex, whether the same standards should apply across the age distribution (when the needs of the work-place are not relevant to the retired, for example), and whether particular weight should be applied to the lowest levels of literacy proficiency.

A harmonised measure of the relationship between the educational attainment level of parents and their children would also be very valuable in capturing the intergenerational transmission of educational disadvantage and thus poverty and social exclusion. As discussed below, the specific module on the "intergenerational transmission of poverty" included in the 2005 wave of EU-SILC has collected comparative information in this respect.

The regional dimension

The set of indicators originally agreed at Laeken, in an effort to give weight to the regional dimension, included as a Primary Indicator the variation in employment rates across NUTS 2 regions. The logic of having a specific regional disparity indicator in a set designed to focus on social inclusion (rather than for example regional cohesion) was questioned by Atkinson *et al* (2002, pages 76–7). We noted the problem of comparing the degree of regional disparities across Member States where the number of NUTS 2 regions varies widely, with some having none or very few and thus not presenting figures for this indicator. For the Member States where values are given, the dispersion of employment rates depends on the number of regions distinguished. Taken together, these considerations mean that international comparability, a key principle for common indicators, is not satisfactory. With the introduction of "context" indicators for social inclusion and rearrangement of Primary and Secondary Indicators in 2006, this regional indicator has now been transferred from the Primary to the "context" set but has been included in the overarching set (Table 2.2a, Appendix 1). Furthermore, a single indicator is not sufficient to capture regional disparities. As has been demonstrated by Stewart (2003), the degree of regional variation differs across indicators. An alternative would be to give, as Secondary Indicators or Context Information, regional breakdowns for all indicators of social inclusion where it is meaningful and data allow. (A breakdown of the at-risk-of-poverty and other indicators by urban versus rural areas would also be valuable and could draw on the EU-SILC primary target variable on the "degree of urbanisation".) This would make explicit the number of regions identified, and the national figures would provide a point of reference. In this way, we would be giving more, not less, prominence to the regional dimension, since it could potentially cover several dimensions of poverty and social inclusion and not just employment. Identifying in this way the differences from the national proportions would highlight the situation of countries like Italy where living in a disadvantaged region may be one of the most important factors leading to poverty and social exclusion.[12]

We recognise that the introduction of more extensive regional breakdowns is not possible in many situations because of data limitations, and some of the Primary and Secondary EU indicators may be more suitable for regional application than others (whereas others may be suitable only after some modification and some may in fact not be appropriate for the purpose).[13] In most Member States, implementing our recommendation would indeed require a significant investment in statistical capacity, to provide samples of sufficient size and sufficiently representative at the regional level. The best way forward would probably be to make full use of the information contained in administrative registers to complement the information collected in the context of EU-SILC and other household surveys. Methodological research into local area estimation techniques to produce sub-national poverty and social exclusion indicators may also prove fruitful. (Verma *et al*, 2005, have analysed how the latter techniques could usefully be used to estimate regional poverty rates relative to both national and regional thresholds, thereby allowing for a powerful illustration of inequalities both within and between regions.)

It is also necessary to consider the possible need for *addition* to the indicators developed primarily for application at national level of other specific indicators able to capture aspects which are essentially regional. A more diverse "portfolio of indicators" is required for the purpose of addressing concerns of regional policy and research. (For an extensive discussion of these and other related issues, see Verma *et al*, 2005.)

Migrants and ethnic minorities

In 2002, when revisiting the EU common objectives set in Nice for the Social Inclusion Process, the Council stressed the need "to highlight more clearly the high risk of poverty and social exclusion faced by some men and women as a result of immigration" (Council, 2002, page 3), which would require that appropriate indicators/statistics should be employed by Member States. Work has been undertaken on this subject within a number of Member States, as reflected in their NAPs/inclusion. The 2001 Dutch NAP/inclusion, to give just one example, described an Integration Monitor. The Indicators Sub-Group has also discussed this issue on a number of occasions, and considered alternative strategies on the basis of a methodological document presenting a detailed and systematic *Overview of third level indicators used in the NAP/inclusion relating to the social inclusion of "foreigners, immigrants and ethnic minorities"* (Indicators Sub-Group, 2004b).

As clearly shown in the Sub-Group document, it is evident that there are a number of technical problems in considering both migrants and ethnic minorities,[14] and in considering the complex question of the social inclusion of migrants and ethnic minorities, we need to bear in mind that, while there is considerable overlap, the two groups are not identical and the issues may differ. It is therefore more appropriate to keep them separate.

Concerning *migrants*, a Primary Indicator has been introduced aimed at capturing the gap in employment rate between immigrants and non-immigrants, calculated on the basis of the Labour Force Survey.[15] This indicator is to be calculated on the basis of clear "mandatory guidelines" according to which the criteria used to define immigrants is the "country of birth", modified as necessary by "nationality at birth"; it is for each country to decide, as appropriate, whether or not to include nationals born abroad (which is why this indicator appears as "NAT" in Table 2.3a in Appendix 1, i.e. as a commonly agreed *national* (rather than *EU*) indicator; see Section 2.6). This indicator is to be supplemented with the relevant available national data covering other key aspects of social inclusion (breakdowns of other social inclusion indicators by migrant/non-migrant status). This requirement aims to reflect the importance of the multi-dimensionality of inclusion of immigrants – even more than for others, for immigrants having a job does not automatically mean being "socially included" (Indicators Sub-Group, 2005c).[16]

Concerning *ethnic minorities*, the Indicators Sub-Group has rightly acknowledged that "no single criteria can be used to adequately define ethnic minorities across countries for the purpose of data collection" (examples of criteria used include: nationality, skin colour, religion, etc), and has therefore agreed to cover ethnicity "at the third level in the form of existing social inclusion indicators broken down by ethnic groups, where national data is available". Countries are then "encouraged to use their own classifications" (Indicators Sub-Group, 2005c; see also European Commission, 2006h).

In view of the above, Member States should be invited to supply two types of information relating to the situation of migrants and ethnic minorities (on top of the employment gap for migrants/non-migrants as described above). First, they should provide a breakdown by migrant status and/or ethnicity (and possibly recent migrant status) of *all* relevant common indicators, where possible and meaningful, employing, subject to certain guidelines, the breakdowns that make sense in their national context. Secondly, they should complement this with third level indicators reflecting the specificities of their national situation. In the context of our suggested *children mainstreaming*, they should, wherever possible and meaningful, emphasise the particular situation of children.

Homelessness

One of the most important areas not currently covered by the agreed indicators is housing; it has been agreed that a Primary Indicator will cover this area, but the indicator to be used is still under discussion. The Social Protection Committee in its report endorsed by the December 2001 Laeken European Council (see Chapter 2) recognised the importance of the area but could only recommend that individual Member States in their NAPs/inclusion present quantitative information on decent housing, housing costs, and homelessness and other precarious housing conditions, and that obtaining better comparable data and reporting on these topics be a priority. This recommendation has been usefully recalled in Indicators Sub-Group (2006b).

Homelessness is, of course, the most pressing concern in the housing area, and clearly one of the most serious and visible forms of social exclusion. It is, however, particularly problematic from a measurement point of view: both defining precisely what is meant by homelessness and then capturing that empirically are difficult in any country, and doing so in a consistent fashion across countries is even more challenging. At the conceptual level, homelessness could conceivably cover a very wide spectrum of circumstances, ranging from sleeping rough without a roof over one's head to living in over-crowded housing or without secure tenancy status. As far as measurement is concerned, gathering data on a small, mobile population that fluctuates for seasonal and other reasons is bound to be difficult, and conventional statistical tools are not designed to reach such populations. People who are homeless or living in very precarious and temporary accommodation tend not to be included in household surveys and other statistical data sources, which is why many countries rely on administrative sources and service providers for data, though this may give a partial or even misleading picture depending on the structures in place in the country.

Following the recommendations by the SPC, a European Task Force was set up in 2001 by Eurostat to help the Commission and Member States tackle these complex housing issues, including both representatives of the national statistical institutes and Non-Governmental Organisations active in this area. Despite a sustained focus on the area since then by the Commission and Member States, and a very valuable in-depth report on the topic by the French national statistical office INSEE (Brousse, 2004), it appears that progress towards anything approaching a harmonised measure of homelessness may be achievable but will be slow.[17] This is readily understandable given the starting point. There is not at present an agreed definition of the underlying concept of homelessness, an indispensable starting point for a statistical framework for gathering data relating to that concept. The most useful data on homelessness at national level are generally gathered by public bodies in the course of administration of housing policies, and the nature of the data consequently varies with the institutional setting. It is simply not valid to place figures derived in such a fashion in a comparative table. Household surveys, the primary source for many of the common social inclusion indicators, miss those who are currently homeless because they are either not in the sampling frame in the first place or if in the frame will not be contacted (although retrospective questions about episodes of homelessness in the past can yield some interesting information). Special surveys of the homeless in particular countries, while producing very useful information, adopt different definitions and procedures and rarely produce data that is comparable across time, and even less so between countries.

Despite this point of departure and the difficulties in making progress, a measure of homelessness on a harmonised basis would be valuable and its production should be adopted as an objective. Progress can then be made incrementally. The first step would be an agreement on a common definition of what constitutes homelessness. The debate here largely centres on how narrowly or broadly the net is cast, with the range of views illustrated by the consultation process carried out as part of the aforementioned Brousse report. Some respondents argued for a definition that focuses purely on those sleeping rough or in emergency accommodation, and not, for example, those living with friends or relatives, in short-stay accommodation, or in unsuitable/unacceptable housing. On the other hand, others argued for a definition that encompasses not only all those groups but also those threatened with eviction, or in insecure tenancy arrangements. (The range of different circumstances one might consider is illustrated for example in the typology put forward by FEANTSA,[18] ranging from rooflessness at one extreme to forms of insecure and inadequate housing at the other.)

The Brousse report puts forward an interim working definition that seems a sensible point of departure and would allow progress to be made. This would focus on those who are sleeping rough, in shelters or short-stay hostels, or other temporary accommodation because they do not have access to acceptable accommodation. It would not count as homeless those in insecure housing situations, such as without legal tenancy agreements or facing eviction orders, or those living in unfit or overcrowded housing – though insecure or inadequate housing could be measured separately. The next stage would be to agree on the preferred measure – providing, for example, a count of the number of persons experiencing homelessness on a given night or nights, which could be expressed as a homelessness rate. The best approach to producing data relating to this agreed definition and measure, whether it be via the Census of Population, administrative sources or special surveys, could then be investigated. Although EU-SILC itself is not a suitable vehicle for data on homelessness, the philosophy underlying it – that harmonised target variables are tightly specified at EU level but national statistical offices have freedom to decide how best to collect the required information – is directly relevant. It is important that there be clear official responsibility, to ensure oversight of the collection of appropriate data in close collaboration with the organisations working in the area. As progress is made towards a harmonised measure that would serve as a Primary Indicator, Member States will in the meantime be expected to report on the basis of national statistics as a "level 3" indicator (as required under the December 2001 Laeken agreement).

Housing quality and adequacy

As well as the extreme of homelessness, less severe but still substantial problems with housing adequacy and the cost of attaining it need to be captured in a social inclusion context. We have noted that housing is included among the set of Primary Indicators, but the indicator itself is under development, involving both data and conceptual considerations. EU-SILC enables the production of harmonised measures relating to housing costs. And, like the ECHP before it, EU-SILC also collects information on housing quality and housing deprivation. In particular, this covers not only the presence or absence of basic amenities (such as a shower/bath and an indoor flushing toilet) and density/overcrowding, but also whether the household perceives problems in terms of the presence of damp walls, leaking roof, rot in windows, adequacy of lighting, exposure to noise, exposure to pollution, exposure to vandalism and crime. One useful approach to employing this information would be to construct an aggregate measure of poor or inadequate housing, based on an index counting the number of different types of housing-related "bads" the household reports. Such an indicator is worth considering as a Primary Indicator, though there are significant issues to be addressed in constructing and using it which we discuss shortly when we come to the use of non-monetary deprivation indicators.

One important point that we emphasise then is that there is a distinction between poor housing and local environmental "bads". Some of the EU-SILC indicators relate to problems in the neighbourhood, and empirical investigation using the ECHP has shown these are related only loosely if at all to problems with housing quality *per se* (see for example Whelan *et al*, 2002 and Indicators

Sub-Group, 2005a). This is an argument for treating the two phenomena separately and studying the relationship between them, rather than merging them into a single aggregate measure and obscuring their differing impacts. In the current context, where the major gap to be filled relates to poor housing, it would seem sensible to give priority to a measure of housing problems *per se*. Housing problems themselves, as captured in the ECHP, have also been seen to be rather loosely related to risk of poverty (in the sense of being below relative income thresholds) or other aspects of deprivation. Again the logic is that they should be clearly distinguished from other aspects of deprivation more generally and the inter-relationships with other forms of exclusion studied – which we shall have more to say about in discussing the use of non-monetary deprivation indicators more broadly below. A final issue, which also arises in the use of non-monetary deprivation indicators more broadly, relates to the point of reference: in effect, should the same standard be applied across all the Member States, or is a country-specific point of reference more appropriate in assessing "adequacy"? While housing is an area where specific considerations arise, we reserve discussion of this issue for the broader context below.

Concern has also been expressed about the burden imposed by housing costs, and the desirability of capturing situations where an "excess burden" is being imposed on the household by these costs. Such a concept needs to be interpreted and used with care. On the housing expenditure side, measures of financial "burden" associated with housing can be constructed by taking expenditure on housing (principal residence) as a proportion of total income. However, a household in the top half of the income distribution spending a substantial proportion of its income on housing may be regarded as having a significant burden, but not one that is directly relevant from a social inclusion perspective. In considering the situation of those further down the distribution but spending a sizeable proportion of their income on housing, the institutional context is all-important: in some cases that expenditure may be fully covered by social transfers included in income, in which case they do not represent an immediate burden for the household. Reliance on crude financial measures of "burden" can therefore be hazardous. It is worth exploring whether a measure of the "uncompensated burden" of housing costs that focuses on those on low incomes could be constructed in a way that is meaningful across countries. One way of approaching this would be to subtract cash transfers aimed at covering housing costs from total household income, and calculate the proportion that the "uncovered" housing costs (that is, expenditure on housing less support received to cover it) comprise of that income.[19] Those with income "net of housing support" falling below some income threshold whose uncovered housing costs comprise more than a certain proportion of income (net of housing assistance) could be identified as seriously at risk of poverty/exclusion due to housing costs – with the appropriate income threshold and critical proportion themselves the subject of analysis. The difficulty may well arise that support for housing costs is not always distinguished from other forms of social transfer, but such an approach is well worth investigation, particularly with the enhanced data that EU–SILC provides, and Eurostat has already made significant progress in this direction.

Health

The relevance of ill-health, both in terms of physical and of mental health, to social exclusion is evident. Yet, in the health area, the ISG faced the very real difficulty that while a good deal of comparative data on health was available, very little of it had a specific focus on poverty and social exclusion. Two health-related indicators were included among the original Laeken indicators: life expectancy and a measure of inequality in self-assessed health, calculated for the first and fifth quintiles. The adoption of these two as Primary Indicators reflected the importance of health in the social inclusion context, but they also had serious limitations.[20]

The problem with life expectancy was not with the indicator itself but with its relevance to social inclusion. Differences in life expectancy across Member States are relevant to the social cohesion of the EU as a whole, but do not have anything to say about disparities within countries or the extent to which some individuals and groups in each country are disadvantaged or experiencing social exclusion. One country may have higher mortality than another, on account of dietary, smoking or other behavioural differences, but this does not necessarily imply a problem of social exclusion within that country. Thus it is not mortality as such that is central in a social inclusion context but rather differential mortality – and more broadly differences in health – according to socio-economic characteristics. The only case that can be made for inclusion of life expectancy *per se* is in the context of Enlargement, and the generally significantly lower life expectancy in the new Member States (see Section 3.3). The second health indicator in the original Laeken set, based on self-assessed health, did aim to capture such disparities in health. However, the figures produced by the ECHP for this indicator seem problematic: the variation across countries, and across income groups within countries, cannot necessarily be taken as a reliable reflection of underlying health. The ability of the indicator to capture change over time in socio-economic health inequalities within countries is also unproven. Eurostat has started methodological investigation on this indicator on the basis of the available EU–SILC data.

These two health indicators have now been dropped from the Primary and Secondary sets of the social inclusion portfolio, although life expectancy is included as a context statistic (see Table 2.3c in Appendix 1) and an indicator of "healthy life expectancy" at birth and at 65 (based on mortality tables combined with survey responses on the extent of disability at different ages) is included among the overarching indicators (see Table 2.2a in Appendix 1).

The indicator of health inequalities that has played a key role in national monitoring and debates in some countries is socio-economic differentials in premature mortality. Mortality data broken down by socio-economic characteristics can either be derived from death registers directly, from a linkage between the death certificate and other registers containing socio-economic information, or from specific surveys based on sub-samples of the census. However, the available socio-economic information available from death registers differs from one country to the next, and often relates to occupation, which may not be the most relevant since at the time of death persons are often "retired" – income or educational attainment would probably be the most pertinent. This is a typical example of an area where statistical capacity building would be welcomed urgently and where good practice on the use of administrative registers could be exchanged usefully. We strongly believe that the development of an indicator of premature mortality by socio-economic status should be a priority at both the national and EU level. Significant progress may take a few years and a harmonised indicator of socio-economic differentials in mortality or life expectancy will not be immediately available, but this should be given very high priority. (Given the data demands, and the fact that the indicator is likely to change slowly over time, it should be stressed that the indicator would not need to be produced every year.)

Progressing to the point where *healthy* life years could be compared for different socio-economic groups would be enormously valuable, providing an indicator that could complement and deepen a measure of socio-economic differentials in mortality/life expectancy. Indeed, focusing directly on the extent and impact of health-related limitations in people's daily activities is itself potentially very valuable in thinking about indicators. From a social inclusion perspective, the impact that illness and disability have on ability to participate fully in the life of society is critical. Those who are severely limited may well face severe obstacles in obtaining access to schooling, employment, independent housing and other aspects of participation. However, one has to be confident that available measures capture limitations in activity reliably, not only across countries but also across socio-economic groups within countries. EU-SILC is producing information on such limitations in a way that is likely to lead to more robust data than those that were collected in the ECHP (the national translations of the question in particular have been carefully checked centrally by Eurostat, and the question is no longer asked solely of those suffering chronic diseases but of the whole population aged 16 and over). An indicator comparing the extent of such limitations in activity towards the top versus the bottom of the income distribution (by age and gender) has been included in the Context Information for the social inclusion portfolio, and when its robustness has been fully tested may prove suitable as a Primary or Secondary Indicator. (For a study on children and disability that covers a number of the new Member States, see UNICEF (2005b).)

The impact of ill-health is one concern in a social inclusion perspective but inability to access adequate health care is a distinct concern that also needs to be captured in the set of indicators. As well as inequalities in health, inequalities in access to health care and in particular failure to access care due to financial constraints are particularly salient from a social inclusion perspective, and the

Indicators Sub-Group has singled out indicators capturing barriers to accessing health care for attention (see Table 2.3a in Appendix 1). The new EU-SILC instrument provides for the first time at EU level important new information on this topic, focused on perceptions of difficulties in accessing medical examination or treatment and in accessing dental examination or treatment.[21] Eurostat and the ISG's first evaluation of the results from 2004 EU-SILC data in this regard suggest that an indicator of perceived unmet need for health care (medical and/or dental examination) would indeed be valuable – focusing in particular on where respondents say need was unmet because they were unable to afford it, because there was a waiting list, or it was too far or difficult to travel (i.e. those reasons more clearly linked to social protection and social inclusion aspects). A breakdown by broad age groups (e.g. 18–64 versus 65+) and gender would also be helpful.

It is also important to continue researching disparities in the utilisation of health care services across socio-economic groups, seeing utilisation as a proxy for access. This has been intensively researched in a series of studies by Van Doorslaer and colleagues using both the ECHP and national data sources (Van Doorslaer, Masseria and members of the OECD Health Equity Research Group, 2004; Van Doorslaer, Koolman and Jones, 2004; Van Doorslaer, Koolman and Puffer, 2001; Van Doorslaer *et al*, 2000). This has yielded valuable insights into how patterns of health care utilisation vary across the income distribution (for people of the same gender and age group) in different countries, and the extent to which influences on utilisation vary across countries and health care systems. Differences in "needs" (other than those related to age and gender) are hard to take into account; subjective assessments of health status reported by survey respondents provide some basis for doing so but may not be sufficient. The capacity of this approach to distinguish changes over time in the access of different income groups to health care controlling for needs remains to be demonstrated. Nonetheless, measuring differences in the actual utilisation of health care services across income levels and socio-economic groups has to be one important element in monitoring equity in access.[22]

It is worth noting in conclusion the relevance of broader European statistical developments in the health area for the Social Inclusion Process. Eurostat has been investing considerable energy into the development of public health statistics, and together with Directorate-General SANCO of the European Commission has been developing the framework of what is known as the *European Health Survey System* (EHSS).[23] This incorporates:

- the *European Core Health Interview Survey* (which consists of the annual component on health included in EU-SILC, and a *European Health Interview Survey* expected to be launched in 2007–8 and carried out every five years, covering more elaborated modules on health status, health care and determinants of health);
- special surveys aimed at specific topics (where research groups may have a role to play in identifying the demands); and

- a database of certified standards and recommended reference instruments for health interview surveys.

This is a most important development and one that promises valuable information for the Social Protection and Social Inclusion Process on health status and health care utilisation (and of course also for the OMC in the field of health and long-term care). It is essential that the social inclusion perspective continues to inform the development of this broader framework.

Non-monetary indicators

In considering the potential value of non-monetary indicators, we need to distinguish two reasons for their inclusion. The first is that they can supplement information about income, which is subject to mis-measurement and may not always be a reliable guide to "permanent income". Those on low income for a number of years face a very high probability of experiencing genuine poverty, and where longitudinal data are not available, direct measures of deprivation may provide a useful substitute. As we discussed in Section 5.1, the switch from the ECHP to EU-SILC will produce a particularly long gap in data on the prevalence of persistent low income so that non-monetary indicators may help fill this gap. The second reason is that non-monetary indicators help to capture the multi-dimensional nature of poverty and social exclusion. Direct measures of deprivation are not simply another way of capturing persistent low income. Other factors also contribute to producing high levels of deprivation (see for example Boarini and d'Ercole, 2006, and Whelan *et al*, 2004). In Chapter 3, we have seen how low the correlation is between the income-related and some of the non-income-related indicators. As discussed there, and in Section 5.2, non-monetary indicators have become even more important in the context of the enlarged Union. They can augment income-based measures in identifying those at risk of poverty; they provide a better understanding of the concrete living conditions of the "poor", and they give information about those domains where income-based indicators are least helpful.

Some fruitful approaches combine deprivation with low income, as in Ireland and Austria. If those falling below a relative income threshold are indeed "at risk of poverty" rather than "poor", then non-monetary indicators may allow us to hone in on the sub-set of those "at risk" who are in greatest need and should be prioritised in framing policy. This is certainly a strong motivation in the context of a particular country, where indicators appropriate to that society and point in time can be selected. Although not insurmountable, serious obstacles need to be overcome before this sort of "low income *and* deprived" ("consistent poverty") measure can be meaningfully employed in a cross-country context.[24] We focus instead on the role non-monetary indicators can play as a complement to other social inclusion indicators, in particular in capturing differences in absolute levels of deprivation and in tracking change over time. This is something to which both Eurostat and the ISG have already devoted considerable attention.

While accepting that poverty is relative, many would still see changes in real living conditions as relevant and not to be ignored in framing social inclusion indicators.[25] Deprivation indicators can reflect such changes in a way that can be easily understood and conveyed to a broad audience – which is one of the desiderata for EU social inclusion indicators. The substantial number of non-monetary items included in the ECHP has allowed this to be studied in some depth, and EU-SILC also obtains such information though on a more limited range.[26] It is therefore well worth focusing on how best to use this information. We discuss first the broad approaches that might be adopted, and then turn to more detailed issues relating to the selection and grouping of items. In doing this, we take account of the particularly valuable work carried out by Eurostat on this topic to inform the discussions at the ISG (Indicators Sub-Group, 2005a, 2006a).

A straightforward approach is to take a set of suitable non-monetary items, look at deprivation levels in terms of these items across each of the Member States, and see how those levels change over time. Both individual items, and a summary index showing the number of "deprivations" experienced by a household, could be used. Because a common standard is being applied across countries, rather than a relative standard that takes the median level of living in the country into account, there will be much wider gaps between countries at a point in time than with for example relative income poverty rates, as results from the ECHP have demonstrated.[27] Furthermore, if the same set of items is used from one year to the next, then progress is being measured against a fixed standard rather than one that reflects the evolution of median levels of living over time. Such an "absolute" approach, applying the same standard to countries with very different levels of income and living standards, would certainly not be suitable as the only, or even the main, measure of poverty and social exclusion, but as one in a set it has a real added value.

To complement that approach, non-monetary items could also be used to try to capture social exclusion due to lack of resources using a more relative standard. A purely relative approach could use different items for different countries, but this poses significant (though not necessarily intractable) conceptual and analytical problems. There is currently no agreed methodology for the selection of country-specific items tapping the same underlying phenomenon of social exclusion, and conveying to a general audience what such a varying set represents is likely to be difficult. Instead, as a first step, a common set of items across all countries could be used, but in a way that takes average levels of living in the country in question into account – e.g, by constructing a summary deprivation index in which each item is weighted by the percentage not deprived of it in the country in question. So it would be a more serious deprivation to be unable to afford a particular item in a country where most people can afford it than in one where most people have to do without it. This can be seen as a summary measure of relative deprivation at a point in time. In looking at trends over time, the weights for each item in each country would adjust automatically as the extent of deprivation in the country on each item changed. Thus, continuing to be unable to afford an item that more and more people in one's own country have would be given an increasing weight over time. This might not be sufficient to capture changing living patterns and expectations over any prolonged period, so the set of items would have to be adapted at some point, but over say a five-year period there would be major advantages in focusing on a set of items that is common across countries and over time, but with varying weights. This would complement results from the approach where the same items *and* weights are used across countries and over time – just as the purely relative and "anchored at a point in time" income-based indicators complement each other.

Both these approaches have been considered by the Indicators Sub-Group, and a key objection raised to the varying-weights version is a lack of transparency (2006a). While clearly valid, this does not appear insurmountable. The key indicator could be a deprivation score, and mean deprivation scores could be compared across countries, with the gap between countries then being narrower than for a summary index with items weighted equally across countries. Alternatively, the percentage scoring above a threshold level – to be determined – could be presented. We see merit in both but the introduction of the more straightforward "fixed-weights" indicator first seems the best way to make immediate progress.

This leaves the issue of the selection and grouping of items. This has already been analysed in some depth using data from the ECHP,[28] and has also been explored with emerging data from EU-SILC (Guio, 2005b; Indicators Sub-Group, 2005a and 2006a; Guio and Museux, 2006). As far as a choice of items is concerned, some of the items available in the ECHP seem not to be transferable across countries – for example "buying second-hand clothes" seems culture-specific, and needing central heating seems geographically specific (which is why those variables have not been included among the EU-SILC variables). While such items have to be excluded, otherwise keeping the set as broad as possible helps to ensure that individual, potentially idiosyncratic items do not have undue influence on the results. Another issue is whether the items should be confined to "objective" possession/absence or non-participation or whether they should include "subjective" assessments of respondents about their own circumstances. However, this distinction is not as clear-cut as it might appear at first sight. Respondents' assessments of whether they are doing without specific items or activities because they cannot afford them (as opposed to not wanting them) have considerable value, and we would favour using such information in framing indicators. The broad question included in the ECHP and EU-SILC about the extent to which the household has "difficulty making ends meet" is in a different category: rather than simply include it in constructing an indicator of deprivation, we would prefer to keep it distinct and study the relationships between deprivation, income, and this measure of self-assessed economic strain. (EU-SILC includes the more specific question as to whether the household has the financial capacity to face unexpected *required* expenses, and the argument for including this in a non–monetary index seems stronger, along with for example being in arrears on utilities bills.[29])

We now turn to the way the selected deprivation items are used: should one simply present the numbers experiencing deprivation on each of the individual items, or should they be grouped into summary indices? If summary indices are employed, should all the selected items be aggregated into one overall deprivation index or is it preferable to group them, distinguishing different dimensions? As far as the first issue is concerned, simply focusing on the extent of deprivation on individual items certainly has the advantage of transparency: it can be easily understood by a wide audience that for example 10% of people in a particular country cannot afford to heat their home adequately or to have a car. However, the essential interest here is not so much in the individual items *per se* as in the underlying situation of more generalised deprivation that they can help to capture.[30] So we would place most emphasis on indicators produced from groups of individual items, with the individual items themselves presented as background information.

As far as the way items are grouped is concerned, we would emphasise that grouping items into sets or dimensions may produce more valuable indicators than simply adding them all up into one summary deprivation measure. Adding up items of, for example, housing problems and being unable to afford to eat properly may obscure the fact that these often affect different people and different types of people (an illustration of the hazards of using composite indicators that we discuss more generally later in this Chapter). The evidence from both the ECHP and EU-SILC suggests that different dimensions can usefully be distinguished using for example factor analysis. While different methodologies may give somewhat different results, it seems that a reasonably robust distinction can be drawn between at a minimum items relating to housing conditions, items relating to local environmental conditions, and items capturing broad living standards (in terms of food, holidays, "possession of durables", and so on).[31] The common indicators for social inclusion will now have to be based on the non-monetary items included in EU-SILC, and the work carried out by Eurostat is particularly helpful in this respect (Indicators Sub-Group, 2005a and 2006a; see also Guio, 2005b). Eurostat has used EU-SILC data for 14 countries to check the consistency of the results of the factor analysis between EU-SILC and ECHP.[32] The results of Eurostat analyses are as shown in Box 5.1; while separate "economic strain" and "durables" dimensions are distinguished, it is also made clear that they can be combined with little loss of information and gain in simplicity.

This combined index (durables/economic strain) could be the central focus in capturing deprivation broadly conceived, while the housing conditions measure would capture that specific aspect. (A measure of neighbourhood/environmental problems provides very useful information, but in view of its strong urban nature and the absence of a clear link between it and relative financial poverty, this dimension is less central as far as the Social Inclusion Process is concerned.)

Box 5.1: Main potential deprivation items in EU-SILC, by dimensions

Dimension 1 – economic strain

Inability to afford
- keeping the home adequately warm
- paying for a week's annual holiday away from home
- a meal with meat, chicken or fish every second day
- facing unexpected essential financial expenses

Inability to meet payment schedules
- arrears on mortgage payment, or rent, or utility bills or hire purchase instalments

Dimension 2 – durables

Enforced lack of
- a car
- a colour TV
- a washing machine
- a telephone (including mobile phone)

Dimension 3 – housing

Absence of basic housing facilities
- bath or shower
- indoor flushing toilet

Problems with accommodation
- too dark/not enough light
- leaky roof, damp walls, floors or foundation, rot in window frames or floors

Dimension 4 – neighbourhood/environment
- pollution, grime or other environmental problems caused by traffic or industry
- noise from neighbours or from the street
- crime, vandalism or violence in the area

Source: Table based on Eurostat work presented to the Indicators Sub-Group (Indicators Sub-Group, 2005a and 2006a)

So the set of social inclusion indicators could be expanded to first include:

1. an "absolute" indicator of deprivation in relation to broad living standards in the form of an aggregate index, with the same weight being given to each item across the Member States and over time; and
2. an indicator of housing problems in the form of an aggregate index (grouping the four items of dimension 3 in Box 5.1), with the same weight being given to each item across the Member States and over time.

Subsequently, a "more relative" indicator of deprivation in relation to broad living standards in the form of a weighted aggregate index could also be used (in line with the thrust of the proposals set out in Indicators Sub-Group, 2006a, to be the focus of "deepened punctual studies" by Eurostat). The adequacy of the indicators of deprivation, including housing, obtained via EU–SILC will need to be carefully assessed and further items incorporated as necessary.

The importance of dynamics

Finally, we should point to the importance of more systematically monitoring and understanding how the situation of individuals and households changes over time – the dynamics of income, poverty and social exclusion at the *micro-level*, based on longitudinal (panel) data. The common indicator of persistent at-risk-of-poverty already represents an important step in this direction, but it is not sufficient. It would be very useful if countries also included in their NAPs/ inclusion dynamic analyses of movements above and below the relative income thresholds, and the factors/processes/life stages associated with them. Indeed, where possible panel data should also be employed to study the dynamics (at micro-level) of other aspects of social exclusion, not only income. (As well as new longitudinal data as it emerges, data from the ECHP also has still much to offer in this context – and access to it should be facilitated to ensure this potential is exploited.)

Conclusions

It may be useful to conclude this section by highlighting the key points we have made in our discussion of refinement of the existing commonly agreed indicators, and of development of new indicators:

- For the analysis of the "working poor" indicator it would be valuable to have information on the poverty risk run by employees aged 18–59 in full-time employment for the entire reference year, and on the corresponding risk run by those aged 18–59 unemployed all year and those aged 18–59 inactive all year, so their risks can be better compared. A measure of the extent of low pay would also provide a very useful complement.
- The EU indicator of literacy needs to be extended to the adult, or at least working age, population.
- The regional aspects of the risk of poverty and social exclusion would be best reflected by including regional breakdowns for existing indicators, where possible and meaningful. There may also be a need for region-specific indicators to capture aspects which are essentially regional.
- The new Primary Indicator on the employment gap of immigrants is an important step forward, but it is not enough. The specific at-risk position of migrants and ethnic minorities needs to be more systematically analysed and reported on by Member States, by appropriate breakdowns of the common indicators where possible and meaningful, complemented by third level indicators reflecting their specific situations.
- Full use should be made of the potential contribution of administrative data to

improve national and EU knowledge of the regional dimension and of the circumstances of migrants and ethnic minorities.

- Progress on the introduction of an indicator for homelessness should be made incrementally, first agreeing on a relatively tight definition of homelessness, then on the preferred measure and the approach to producing data relating to this agreed measure. Official responsibility has to be clearly assigned for overseeing the collection of appropriate data in close collaboration with organisations working in the area. Member States should in the meantime report on the basis of national statistics as a "level 3" indicator.
- Priority should be given to the development of an aggregate "absolute" indicator of housing quality/adequacy based on EU-SILC data.
- Priority should be given to the development of a harmonised indicator of premature mortality by socio-economic circumstances, to be produced on a regular but not necessarily annual basis. Failure to access health care and health-related limitations in daily activities by income quintile may also provide a useful window on social exclusion.
- An "absolute" common indicator of enforced deprivation in relation to broad living standards should be developed in the form of an aggregate index using data from EU-SILC, accompanied in time by a "more relative" (weighted) common indicator based on the same EU-SILC items.
- Countries should more systematically analyse in their NAPs/inclusion how the situation of individuals and households changes over time; the dynamics of income, poverty and social exclusion at the *micro*-level, based on panel data, and the factors/processes associated with it.

5.4 Presentation and use of the indicators

As well as the content and coverage of the indicators, their presentation is critically important since they are intended to have a wide impact going well beyond those directly engaged in policy formation. From this perspective, we recommended (in Atkinson, Cantillon, Marlier and Nolan, 2002) that a restricted set of headline or Primary common indicators be adopted, complemented by further commonly agreed Secondary Indicators and country-specific "third-level" indicators. This tiered approach was followed by the Social Protection Committee and then adopted in Laeken. More recently, as previously discussed, "Context Information" for the three social processes (inclusion, pensions, and health care and long-term care) has been added to the Primary and Secondary sets of indicators. And an "overarching" portfolio of indicators and "Context Information" has been introduced aimed at building (and monitoring) links between the various EU social processes, and also between the streamlined Social Protection and Social Inclusion Process, on the one hand, and the Lisbon goals of employment and growth on the other). Overarching Indicators have emerged as a critical issue since the re-focusing of the Lisbon Strategy on employment and growth agreed upon by the March 2005 European Council. Naturally, the indicators employed in the different social processes and in the social, growth and employment processes have to reflect the specific concerns of the sphere in question, but they also have to fit together as a whole (see Indicators Sub-Group, 2006b). In Chapter 6, we come back on the need for an approach in line with the Sustainable Development Strategy (at sub-national, national and EU levels), which "bridges" in a mutually reinforcing manner all four pillars of the Lisbon Strategy – the three just mentioned and the environment (see Chapter 2).

In the case of the social inclusion portfolio, the introduction of a set of Context Information for the Social Inclusion Process and the agreement on an overarching portfolio have been accompanied by significant rearrangement of the indicators across these two portfolios and introduction of new indicators that are already available or under development. This has helped to significantly tighten the focus of the Primary Indicators for social inclusion, in line with the strong plea we made in favour of a "pruning" of the Primary Indicators in our original report (see Section 2.6 and Table 2.3a in Appendix 1). This revised monitoring framework, including the introduction of the overarching set across the social inclusion, pensions and health area, should enable the indicators to serve their core purpose of tracking progress and informing policy more effectively.

Turning to the linkage between social inclusion, employment and economy, again indicators have an important role to play but their potential can only be realised if care is taken in selecting and aligning indicators across the different areas. To take just one example, the Employment Guidelines adopted by the Council in July 2003 for the period 2003–5 set full employment, improving quality and productivity at work, and strengthening social cohesion and inclusion as the three general objectives of the *European Employment Strategy*, one focus being on "Making work pay through incentives to enhance work attractiveness". Tackling this issue involves mobilising complex (and sometimes contradictory) actions in the social, employment and economic fields, but this is more likely to be achieved if the emergence of different indicators of essentially the same phenomenon in different parts of the EU policy processes is avoided. The "working poor" indicator first adopted by the Social Protection Committee was then taken on by the Employment Committee (see Lelièvre, Marlier and Pétour, 2004) and is now used in the *European Employment Strategy* for monitoring policies that Member States develop with a view to reducing the number of working poor, one example of good practice in this regard.

As well as the way the indicators are presented, the way that they are best used also merits careful consideration. In judging the progress made by individual Member States, rankings on the different dimensions of social exclusion will be inevitable, and they have a role to play in bringing "peer pressure" to bear. However, "the purpose of the establishment of a common set of indicators is not a naming and shaming exercise" (Vandenbroucke, 2002b, page viii). Here we disagree with the proposal of the Kok Report, which said that in the case of the key Lisbon indicators, the European Commission should present league tables with rankings (1 to 25), praising good performance and castigating bad performance – "naming, shaming and faming" (European Communities, 2004, page 43). Indeed, the process can only work effectively with the cooperation of Member States, and this is unlikely to be engaged by castigation. The aim is not to rate relative performance but to help all Member States to do better. The Commission may wish to highlight the best-performing Member States on particular dimensions and encourage other members to emulate them and learn from their experience. It is important, moreover, to stress that the ultimate concern is with the level of performance achieved, and the consequences of policy choices. In the (unlikely) event that all Member States were performing equally badly, a ranking would give no indication of the need for action. Equally, in a situation where all countries are improving their performance, but with no changes in ranking, then no change would be recorded. Finally, indicators are measured with error, and rankings need to take the margin for error into account: one would not want to put too much weight, for example, on a difference of one percentage point in the at-risk-of-poverty rate. So, rankings are necessarily "fuzzy", and their real value, rather than in crude headlines, is in pointing to underlying mechanisms and areas where policy can fruitfully be focused. We return to some of these issues in discussing the best way to set targets for promoting social inclusion in Chapter 6.

Composite indicators

In addition to presenting the individual common indicators, is there a case for trying to summarise some or all of them in a composite measure? The popularity of such an approach has been demonstrated by the most widely known measure of this kind in current use: the UNDP Human Development Index (HDI), which is a composite of three basic components: longevity, knowledge and standard of living. The rationale given for this procedure in 1990, when it was published for the first time, was that "too many indicators could produce a perplexing picture – perhaps distracting policymakers from the main overall trends" (UNDP, 1990, page 11). The combination of separate indices for GDP, life expectancy and educational attainment has certainly served to broaden the focus from looking only at GDP and has therefore been an important step forward. Examples of composite indicators abound in the social indicators literature, and a recent example is the child well-being index produced by Bradshaw *et al* (2006, forthcoming), to which we return in Section 5.5.

There are, however, a number of reasons why we should not rush too quickly to reduce a multi-dimensional phenomenon to a single number. To begin with, it is important to distinguish two different forms of aggregation. The first aggregation combines different characteristics at the individual level (e.g. persons or households), which are then summed over individuals to form an aggregate index. This is for instance the approach we suggested in Section 5.3 for calculating non-monetary indices of deprivation: the focus there is on multiple deprivation at the individual level. An approach based on household welfare then indicates how the separate deprivations should be aggregated into a single indicator for individual persons; alternatively a "counting" approach leads us to focus on those with n, (n-1), (n-2) ... deprivations (see Atkinson, 2003, for an analysis of the differences between these two approaches).

Instead of first aggregating across fields for an individual and then across individuals (first aggregation), the second approach aggregates first across people and then across fields. This second approach is thus a combination of aggregate indicators, as with the HDI. We now concentrate on this second approach – which we refer as "composite" indicators. It is clear that the design of any such indicator requires us to make social judgements, and these are not easy to make. The problem is illustrated in poverty risk/unemployment space in Figure 5.1 for seven hypothetical countries, ranging from A with low unemployment but high poverty risk to G with low poverty risk and high unemployment. Summation, as in the HDI, adds the two scores: the social welfare contours are therefore 45° lines, and country C is ranked the highest. Even with a linear social welfare function, however, there is no reason why the variables should be weighted equally. If we were to attach a greater weight to the risk of poverty than to unemployment, then country E could take over the lead. Moreover, why should we simply add? Alternatives to simple addition are considered, in the context of poverty indices, by Anand and Sen (1997). One limiting case is that of "Rawlsian" social welfare contours, where we rank countries according to the dimension on which they perform least well. The space is then divided into two. Above the 45° line, poverty risk has priority; below the 45° line, unemployment has priority.

One problem with the choice of weights is that these may not conform with those embodied in national policy objectives. This has led Cherchye, Moesen,

Figure 5.1: Aggregating indicators

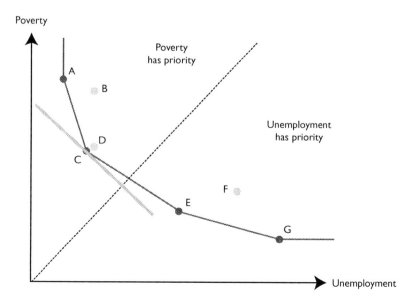

andVan Puyenbroeck (2003) to argue that the weights should vary across countries according to their own national priorities, as revealed in their performance. If a country regards risk of poverty as more important than unemployment, then we should weight poverty more highly when constructing the synthetic indicator for that country. Cherchye, Moesen andVan Puyenbroeck develop this approach by drawing a parallel with Data Envelopment Analysis in production theory. In essence, this involves asking how close countries are to the "efficiency frontier", illustrated in Figure 5.1 by the frontier ACEG. All four of these countries score 100%, since none is dominated by another country. There is, for example, always a dimension on which country E scores better than any other country (it beats G on unemployment and all the others on risk of poverty). They then devise a measure of the distance by which "non-frontier" countries fall short of the frontier, obtaining the weights by solving a linear programming problem. In effect, this is based on the "revealed preferences" of countries – see Figure 5.2.

The efficiency frontier approach is a good example of cross-fertilisation in social science, with a technique developed for one purpose being applied imaginatively to a quite different field. However, it is open to question whether policy makers would find the solution of a linear programming problem less perplexing than consideration of a number of separate indicators. It may appear to be offering a scientific resolution of what is at heart a political problem, ignoring the advice that "weighing together different welfare components should be avoided to the very last so as not to conceal dissensions in a 'scientific' model" (Erikson, 1974, page 279). We could drop the linear programming element, and simply rank each country on the dimension on which they perform best,

Figure 5.2: Revealed preference approach

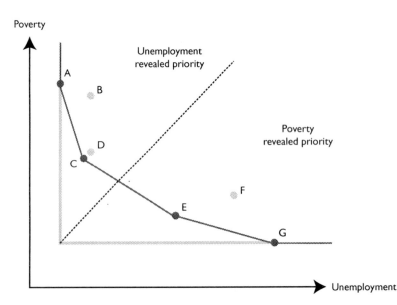

measuring the distance from the best performance. But this would convey the message to (sub-)national Governments that they did not need to make efforts to improve their performance on the other dimensions. Comparing Figures 5.1 and 5.2, we can see that there is a complete reversal of priorities compared with the case of a Rawlsian social welfare function. It is not obvious that this can be justified.

One feature of the objective functions described above is that, in certain situations, the pay-off to improving performance for a particular country can be concentrated on one of the two dimensions. A country judged according to its better performing indicator can only improve its position by doing even better on that indicator: it invests in success. If the social welfare function is Rawlsian, it can only improve its position by doing better on the dimension where its performance is less satisfactory. In both cases, there is a risk that countries will pursue "bang bang" policies, concentrating on a single objective, rather than a balanced approach to different dimensions of deprivation.

If combining different indicators into a single number is certainly appealing at first sight, this approach thus raises serious technical issues but also, and this is most fundamental for our purpose, political questions. Those technical and political issues become even trickier if such indicators are to be used for international comparisons and for measuring changes over time. For these reasons, even though composite indicators, like the Human Development Index, undoubtedly can play a valuable role in certain contexts, we do not feel that they should be employed as part of the current EU Social Inclusion Process.

Comparisons with non-EU countries

In the previous Chapter, we made the obvious point that EU Member States could learn from comparisons with other industrialised countries, such as the US, Canada, Japan, Australia, and New Zealand. We noted that in 10 of the 15 cases, the EU Structural Indicators have been extended to include Japan and the US, but not, unfortunately, the at-risk-of-poverty rate. It would be helpful if the full set of Structural Indicators could be given, as a minimum, for Japan and the US, and if consideration could be given to developing values for the US for the long list of Structural Indicators for social cohesion.

More generally, as is argued by Room (2005), the Lisbon process starts from a global diagnosis but the indicators have remained largely rooted at an EU level. We recommend that the EU institutions consider, in collaboration with OECD, the extension of the common social indicators to include comparable data for (as a minimum) Japan and the US. In some cases, such as life expectancy, this should be possible using readily available comparable statistics. In the case of the income-related indicators, it will involve aligning the necessary data (for Japan, the US, etc.) with the EU-SILC process.

5.5 Children mainstreaming: looking to the future

Since the initial list of indicators was prepared, growing attention has been paid to the position of children. The SPC and its Indicators Sub-Group have increasingly moved towards "children mainstreaming". As we have seen, the two roles of social policy are well illustrated by the explicit reference to child poverty in the EU Presidency Conclusions of March 2005 and March 2006. In the 2006 Conclusions, the European Council specifically asked the Member States "to take necessary measures to rapidly and significantly reduce child poverty, giving all children equal opportunities, regardless of their social background". More generally, both European Councils stressed the need for investment in the youth of Europe. The 2005 European Council specifically adopted the European Pact for Youth and the 2006 European Council urged its implementation.

In line with these policy statements by EU leaders, and as already highlighted in the 2004 Joint Inclusion Report (Statistical Annex), "children and the elderly population must be given a special focus within indicators of social exclusion and poverty. In particular, it is recognised that it is especially important not to base the examination of child poverty and social exclusion on one single at-risk-of-poverty indicator" (European Commission, 2004b, Annex, page 6). The ISG has recommended to "apply a standard breakdown by broad age groups to all Laeken indicators, where relevant and meaningful" (European Commission, 2004b, Annex, page 6). All the current Primary and Secondary Indicators relating to poverty risk and the Primary Indicator on "jobless households" include a breakdown for "children" (now meaning generally the age group 0–17), while the indicator of low reading literacy performance is focused on 15-year-old pupils (see Tables 2.3a and 2.3b in Appendix 1).

The coverage of other dimensions of social exclusion is however, from the perspective of children, rather limited and the "yet-to-be-developed" indicators set out in Tables 2.3a and 2.3b for which a children breakdown should also be provided will significantly contribute to improving the situation (namely housing and material deprivation). From the at-risk-of-poverty indicators, the user can draw significant conclusions regarding the risk of child poverty, as we have seen in Chapter 3. At the same time, that is approaching the issue in the order – indicators, then breakdown. In our view, it would also be valuable to approach the table in the other direction – breakdown, then indicators. For example, a life course perspective suggests that we should consider the different, but inter-related, phases of the life-cycle. For each phase, there will be certain dimensions of social exclusion that are particularly pertinent. In part, these are household variables, such as housing quality and adequacy, and in this case the age breakdown approach will capture what is needed, when an indicator is adopted for this dimension. In other cases, the variables concern individuals, as is the case with health status and education. For an example of an approach to the social exclusion of children that starts from the needs of children, see Ben-Arieh *et al* (2000) and Aber, Gershoff and Brooks-Gunn (2002), the latter referring to the US.

As has been argued by Ruxton and Bennett (2002) in their report *Including Children?*, we need to look at poverty and social exclusion from a children's perspective. This leads them to emphasise, in addition to the dimensions already covered, other mediating factors that may influence later development, including the quality of neighbourhood services. They note the importance of the timing of periods of childhood spent at risk of poverty, and suggest that certain points of transition during childhood may be "particularly sensitive to the damage caused by poverty and exclusion. It is not sufficient to publish only one figure for the total number of under-16s or under-18s living in poor households" (Ruxton and Bennett, 2002, page 37). Their study also contains findings from a Euronet-coordinated project to listen to children's own views about poverty and social exclusion. From these and other considerations, we may wish to consider finer breakdowns of the child population where data allow. These may involve more age categories; they may distinguish rural and urban populations; they may give particular attention to single parent families, and so on.

In a similar vein, the recent study by Bradshaw *et al* (2006, forthcoming) uses available data to make a multi-dimensional comparison of child well-being across the EU-25. They use 51 indicators in all, combined into 23 domains and eight clusters – namely material situation, housing, health, subjective well-being, education, children's relationships, civic participation and risk and safety. This demonstrates impressively the breadth of the areas that are important in children's lives, as well as what can be done by combining available data from different sources. Ideally (see sub-section "composite indicators" above), one would seek to encompass a similar range in monitoring progress in a social inclusion context, but with a distinctive emphasis on socio-economic disparities and the position of children in disadvantaged circumstances.

The present indicators do not, therefore, seem particularly well-adapted from the perspective of children. It is true that the difference between life expectancy at 0 and life expectancy at 1 provides an impression of the extent of infant mortality (in the first year); and, in contrast to the life expectancy at 60, can be more properly seen as a measure of differential deprivation. There is a good case for considering the under-five mortality rates, as investigated by Micklewright and Stewart (2001) in their study of child well-being in the EU and the impact of Enlargement. But consideration should be given to child health and not just mortality, and the present self-defined health status indicator relates only to those aged 16 years and over. In the same way, for education we need to look at younger ages. The early school leavers indicator relates to those aged 18 to 24, not to those missing primary education (see Micklewright and Stewart, 2001, for discussion of enrolment rates), or repeating their early secondary school years.

Children mainstreaming suggests starting earlier. Indicators that reflect the current experience of children are needed, and the ISG has in fact recently decided that there should be a Primary Indicator relating to "child well-being", with the choice of specific indicator as yet left open. Presumably this will relate to a non-income-related dimension, and a number of options merit consideration. To give an example, it would be very desirable to develop an indicator for the health of children. With the introduction of the European Health Interview Survey (see Section 5.3 above), using existing data and fieldwork, it may be possible to build a module for child health. Or the child-focused indicator could relate to schooling, where we need direct measures of early school attendance and performance, to supplement the attainment measures at age 15 or later. These could cover school truancy or drop-out rates. The Key Priority focus on children in the 2004 Joint Report was particularly concerned with "early intervention and early education initiatives which identify and support children and poor families" (European Commission, 2004b, page 36). This suggests that we need to consider the evidence that can be assembled for educational performance at earlier ages. There are evidently serious difficulties in achieving comparable indicators, given the institutional differences across Member States, but Member States could be encouraged to include national indicators in their National Action Plans. These are an important part of human capital investment.

The essentially dynamic nature of the life course approach means that we should give explicit attention to the timing of different variables (an aspect to which we have already drawn attention and that is emphasised by Erikson, 2002). We are concerned about social exclusion both in terms of its immediate consequences and of its impact on future outcomes. We need to have forward-looking indicators, capturing the investment that is, or is not, being made in the future of children. Here there may be an important role for indicators of public services. Moreover, current indicators may measure the impact of past exclusion. For instance, the early school leaver indicator (see Table 2.3a in Appendix 1) may be interpreted as capturing the effects of *past* deprivation. The person aged 20 without educational qualifications in 2004 may have been the child of 10 in 1994 who was truant from school.

It will also be important for Member States, when developing strategies in relation to children, to use a more extensive and multi-dimensional set of child-centred indicators, and the Commission could do likewise when reporting in more depth on policies in relation to child poverty and exclusion. In that context it would be helpful if guidelines could be developed for countries on the range of indicators that they would need to take into account when considering questions of child well-being.

Inter-generational transmission of disadvantage

An important element in the life course approach is the inter-generational transmission of disadvantage. As mentioned earlier, EU–SILC has included, as one of its annual thematic modules, a 2005 module focusing on the intergenerational transmission of poverty. Several distinct strategies have been employed by social scientists to capture the overall degree of association between the socio-economic circumstances of parents and that of their offspring.

Sociologists have tended to concentrate on either educational attainment or occupation, whereas economists have tried to study income and earnings. All face challenges, both in data collection and in the interpretation of the findings.

The data issues have been extensively considered, notably those concerning the situation where retrospective information is being obtained in a cross-sectional survey from the offspring about the circumstances of the older generation many years ago. This makes the relationship between current and parental income, for example, particularly difficult to capture reliably via such an approach. Since the educational attainment level of their parents, or their occupation, are more likely to be known by offspring, the relationship between educational outcomes across the generations could be a better indicator of transmission on which to focus. Social class mobility, as captured by occupation-related information and categorised in a common framework such as the commonly used Erikson-Goldthorpe class schema,[33] would represent an alternative. The comparison of mobility across countries has been an active research field (see Breen, 2004). In a number of Member States, for example the Czech Republic and the UK, there is concern about the differential chances of entering university education depending on the education of parents.

It is important, however, to remember that the indicator is being employed in a social exclusion context. We are not here concerned with mobility *per se*. We are interested in the parental background to the extent that it helps us understand why certain children are disadvantaged and why they are unable to acquire the skills and capabilities required in today's labour market. (We concentrate here on education.) It is here that the human capital perspective is invaluable. There is a great deal of difference between seeing mobility in terms of competition for a fixed number of scarce places and seeing mobility in terms of allowing the disadvantaged to join the better qualified. To use a sporting parallel, in the former case there is a swimming race; in the latter case we are seeking to ensure that all win swimming certificates.

This perspective helps resolve some of the understandable concerns about how to interpret parent–child correlations in a situation where the world of the parents was very different from that of the children today. For example, it is argued that the expansion of educational participation, and thus shifting proportions in different educational categories over time, makes it difficult to make sense of observed changes in the degree of association. If the level of educational attainment has intrinsic value, and is not simply a ranking device, then it can be expected to have a positive relation with the capacity of the children to themselves progress in acquiring education. This in turn provides an instrumental reason for concern with the Primary Indicator (see Table 2.3a in Appendix 1), the proportion of people aged 18 to 24 with only lower secondary education and not in education or training. A reduction in that score today pays dividends in the future.

Drawing conclusions about mechanisms from the observed association of status across generations depends on a degree of stability in the underlying structure.

In the present EU, there are a number of countries where this assumption is questionable. As was noted by the Statistical Bureau of Latvia, "Latvia has experienced fundamental political and socio-economic changes (repression, communism, collapse of the Soviet Union). [This] could be a hindrance in analysing the factors of the respondents' and their parents' welfare and making conclusions about the intergenerational transmission of poverty" (communication to the authors).

Conclusions

In this Section, we have explored some of the implications for the design of social indicators of approaching social inclusion from the perspective of children. Rather than developing the indicators and then seeking interesting breakdowns, we have started from the needs of a potentially vulnerable group and asked what indicators are suggested. The ISG has singled out the need to develop a Primary Indicator on "child well-being", and this should relate to a non-income-related dimension; the choice of dimension could be for instance child health or child educational performance/attendance at a younger age.

5.6 Concluding comment

As we noted at the outset, the design of the common indicators is a dynamic process for the EU. The Laeken indicators were only the first step and have since been adapted and complemented by indicators adopted under other areas of the Open Method of Coordination. It was recognised at the time that indicators needed to be developed for homelessness and that the health indicators needed to be enriched. The arrival of the new EU-SILC data source has provided an impetus to develop the indicators further, Enlargement has brought out new features, and we have considered the role of EU-wide indicators and of the new deprivation indicators that are under discussion. There are new policy concerns, which we have illustrated by reference to the risk of child poverty.

There are two points that we would like to emphasise in conclusion. First, the income-related indicators, whatever their limitations, are now relatively well developed, and the non-income-related indicators should now be the principal focus of attention. As we have shown in Chapter 3, they present a rather different picture of the position of Member States, and the degree of correlation has been changed by Enlargement. Secondly, a balance has to be struck between adding to, refining and improving the indicators and having a reasonably stable and succinct set of agreed measures with which to capture progress.

Notes

[1] Regulation (EC) No 1177/2003 of the European Parliament and of the Council of 16 June 2003 concerning Community statistics on income and living conditions

(EU-SILC), amended by Regulation (EC) No 1553/2005 of the European Parliament and of the Council of 7 September 2005.

[2] See, for example, the study of France by Driant and Jacquot (2005); Belgium by van den Bosch (1998); Luxembourg by Berger (2004); Finland and other countries by Ritakallio (2003); Germany, Great Britain and the US by Frick and Grabka (2003); and a range of countries by Fahey, Maître and Nolan (2004).

[3] In this respect, imputed rent seems to us different from the value of self-consumption and company cars. If the elderly person in the example is cultivating 100kg of potatoes, then all of this *should* be included when assessing her standard of living.

[4] We have noted in Chapter 3 the observation in the NAPs/inclusion for Cyprus and Greece that owner-occupation is high among the population at risk of poverty.

[5] The figures in PPS for a single-person household were 2,064 for Latvia, 9,176 for Denmark, and 9,175 for Germany (European Commission, 2006b).

[6] See, for example, Diener *et al* (1999) or Ryan and Deci (2001) for reviews.

[7] It should be remembered that in the "jobless households" indicator, students aged 18–24 years who live in households composed solely of students are counted in neither numerator nor denominator.

[8] This definition is somewhat arbitrary, driven by the fact that the income measure on which poverty risk is being calculated is itself an annual measure. For a detailed discussion of the working poor indicator (concepts and methods), which is thus much stricter in terms of months actually worked than the well-known official US and French definitions, as well as a description of the EU context in which it was agreed (Social Inclusion Process and European Employment Strategy), see Lelièvre, Marlier and Pétour (2004). See also Bardone and Guio (2005) for a detailed discussion of concepts and methods, and see European Commission (2006b) for the most recent in-work poverty figures relating to all EU-25 Member States. For a comprehensive and analytical review of the literature on working poverty, see Peña Casas and Latta (2004).

[9] It should be highlighted that the new EU monitoring framework (Indicators Sub-Group, 2006b) usefully includes the breakdown full-time/part-time of the working poor indicator in the Context Information set for the social inclusion portfolio (see Table 2.3c in Appendix 1).

[10] PISA is an internationally standardised assessment that was jointly developed by participating countries and administered to 15-year-olds in schools. The survey was implemented in 43 countries in the first assessment in 2000, and in 41 countries in the second assessment in 2003; it covered all the then 15 Member States but only some of

the 10 countries which joined the EU as of May 2004 It is expected that at least 58 countries will participate in the third assessment in 2006, including most of the current Member States (with the exception of Malta and Cyprus, which have not yet committed to doing so), and the four acceding/candidate countries (Bulgaria, Croatia, Romania and Turkey). Comprehensive information on PISA can be obtained from: http://www.pisa.oecd.org.

[11] See, for example, results on literacy and numeracy among the adult population in France from the survey "Information et Vie Quotidienne" carried out by INSEE (Murat, 2004).

[12] The value of examining the regional breakdown of different dimensions of exclusion is illustrated for Italy by Barca *et al* (2004).

[13] For instance, certain more complex poverty risk and inequality measures, which are sensitive to details and irregularities of the empirical income distribution, are less suited for disaggregation to small populations and small samples. For the same reason, longitudinal indicators defined over short time periods (such as over *pairs of adjacent years*), which can be aggregated over time, are likely to be more practical. Greater emphasis may have to be given to cross-sectional as distinct from longitudinal/panel measures, in so far as the former are less demanding in terms of the data required. (see Verma *et al*, 2005).

[14] In some countries there are legal or institutional obstacles to collecting information on some of these groups. There are major problems of definition: very definite limits may be imposed by sample sizes (as already suggested for the regional dimension, the way forward may then be to make use of the information contained in administrative registers to complement the information collected in the context of EU-SILC and other household surveys), etc.

[15] The employment gap can be expressed either in absolute terms or as a proportion of the employment rate for the non-migrant population. It should be noted that the ISG rightly pointed out that *adjusted* gap measures (to take account of differences in educational/ skills levels, demographic characteristics, and so on between the migrant and non-migrant populations) would allow better identification of the role of immigration *per se* on the deficit of inclusion of immigrants. Countries able to produce such measures are encouraged to do so.

[16] "Depending on immigration policies and histories, immigrants currently in employment might remain in precarious situations (e.g. temporary residence permit), with or without their families, accommodated in poor quality housing, and have poor access to health care and education" (Indicators Sub-Group, 2005c).

[17] An international study funded by the European Commission (DG EMPL) and led by the Joint Centre for Scottish Housing Research (University of Dundee, Scotland) is investigating further the complex issues raised by the "Measurement of Homelessness at EU level"; this includes in particular identifying methodologies and practices, and common basic tools (definitions, nomenclatures) for the development of the information base required for the measurement of housing deprivation and homelessness. A report summarising the main results of the study is planned for 2007. More information on this study can be found at: http://feantsa.horus.be/code/EN/pg.asp?Page=538.

[18] FEANTSA stands in French for "Fédération Européenne d'Associations Nationales Travaillant avec les Sans-Abris", i.e. the European Federation of National Organisations working with the Homeless.

[19] Suppose for example that a household in country A had total disposable income of €1,000 with no cash housing assistance, and spent €200 on housing, whereas a household in country B had total income of €1,200 including €200 in housing allowances, and spent €400 on housing; the uncovered housing costs as a proportion of income net of housing support would be the same – (200/1000) in one case, and (400–200)/(1200–200) in the other. Note that for those repaying mortgages, one would probably want to include both interest and capital repayments as housing expenditure, since the latter, although it represents savings, is not discretionary in the shorter term; also for this specific purpose it would not seem appropriate to include imputed rent in household income.

[20] A substantial amount of work on the topic has been carried out subsequently by the ISG and Eurostat, in the context of both the Social Inclusion Process and the extension of the Open Method of Coordination to health care and long-term care. This has involved the collection of information from Member States on their available health indicators, including a helpful discussion of methodological as well as data issues, which served as a useful basis for seeing where and how progress can be made (see Indicators Sub-Group, 2004a).

[21] Respondents are asked whether there was during the previous year any time when they "really needed" a medical (respectively dental) examination or treatment but did not receive it, and if they say yes are asked whether the main reason was that: they could not afford it (too expensive); there were waiting lists; they could not take time off from work or caring duties (children or others); too far to travel or no means of transportation; fear of the doctor/hospital/examination/treatment (respectively dentist); they wanted to see if the problem got better on its own; they did not know a good doctor/specialist (respectively dentist); or "other".

[22] From this perspective it is problematic that the information prescribed for collection via EU-SILC does not include actual levels of utilisation of different health services, such as general practitioners, specialists and hospitals, which were included in the ECHP.

[23] For more information on EU public health statistics, see the Eurostat website: http://forum.europa.eu.int/Public/irc/dsis/health/home. See also 'Analysing and reporting on health' on the website of the "Health and Consumer Protection" Directorate-General (DG SANCO) of the European Commission: http://ec.europa.eu/health/ph_information/reporting/analysing_reporting_en.htm. The latter website includes the various health reports produced by the European Commission (DG SANCO, Eurostat and other DGs) and some other bodies (OECD and so on) as well as various links (in particular to the health reporting systems at national level).

[24] See Förster (2005) for a cross-country application of the "consistent poverty" approach.

[25] The agreed set of common indicators complements the "at-risk-of-poverty rate" based on purely relative income lines with the value of that threshold for 2 different household types. In addition, a context statistic shows the percentage falling below income thresholds held fixed in real terms over a period (currently 4 years) described as the "at-risk-of-poverty rate anchored at a moment in time". The value of the relative threshold is obviously important contextual information in interpreting the at-risk-of-poverty rate, as we discussed earlier, and the anchored measure is very useful in capturing the impact of short-term changes in real incomes, but even taken together they may still fail to adequately capture and convey changes in living conditions.

[26] Whelan and Maître (2006) have analysed the EU-SILC deprivation indicators and the broader ECHP set using data for Ireland (which retained the larger set in its EU-SILC), and conclude that the former still contain much of the information required to identify those who are "economically vulnerable".

[27] See, for example, Eurostat (2000).

[28] See, for example, Eurostat (2000 and 2003), Fusco (2005), Whelan *et al* (2001 and 2002).

[29] The question reads as follows: "Could your household afford an unexpected required expense of (*amount to be filled*) with its own resources?" "Own resources" means that: "your household cannot ask for financial help from anybody; your account has to be debited within one month; and your situation regarding potential debts does not deteriorate (you cannot intend to pay on instalments or with a loan the expenses that you used to pay in cash)". The amount to be used is the monthly national at-risk-of-poverty threshold for a one-person household.

[30] A useful analogy may be the way a battery of different survey responses can be used to categorise respondents by, say, personality type: any one response item may not be a reliable indicator, but taken together a set of responses can provide a very much more reliable basis for categorisation.

[31] On these various issues, see, for example, Whelan *et al* (2001 and 2002), Eurostat (2003) and Indicators Sub-Group (2006a).

[32] They have done this through a "confirmatory factor analysis" on the EU-SILC data, which has allowed them to test the adequacy of the factor structure identified through an "exploratory factor analysis" on the ECHP items that have been retained in EU-SILC (see Indicators Sub-Group, 2005a and 2006a).

[33] This sees individuals as occupying a limited number of common positions in the social structure in terms of social power, based on possessing similar resources and consequently facing similar possibilities and constraints in terms of life-chances (see Erikson and Goldthorpe, 1992).

Taking forward the
EU Social Inclusion Process

In Chapter 2, we described the new context within which the Social Inclusion Process is now being taken forward. Alongside the new Lisbon governance cycle launched in 2005, there will be a simplification and streamlining of the reporting mechanisms under the Open Method of Coordination on social protection and social inclusion (European Commission, 2005h, 2005i, and 2005l; Social Protection Committee and Economic Policy Committee, 2006). Separate reporting will continue as part of this OMC. The annual Joint Report on Social Protection and Social Inclusion will remain a separate document, not be integrated into the "renewed" Lisbon Strategy, although information relevant to the Lisbon goals of employment and growth are also expected to be reflected in the National Reform Programmes (see Section 2.3).

In the preceding three Chapters, we have sought, in Chapter 3, to learn from the evidence about poverty and social exclusion contained in the body of aggregated information now represented by the commonly agreed social indicators, to describe in Chapter 4 how policy analysis in the EU can be strengthened, and to further develop in Chapter 5 the set of EU social indicators. In this Chapter, we ask how the EU Social Inclusion Process can be taken forward in the context just outlined. In particular, we consider two ways in which the process can be deepened. The first is the use of targets at national and EU level. The desirability of setting targets has already been recognised at the highest EU political level, at the Barcelona European Council in spring 2002. In this Chapter we look at the role which target setting has played to date in the Social Inclusion Process, and discuss how the setting of ambitious but achievable targets might assist the Process to reach its full potential. This involves an examination of the varying roles assigned to national targets by different Member States in their National Action Plans on social inclusion (NAPs/inclusion), followed by consideration of key issues in pushing forward the use of national targets, and finally a discussion of how EU-wide targets might best be approached, balancing ambition and achievability.

The second form of deepening involves embedding the Social Inclusion Process more firmly in domestic policy making. A necessary condition to guarantee a credible and meaningful Social Inclusion Process is to truly embed it in national and sub-national policy formation, and in particular work towards integrating social inclusion, employment and economic policies. In this context, the Chapter underlines the pivotal role of *restructured* NAPs/inclusion, which will be preserved under the streamlined process, and makes practical suggestions to assist in the re-focusing of the NAPs/inclusion so that they become real "action plans" with a truly strategic and focused approach, as envisaged in the *Guidelines for Preparing National Reports on Strategies for Social Protection and Social Inclusion* agreed upon between the Social Protection Committee and the European Commission (Social Protection Committee, 2006). Following on from this, the Chapter emphasises the need for *joined-up Government*, committed political and administrative leadership, and parliamentary scrutiny to guarantee a credible and meaningful Social Inclusion Process. It also discusses the need to establish a scheme of systematic policy assessment (both *ex ante* and *ex post*) as well as the importance of raising awareness of the EU Social Inclusion Process, and of further mobilising the different actors involved in the fight against poverty and social exclusion at the sub-national, national and EU levels.

6.1 Streamlining the EU Social Processes

As explained in Chapter 2, the Council decided in October 2003 to implement a "streamlining" of the EU social processes covering the fields of social inclusion, pensions, and health and long-term care. In its Communication (European Commission, 2003c), the Commission referred to *Social protection* rather than *Social protection and social inclusion*. However, to better stress the diversity and specificity of the social policy issues covered, and in line with the separate treatment of social inclusion and social protection in the Social Policy Agenda adopted by the December 2000 Nice European Council, the Commission and Member States have agreed that an explicit reference to both social protection *and* social inclusion was more appropriate. This is important as it is indeed essential that social inclusion is seen not as synonymous with social protection, but rather as an issue for economic and employment policy as well as social policy. Streamlining of open coordination in the social field was to have been accompanied by a synchronisation of the timetable for the various EU processes – social, employment and economic. Although this "double streamlining" has not fully materialised in the present cycle (see Chapters 1 and 2), it is intended to move progressively in this direction with full synchronisation from 2008.

The single streamlining, that is to say the synchronising and rationalising of existing individual EU social processes, which has been agreed, poses a major challenge. This is particularly the case given that during the lead up to streamlining, significant actors expressed concerns that it might lead to a weakening and not deepening of the Social Inclusion Process. It is thus encouraging that in the new streamlined arrangements that have been agreed Member States and the EU have committed themselves, both politically and administratively, to work together towards ensuring the robustness of the individual EU social processes. The importance of maintaining the distinctive identity of each "strand" is stressed. However, there remains the challenge that future NAPs/inclusion be anchored nationally and integrated with Member States' policies.

Individual Social Processes

The new *Guidelines* allow for the preparation of distinctive plans for social inclusion, pensions, and health care and long-term care within an overall National Report on Strategies for Social Protection and Social Inclusion (Social Protection Committee, 2006). However, it will still remain a considerable challenge to ensure that the new plans put a stronger focus on delivery and synergies across the different strands (social inclusion, pensions, and health and long-term care), while respecting the distinct *identity* and *visibility* of the individual processes.

One could (rightly) argue that the real risk of weakening the individual processes is not so much their streamlining as the political options taken by individual Governments – either in the name of subsidiarity ("we know how to solve our domestic problems without help from the EU") or in the name of very "liberal"/anti-welfare ideologies. It is true that the decision to integrate NAPs/inclusion with domestic policy formation is first and foremost a national (and sub-national) *political act*. Even under the yet-to-be-ratified *Treaty establishing a Constitution for Europe*, at least until the suggested Article I-15 is given some real flesh,[1] the progress of the Open Method of Coordination will always depend on the voluntary adhesion of Member States based on the belief that it is useful for policy exchanges and does not create too many additional constraints. This being said, in our view it is essential that in implementing the Social Protection and Social Inclusion Process in the future those responsible continue to respect (and in fact build upon) the specificity of the individual processes. The reason is that the (currently) three social processes that are being streamlined all have quite different characteristics and challenges. They relate (partly) to different populations, require the involvement of (partly) different stakeholders, and are at different stages of maturity. The necessary involvement of the various EU-level Committees (those concerned with social protection and social inclusion, with employment, with economic policy coordination, with health and long-term care) and of the various Council formations also differs over these areas.

The new Common Objectives on Social Protection and Social Inclusion that have been agreed at EU level (see Appendix 2b) demonstrate an encouraging recognition of the importance of maintaining a distinctive identity for each strand containing, as they do, three specific objectives. The three social inclusion objectives, under the very welcome aim of "making a decisive impact on the eradication of poverty and social exclusion", are largely consistent with the original social inclusion objectives agreed at Nice in 2000. Essentially the first two of these new objectives encompass the main elements of the first three Nice objectives, albeit in a more generalised form. The new third objective maintains the intention of the fourth Nice objective of putting the focus on the mobilisation of actors and good governance which has been such a distinctive feature of the Social Inclusion Process to date. This is further reinforced by the third overarching objective that also stresses good governance issues across the whole streamlined process. There are of course some risks in the necessary simplification and generalisation of the objectives that has taken place under streamlining. In particular there is a risk that, because a number of specific policy areas are no longer mentioned by name (e.g. health, housing, justice, culture, sport and leisure), a multi-dimensional approach may be weakened. Also the balance implied in the original objectives between preventing poverty and social exclusion arising and helping those who are most vulnerable is less explicit, as is the need for a balance between policies aimed at promoting the inclusion of the generality of people and more targeted interventions in favour of specific groups at high risk. However, it is quite encouraging that the new Guidelines for preparing the new National Reports (Social Protection Committee, 2006) address these issues in more detail. It will be very important that in the next phase of the NAPs/inclusion Member States do maintain a multi-dimensional approach to the issues they focus on and that they do not lose sight of issues that have emerged as being important in the course of the process to date, such as access to culture and transport, indebtedness or micro-credit. It will also be essential that Member States continue to ensure a balance between increasing the access of all to services while developing specific supports for people facing particular difficulties.

Another strength of the new objectives is that they should help to ensure there will, in future, be a greater consistency and interaction with the "Integrated Guidelines" that now bring together the Broad Economic Policy Guidelines and the Employment Guidelines (see Chapter 2).

While the new objectives are one important element in ensuring the continuing distinctive identity of each strand, another key element is the role played by specific reports and *peer reviews* on each strand. The continued preparation of such separate reports and peer reviews is less clear under the new arrangements. In our view the essential critical analysis of the individual social processes requires *separate* reports (NAPs/inclusion, National Strategy Reports for pensions, National Strategy Reports for health and long-term care), providing detailed and contextualised information (see for instance Vandenbroucke, 2002a; Sakellaropoulos and Berghman, 2004). In order to boost mutual learning between countries and identify good (and bad) practices, these reports need to be reviewed by Member States and the Commission in *specific* peer reviews, focused on a single process (e.g. only on NAPs/inclusion as far as the Social Inclusion Process is concerned), rather than *general* peer reviews (covering the various processes). The separate exchanges of information and peer reviews for each of these quite heterogeneous processes are key conditions for fruitful exchanges. Put simply, one cannot expect participants in peer reviews to have a range of expertise that covers all of the social domains. As we have argued in Chapter 4, policy analysis needs to become more, not less, professional. The new arrangements clearly provide for an annual Joint Report on Social Protection and Social Inclusion which brings together the main messages from all three strands into one "overarching document" so that these can be fed each year into the EU's key policy making forum, the annual Spring European Council. This is most welcome but not sufficient. Behind the Joint Report, there need to continue to be detailed and free-standing reports which make visible the main developments of each strand. Without this there is a significant risk that the visibility of the Social Inclusion Process will gradually be lost within the overall Social Protection and Social Inclusion Process.

Preservation of the distinct *identity* and *visibility* of the individual social processes will continue to be crucial for an effective Open Method of Coordination: awareness of the process is a condition for public and political attention, which in turn is a *sine qua non* for successful open coordination. If, as we believe, the final goal of the open coordination is to improve performance of all the Member States and try to bring them all to a high level, then the awareness of the process has a role to play in bringing to bear the necessary *peer pressure*. However, for the streamlined Social Protection and Social Inclusion Process to be effective, especially in view of the re-focused Lisbon Strategy on growth and jobs, it is also important that each Member State bring together, without "merging" them for the reasons just explained, the NAP/inclusion with the equivalent Strategy Reports on pensions and on health care and long-term care. Thus we also support the proposal in the new Guidelines for an overarching section drawing out common/horizontal themes between the reports relating to the individual social *strands*.

6.2 The role of targets in the Social Inclusion Process

Against the background of a Social Inclusion Process that is streamlined in the way described above, we can go on to consider the deepening of this process, beginning with the issue of target setting. In the first round of NAPs/inclusion, submitted in 2001, only a minority of the then 15 Member States had outcome targets. Furthermore, not all these targets were systematically linked to indicators to be used for monitoring progress towards achieving them. A few did have high-level national targets, notably Ireland which already had such a target at the core of its *National Anti-Poverty Strategy*, framed in terms of a domestically developed measure of "consistent poverty", which combines being at risk of poverty with experiencing basic deprivation (see Chapter 5). The UK presented a number of specific targets relating to the activities of different Government departments, as well as a commitment to eradicate child poverty; the Netherlands set targets for reducing early school leaving, illiteracy and "unhealthy life years"; and Sweden set out a target for reducing welfare dependency (as well as increasing employment). Overall, though, the setting of targets for key outcomes was rare and their coverage extremely patchy.

When it came to the second round of NAPs/inclusion, the Presidency Conclusions of the March 2002 Barcelona European Council stated: "*The European Council stresses the importance of the fight against poverty and social exclusion. Member States are invited to set targets, in their National Action Plans, for significantly reducing the number of people at risk of poverty and social exclusion by 2010.*" The thinking behind this, and a detailed elaboration of how Member States might approach target-setting, was contained in the Common Outline for the 2003–5

NAPs/inclusion agreed upon between the SPC and the Commission (Social Protection Committee, 2003b). The point of departure was that Member States were encouraged to take into account lessons and weaknesses identified from the first round of NAPs/inclusion. In that light, more attention was to be given to, *inter alia*, setting clear objectives and specific targets for the reduction of poverty and social exclusion. To meet the EU objective of making a decisive impact on the eradication of poverty and social exclusion by 2010, an overall coherent strategy for tackling and preventing the risk of poverty and social exclusion should be presented. This should contain long-term objectives for the eradication of poverty and social exclusion. The priorities for the two-year period from July 2003 should also be specified.

It was clear from the Common Outline that these statements of objectives and priorities were intended to go beyond the general and aspirational. It spelt out that quantified targets should be set for reducing the number of people at risk of poverty and social exclusion. These should draw as appropriate on the commonly agreed indicators but also take into account other issues identified in the Report on indicators for social inclusion prepared by the SPC and endorsed by the December 2001 Laeken European Council (see Chapter 2) – such as access to health care, housing and homelessness, literacy and numeracy. When necessary they should also draw on national data where these data reflect better those aspects of the risk of poverty and social exclusion that are a priority for a Member State, or where national data are more timely than those available on a comparable basis. The Common Outline emphasised the importance of statistical capacity in this context, since the setting of targets and indeed the use of indicators to monitor progress depends on the availability of relevant and timely data. Thus, as well as setting targets in their NAPs/inclusion, it encouraged Member States to identify gaps in existing data and to further develop their statistical infrastructure.

The Common Outline explained that such targets are important for a number of reasons. They can be a significant political statement of purpose, a goal against which to measure progress, a tool for promoting awareness of the process and mobilising support around it, and a focal point around which to concentrate effort. The distinction was drawn between outcomes versus policy effort targets, with a clear preference for the former: "Although performance or outcome indicators are strongly preferred, policy effort indicators could be used when performance or outcome indicators are not measurable." Given the multi-dimensional nature of poverty and social exclusion it would be useful to have targets that cover a number of key dimensions. For targets to make a political impact and to contribute to awareness raising, selecting a small number of headline or global targets for poverty reduction by 2010 should be considered, complemented by more detailed targets covering very specific aspects and intermediate targets that allow progress from one plan to the next to be assessed.

The targets envisaged for the NAPs/inclusion at this stage of the Social Inclusion Process are clearly national, rather than EU-wide targets. At the same time, it was envisaged that some Member States might make use of the common indicators to help them to benchmark their performance against other Member States – for example by using the average performance of the three best performing Member States on a particular indicator to set a benchmark of what is to be achieved. The new common objectives and working arrangements, including the new Guidelines for preparing the next NAPs/inclusion (Social Protection Committee, 2006), reinforce the existing position on the importance of setting national level quantified outcome targets.

We review below the role that targets play in the NAPs/inclusion prepared by the 15 Member States (submitted in 2003), and in the plans prepared by the ten new Member States (submitted in 2004, just a couple of months after their accession). We then consider in the following Section a range of issues in relation to such national target setting, many of them highlighted by the gap between the approach suggested in the Common Outline and the actual treatment of targets in the national plans.

Targets in the 2003 NAPs/inclusion in the EU-15

There was wide variation across the 15 EU members in the way they responded to the Barcelona European Council invitation to set targets in their 2003 NAPs/inclusion, as is illustrated by Box 6.1 (drawn from European Commission, 2004b). Overall there was certainly a greater emphasis on targets than in the first round,

Box 6.1: Use of quantified targets in the NAPs/inclusion in the EU-15

Country	Direct outcome targets		Intermediate outcome targets	Input targets
	Laeken	Non-Laeken		
Belgium				
Denmark			*	
Germany			*	
Greece	*		*	
Spain	*			
France		*	*	*
Ireland	*	*	*	*
Italy			*	
Luxembourg			*	*
Netherlands		*	*	*
Austria		*	*	*
Portugal	*	*	*	*
Sweden			*	
Finland			*	*
United Kingdom	*	*	*	*

Source: European Commission, 2004b, page 40 .

and a number of Member States set targets in terms of the Laeken common social inclusion indicators. Notably, Spain, Greece, and Portugal set quantified targets that include the "at-risk-of-poverty" rate. The three countries in fact adopted similar structures in framing targets, setting out ten (Greece, Spain) or twelve (Portugal) main objectives, national social targets, or major challenges, of which the first related to the at-risk-of-poverty indicator. In the case of Spain, the stated aim was to reduce the number of people with a level of income below 60% of the average by 2% during the period of the plan. For Greece, the aim was that by 2010 the percentage of individuals at risk would be down to the EU-15 average. For Portugal, the aim was that the risk-of-poverty rate would be brought down by three percentage points by 2005.

Several points are worth making about the way these targets are framed. To do so, we take the three countries – Spain, Greece, and Portugal – for purposes of illustration, but this should not be taken as implying criticism on our part. Indeed, the three countries are to be commended for having made a positive response to the invitation to set targets in terms of the Laeken indicators. The first point is that in setting a quantitative target, the exact definition of the indicator to be employed is critical. In this instance, only the Portuguese plan is entirely transparent, in that it also states that the base level for the indicator in question was 21% in 1999. For Spain, 60% of average income seems likely to refer to the median rather than the mean, since the former is employed in the Laeken indicators, but there is some scope for ambiguity; in the case of Greece the reference is simply to the percentage at risk of poverty: the 60% of median threshold is the central one employed in the Laeken set but 40%, 50% and 70% of the median are also included, so again the precise target is open to interpretation.

The second issue is the time-scale: both Spain and Portugal specify targets for the life of the current plan, to 2005, whereas Greece presents a target for 2010 that is consistent with the Lisbon agenda time-frame. Both approaches to specifying the time-scale have limitations: the former does not constitute a vision or medium-term societal goal, while the latter could be taken to imply, but does not state explicitly, intermediate goals for monitoring purposes along the way. Ideally, a fully worked-out strategy would include both the desired position to be reached by 2010 and a set of intermediate targets to allow progress towards that aim to be monitored, with a feed-back loop to allow policy to respond if it looks to be falling short.

The third issue is whether the target is framed in national or comparative terms: both Spain and Portugal specify a percentage point reduction in their rate, whereas Greece specifies an improvement vis-à-vis the EU average. Finally, and perhaps most importantly, there is little direct linkage between the poverty target and the strategy/policies elaborated in detail in the plans: it is not clear whether these represent a realistic response to the challenge of meeting the target and how this is to come about.

The target for the risk-of-poverty rate is distinctive even in these three plans in being directly framed in terms of one of the Laeken common indicators. The rest of the set presented in the Spanish plan mostly represent broad goals rather than quantified targets – such as improving coordination of policies, promoting reconciliation of work and family life, strengthening access to new technologies – or relate to specific policy measures, both common across many of the other Member States. The Portuguese plan does set out other quantified targets, relating to for example active labour market measures, childcare and minimum pensions, but these are mostly in terms of policy inputs rather than quantified outcomes.

The Greek plan is unusual in setting out other quantified targets linked to the risk of poverty. These include halving the poverty risk for the over-65s compared with the national average, tackling child poverty so that the situation in Greece for children will be better than the average for the seven best countries in the EU-15, and in terms of persistence ensuring that one in three of those currently at risk have escaped by 2010. It is also interesting that as well as reducing the risk-of-poverty rate, which is a purely relative measure, the Greek plan also has the aim that the average income of individuals at risk will have risen in real terms by at least a third by 2010. (Again it is worth noting that as stated these targets are not entirely unambiguous.)

Some other countries from the EU-15 did present in their NAPs/inclusion key targets in quantified terms relating to headline outcome indicators, but not framed in terms of a Laeken indicator. Ireland, for example, continued the approach adopted in its first report of highlighting the overall goal of reducing "consistent poverty". Poverty on this indicator is to be brought below 2%, and if possible eliminated, by 2007. In pursuing this overall target specific attention is to be paid to particular vulnerable groups. Quantified targets in some other dimensions are also presented, notably in health and education. These include reducing by at least 10% the gap in premature mortality from specific causes between the lowest and highest socio-economic groups, and increasing completion of upper second-level education to 90% of the cohort by 2007. These then are examples of quantified outcome targets in other dimensions of social inclusion covered by the Laeken indicators, but once again using (mainly) national rather than commonly agreed indicators. Some other targets set out in the Irish plan either relate to policy measures or variables – such as social protection levels – rather than outcomes, or are framed in broad aspirational rather than quantified form, again a common feature of many of the targets in the NAPs/inclusion from various countries. Furthermore, no link is made between the "consistent poverty" indicator and the Laeken "at-risk-of-poverty indicator" in the Irish NAP/inclusion.

The UK 2003 NAP/inclusion described the specific targets relating to the activities of different Government departments, set out at the time as part of the process of Public Service Agreements (PSAs). There were around 130 targets covering key areas and intended to focus on outputs and outcomes – for example raising standards in education, improving health etc. The UK NAP/inclusion then states that the National Action Plan sets targets based on the PSAs deemed most relevant to tackling poverty, as well as key targets set by the devolved administrations in Scotland, Wales and Northern Ireland. PSA Target 1 for the Department for Work and Pensions (DWP), for example, is concerned with child poverty, and the UK highlights its commitment to ending child poverty, stating that this is the Government's main focus. The aim is to halve child poverty by 2010 and to eradicate it by 2020. The UK Government has consulted widely on the appropriate measure to be used in monitoring progress, and, as a result, has decided to adopt a "tiered approach", using a set of inter-related indicators, while keeping income at the core (UK Department for Work and Pensions, 2003). The document refers to the Laeken indicators (paragraph 33), but does not give them any central role.

The NAP/inclusion for Belgium is interesting in explicitly discussing the rationale for the approach it adopts to target setting. This states that the experience of other Member States (such as the Netherlands, the UK and Ireland) shows that formulation of global and central targets is not straightforward. For this reason, the Belgian plan has decided to work with specific targets, which have the advantage that they are more concrete and can be more easily attained by specific policy instruments, and are thus easier to address. Also, it argues, setting numerous and varied targets is a better response to the multi-dimensional character of poverty. Such an approach also has an analytical advantage, in allowing the areas where progress is and is not being made to be distinguished. Finally, and importantly in the Belgian context, this approach allows the responsibility to rest with the political level which has competency in the specific area in question. While subsidiarity is much discussed in relation to Member States, we tend to lose sight of the operation of this principle *within* Member States. The Belgian Plan does not then set out a list of the specific targets set, and the subsequent discussion relates to policy measures being implemented. So although the arguments for setting various and concrete targets are articulated, no targets are in fact set out.

The NAP/inclusion for the Netherlands presents a series of "main objectives", for most of which a set of targets is given, some broad and unspecific but others quantified. The latter are most common in what is labelled the "social participation" area, but turn out to relate for the most part to employment and unemployment. There are, however, some other quantitative targets, such as reducing waiting lists for care, reducing early school-leaving and increasing the life expectancy of people of low socio-economic status. Where the targets are concrete, the time-period involved is most often that of the plan – to 2005 – but the one for life expectancy relates to 2020.

Most of the other NAPs/inclusion for the EU-15 make little use of quantified outcome targets, some having virtually no such targets at all other than those in the employment area that had already been adopted in the context of the European Employment Strategy. Sweden, for example, reiterates its targets of an employment rate of 80% and of halving dependence on social assistance between 1999 and 2004. It also expresses concern about the economic impact of sick leave from work, and aims to halve the number of sick days between 2002 and 2008. However, despite a lengthy description of objectives and policies in various areas, other quantitative targets are eschewed. The NAP/inclusion for Luxembourg also focuses on strategic approaches and detailed policy measures and budgetary allocations for different areas, rather than on quantitative outcome targets (with only a few exceptions). The Austrian NAP/inclusion presents a set of key targets that are mostly broad-ranging, such as better coordination of economic, fiscal, employment and social policies or adaptation of the social security systems to the changes in the labour market, and again the focus is on policy measures being implemented in different areas.

In the case of Denmark, the thinking behind the approach to targets is discussed in the following terms:

> When mapping out the implications of new legislation, Denmark often applies indicators for changes in income distribution, and distribution considerations generally form an integrated part of economic-policy planning. However, no specific, quantitative targets are set for Danish income distribution development. Consequently, the above indicators do not constitute independent variables for economic policy. However, legislation and action plans, etc., prescribe certain quantitative targets, e.g. for the development in total employment, which may indirectly affect the development of the mentioned indicators. To some extent, other targets and indicators are applied in Danish social and employment policy – often in more specific policy areas. In terms of Danish policy aimed at the most disadvantaged and marginalised groups, the targets typically pertain to the scope of the effort and the range of offers in relation to these groups. (Government of Denmark, 2003, page 7)

This approach can be interpreted in terms of the matrix set out in Chapter 4: it starts from a definition of vulnerable groups, but there is considerable distance between such a perspective and the placing of quantitative outcome targets for key dimensions centre-stage in the social inclusion strategy.

The NAP/inclusion for Finland also includes some discussion of the role of targets, when summarising the results of an evaluation of the previous plan whereby a range of experts submitted their views. In that context it was noted

> Quantitative goals were considered advantageous in that they made the Plan more tangible, making it easier to monitor its implementation and to evaluate its impact. On the other hand, social exclusion is a multi-dimensional cumulative phenomenon and therefore difficult to reduce to specific targets. [...] The value of quantitative targets is linked to whether the selected indicators measure the right things and how reliable they are. [...] fixed-term targets (both qualitative

and quantitative) were proposed, to be revised at regular intervals. (Government of Finland, 2003, page 17)

The Finnish plan itself then sets out national objectives across a range of areas, mostly relating to direction of change or broad goal – reduce need for income support, reduce poverty among families with children and prevent inheritance of social exclusion, reduce long-term unemployment, reduce differences in health between population groups, improve availability and quality of services.

The NAP/inclusion for Germany provides another example, using the Laeken Indicators as the framework to describe trends and identify vulnerable groups as other Member States do but not specifying quantitative targets, either for these or national indicators (again with the exception of the employment rate for women). Instead, broad political goals are set out:

• securing social equilibrium, improving capabilities;
• organising the participation of people, preventing poverty and social exclusion;
• strengthening responsibility and activating existing potentials; and
• making social security poverty-proof.

The French NAP/inclusion states that priority is to be given to:

• restoring independence and dignity for the most vulnerable;
• striking the right balance between protection and empowerment;
• reactivating integration and access to economic activity; and
• promoting local initiatives and solidarity.

In a wide variety of areas, aims, strategies and new initiatives under the National Plan are described.

The NAP/inclusion for Italy sets out three main objectives in the fight against extreme poverty: to reduce the number of people living in conditions of extreme poverty; to increase local services for people living in extreme poverty, and to make the homeless "socially visible". The quantified targets relate solely to the employment rate.

It is worth noting that assigning a limited role to target setting does not necessarily reflect a lack of focus on quantifying outcomes. The French NAP/inclusion, for example, devotes particular effort to carefully specifying indicators used in tracking progress across different areas, and the Scandinavian countries and Germany provide other examples of countries that place considerable emphasis on quantitative indicators of progress and change. Indeed, some of the countries assigning a prominent role to targets are in a relatively weak position with respect to the depth and comprehensiveness of indicators available. The wide variation across countries in the role assigned to targets to date appears to reflect differing attitudes to the value and appropriate use of public pre-commitment to goals specified in terms of outcome indicators, rather than to the use of such indicators *per se*.

Targets in the 2004 NAPs/inclusion in the "new" Member States

The countries that joined the EU in 2004 drew up NAPs/inclusion for the period 2004–6, following the aforementioned "Common Outline" put forward by the SPC and the Commission (Social Protection Committee, 2003b), and we now look at the stance they adopted to target setting. Overall, we can see a similar spectrum to that described in relation to the EU-15, with those giving prominence to quantified targets for key outcomes towards one end, and those emphasising broad objectives and policy measures towards the other (see Box 6.2, drawn from European Commission, 2005c). Most of the new Member States are closer to the latter, but there are a number of exceptions, and targets framed in terms of the Laeken indicators themselves are actually more common than in the EU-15.

The NAP/inclusion for Estonia, for example, presents long-term objectives framed in broad terms – e.g. achieving the highest possible employment rate for the working-age population, preventing long-term unemployment – but also some quantified targets for 2006, when the current plan ends. These include not only targets for employment rates but also for the Laeken at-risk-of-poverty indicator – that no more than 15% fall below the relative poverty line (compared with 18% in 2003), and that the number of children below the relative poverty line be reduced by 2% compared with 2003. Other quantified outcome targets include school completion and life expectancy, while there are also targets set for social protection levels.

Box 6.2: Use of quantified targets in the NAPs/inclusion in the 10 "new" Member States

| Country | Direct outcome targets | | | | | |
	Income/ deprivation	Long-term unemployment/ employment of vulnerable groups	Education	Health	Direct outcome targets	Input targets
Cyprus						
Czech Republic					*	
Estonia	*	*	*	*	*	*
Hungary		*	*	*	*	*
Latvia					*	*
Lithuania	*	*			*	*
Malta		*	*		*	
Poland	*	*	*	*	*	*
Slovak Republic					*	*
Slovenia		*	*		*	*

Source: European Commission, 2005c, page 37

Poland's NAP/inclusion sets out a long list of objectives for the desired direction of change in key indicators, such as increasing the number of children participating in pre-school education, promoting tertiary education and adjusting it to the demands of the labour market, radically reducing extreme poverty, limiting long-term unemployment, extending average healthy life expectancy, and so on. Underpinning these are specific targets set out in the National Social Inclusion Strategy (NSIS) (also presented in Annex 2 of Poland's NAP/inclusion). For all these, the concrete indicator against which progress is to be made is specified; some examples being raising the percentage of youth in the relevant cohort in tertiary education to 60%, reducing the long-term unemployment rate to 5%, extending healthy life expectancy to the average level for EU countries, reducing the share of the population living below the subsistence minimum to 5%, and having the Gini coefficient no higher than the average level for EU countries.

The plan for Lithuania sets out a lengthy list of broad objectives, such as upgrading the labour market, expanding public health care, and so on, but some outcome targets are included, notably reducing the relative poverty rate of the poorest population groups by five to ten percentage points by 2010 and eliminating "extreme poverty" – "Anyone short of food, shelter or warm clothes will be provided with these prerequisite means" (Government of Lithuania, 2004, page 24). (Neither of these targets is entirely transparent, in that it is not clear exactly what is intended in the first case nor how the relevant outcomes are to be measured in the second.) Other targets include increasing employment and reducing the duration of unemployment, reducing school dropout, and increasing life expectancy.

In the case of Latvia, on the other hand, a very extensive list of long-term objectives is presented across various areas, and for each specific indicators are noted which will be used to measure progress. On these indicators, sometimes a specific target is given, but more often a desired direction of change is simply stated; indeed, sometimes just the indicator is specified and the desired direction of change is left implicit. The plan for Slovenia identifies target groups and key challenges and objectives in various areas, but includes only a few specific outcome targets to be achieved by 2006, in the employment and education fields. In other areas most of the objectives are set out in very broad terms, such as reducing dependence on social transfers or easing access to health services for people with the lowest incomes. The Slovakian plan sets out for each area a list of target groups, targets, and indicators, but those targets are broad rather than specific and generally not quantified except in the employment area.

The Hungarian plan sets out a detailed list of targets in different areas, including not only employment but also increasing life expectancy and school completion. As far as poverty and social exclusion are concerned, though, most of the targets are either broad or relate to policy interventions – for example, revising and modernising social legislation, designing a social minimum and introducing general subsistence benefit, or improving the situation and life chances of children living in deep poverty by expanding benefits in kind and in cash. (Exceptions are reducing the number of homeless persons living on the street and reducing the dropout rate of young people from vocational training schools by 15%, and there are also some quantified output targets in the health area.)

The plan for the Czech Republic sets out key challenges – for example, to respond to on-going structural change and its repercussions on the labour market, to support the long-term unemployed in seeking employment, to address disadvantage in education for groups at risk of social exclusion, to adapt the social protection and health care systems, and to improve access to affordable good quality housing – but not time-bound quantitative targets for outcomes in these areas.

The plan for Malta identifies a set of 12 "Key Priorities", and gives key data relating to each, but specifies quantified targets for education and employment. The NAP/inclusion for Cyprus does not set any targets, but does present a rationale for the approach taken: "Setting targets, at this point in time, would be premature (and possibly counter-productive), since Cyprus is at the stage of first production and evaluation of the statistical information. Given the lack of experience in the use of indicators, it is not known at which level of *effort* a particular *outcome* target corresponds to. An important point of the process which will take place within Cypriot society, during the period of execution of the NAP/inclusion, is the analysis, public discussion (with the involvement of all the players concerned) and finally, the adoption of a cohesive, ambitious and realistic set of targets for 2010." (Government of Cyprus, 2004, page 23). However, the following year, having had time to reflect more on the issue and with new up-to-date data becoming available, Cyprus reviewed its NAP/inclusion and introduced a number of important quantified targets.

6.3 Key issues in setting national targets

We have seen that there was wide variation across the EU-15 Member States in their approaches to setting targets in their 2003 NAPs/inclusion. To some extent, this is not surprising, in view of the diversity across Member States in the extent and nature of poverty and social exclusion. Account has also to be taken of the diversity of institutional structures, particularly regarding multi-level Governments. Nonetheless, having said that, and acknowledging the role assigned to targets by some of the new Member States in particular, one can only characterise as "disappointing" the overall response of Member States to the Barcelona European Council's invitation to set targets. This is the case across a range of dimensions, and it is worth considering these in some detail, with the approach suggested in the aforementioned Common Outline for the NAPs/inclusion as a useful point of reference.

First and foremost, most countries did not set what could reasonably be construed as targets "for significantly reducing the number of people at risk of poverty and social exclusion by 2010" (Presidency Conclusions, March 2002 Barcelona European Council), although a minority did so. Others either set out poverty objectives and priorities in a general, unquantified way or specified quantitative targets that related either to policy inputs rather than outputs, or mostly to very specific rather than high-level outcomes. The Barcelona invitation to set targets flows directly from the Lisbon goal of making a decisive impact on the eradication of poverty and social exclusion by 2010, and has to be seen in the light of that concrete goal rather than in the abstract. This "decisive impact by 2010", the need for which was explicitly recalled by EU leaders at their March 2006 European Council, has to be measurable and demonstrable to the citizens of the Union. By setting targets for 2010 that relate to high-level broad indicators of poverty risk and social exclusion, a Member State *inter alia* sets out a standard against which success or failure could be measured for the country in question. In the absence of such national targets, other benchmarks against which to assess the Lisbon agenda will be required. (Even a comprehensive set of national targets framed without reference to each other would not be the only point of reference in assessing whether the Lisbon goal has been reached, but such a set would play a central role.)

The core role envisaged for targets goes beyond this, to playing a key role in the development of the anti-poverty strategies themselves (see below). Setting targets is intended to serve as a spur to the development and implementation of strategies for attaining them. Tight linkage and coherence between targets and strategy is critical if targets are to be more than simply a statement of intent. Here again, this was followed through to a limited extent even in those Member States that did set out high-level targets in their NAPs/inclusion. For the most part one does not get a clear sense of exactly how the stated goals are to be achieved: both broad approaches and detailed policies are often described, but the linkage between those and the achievement of the quantitative outcome targets is left open. Filling in this gap is clearly a very real challenge, not least in analytical terms as we discussed in Chapter 4, but it represents a fundamental part of the development and implementation of national (including sub-national) social inclusion strategies.

Another issue about the way targets are framed relates to the time-period involved. The Barcelona Summit referred specifically to targets for 2010, consistent with the Lisbon agenda, but Member States more commonly set targets for the period of the current National Action Plan. Clearly both are needed: one would want to see high-level targets for 2010, together with shorter-term targets for intervening points to allow progress towards the longer-term goal to be monitored. It is also worth highlighting that a small number of headline targets may be much more effective as a motivating and mobilising device than a large undifferentiated set including both very specific and very broad targets. The headline set might well be accompanied by a series of more detailed targets, but they should be clearly distinguished.

Similarly, a clear distinction needs to be drawn between outcome and input targets, currently often presented together without differentiation. The role of indicators relating to policy effort and inputs versus outcomes has already been discussed in Chapter 4, but here we wish to draw out the implications for target setting. Member States may well differ in their choice of methods by which common objectives are to be realised, and a primary focus on outcomes in framing targets is consistent with the core principle of subsidiarity. Targeting outcomes means that Member States, in reporting on policy, are encouraged to relate those interventions to the desired/planned impact on outcomes, rather than simply present a catalogue of policy measures, as is often the temptation for Governments. One of course also wants to know about the impact of specific policy interventions on the outcomes of interest, something that by its nature is often difficult to assess. However, with targets focused on key outcomes, input and impact-related indicators can then help countries to learn from each other about what efficiently works in improving those outcomes. They play their appropriate role, as means to an end, rather than as they are so often presented, as if they were ends in themselves.

Ambitious and achievable targets

General principles regarding the best way to frame targets also need to be given more prominence, as experience to date shows that they are often not fully reflected in the targets adopted. As well as being quantified, measurable and time specific, targets should be ambitious *and* achievable. This poses a real dilemma because it may be difficult, in the current state of knowledge, to actually decide what is realistic. However, the Open Method of Coordination focuses attention *inter alia* on cross-country comparisons, and the best-performing countries in particular domains serve to demonstrate what can be achieved. Initial conditions in each Member State and national institutional structures are, of course, extremely important, and long-term underlying societal trends such as demographic shifts and the reduction of the share of the population engaged in agriculture affect income inequality differentially in different countries. One needs to separate out the elements due to policy choice and design. As discussed in Chapter 4, there exist methods for this purpose. Analytical tools such as tax-benefit simulation can help in projecting forward benchmark scenarios against which the level of ambition of targets can be assessed. Significant scientific work is required in this complex area, and researchers have a major contribution to make in deepening the information base for decision makers.

The problem of linking targets and policy is a major reason why Member States have made relatively little use of the commonly agreed social inclusion indicators in framing targets. Although the Common Outline suggested that this would be preferable where possible, the use of the common indicators in framing targets in the NAPs/inclusion was in fact very limited, with the notable exception of some of the new Member States. Clearly there were – and still are – areas not currently covered by these indicators, such as housing and homelessness, which some Member States wished to highlight. Even if the scope of the common indicators is extended (see Chapter 5), there will remain areas where national measures represent the only option, but where possible use of the common indicators would be very helpful for the process as a whole. It is worth considering why this has not been the common practice to date. A number of factors may be at work. One reason is that some Member States may be more comfortable with targets framed in terms of outcomes that are domestically the focus of long-standing attention, whereas the common indicators may not be as familiar. National indicators may have a specific meaning in the Member State. The most important reason, though, may be that Governments are not confident that they have the policy levers to achieve targets framed in terms of the common indicators. How confident can they be, for example, that a stated reduction in the numbers below relative income thresholds or in income inequality is achievable and likely to be produced by implementing a specific strategy of policies? And what about other factors influencing the outcome that may develop adversely and make the target more difficult to reach? The perceived absence of clear linkages between domestic policies and the common indicators, and the uncertainty about the determinants of those outcomes, may thus be the greatest obstacles to the adoption of targets framed in terms of those indicators.

Policy making is always surrounded by uncertainty, and there is much scientific work to be done to assist policy makers, but it must be emphasised that this holds true in other areas where target setting has nonetheless been widely adopted. In the labour market area, for example, Governments have adopted targets for reducing unemployment and increasing employment without being entirely sure in advance how those targets are to be met. Setting a target is not a guarantee; it is a statement of the importance attached to the outcome in question and a commitment to implementing policies that have a serious chance of producing the desired outcomes. It is difficult to see how National Action Plans can be effective without stating at the outset what they aim to achieve, in terms of a limited set of key objectives and headline targets. While it is not imperative that these be framed in terms of the common indicators, it is essential – if mutual learning and peer review are to be meaningful – that at a minimum the *links* be made between these headline targets and the common indicators. To take one example, if a Member State sets a target for the numbers falling below a nationally defined income threshold, the likely implications for numbers at risk of poverty according to the commonly agreed definition in the Laeken indicators should also be brought out. In effect, the implied targets framed in terms of the common indicators should be spelt out quantitatively where possible, or if this is not possible they should at least be discussed in a qualitative way.

In our view, whether targets are framed in terms of national or commonly defined indicators is not the critical issue at this point in the evolution of the process. What matters most at this stage is that key outcomes are the focus for monitoring progress and setting targets. Ensuring that the relationship between inputs and outputs is put in proper perspective, moving away from a focus purely on inputs and actions, is the essential step. We need feasible action plans for attaining the desired targets. It would then certainly be helpful for those key outcomes to be based on common indicators or at least linked to common indicators, but bringing about the shift in focus is the critical advance.

The focus of our discussion to this point has mostly been on national rather than EU-wide targets (whereas EU-wide targets are at the centre of the Employment Strategy). The next step in our view is that there should be EU-wide targets set in terms of the agreed common indicators. We discuss in the next Section how such EU-wide targets might be framed, suggesting in particular that the approach adopted in the European Employment Strategy – of specifying a common level on a specific indicator that each country should seek to reach – may not be the best approach.

6.4 Framing EU-wide targets

In its Communication to the Spring European Council in Barcelona, the European Commission proposed that the European Council should set the target of halving the EU-wide risk-of-poverty rate from 18% to 9% by 2010 (2002c, page 16). While this proposal was not accepted, the setting of EU-wide targets is likely to remain on the agenda as an idea. Indeed the December 2005 Commission's Communication on Sustainable Development specifically raises this issue (European Commission, 2005k). It is therefore important to ask – before there is any serious attempt to garner political support – what would be involved in such an EU-wide target. Would it be a sensible and productive approach? Can we learn from the example provided by the European Employment Strategy? (The Employment Strategy has *inter alia* established the goal of having at work 70% of the population of working age in each Member State by 2010.)

The crucial prior question is, of course, whether EU targets in the area of social inclusion would actually be a good idea: what would they add to national targets? We see two distinct and substantial arguments in favour. The first is that adoption of such targets would highlight that promoting social inclusion is a key aim of the European Union itself. This could have a significant impact on the perception of the EU by its citizens, and assist in ensuring that social objectives are accorded due weight vis-à-vis economic and employment policy as the EU evolves. (We have seen in this respect the political saliency of the EU employment target.) The second is that Member States might well find it helpful in framing national targets and policies to have a broader frame of reference than the purely domestic one. Again the experience of the Employment Strategy suggests that a common framework for target-setting and policy review has helped Member States to make progress domestically. It may well be that a more ambitious approach, in terms of setting out what can and should be achieved, is encouraged by operating within such a common and comparative framework.

On the other hand, the introduction of EU-wide targets may be counter-productive. It makes no sense to proclaim targets where there is no realistic prospect that they are achievable. Targets can only play the roles described above if they are realistic. This brings us back to the crucial role of policy analysis (see

Chapter 4). In order to establish whether targets are achievable, we need a demonstration of feasible policies to bring about the desired outcomes.

This in turn depends on how the EU targets are formulated. We illustrate the general issues by considering a particular dimension/indicator: the risk of poverty. There are a number of possible forms that a European target for this indicator could take, including:

1. a common target for all Member States (e.g. poverty risk down to x% in all countries), as with the Employment Strategy;
2. an overall target for the European Union, set in terms of the poverty rate for the EU as a whole (the proportion of the total EU population at risk of poverty);
3. different targets for each Member State, scaling poverty risk down to zero;
4. Member States asked to emulate the best performing Member States.

A common target would seem unrealistic given the existing wide differences in performance. Currently available figures for the EU show the percentage falling below the 60% of national median income threshold varying from high single figures up to over 20%. A common poverty target would be very challenging for some Member States and irrelevant for others. An EU-wide target, on the other hand, would in effect mean the largest Member States taking responsibility. As we have seen in Chapter 3, there is considerable concentration of the at-risk population. Put differently, a situation in which a small country had a risk-of-poverty rate of 50% might make little difference to the EU-wide statistic but be incompatible with European social cohesion. The third method takes account of the existing differences. It would require say that a risk-of-poverty rate of 21% be reduced to 15% and one of 7% reduced to 5%. But in the latter case the required reduction might be small in relation to the measurement error, and there seems then a case for a target of the fourth kind, which also seems in the spirit of the OMC. Member States would be set the target of closing the gap on, say, the best three performing countries. Such a criterion should be seen, not as a ranking exercise, but as an application of peer review. The UK Department for Work and Pensions refers in a footnote to such an approach in its report on child poverty:

> Possible ways to define being "among the best in Europe" could include: having a relative child poverty rate no higher than the average of the best three countries in Europe; having a relative poverty rate no higher than the average of the best four countries in Europe; and, having a relative child poverty rate that was within 2 percentage points of the average of the best three countries in Europe. Achieving any of these on current definitions would mean having a poverty rate between that of Sweden and Denmark. (UK Department for Work and Pensions, 2003, footnote 22)

Does this mean that the three best performing Member States in terms of poverty risk can rest on their laurels? This would only be the case if they were also the best three performers on all other dimensions. (Even then, depending on the level of their performances, they should be encouraged to either remain (within a certain range) at the already achieved level or improve further.) As we have seen in Chapter 3, the rankings of Member States differ across indicators. Nearly half (12) of the EU-25 countries are in the top four on one of the four indicators considered there (see Figure 3.11 and Box 3.2). Social inclusion is inherently multi-dimensional, and that is precisely why a set of indicators seeking to capture key aspects was recommended by the SPC and adopted by the Laeken European Council. Having explicitly recognised this central characteristic in agreeing indicators, it would be inconsistent to now seek to focus target setting on one indicator, however important. Instead, following through on the approach adopted so far would point towards encouraging Member States to set targets across the dimensions. This would face Member States with complex and inter-related challenges but allow real progress to be registered in the different dimensions of social exclusion. Once again, rather than thinking in terms of targets representing a common level for an indicator across the Member States, it may be best to seek to emulate the best performing countries (an approach adopted in a few cases in the 2003/2004 NAPs/inclusion). Where appropriate, national targets may also then be translated into regional or local targets.

6.5 Embedding the Social Inclusion Process in domestic policies

So far in this Chapter, we have concentrated on the EU Social Inclusion Process and the interaction with Member States. We turn the spotlight now on deepening the Process within Member States, and ask how progress could be made towards better anchoring the process in domestic policies. We have identified a number of the key elements – diagnosis, policy evaluation, and definition of outcome indicators – and we want to suggest how these can be employed to aid the implementation of effective national and sub-national strategies to combat poverty and social exclusion.

Ireland was the first Member State to adopt a national poverty reduction target. It did so in the context of its *National Anti-Poverty Strategy*, which was launched in 1997 (following on from the 1995 United Nations Social Summit in Copenhagen) and thus pre-dated the EU Social Inclusion Process. The way Ireland handled the EU process, a few years later, is therefore informative. The aim of the Irish National Anti-Poverty Strategy was to provide a framework for the efforts of various Government departments and agencies and for non-governmental actors. Based on a stated understanding of the key causes of poverty and social exclusion, and an explicit definition of poverty, the Strategy set out both a global poverty reduction target and five sub-targets. The revision of the Irish Strategy was only due for completion in February 2002, i.e. several months after the deadline for submission to the Commission of the first (EU) NAPs/ inclusion.

It is with this specific social reporting history in mind that we should interpret a recommendation which the Irish National Economic and Social Council, composed of representatives of Government and the Social Partners, made in a report issued in March 2003:

> The National Anti-Poverty Strategy should be aligned fully with the EU NAPs/inclusion and should be included in the Open Method of Coordination developing across the EU. As in other areas, there is good evidence that policies for tackling social exclusion in Ireland will benefit from the discipline and systematic comparison involved in participating in peer review at the EU level. It should be a once-off and not insurmountable challenge to subsume the timetable and review procedures of [the National Anti-Poverty Strategy] within those that have been adopted at the EU level for the NAPs/inclusion. (Irish National Economic and Social Council, 2003, page 355)

This illustrates the added value which the Social Inclusion Process can have for domestic policies, and in fact does have in various countries. In this (potential) added value we also include the progress made by the new Member States before their accession, in the context of the *Joint Memoranda on Social Inclusion* exercise. Thanks to this bilateral cooperation process (Commission/individual country) already launched in 2002, the new Member States were able to submit their first NAPs/inclusion, and thus to fully participate in the Social Inclusion Process, only a couple of months after their accession. In this Chapter, we do not try to assess the impact that the Social Inclusion Process has actually had on Member States' national policies (on this, see Section 2.5). Our objective here is rather to put forward some practical suggestions on ways of helping to embed the Social Inclusion Process in domestic policy making, so that policies can benefit more substantially from its (potential) input.

In our view, NAPs/inclusion have a *pivotal role* to play in anchoring the Social Inclusion Process in national and sub-national policies. It is only if NAPs/inclusion truly become instruments for furthering both the domestic and EU policy debate that the Social Inclusion Process can attain a credible and meaningful status. *In turn*, if the EU process gets this status both politically and popularly, and, as a result, becomes increasingly visible, then countries will more likely feel that they will be held to account for achieving the common objectives set for the EU as a whole.

6.6 The pivotal role of *restructured* NAPs/inclusion

The key role played by the NAPs/inclusion in anchoring the Social Inclusion Process in Member States' policies should be maintained under the new arrangements which emphasise their distinct *identity* within the new streamlined Social Protection and Social Inclusion Process that has been launched in 2006. In line with the agreed streamlining, the first National Reports, to be submitted to the Commission in September 2006 will be on a two yearly basis (2006–8). They will then subsequently be on a three-yearly cycle to bring them into line with the revised Lisbon process on jobs and growth. The future NAPs/inclusion, as one distinct element of the National Reports, will thus follow the same time-scale. (See Chapter 2 for a more detailed discussion.)

For NAPs/inclusion to play this central role, it is however essential that Member States no longer consider them essentially as a "reporting" exercise, mainly aimed at providing information to other Member States and the EU, but rather as a strategic planning exercise the goal of which is to actually develop an "action plan". The NAPs/inclusion should not simply be catalogues of major and minor policy measures having some link with fighting poverty and social exclusion, as is often the temptation for Governments. The proper starting point is a diagnosis of the underlying causes of poverty and social exclusion (also supported by evidence about poverty and social exclusion dynamics; see Section 5.3). From this, one can develop an understanding of the potential policy responses, and the linkages between policies and outcomes. As we have seen in Chapter 4, there is at present a lack of penetrating policy analysis in both the NAPs/inclusion and their analyses by the Commission and Member States. There are tools that can be employed – such as the complementary model families analysis and micro-simulation modelling – and, while these have limitations, they offer the prospect of a first step in a systematic process of policy analysis.

It is encouraging that the 2006–8 NAPs/inclusion will be revised in both content and structure. The new arrangements agreed between Member States and the European Commission (Social Protection Committee, 2006) emphasise that in order to be more concrete and to develop into "action plans" the NAPs/inclusion should in future be strictly *objective-driven*. As we argued in our original report to the 2005 EU Luxembourg Presidency Conference, future NAPs/inclusion should concentrate on a carefully selected *shortlist* of key national policy objectives, expressed in terms of social outcomes (for the reasons already explained) and framed according to the relevant common objectives. In this highly focused framework, NAPs/inclusion should then solely consider those policy measures aimed at realising the short-listed national priorities, while keeping in mind the need to address all the relevant policy domains in deciding on the measures to be implemented. The selection of policy measures should systematically be based on *ex ante* impact assessments (as discussed in Chapter 4). Countries would therefore need to develop their own social inclusion monitoring framework, responding to their national specificities, and including targets and indicators built on reliable and timely data. This national framework should allow clear links with the general EU framework (in particular, the Laeken indicators and the Laeken methodological framework – even more so, since this framework has been usefully revisited as a result of streamlining; see Chapter 2) and with the national frameworks of the other Member States (along the lines suggested in Figure 2.1). For this, countries would also need to build the required statistical and analytical capacity.

Once these policy measures are adopted, *headline* outcome targets should be set, with the number of such targets having to be small for them to make a political impact; they need to represent concrete statements of purpose and to contribute to awareness raising. As appropriate, headline targets should be complemented by more *detailed* targets covering very specific aspects, and by *intermediate* targets for the time-span of the measures (to allow progress from one NAP/inclusion to the next to be assessed and to serve policy planning purposes); they could also usefully be linked to relevant input targets. All those outcome targets (and possible related input targets) should be linked to concrete indicators for monitoring progress towards achieving them; some (not necessarily all) targets should ideally be framed in terms of the Laeken indicators. The changes that we proposed in our original report for the format of the NAPs/inclusion are essentially the same as what has now been agreed by the Commission and Member States in the new Guidelines for preparing the 2006–8 NAPs/inclusion (Social Protection Committee, 2006).

For these changes to happen strategies put in place by countries will need to be broad. As much as possible, they should follow a multi-dimensional approach cutting across and integrating a range of policy domains, calling for *joined-up Government* (see Section 6.7) as well as the *active participation* of all the relevant actors and bodies (see Section 6.8). There has to be widespread "ownership" of the Social Inclusion Process.

We can summarise the above by stating that the *restructured* NAPs/inclusion should follow a focused, targeted and monitored approach, based on what ought to become a "logical flow" (see Figure 6.1; see also Figure 2.1).

Moving from the previous to the new NAPs/inclusion clearly represents a challenging task for Member States. Countries are being asked to *combine a multi-dimensional with a focused approach*, in order to create a number of truly *integrated strategies*. For this, using the common objectives as their analytical framework, they have to carry out a thorough multi-dimensional analysis of the national situation with regard to poverty and social exclusion across all important areas. On the basis of this analysis, they should then identify (and "justify") a shortlist of three or four key national policy objectives for the period 2006–8. Finally, for each key national objective, they will have to develop an integrated strategy, looking explicitly at how each main policy domain can best contribute to addressing it and how the different policy areas can mutually reinforce each other. As we have already discussed, academic research can play an important role, particularly in the diagnosis of the causes of social exclusion and the analysis of the impact of policies on outcomes.

Figure 6.1: Restructured NAPs/inclusion – a focused, targeted and monitored approach

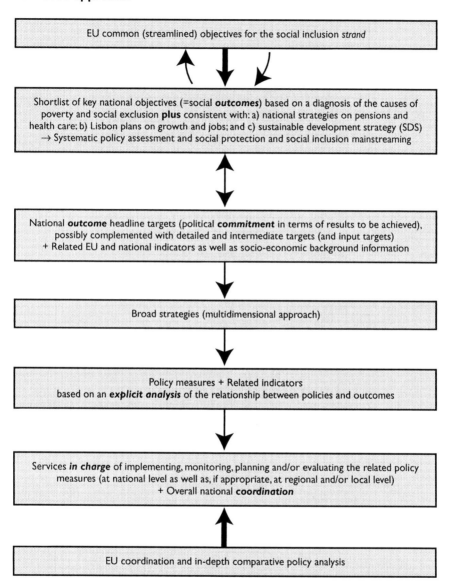

Reviewing the NAPs/inclusion

Re-focusing fundamentally NAPs/inclusion and then maintaining them under the streamlined process after 2006 will only prove to have been sensible if NAPs/inclusion are properly reviewed in future. The method used for the preparation of the 2001 and 2003 (EU-15) Joint Reports on Social Inclusion, whereby the first draft report is produced by the Commission and then finalised between the Commission and the Council, should, we think, also be used for the analysis of future NAPs/inclusion. (This same method is used for the preparation of the Joint Employment Reports.) It should be noted that the draft Joint Report is produced by the Commission and then published as a Commission's Communication in the form of a "Draft Joint Report". This way of analysing national contributions is indeed the critical element of the Social Inclusion Process in that it builds on all the components of the Open Method of Coordination: the EU common objectives, the common indicators, the peer reviews and the exchange of experiences and good (and bad) practices.

The final aim of the OMC is to improve performance by all Member States and, ideally, bring them all to a high level. To achieve this, hard-headed analysis is necessary. The European Commission, as the independent EU body, can and must play a central role in conducting such a critical evaluation. Together with the EU Social Protection Committee, it has to be the *driving force* of the Social Inclusion Process, and more generally of the whole open coordination in the social field. The Commission has a number of instruments at its disposal: the peer review process, specialist studies, and the EU documents summarising NAPs/inclusion. The last of these, whether "Joint Reports" *per se* or "Commission Staff Working Papers" (see Chapter 2), can be really useful *only* if they go beyond simple, purely descriptive reporting.

In the European Employment Strategy, country-specific recommendations may be issued upon a proposal by the Commission on the basis of the Joint Employment Report. This is a major difference with the EU Social Inclusion Process where, at the moment, this possibility does not exist. In our view, the time is now ripe to give the Commission the same possibility in the EU Social Inclusion Process, which could be seen in the context of the renewed Sustainable Development Strategy. Once it has assessed the individual NAPs/inclusion, the Commission should then have the power to make recommendations to Member States. This would give something very concrete for national and sub-national policy makers to focus on, and for the Commission to monitor. For the same reason, we believe that the "implementation reports" on the NAPs/inclusion (see Chapter 2, Section 2.5), in which countries are to explain how they have actually implemented the objectives they established in their NAPs/inclusion, are extremely useful as explicit requirements for Member States in relation to evaluation, monitoring and reporting. Also the fact that Member States are specifically being asked in their new (2006–8) NAPs/inclusion to say how they will monitor each objective and which indicators they will use for assessing progress (Social Protection Committee, 2006) should lead to a more analytical approach in future Implementation Reports. In addition, the Commission's monitoring role is essential here to ensure the ambition of the process. But in order for the Commission to carry out this function, it needs the necessary analytical capacity. The research already underway in collaboration with the OECD is an important building block (see Chapter 4), and it would be desirable if the techniques of comparison being developed could be applied to the review of the implementation of the NAPs/inclusion. The potential role of an EU-wide micro-simulation model in the evaluation of the NAPs/inclusion was discussed in Chapter 4 (see also Atkinson, 2002).

EU documents summarising NAPs/inclusion may then be seen as providing a framework within which other actions may unfold: the analysis and monitoring of the impact of different policies, as well as the structured exchange of information, experiences and practices, which can evolve semi-spontaneously as the Open Method of Coordination matures.

As mentioned in Section 2.3, an important aim of the 2002-2006 "Programme of Community action to encourage cooperation between Member States to combat social exclusion" is to boost the exchange of experiences and practices. In this context, the Commission launched a peer review programme specifically focused on this aspect of the process. Contrary to the "general peer review" of NAPs/inclusion, organised jointly between the Commission and the Social Protection Committee (and already referred to several times in this book), each of these "good practice peer reviews" is hosted by the Member State that submits the practice for review. These highly targeted reviews, which therefore aim at supplementing the general ones, are carried out by a group of decision makers from peer countries, European Commission representatives, independent experts and stakeholders' representatives – who all share a special interest in the experience and transfer of the policy. They are intended to assess whether and how each reviewed policy, regarded as a good practice in a given Member State, can effectively be transferred to other Member States. For this reason, they are expected to be based on existing evaluation or early monitoring data even though, in the practices selected so far, this crucial assessment/monitoring aspect may not always have sufficiently been present.[2]

To date, when people have considered the exchange of practices, they have tended to have in mind policies rather than institutional or process issues (though this is not the case in the "transnational exchange projects"). In our view, however, practices in terms of processes are at least as important and should therefore be more systematically identified, especially in the areas of social policy monitoring and statistical capacity building.[3] It should be noted that specific national characteristics, and therefore also related subsidiarity issues, are likely to be much less of an issue for these practices than for actual policies; the "transferability" of these practices among countries could then be greater than that of specific policies. Some of the 31 projects of the current Transnational Exchange Programme[4] deal with process rather than specific policy areas. For example the Irish Combat Poverty Agency-led project (Combat Poverty Agency, 2006) has examined approaches to mainstreaming social inclusion in national policy making, and the project led by the UK University of Warwick has looked at the role of local authorities and social inclusion and how to develop local anti-poverty strategies. Some of the aforementioned "good practice peer reviews" have also addressed process issues at local level, which include an examination of the question of the mobilisation of all relevant stakeholders and public authorities to tackle poverty and social exclusion.

6.7 Working towards more *joined-up* Government

As already emphasised, combating poverty and social exclusion in its multi-dimensionality requires coordinated actions between various agencies of the national Government as well as, depending on national institutional arrangements, various agencies of the sub-national Governments. All the social inclusion policies indeed potentially involve joint action by different agencies. NAPs/inclusion provide therefore a unique opportunity for all levels of Government to come to a shared focus on social inclusion, and to work together on setting shared outcome targets and developing related successful anti-poverty and social exclusion strategies; the Open Method of Coordination is thus to be seen as a means to promote coordination not just *across* Member States but also *within* individual countries, across different Government departments and between national and sub-national Governments. The EU choice to primarily focus on social outcomes rather than the means and financial resources by which they are achieved should ease the required cooperative attitude between the various bodies that have competence in these areas.

The extent of devolution of responsibility from the national to regional and/or local Governments varies across Member States, but the NAP/inclusion, together with its targets and indicators, provides a focus for all levels of Government. When Member States are setting national targets, it is to be hoped that lower-level Governments will be involved in the definition of these targets and in the related monitoring of the sub-national performance. This is especially important where responsibility for provision of services etc. is being devolved to the sub-national level, where it is essential to monitor that this does not lead to new inequalities. Indeed in these situations it may well make sense to develop Regional Action Plans and/or Local Action Plans on social inclusion with their own objectives and targets. These Plans should be closely linked with Regional or Local Development Plans. They should also be carefully interconnected with the overall National Action Plans so as to directly contribute to achieving the country's overall objectives for social inclusion.

There are two particular arguments for developing Regional or Local Action Plans within the context of the NAPs/inclusion. The first is that in Member States the policy responsibility in many of the policy domains that are key to promoting greater social inclusion lies at the regional or local level. The second is that even where policy responsibility remains at national level the responsibility for delivery of policies rests with regional or local levels of Government. Furthermore, effective delivery of policies to promote social inclusion, particularly if they are to reach those who are most vulnerable, needs to be coordinated and accessible at a very local level. Indeed the lack of such local coordination may have been an important factor in the implementation gap in the delivery of the

Social Inclusion Process to date. There is a growing body of experience and good practice on the development of regional and local plans within the Social Inclusion Process that should provide a good basis for further development in this area. For instance, Spain has already given a high priority to the development of regional action plans within its NAPs/inclusion and several of the Transnational Exchange Projects and Peer Reviews under the Community action programme on social exclusion (see above) have addressed the question of regional/local action plans.

Streamlining makes joined-up Government even more important, and a key objective of integrating NAPs/inclusion with domestic policy formation should be to ensure that a concern with poverty and social exclusion is *mainstreamed* into all policy areas – that every agency, belonging to the different levels of Governments, should be required to make tackling/preventing poverty and social exclusion a core objective built into its annual work programmes and possible strategic plans (see below). In line with the approach agreed in Lisbon, it is essential in particular that Member States coordinate the preparation of the NAPs/inclusion and NAPs/employment, so that each reinforces and complements the other. To the extent possible, Member States should also indicate what budgetary resources are being committed to each major policy measure adopted in the context of the NAPs/inclusion and any additional resources that might be committed over the period covered by the NAPs/inclusion; in doing this, they should also specify the contribution of EU Structural Funds, especially the European Social Fund, whose potential in the fight against poverty and social exclusion should be exploited to the full. It is significant that Member States are encouraged to do this in the Guidelines for the 2006–8 NAPs/inclusion (Social Protection Committee, 2006). The targets set in the NAPs/inclusion "need to be borne more in mind by Member States when setting overall expenditure priorities, including the expenditure of Structural Funds. And more needs to be done to ensure that economic, employment and social policies are *mutually reinforcing*" (European Commission, 2004c, page 19). This thus "operationalises" the intention behind the third streamlined common objective for the social inclusion strand (see Appendix 2b), which asks Member States to ensure "that social inclusion policies are well-coordinated and involve all levels of Government and relevant actors, including people experiencing poverty, that they are efficient and effective and mainstreamed into all relevant public policies, including economic, budgetary, education and training policies and structural fund (notably ESF) programmes". It is essential to see Government policy as a whole. The overall impact of the Government budget, for example, has to take account of the interaction between different policy measures.

To help anchor the Social Inclusion Process firmly in domestic policy making, countries should aim at building the objectives and targets contained in their NAPs/inclusion into other core policy Government's documents such as national development plans, Government programmes or Structural Funds Plans.

Implementing this in a coordinated manner requires a strong, committed political leadership at the national and sub-national levels. Political responsibility for the NAP/inclusion should, we believe, be assigned to a single Minister whose activities in the context of the plan would benefit from being supported by an inter-ministerial committee; this committee should consist of Ministers coming from all the relevant levels of Governments. Ideally, the committee would be chaired by the Prime Minister, who could more easily give overall political direction to the process. Political leadership at EU level would also be necessary. In our view, for instance, the Commissioner in charge at the European Commission should regularly discuss at the Council the implementation of the Social Inclusion Process; not only with the social affairs Ministers of the different Member States, but also with both Ministers responsible for Employment and Finance Ministers. And at their annual Spring European Councils, when discussing the shape of policies designed to drive progress with the Lisbon ("re-focused") Strategy and the implementation of concrete actions to be taken in this context, EU leaders, together with the President of the European Commission, should also specifically address the issue of progress made under the Social Inclusion Process. The fact that the Conclusions of the 2006 Spring European Council state that "The Commission and the Council will inform each Spring European Council with the Joint Report on the progress in the area of social protection and social inclusion" makes this more likely.

This increased (committed) political leadership should go together with an increased parliamentary scrutiny, in order to satisfactorily cope with the *democratic deficit* of the Open Method of Coordination currently applied to the Social Inclusion Process and in fact to the OMC in general. (The Commission expressed the view, in its May 2003 Communication on the streamlining of the EU Social Protection and Social Inclusion Process (European Commission, 2003c), that in creating a streamlined process in the social policy field, methods to involve the European Parliament as appropriate and practical should be seriously explored.) For this reason, we think that NAPs/inclusion ought to be debated in national (and where appropriate sub-national) parliaments, and that their actual implementation should be regularly monitored by the parliament(s) and relevant parliamentary committees. Similarly, the role of the European Parliament in scrutinising the whole process would have to be strengthened, and links between the European Parliament and national (sub-national) parliaments in this respect ought to be encouraged (possibly through the *Conference of Community and European Affairs Committees of Parliaments of the European Union* (COSAC), which aims to ensure cooperation between committees of the national parliaments dealing with European affairs and representatives from the European Parliament[5]).

Apart from strong political leadership at both country and EU levels, implementing NAPs/inclusion will obviously also necessitate strong administrative leadership and coordination. As is already the case in several Member States, we believe that countries should have a committee of senior civil servants from all relevant departments to oversee the concrete implementation of NAPs/inclusion.

Reporting to this committee, an inter-departmental group of officials should then coordinate the development of NAPs/inclusion as well as their implementation and monitoring on an ongoing basis (liaison officers responsible for the NAPs/inclusion in each ministry/department could also be appointed). This inter-departmental group would also be tasked with developing poverty and social exclusion impact assessments (both *ex ante* and *ex post*) for policies not included in NAPs/inclusion and not specifically aimed at increasing social inclusion, so that policy proposals coming before Government all have to take into account the potential (positive or negative) impact they may have on poverty and social exclusion. Existing policies should also regularly be reviewed for their impact on poverty and social exclusion.

With the same logic and, as agreed in Lisbon, with a view to further integrating social inclusion, employment and economic policies, the same group could also usefully monitor and report on the impact of specific employment, economic and also sustainable development policies on social inclusion; it could then systematically work at identifying possible ways (links/synergies) of adjusting such policies to strengthen their contribution to promoting social inclusion. In this regard the EU's renewed *Sustainable Development Strategy* (SDS) may prove a useful reinforcement of the Social Inclusion Process – in particular, the emphasis in the Strategy on impact assessments when developing policies and the encouragement of wider use of evaluation to assess the *ex-post* impact of policies can reinforce this important aspect of the Social Inclusion Process (see Section 2.5). A good example of the need for joined-up thinking is provided by the research agenda identified earlier in the book. We have argued that the strengthening of policy analysis and evaluation depends on social science research. At a European level, EU RTD Framework Programmes have supported such research, and this needs to be taken into account in the design of the seventh and subsequent Framework Programmes. The potential support of the Community action programme to combat social exclusion, and from 2007 its replacement PROGRESS, should also be exploited to the full.

This combination of developing and integrating the regional and local levels into the NAPs/inclusion, ensuring the mobilisation of all stakeholders, improving the integration and coordination of policy at national level (following an SDS approach integrating the social and environmental objectives and those of the Lisbon goals of growth and jobs), strengthening political leadership, mainstreaming social inclusion goals into national policy making, and linking the NAPs/inclusion into financial and budgetary decision-making process is a complex and sophisticated process that will need to vary depending on the particular governance arrangements in different Member States. An indication of how some of the key elements might interact is given in Figure 6.2 (Marlier, 2006).

The interconnections need, of course, also to take account of the EU dimension and in particular the common objectives on social inclusion (and social protection). Thus there should be a flow in both directions from overall EU objectives to national objectives, to national targets, to national plans with specific measures at

Figure 6.2: The need for *joined-up Government* – a country perspective

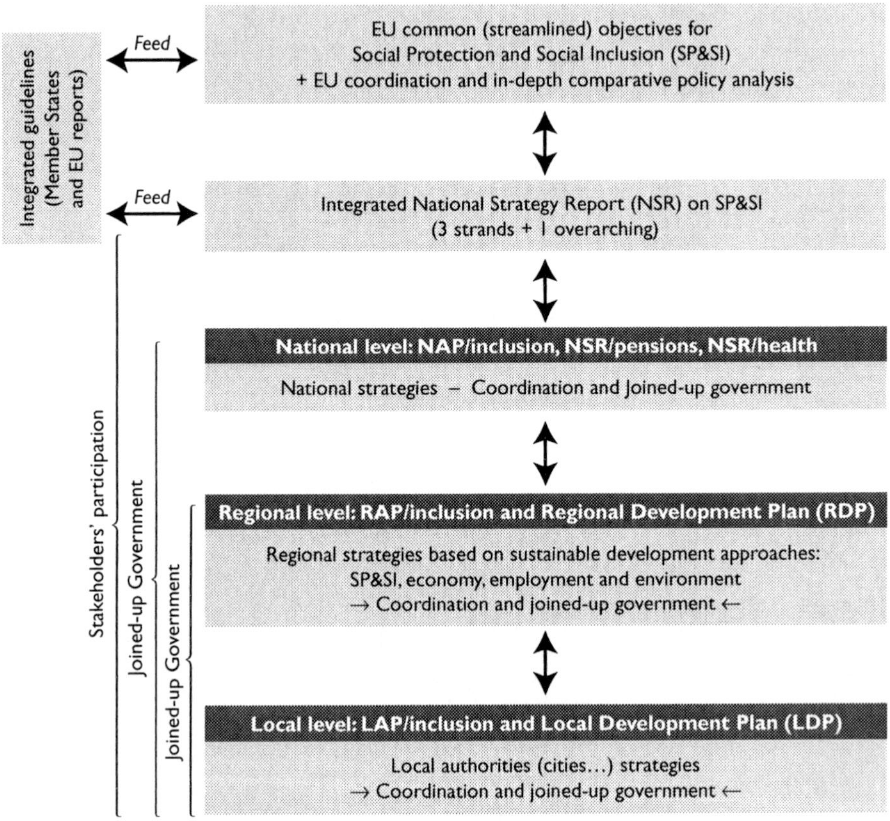

Source: Marlier, 2006
Notes: NAP/inclusion = National Action Plan on social inclusion; RAP = Regional Action Plan; LAP = Local Action Plan; NSR/health = National Strategy Report on Health Care and Long-term Care

both national and regional/ local levels and vice versa. Figure 6.3 tries to capture these different elements.

Properly joined-up Government, political and administrative leadership, parliamentary scrutiny, and research, should help ensure that the social dimension gets proper attention and is not treated as purely subsidiary. They should also help ensure that support and advocacy for the *three*-pillar strategy reaches beyond Governments through an extensive participatory approach, which brings us to the next Section.

Figure 6.3: The need for *joined-up Government* – an EU perspective

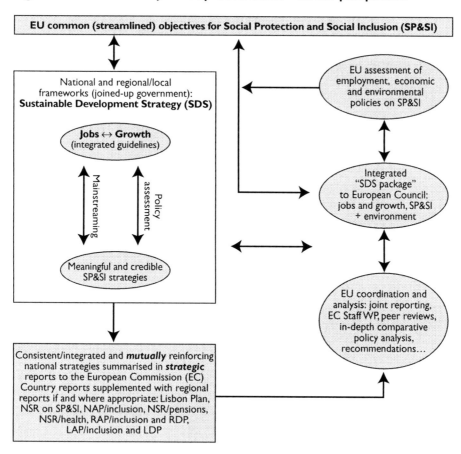

Source: Marlier, 2006
Notes: NAP/inclusion = National Action Plan on social inclusion; RAP = Regional Action Plan; LAP = Local Action Plan; NSR = National Strategy Report; NSR/health = NSR on Health Care and Long-term Care; RDP = Regional Development Plan; LDP = Local Development Plan; EC Staff WP = European Commission Staff Working Papers

6.8 Mobilising all relevant actors and bodies

A core objective assigned by the December 2000 Nice European Council for the EU Social Inclusion Process, and confirmed by the EPSCO Council two years later, is "to mobilise all relevant bodies". In the Conclusions of their 2004 Spring meeting in Brussels, EU leaders stressed that "support and advocacy for change must reach beyond Governments" and, in order to generate this support, they invited Member States "to build Reform Partnerships involving the social partners, civil society and the public authorities, in accordance with national arrangements and traditions". They went on to declare:

> Such national Reform Partnerships should promote complementary strategies for change, addressing the broad range of policies – economic,

social and environmental – encompassed by the Lisbon Agenda. These strategies should be reflected in clear national policies and objectives and should be taken into account by Governments in the course of preparing national contributions to the mid-term review of the Lisbon agenda. (Spring 2004 European Council, Presidency Conclusions, para 44)

A participatory approach, at the sub-national, national and EU levels, contributes to disseminating knowledge and to greater transparency and awareness of the EU Social Inclusion Process; it is a necessary condition for making the process credible and meaningful, both politically and popularly. If the Social Partners are not fully engaged in the process, then it will stand little chance of ultimate success. It is therefore crucial that *all* aspects of the (national/sub-national and EU) work on social inclusion are as open as possible to the active participation of the different non-governmental actors and bodies involved in the fight against poverty and social exclusion, including social partners, non-governmental and grass roots organisations (at EU, national and sub-national levels), the socially excluded people themselves, and academics. Structuring and supporting such participation should be a key component of national strategies, as usefully recalled in the overarching common objectives for the streamlined OMC on social protection and social inclusion (see Appendix 2b).[6] Such a development has also been reinforced by the annual European Meetings of People Experiencing Poverty and is a specific recommendation of the fifth meeting held in May 2006 under the auspices of the Austrian Presidency of the EU (see below).

Consultation

Significant efforts have already been made in this direction at EU level. An important one is the *European Round Table on Poverty and Social Exclusion* organised annually, with the support of the European Commission, by the country holding the Presidency of the EU in the second half of the year (around the 17 October, i.e. the UN International Day for the Eradication of Poverty). These Round Tables allow EU and national actors and bodies involved in the fight against poverty and social exclusion to exchange information and views on the Social Inclusion Process, to discuss progress towards the Lisbon goal of making a decisive impact on poverty and social exclusion by 2010, and to suggest ways of further strengthening the process. The first such Round Table was organised by the Danish Presidency (Aarhus, Denmark, October 2002). It was followed by a second one organised by the Italian Presidency (Turin, Italy, October 2003), a third one organised by the Dutch Presidency (Rotterdam, the Netherlands, October 2004) and a fourth one by the United Kingdom Presidency (Glasgow, UK, October 2005). The next one, organised by the Finnish Presidency, is taking place in October 2006.

The *European Meetings of People Experiencing Poverty* constitute another important

EU initiative in this context. They aim at giving a voice to the poor and socially excluded people and are a first step towards their active participation in the Social Inclusion Process. They are also organised with the support of the European Commission and they largely build upon the expertise of EAPN. The first such meeting was organised by the Belgian Presidency (Brussels, December 2001). The Greek Presidency Conference "We also Participate in Europe!" (Brussels, May 2003) was the second such meeting and the Irish Presidency Conference "Participation of People Experiencing Poverty – From Theory to Practice" was the third one (Brussels, May 2004). The Luxembourg Presidency organised the fourth such meeting in June 2005 (on "Images and Perceptions of Poverty) and the Austrian Presidency the fifth meeting in May 2006 (on "How Do We Cope with Everyday Life?").[7]

Twice a year, with these quasi "institutionalised" EU events (the Meeting of people experiencing poverty in the first half of the year and the Round Table on poverty and social exclusion in the second half), Member States, together with the European Commission, are therefore working towards an increased involvement of relevant actors and bodies in the Social Inclusion Process. In addition, as can be seen from the 2003 and 2004 NAPs/inclusion (respectively for EU-15 countries and the 10 new Member States) and the 2005 Implementation Reports (EU-15), a majority of countries have also implemented strategies in this direction.

EU demonstration projects and experiments

We have referred to current EU activities, but we can also draw lessons from the earlier Poverty Programmes. These Programmes, described briefly in Chapter 2, included pilot and demonstration projects. The Poverty 1 Programme for example supported some 60 action projects, which were intended to test out new methods to help the poor, to be relevant to more than one Member State, and for which it was a condition that the projects be "planned and carried out as far as possible with the participation of those concerned" (Dennett *et al*, 1982). They involved organisations such as ATD, London Voluntary Service Council, Irish National Committee on Pilot Schemes to Combat Poverty, and the Comité Général d'Action des Marolles. It was widely believed that these projects, while small and local in scale, did much to heighten public awareness of poverty and social exclusion. Whereas the EU has made great progress in developing a strategic approach to social inclusion, this approach still often appears far removed from what is happening on the ground. There is a case for considering, particularly after the Enlargement, whether there should be a return to the direct funding of demonstration projects of this type. Initiatives to combat poverty and social exclusion should be "bottom-up", as well as "top-down".

The European Poverty Programmes carried echoes of the War on Poverty in the US, and a second US innovation from which the EU may learn is that of policy experimentation. Most celebrated were the negative income tax experiments of the 1960s and 1970s, when a sizeable sample of households were presented with an alternative tax/transfer schedule, and their behaviour was compared with that of a control group. Experiments have since been conducted in a number of countries, covering taxation, transfers, active labour market policies, and investments in human capital. The UK, for instance, piloted an earnings top-up scheme using test areas and control areas (UK Department of Social Security, 1995). It can be debated how much extra one learns about behavioural responses from experimental, as opposed to other forms of evidence (see for example, Killingsworth, 1983, Chapter 6), but the point that we wish to make here is that such experiments have the potential to generate considerable public engagement and interest. An EU experiment as to the relative effectiveness of different anti-poverty measures, involving those Member States willing to participate, might serve to raise the profile of the Social Inclusion Process as well as adding to our knowledge about behavioural responses (about which, as we suggested in Chapter 4, we have much to learn).

Actions by Member States

Despite these efforts, a lot remains to be done to raise public and political awareness of the process, and we think that further efforts should be made to engage a wide(r) range of actors at both Member States and EU levels, including steps to incorporate these events into the regular consultative processes, such as those involving the Social Partners. As has been argued by de la Porte *et al* (2001), there are grounds for adopting a positive perspective. There are already-present forces for "bottom-up" benchmarking, "drawing its dynamic from the pressures for accountability coming from below" (de la Porte *et al*, 2001, page 303). In terms of national governance, there are action groups, and civil society organisations, with experience of lobbying Government and of taking forward the public debate. For these groups, the European dimension offers opportunities.

There are, therefore, forces on which one can and should build. However, we believe that this stronger involvement of stakeholders will not be sufficient on its own to create the necessary awareness and, directly linked to this, the necessary political commitment to the Social Inclusion Process. In our view, what is needed (on top of what has just been mentioned) is that Member States, as part of their NAPs/inclusion, be required to develop a genuine public awareness-raising *strategy*. The focus of national (and sub-national) strategies should be on creating greater public awareness of the extent and nature of poverty and social exclusion in the country and the EU, and how the Process is addressing the problem at both country and EU levels. An objective of strategies should be to strengthen people's belief in (potential) valuable outcomes of the Process or, put differently, to embed the process in the hearts of EU citizens. An awareness-raising strategy would also be needed at EU level.

As a concrete example, this means, for instance, the translation into the national language(s) of concepts such as "social exclusion" and "social inclusion". The meaning of the EU lexicon, "Open Method of Coordination", "Process", "Mainstreaming", "National Action Plan", and so on, would also need to be discussed/debated in this context. Embedding the Social Inclusion Process in people's hearts and thinking requires that they can understand not only its objectives but also its vocabulary. A second example is provided by the suggestion in Chapter 5 that contextual information, both quantitative and qualitative, should be provided to help understand the living standard achievable at the at-risk-of-poverty threshold in each Member State, building in particular on the concrete experience of people living in poverty and social exclusion. Engagement of civil society in this process would help advertise the Social Inclusion Process.

On this very issue, it is worth mentioning the NAP/inclusion for Cyprus submitted to the Commission in July 2004. As already noted this NAP/inclusion did not set targets, on the grounds that it would be "premature (and possibly counter-productive) since Cyprus is at the stage of first production and evaluation of the statistical information. Given the lack of experience in the use of indicators, it is not known at which level of effort a particular outcome target corresponds to." And the NAP/inclusion concluded that "an important point of the process which will take place within Cypriot society, during the period of execution of the NAP/inclusion, is the analysis, public discussion (with the involvement of all the players concerned) and finally, the adoption of a cohesive, ambitious and realistic set of targets for 2010" (Government of Cyprus, 2004, page 23; see also Section 6.2).

Finally, it scarcely needs underlining that the single most effective way of engaging public support is if the Social Inclusion Process can demonstrate significant progress in reducing poverty and social exclusion in the European Union.

6.9 Concluding comment

In this Chapter, we started from the streamlining of EU processes that is being implemented since January 2006. There are concerns that this streamlining means a loss of post-Lisbon momentum. In order to allay such concerns, it is necessary that there be mutually reinforcing feedback between the economic/employment policy processes, on the one hand, and the social processes, on the other. This has become even more important with the re-focused Lisbon Strategy agreed at the 2005 Spring Summit. Secondly, the streamlining of EU social processes has to be accompanied by measures to deepen the Social Inclusion Process. Streamlining alone will not automatically create this. It requires that countries and the EU commit themselves, both politically and administratively, to work together to take the Process forward. An effective streamlining can only be achieved while retaining the specificity of each individual process, given that the three social processes that are being streamlined all have quite different characteristics and challenges. It is thus important that NAPs/inclusion, as well as National Strategy Reports, are being maintained as *specific components of a unified social protection and inclusion framework.* This is the only way in our view to ensure a sufficiently incisive approach to policy evaluation.

Against the background of a Social Inclusion Process that is streamlined in the way described above, we have considered the deepening of this Process, beginning with the extension of target setting. Currently only a minority of countries have assigned a significant role to targets, and these may or may not be directly linked to the common indicators. Targets are far from being a panacea or a "magic bullet". The challenge is that of framing targets that are ambitious but realistic. This brings us back to the crucial role of policy analysis. In order to establish whether targets are achievable, we need a well-founded understanding of the causes of poverty and social exclusion, and a demonstration of feasible policies to bring about the desired outcomes. It requires that targets be properly designed. Given the great divergences within the European Union in the case of EU-wide targets, the approach adopted in the European Employment Strategy – of specifying a common level on a specific indicator that each country should seek to reach – is not the best approach for poverty and social exclusion. Rather, we recommend that Member States be set the target of closing the gap on, say, the best three performing countries. Such a criterion should be seen, not as a ranking exercise, but as an application of peer review.

The second form of deepening involves embedding of the Social Inclusion Process more firmly in domestic policy making. In this context, the Chapter has underlined the pivotal role of the *restructured* NAPs/inclusion, and made suggestions to assist Member States in re-focusing their 2006–8 NAPs/inclusion as actual "action plans" (i.e. strategic planning documents). The NAPs/inclusion can be really useful *only* if they go beyond simple, purely descriptive reporting; they have to meet the challenge of providing the basis for a sound critical analysis. The Chapter has emphasised the need for *joined-up Government*, committed political and administrative leadership, and parliamentary scrutiny to guarantee a credible and meaningful Social Inclusion Process. It has then stressed the importance of mobilising the different actors involved in the fight against poverty and social exclusion, and incorporating them into the regular consultative processes.

Notes

[1] Article I-15 on "the coordination of economic and employment policies" (Part 1 of the Treaty) opens the way to coordination rather than intergovernmental cooperation in the social field (see Section 2.2).

[2] For more information on peer reviews of good practices, see: http://www.europa.eu.int/comm/employment_social/soc-prot/soc-incl/prp_en.htm. Newsletters issued in this context can be downloaded for free from: http://www.peer-review-social-inclusion.net/.

[3] This is a point also made in the recent European Parliament Report on social inclusion in the new Member States, where two-way exchange of experience and good practice in this respect is encouraged (European Parliament 2005, page 6).

[4] See: http://www.europa.eu.int/comm/employment_social/social_inclusion/ tep_en.htm.

[5] COSAC was created in May 1989 at a meeting in Madrid, where the speakers of the Parliaments of the EU Member States agreed to strengthen the role of the national parliaments in relation to the community process by bringing together the European affairs Committees. The first meeting of COSAC took place in Paris in November 1989.

[6] Such participation is enormously valuable not just in framing policies and strategies but also in measuring progress – see for example the report on poverty indicators by Horemans (2003), which tapped the views of those directly affected by poverty and social exclusion.

[7] See http://www.eapn.org.

SEVEN

The EU and social inclusion: facing the challenges

At the March 2000 European Council in Lisbon, the EU committed to taking steps "to make a decisive impact on the eradication of poverty". At their 2005 Spring Summit in Brussels, EU leaders stressed that "it is essential to relaunch the Lisbon Strategy without delay and re-focus priorities on growth and employment"; they also reaffirmed that "social inclusion policy should be pursued by the Union and by Member States". And one year later, in March 2006, they restated "the objective of the Partnership for growth and jobs that steps have to be taken to make a decisive impact on the reduction of poverty and social exclusion by 2010". The Social Inclusion Process has a central role to play in this regard. This book has sought to provide an analysis of the challenges facing this Process and how it can be taken forward, in a context where the interdependence of the Union's economic, employment, social and environmental goals is to the fore. The importance of ensuring close links between the Social Protection and Social Inclusion Process and the revised Lisbon agenda on jobs and growth has been made clear, with active social policy expected to contribute in particular both to the reaffirmed social inclusion objectives and to economic and employment goals.

In this context, we have argued that the effectiveness of the Social Inclusion Process can be strengthened by improved policy analysis, monitoring and reporting on progress, and by ensuring that Member States' National Action Plans on social inclusion (NAPs/inclusion) become more strategic, focused, and better mainstreamed into national policy making. This book has set out a range of concrete suggestions as to how to make progress in that direction. First, though, we began with a brief historical account of the development of EU cooperation in social policy since the Treaty of Rome and more particularly since the Lisbon European Council, which is necessary to understanding what has been achieved to date and the challenges currently facing the Social Inclusion Process.

7.1 EU cooperation in social policy

A great deal can be learned from the history of the development of EU cooperation in social policy: "those who cannot remember the past are condemned to repeat it" (Santayana, 1980). There is considerable continuity in the basic ideas underlying the development of EU cooperation in social policy: the setting of common objectives, with Member States free to determine how they are achieved, according to the principle of subsidiarity. Since Lisbon, three EU social "processes" have been launched: first the *Social Inclusion Process*, then the *Pensions Process* and finally the *Health Care and Long-Term Care Process*, each being taken forward via the Open Method of Coordination (OMC). The machinery of the Social Inclusion Process has been established, including the NAPs/inclusion, their analyses by the European Commission and Member States, the agreement on and construction of the commonly agreed indicators, as well as the exchange of learning and the identification of good (and bad) practices. Against this background the book has then explored in some depth the potential for a systematic comparative analysis of the performance of Member States, using common indicators; how policy analysis can be strengthened; how the social indicators can be developed to fill gaps, refine existing indicators, respond to Enlargement, and widen their use; and how the Social Inclusion Process can be taken forward and embedded more firmly in domestic policies (both at national and sub-national levels). As we have sought to bring out, the Process has been considerably developed, but it needs to have traction in terms of concrete reductions in poverty and social exclusion.

7.2 Poverty and social exclusion in the EU

Examination of the rich information provided by the common indicators reveals considerable diversity in social performance in all dimensions. While the level of relative poverty in Europe is substantially lower than in the United States, the headline EU figure of 16% for the proportion of its citizens at risk of poverty remains unacceptably high. Enlargement has increased only marginally the degree of diversity of rates of poverty risk in the EU. However, the differences in ranking of countries on different indicators underlines the importance of a multi-dimensional approach, and this has become even more so with Enlargement. This is illustrated by the fact that 11 of the 25 Member States (including five new Member States) are in the "top three" on one of four indicators: poverty risk, long-term unemployment, joblessness, and early school leaving. There is ample room for improvement on one or more dimensions of poverty and social exclusion in all Member States.

Much can be learned from the analysis of the common indicators, but the underlying processes are complex, multivariate, and need to be disaggregated. Empirical conclusions need to be based on a theoretical framework linking the different mechanisms in operation. Simple correlations may be suggestive, but one cannot stop there, as was demonstrated by our examination of the relation between the at-risk-of-poverty rate and, on the one hand, social protection expenditure, and, on the other hand, employment growth. One can learn by comparing the relationships found for the EU-15 with those for the full EU-25, and also by comparing, not levels, but changes over time.

7.3 Strengthening policy analysis

The NAPs/inclusion and the EU summary documents (Joint Reports and Commission Staff Working Papers) have contributed a great deal to advancing the Social Inclusion Process, but policy analysis needs to be further developed in those documents and through other instruments (peer reviews, "transnational exchanges" and analytical reports). An adequate analysis of the baseline policy situation and a "counterfactual" for the outcome indicators (in other words, how the situation would evolve in the absence of the policy reform being considered) is required; the total effects of policies on poverty and social exclusion need to be investigated, as well as the contribution of each individual policy; and policy analysis to date is still insufficiently comparative, despite recent advances in that regard.

We have outlined a matrix approach, with vulnerable groups along one dimension and policy interventions along a second dimension, which would be helpful in framing policy questions. In addition, specific policies and their impacts can only be properly understood in the context of the broad institutional setting in which they operate (e.g. in terms of labour market regulation and collective bargaining arrangements). Some may therefore be more easily transferred across countries than others, and system-wide analysis is also required.

We need to be particularly concerned with the three-way linkage between policy, vulnerable groups and indicators. At the moment there is a tendency to approach issues either from the perspective of policies, or from the perspective of vulnerable groups, or from the perspective of indicators. But the intersection between those three perspectives, the contents of the three-dimensional box, is only just beginning to be filled out.

We have described two important tools for policy analysis that we believe could particularly strengthen the Social Inclusion Process. The model families approach has the merit of simplicity and limited data requirements. Results can be produced and brought up-to-date very quickly and without a sophisticated statistical apparatus. At the same time, they cannot fully reflect the variety of household circumstances, and there is no satisfactory method for aggregation unless recourse is had to distributional data. Micro-simulation models incorporate evidence about the distribution of household characteristics and automatically allow aggregates to be derived using distributional weights, but are resource-intensive and the validity of their results depends crucially on the accuracy of the underlying data. The model families analysis and micro-simulation modelling are best seen as complementary, and as part of a unified approach to policy modelling; this approach needs to be developed, notably by treating behavioural change and by extending the scope beyond income-related indicators.

It would be a major step forward if a common framework could be established by the EU for the analysis of Social Inclusion policy, with this framework making explicit the institutional differences between countries. An EU-wide model families analysis would be a first step towards a common analytical framework, facilitated by agreement on the range of family types to be examined (building on the typology of households used for the commonly agreed indicators and on the joint OECD/European Commission experience with tax-benefit models). Consideration should be given to the construction of an EU-wide micro-simulation model for the enlarged Union.

The strengthening of policy analysis and evaluation will require an investment in social science research. The needs of the EU Social Inclusion Process should be taken into account in the design of the seventh and subsequent EU RTD Framework Programmes. The potential support of the Community action programme to combat social exclusion (and, from 2007, its replacement, PROGRESS) should also be exploited to the full, including for the required strengthening of analytical expertise at sub-national, national and EU levels.

7.4 Commonly agreed indicators for social inclusion

The introduction of EU-SILC represents a major step forward in social statistics, but the transition from the ECHP will need to be taken into account in the construction and use of social indicators. As well as on-going work on the new data by Eurostat (the statistical office of the European Communities) with the national statistical institutes, independent researchers have an important role to play. Having data widely used by researchers, which requires in particular reasonable pricing conditions as well as appropriate documentation on survey and data processing, allows data quality to be assessed and problems identified, as well as raising the visibility and public acceptance of the data source. We strongly support efforts of Eurostat together with Member States to set in place appropriate data access arrangements for the scientific community to ensure effective use of EU-SILC micro-data (and other key EU statistical micro-data sources); these efforts should be pursued further without of course breaching confidentiality rules. This could be taken further through the establishment of an *EU-SILC Users Group* at EU level.

The advent of the EU-SILC data also raises a number of issues surrounding the definition of income: the treatment of negative incomes, self-employment incomes, imputed rent on owner-occupied housing, and the valuing of own-consumption. These issues need to be given full consideration, and we have suggested that the definition of income should be tailored to the purpose for which it is used, which may mean different definitions for different purposes.

We argue that the Social Inclusion Process should continue with its existing poverty risk indicators based on country-specific poverty thresholds, but that the Commission should consider complementing these with a background "2005 Lisbon mid-term social cohesion statistic" based on numbers falling below a threshold based on the median income in the EU-25 as a whole. Making a bridge between the risk-of-poverty indicators based on relative income thresholds and "more absolute" measures of poverty is also important. Contextual information, both quantitative and qualitative, would help in understanding the actual living standard achievable at the risk-of-poverty threshold in each Member State, building in particular on the concrete experience of people and households "at risk". Such an approach would make more meaningful the otherwise arcane statistical procedures on which the poverty risk indicator is based.

In the light of the sensitivity of income-based indicators to the choice of equivalence scale, we have suggested that *background* information should be produced with both the modified and original OECD scales for the most sensitive figures whereas the income indicators *per se* should all be calculated with the OECD modified equivalence scale. Member States particularly concerned about the relevance of the OECD modified scale (used at EU level) should be encouraged to introduce country-specific third level indicators, but these should not replace the Primary and Secondary Indicators.

We have also set out a number of specific suggestions with respect to the set of commonly agreed social inclusion indicators, aimed at filling some widely recognised gaps (to which the Indicators Sub-Group and Eurostat have already devoted considerable attention). These include the following:

- An EU indicator of literacy for the adult, or at least working-age, population would be a useful complement to that for pupils.
- The regional aspects of poverty and social exclusion could be taken into account by including regional breakdowns (and breakdowns by the degree of urbanisation) for existing indicators, where possible and meaningful. Region-specific indicators may also need to be developed.
- Similarly, the new Primary Indicator on the employment gap of immigrants is an important step forward, but it is not enough to deal with the important issue of the position of migrants and ethnic minorities. Each Member State ought to include breakdowns appropriate to their country of the common indicators, complemented, where possible and meaningful, by third level indicators reflecting their specific situations.
- Administrative data have significant potential to improve national and EU knowledge of the regional dimension and of the circumstances of migrants and ethnic minorities and this should be investigated in depth.
- As far as homelessness is concerned, it should be possible to first agree on a relatively tight definition of homelessness; the next stage would be to agree on the preferred measure and the approach to producing data relating to this agreed definition and measure. It is important that official responsibility be clearly assigned for overseeing the collection of appropriate data in close collaboration with organisations working in the area; Member States should in the meantime report on the basis of national statistics as a "level 3" indicator.
- Priority should be given to the development of an aggregate indicator of housing quality/adequacy, based on data from EU-SILC.
- Inability to access health care might well be captured in an indicator based on

information in EU-SILC, and health-related limitations in daily activities by income level may also provide a useful window on social exclusion.

• Priority should also be given to the development of a harmonised indicator of premature mortality by socio-economic circumstances, to be produced on a regular but not necessarily annual basis.

• A common indicator of enforced deprivation in relation to broad living standards conceived in "absolute" terms, in the form of an aggregate index using data from EU-SILC, should be introduced as a Primary Indicator; in time this could be complemented by a "more relative" (with country-specific weights) common indicator based on the same EU-SILC items.

• For the analysis of the "working poor" indicator it would be valuable to have information on the poverty risk run by employees aged 18–59 in full-time employment for the entire reference year, and on the corresponding risk run by those aged 18–59 unemployed all year and those aged 18–59 inactive all year, so their risks can be better compared. A measure of the extent of low pay would also provide a useful complement.

As background to the indicators based on household income, it would also be valuable to study more closely the individual share of income going to adults in a household. Countries should more systematically analyse in their NAPs/ inclusion how the situation of individuals and households changes over time; it is essential to deepen our understanding of the dynamics of income, poverty and social exclusion at the *micro*-level, based on longitudinal (panel) data, and the factors/processes associated with it. In using the portfolio of common indicators, whatever the value of composite indicators (such as the Human Development Index) in other contexts, we do not feel that they should be employed as part of the current EU Social Inclusion Process in view of the specificities of the OMC. Finally, the EU institutions should consider, in collaboration with OECD, the extension of the common social indicators to cover at a minimum the US, in view of the importance attached to learning about what does and does not work from across the Atlantic, as well as Japan. Canada, Australia and New Zealand could also usefully be covered.

It is clear that indicators can play a valuable role in linking across the different social policy processes (with at-risk-of-poverty rates for older people and mortality by socio-economic circumstances as concrete examples) as well as between the EU social, economic and employment processes (with the working poor as an important example). However, the "performance" information conveyed by the common indicators needs to be supplemented with background information/ statistics that allow a better linkage between policies and social outcomes.

Last but not least, when analysing indicators calculated from household surveys data (EU-SILC, Labour Force Surveys, etc.), it is essential to keep in mind that they generally cover only people living in private households. Some vulnerable groups that are in fact living in these households may also be underrepresented because they are not easy to reach. Statistical efforts need to be made at the sub–national, national and EU levels to collect (better) statistical socio-economic information on these groups, which include people living in institutions, migrants and ethnic minorities, and other vulnerable groups including the homeless, people with disabilities, those with addiction problems, etc.

7.5 Children mainstreaming

We have also suggested that the social inclusion indicators include a *children mainstreaming* approach. This should not imply picking out children as a particular priority group; the fight against poverty and social exclusion needs to be a universal one. Rather, as with gender mainstreaming, it suggests a perspective for approaching the general issue of poverty and social exclusion. In combating "child poverty", it is essential that Member States and the Commission focus on child "poverty and social exclusion"; here also we need to think in multi-dimensional terms. Fighting child poverty requires therefore a comprehensive and integrated strategy of child, family and women-friendly policies. From the perspective of children, we need to approach the design of indicators from a specific direction, not simply through age breakdowns as is currently the case (though each time where possible and meaningful the "yet-to-be-developed" common indicators should include an age breakdown distinguishing children). We welcome the recent introduction of a Primary social inclusion indicator on the circumstances of children, with the dimension(s) of disadvantage to be covered and specific indicators as yet to be developed. It will also be important for Member States, when developing strategies in relation to children, to use a more extensive and multi-dimensional set of child-centred indicators, and the Commission could do likewise when reporting in more depth on policies in relation to child poverty and exclusion. In that context it would be helpful if guidelines could be developed for countries on the range of indicators that they would need to take into account when considering questions of child well-being.

7.6 Facing the challenges: taking forward the EU Social Inclusion Process

In thinking about how the EU Social Inclusion Process can be taken forward, a variety of issues relating to the structuring of that process were also considered. Focusing first on the "streamlining" of the EU's social processes that is being implemented from January 2006, this offers the opportunity to advance policy making, but mutually reinforcing feedback between the economic/employment policy processes, on the one hand, and the social processes, on the other has become even more important with the re-focused Lisbon Strategy agreed at the 2005 Spring Summit. The streamlining of EU social processes also has to be accompanied by measures to deepen the Social Inclusion Process, which requires that countries and the EU commit themselves, both politically and administratively, to work together to take the Process forward. An effective streamlining can only be achieved while retaining the specificity of each individual process, given that the three social processes that are being streamlined all have quite different characteristics and challenges. It is thus important that NAPs/inclusion, as well as National Strategy Reports on pensions and also on health, are being maintained as specific components of a unified social protection and social inclusion framework. In our view, this is the only way to ensure a sufficiently incisive approach to policy evaluation.

We have argued that such a streamlined Social Inclusion Process needs to be strengthened and deepened in several respects. The Social Protection Committee and its Indicators Sub-Group play a central role in the Process; given the importance of the work of the ISG, the Commission might usefully consider having an independent analysis of its operation carried out. It would be very valuable if the key working documents of the ISG, including the minutes of meetings, could be made publicly accessible, along with the reports made to the Social Protection Committee when endorsed. The publication of the original report endorsed by the Laeken European Council in 2001 has demonstrated the value of such transparency. In view of the extent of inter-connections between different fields, in terms of topics covered (income, employment, health, housing and homelessness, education and so on) but also methodology and data sources, it is important that there be close liaison between ISG delegates and the national experts involved with other bodies, in particular EU (Council bodies, Eurostat Task Forces and so forth) and OECD bodies, UN and other groups concerned with social statistics. Finally, it would be very helpful to have a further development of the information already provided, in the form of an ISG statistical/methodological document providing a sort of an "ID card" for each commonly agreed indicator.

In deepening the Process, we believe that the setting of ambitious but achievable targets in NAPs/inclusion has an important role to play in focusing policy development and highlighting social objectives. Currently only a minority of countries have assigned a significant role to targets, and these may or may not be directly linked to the common indicators. Targets are far from being a panacea or a "magic bullet". The challenge is that of framing targets that are ambitious but realistic. This brings us back to the crucial role of policy analysis. In order to establish whether targets are achievable, we need a well-founded understanding of the causes of poverty and social exclusion, and a demonstration of feasible policies to bring about the desired outcomes. It requires that targets be properly designed, including (where relevant) involving lower-level Governments in the definition of these targets and in the related monitoring of the sub-national performance. EU-level targets are also worth serious consideration as has been suggested in the recent Commission Communication on the EU's Sustainable Development Strategy. Given the great divergences within the European Union, the approach adopted in the European Employment Strategy – of specifying a common level on a specific indicator that each country should seek to reach – is not the best approach for poverty and social exclusion. Rather, Member States should be set the target of closing the gap on, say, the best three performing countries. Such a criterion should be seen, not as a ranking exercise, but as an application of peer review.

Deepening involves embedding of the Social Inclusion Process more firmly in domestic policy making. NAPs/inclusion can play a pivotal role, but only if they are fundamentally restructured so as to become true strategic "action plans", not just a purely descriptive reporting exercise. They should contain a multi-dimensional diagnosis of the causes of poverty and social exclusion together with explicit analyses of the expected relation between policies and the delivery of outcomes, and be strictly objective driven. More broadly, a true *social inclusion mainstreaming* in sub-national, national as well as EU policy is needed, through establishing a scheme of systematic (*ex ante* and *ex post*) policy assessments. The impact of specific employment, economic and sustainable development policies on social inclusion, and of policies implemented at sub-national (regional, local), national and EU levels, needs to be assessed. It is crucial to reflect on best ways to ensure, at both (sub-)national and EU levels, a mutual, reinforcing feedback between the Broad Economic Policy Guidelines and the Employment Guidelines, on the one hand, and the OMC in the social field (including the Social Inclusion Process), on the other hand.

The Open Method of Coordination could do more to ensure joined-up Government in the field of social policy, bringing together different agencies within national Governments (and, in countries where it applies, different levels of Governments), and bringing together (sub-)national policy makers and the Commission. Given the gap that has been identified between the objectives and policies described in many NAPs/inclusion and their concrete implementation on the ground, increased focus needs to be given to how to ensure effective implementation. This reinforces the need for a much closer link in future between national, regional and local administrations in the planning, implementation and monitoring of actions, calling for Regional Action Plans and/or Local Action Plans. This can also be supported by encouraging more exchange and learning between Member States on good practices in the implementation and delivery of policies and programmes. Mainstreaming of the NAPs/inclusion in national, regional and local policy making will also require a much closer link between social inclusion objectives and national budgetary decision-making processes. In particular, we would strongly urge that decisions made on how to use the new round of EU Structural Funds from 2007 fully take into account the social inclusion priorities that are set in the 2006–8 NAPs/inclusion.

While peer pressure, together with the identification of both good and bad practices, is necessary to maintain the credibility and ambition of the EU Social Inclusion Process, the purpose of the common indicators is not to name, shame and castigate Member States; rather, the aim is to help Member States to do better, and the focus should be on improving the performance of all countries. Good (and bad) practices in terms of processes should be more systematically identified, especially in the areas of social policy monitoring and statistical capacity building. Specific national characteristics are likely to be much less of an issue for these practices than for actual policies; the "transferability" of these practices among countries could then be much higher than that of specific policies. Furthermore, when it has assessed the individual NAPs/inclusion, the Commission should then have the power to make recommendations to Member States, to which Member States would respond in their Implementation Reports on the NAPs/inclusion; this could be developed in conjunction with the Sustainable Development Strategy.

The Social Inclusion Process has so far had limited success in truly engaging key actors (Social Partners, NGOs, the scientific community as well as people experiencing poverty and social exclusion). However, in several countries and in the context of the European Meetings of People Experiencing Poverty there have been an increasing number of good examples of involving civil society and people experiencing poverty in the Social Inclusion Process. These provide good models for transnational learning, which should be used to increase the engagement of key actors in future. Most Member States should develop their own social inclusion monitoring framework, responding to their national specificities, and including targets and indicators built on reliable and timely data collected by independent national and EU bodies; clear links should be made between, on the one hand, the national frameworks, and, on the other hand, the common indicators and the EU methodological framework.

The Social Inclusion Process will only succeed if there is committed political and administrative leadership at sub-national, national and EU levels. Increased parliamentary scrutiny is important: NAPs/inclusion ought to be debated in national (and where appropriate sub-national) parliaments and their actual implementation should be regularly monitored by the parliament(s) and relevant parliamentary committees. Similarly, the role of the European Parliament in scrutinising the whole process will have to be strengthened, and links between the European Parliament and (sub-)national parliaments in this respect ought to be encouraged.

The Social Inclusion Process in effect comprises a set of tools to assist Member States in improving their policies – but their usefulness will be limited without a political commitment to employ them to the full. This needs to be underpinned by widespread "ownership" of the Social Inclusion Process, and the single most effective way of engaging public support is if the Social Inclusion Process can demonstrate significant progress in reducing poverty and social exclusion in the European Union.

References

Abel-Smith, B. and Townsend, P.B. (1965), *The Poor and the Poorest*, G. Bell and Sons, London.

Aber, J.L., Gershoff, E.T. and Brooks-Gunn, J. (2002), "Social Exclusion of Children in the United States: Identifying Potential Indicators", in Kahn, A.J. and Kamerman, S.B. (eds), *Beyond Child Poverty: The Social Exclusion of Children*, The Institute for Child and Family Policy at Columbia University, New York.

Anand, S. and Sen, A.K. (1997), *Concepts of Human Development and Poverty: A Multidimensional Perspective*, Human Development Papers, United Nations Development Programme, New York.

Atkinson, A.B. (2000), *A European Social Agenda: Poverty Benchmarking and Social Transfers*, EUROMOD Working Paper, No. EM3/00, Department of Applied Economics, Cambridge.

Atkinson, A.B. (2002), *Evaluation of National Action Plans on Social Inclusion: The Role of EUROMOD*, EUROMOD Working Paper No. EM1/02, Department of Applied Economics, Cambridge.

Atkinson, A.B. (2003), "Multidimensional Deprivation: Contrasting Social Welfare and Counting Approaches", *Journal of Economic Inequality*, Vol. 1, pp. 51–65.

Atkinson, A.B., Cantillon, B., Marlier, E. and Nolan, B. (2002), *Social Indicators: The EU and Social Inclusion*, Oxford University Press, Oxford.

Atkinson, A.B., Marlier, E. and Nolan, B. (2004), *Indicators and Targets for Social Inclusion in the EU*, Journal of Common Market Studies, Vol. 42, No. 1, pp. 47–75.

Atkinson, A.B. and Meulders, D. (2004), *EU Action on Social Inclusion and Gender Mainstreaming*, EUROMOD Working Paper No. EM8/04, Department of Applied Economics, Cambridge.

Atkinson, A. B. and Micklewright, J. (1992), *Economic transformation in Eastern Europe and the distribution of income*, Cambridge University Press, Cambridge.

Atkinson, A.B. and Sutherland, H. (1988), *Tax-benefit models*, STICERD, London.

Barca, F., Brezzi, M., Terribile, F. and Utili, F. (2004), *Soft and Hard Use of Indicators in Regional Development Policies*, Materiali Uval, Analysi e studi, No. 2, Ministero dell'Economia e delle Finanze, Rome.

Bardone, L. and Guio, A.-C. (2005), *In-work Poverty: New Commonly Agreed Indicators at the EU Level*, Statistics in Focus, Theme 3, 5/2005, Eurostat, Luxembourg.

Beblo, M. and Knaus, T. (2001), "Measuring Income Inequality in Euroland", *Review of Income and Wealth*, Vol. 47, No. 3, pp. 301–20.

Beck, W., van der Maesen, L. and Walker, A. (eds) (1997), *The Social Quality of Europe*, Kluwer, The Hague.

Becker, I. and Hauser, R. (2001), *Einkommensverteilung im Querschnitt und im Zeitverlauf 1973 bis 1998*, Bundesministerium für Arbeit und Sozialordnung, Bonn.

Begg, I., Ferrera, M., Hodson, D., Madsen, P.K., Matsaganis, M., Sacchi, S. and Schelkle, W. (2004), *The Costs of Non-Social Policy*, Report presenting the findings of a research project funded by Directorate-General "Employment and Social Affairs" of the European Commission.

Ben-Arieh, A., Kaufman, N.H., Andrews, A.B., George, R., Lee, B.J., and Aber, J.L. (2000), *Measuring and Monitoring Children's Well Being*, European Centre for Social Welfare Policy and Research, Vienna.

Berger, F. (2004), *L'impact du loyer fictif sur la distribution des revenus*, CEPS/ INSTEAD, Population & Emploi No. 2, Luxembourg.

Berger-Schmitt, R. (2000), *Social Cohesion as an Aspect of the Quality of Societies: Concept and Measurement*, EuReporting Working Paper No. 14, ZUMA, Mannheim.

Berger-Schmitt, R. and Noll, H.-H. (2000), *Conceptual Framework and Structure of a European System of Social Indicators*, EuReporting Working Paper No. 9, ZUMA, Mannheim.

Blair, T. (1999), "Beveridge Revisited: A Welfare State for the 21st Century", in Walker, R., *Ending Child Poverty*, The Policy Press, Bristol.

Blundell, R. (2001), "Welfare Reform for Low Income Workers", *Oxford Economic Papers*, Vol. 53, pp. 189–214.

Blundell, R. and MaCurdy, T. (1999), "Labor Supply: A Review of Alternative Approaches", in Ashenfelter, O.C. and Card, D., *Handbook of Labor Economics*, Vol. 3A, Elsevier, Amsterdam.

Boarini, R. and d'Ercole, M.M. (2006), *Measures of Material Deprivation in OECD Countries*, OECD Social, Employment and Migration Working Papers No. 37, OECD, Paris.

Boarini, R., Johansson, A. and d'Ercole, M.M. (2006), *Alternative Measures of Well-Being*, OECD Social, Employment and Migration Working Papers No. 33, OECD, Paris.

Booth, C. (2002), "Gender Mainstreaming in the European Union: Towards a New Conception and Practice of Equal Opportunities?", *European Journal of Women's Studies*, Vol. 9, pp. 430–46.

Bourguignon, F. (2003), *The Growth Elasticity of Poverty Reduction: Explaining Heterogeneity across Countries and Time Periods*, World Bank, Washington D.C.

Bourguignon, F. and Spadaro, A. (2006), "Microsimulation as a Tool for Evaluating Redistribution Policies", *Journal of Economic Inequality*, Vol. 4, pp. 77–106.

Bradbury, B. and Jäntti, M. (2001), "Child Poverty Across the Industrialised World: Evidence from the Luxembourg Income Study", in Vleminckx, K. and Smeeding, T., *Child Well-being, Child Poverty and Child Policy in Modern Nations*, The Policy Press, Bristol, pp. 11–32.

Bradshaw, J., Ditch, J., Holmes, H. and Whiteford, P. (1993), *Support for Children – A Comparison of Arrangements in Fifteen Countries*, Research Report No. 21, UK Department of Social Security, London.

Bradshaw, J. and Finch, N. (2002), *A Comparison of Child Benefit Packages in 22 Countries*, Research Report No. 174, UK Department for Work and Pensions, London.

Bradshaw, J., Hoelscher, P. and Richardson, D. (2006/forthcoming), "An Index of Child Well-Being in the European Union", *Journal of Social Indicators*.

Bradshaw, J. and Mayhew, E. (2005), *A Comparison of the Tax Benefit Package for Families with Children in Eight European Countries at January 2004*, University of York, York.

Breen, R. (2004), *Social Mobility in Europe*, Oxford University Press, Oxford.

Brewer, M., Goodman, A., Shaw, J. and Shephard, A. (2005), *Poverty and Inequality in Britain: 2005, Commentary 99*, Institute of Fiscal Studies, London.

Brousse, C. (2004), "The Production of Data on Homelessness and Housing Deprivation in the European Union: Surveys and Proposals", Report written on behalf of Eurostat, Office for Official Publications of the European Communities, Luxembourg. [Final report available from: http://epp.eurostat.ec.europa.eu/portal/page?_pageid=1073,46587259&_dad=portal&_schema=PORTAL&p_product_code=KS-CC-04-008].

Bundesregierung (2005), "Lebenslagen in Deutschland - Der 2. Armuts- und Reichtums-bericht der Bundesregierung", available at http://www.bmas.bund.de/BMAS/Redaktion/Pdf/Lebenslagen-in-Deutschland-De-821,property=pdf,bereich=bmas,sprache=de,rwb=true.pdf

Burgess, S., Gardiner, K. and Propper, C. (2001), *Why Rising Tides Don't Lift All Boats?*, CASE Paper 46, London School of Economics, London.

Callan, T. (2005), *Assessing the Impact of Tax/Transfer Policy Changes on Poverty: Methodological Issues and Some European Evidence*, ESRI, Dublin.

Callan, T., Keeney, M., Nolan, B. and Maître, B. (2004), *Why is Relative Poverty so High in Ireland?*, ESRI Policy Research Series, Dublin.

Callan, T. and Nolan, B. (1997), *Income Distribution and Socio-Economic Differences in International Perspective*, ESRI, Dublin.

Cantillon, B., Marx, I. and Van den Bosch, K. (1997), "The Challenge of Poverty and Social Exclusion", in *Towards 2000: The New Social Policy Agenda*, OECD, Paris.

Cantillon, B., Van Mechelen, N. and Van den Bosch, K. (2004), "Best Practices, or, How to Link Policy Inputs and Well-Being Outcomes: the Role of Policy Input Indicator", Paper presented at the ChangeQual seminar, Paris, 17–18 May 2004.

Cazenave, M.-C. (2006), "Travailleurs pauvres et qualité du travail en Europe", in Bourreau-Dubois, C. and Jeandidier, B. (eds), *Economie Sociale et Droit: Economie sociale et solidaire, Famille et éducation, Protection sociale (Tome 2)*, L'Harmattan, Paris, pages 333-46.

Cherchye, L., Moesen, W. and Van Puyenbroeck, T. (2003), *Legitimately Diverse, Yet Comparable: On Synthesising Social Inclusion Performance in the EU*, Centre for Economic Studies Discussion Paper 03.01, Katholieke Universiteit Leuven, Leuven.

Combat Poverty Agency (2006), "Better Policies, Better Outcomes – Promoting Mainstreaming Social Inclusion", Dublin, available at http://www.europemsi.org/.

Conseil de l'Emploi, des Revenus et de la Cohésion sociale (CERC) (2004), *Child Poverty in France*, Report 4, CERC, Paris.

Conseil de l'Emploi, des Revenus et de la Cohésion sociale (CERC) (2005), *Estimer la pauvreté des enfants*, Dossier du CERC, No. 2 (June), CERC, Paris.

Corak, M. (2005), *Principles and Practicalities for Measuring Child Poverty in the Rich Countries*, UNICEF Innocenti Working Paper No. 2005-01, UNICEF Innocenti Research Centre, Florence.

Corak, M., Lietz, C. and Sutherland, H. (2005), *The Impact of Tax and Transfer Systems on Children in the European Union*, UNICEF Innocenti Working Paper No. 2005-04, UNICEF Innocenti Research Centre, Florence..

Cornia, G.A. and Danziger, S. (1997), *Child Poverty and Deprivation in the Industrialized Countries*, Clarendon Press, Oxford.

Council (1974), Resolution Concerning a Social Action Programme, OJEC, C 13, Brussels.

Council (1975), Council Decision of 22 July 1975 Concerning a Programme of Pilot Schemes and Studies to Combat Poverty", 75/458/EEC, OJEC, L 199, Brussels.

Council (1980), "Council Decision of 22 December 1980 Concerning a Supplementary Programme to Combat Poverty", 80/1270/EEC, OJEC, L 375, Brussels.

Council (1985), "Council Decision of 19 December 1984 on Specific Community Action to Combat Poverty", 85/8/EEC, OJEC, L 2, Brussels.

Council (1989a), "Resolution of the Council and of the Ministers for Social Affairs Meeting within the Council of 29 September 1989 on Combating Social Exclusion", OJEC, C 277, Brussels.

Council (1989b), "Council Decision of 18 July 1989 Establishing a Medium-Term Community Action Programme Concerning the Economic and Social Integration of the Economically and Socially Less Privileged Groups in Society", 89/457/EEC, OJEC, L 224, Brussels.

Council (1992a), "Council Recommendation of 27 July 1992 on the Convergence of Objectives and Policies in Social Protection", 92/442/EEC, OJEC, L 245, Brussels.

Council (1992b), *Council recommendation of 24 June 1992 on common criteria concerning sufficient resources and social assistance in social protection systems*, 92/441/EEC, OJEC, L 245, Brussels.

Council (1999), "Council Conclusions of 17 December 1999 on the Strengthening of Cooperation for Modernising and Improving Social Protection", OJEC, 12.01.2000, C8/7, Brussels.

Council (2002), "Fight Against Poverty and Social Exclusion: Common Objectives for the Second Round of National Action Plans", 14164/1/02 REV 1, 3 December 2002, Brussels.

Council (2003), "Council Conclusions on Structural Indicators", Annex, 15875/03, 8 December 2003, Brussels.

Council (2005), "Key Messages for the Spring European Council from the EPSCO Council", Brussels.

Council (2006a), *Key Messages from the EPSCO Council to the Spring European Council*, Brussels.

Council (2006b), "Review of the EU Sustainable Development Strategy (EU SDS) – Renewed Strategy", Note and Annex, Brussels.

de Beer, P. (2001), *Over werken in de postindustriële samenleving*, SCP, The Hague.

de la Porte, C., Pochet, P. and Room, G. (2001), "Social Benchmarking, Policy Making and New Governance in the EU", *Journal of European Social Policy*, Vol. 11, No. 4, pp. 291–307.

de Vos, K. and Zaidi, M.A. (1998), "Poverty Measurement in the European Union: Country-Specific or Union-Wide Poverty Lines?", *Journal of Income Distribution*, Vol. 8, No. 1, pp. 77–92.

Deaton, A. (2002), *Data for Monitoring the Poverty MDG*, Research Program in Development Studies, Princeton University, Princeton.

Delors, J. (1971), *Les indicateurs sociaux*, Futuribles, Paris.

Dennett, J., James, E., Room, G. and Watson, P. (1982), *Europe Against Poverty: The European Poverty Programme 1975–80*, Bedford Square Press, London.

Dennis, I. and Guio, A.-C. (2004), *Monetary Poverty in New Member States and Candidate Countries*, Statistics in Focus, Theme 3, 12/2004, Eurostat, Luxembourg.

Diener, E., Suh, E.M., Lucas, R.E. and Smith, H.E. (1999), "Subjective Well-Being: Three Decades of Progress", *Psychological Bulletin*, No. 125, pp. 276–302.

Driant, J.-C. and Jacquot, A. (2005), *Loyers imputés et inégalités de niveau de vie*, Documents de Travail F0407, Institut National de la Statistique et des Etudes Economiques, Paris.

Employment Committee and Social Protection Committee (2005), "Joint Opinion of the Employment Committee and the Social Protection Committee on the Integrated Guidelines for Growth and Jobs (2005–2008)", Brussels, available at http://eapn.horus.be/module/module_page/images/pdf/pdf_publication/Non-EAPN%20Publications/intguide-emco_final.doc.

Employment Committee and Social Protection Committee (2006), "Joint Opinion of the Employment Committee and the Social Protection Committee on the Review of the Sustainable Development Strategy (i.e., the Commission Communication COM(2005)706 final)", Brussels.

Erikson, R. (1974), "Welfare as a Planning Goal", *Acta Sociologica*, Vol. 17, pp. 273–88.

Erikson, R. (2002), "Social Indicators for the European Union: Comments", *Politica Economica*, Vol. 18, No. 1, pp. 69–73.

Erikson, R. and Goldthorpe, J.H. (1992), *The Constant Flux*, Clarendon Press, Oxford.

Erikson, R. and Uusitalo, H. (1987), "The Scandinavian Approach to Welfare Research", in Erikson, R., Hansen, E. J., Ringen, S. and Uusitalo, H. (eds), *The Scandinavian Model: Welfare States and Welfare Research*, M.E. Sharpe, Armonk, NY.

Esping-Andersen, G. (1990), *The Three Worlds of Welfare Capitalism*, Polity Press, Cambridge.

European Anti-Poverty Network (2003), "Where is the Political Energy?", EAPN's response to the second round of Plans, Brussels.

European Commission (1981), "Final Report of the Commission to the Council on the First Programme of Pilot Projects and Pilot Studies to Combat Poverty", COM(81)769, Brussels.

European Commission (1989), *The Fight Against Poverty: Interim Report on the Second European Poverty Programme*, Supplement 2/89, Social Europe, Brussels.

European Commission (1992), "Towards a Europe of Solidarity: Intensifying the Fight Against Social Exclusion, Fostering Integration", Communication from the Commission, COM(92)542, Brussels.

European Commission (1993a), "Social Protection in Europe", Communication from the Commission, COM(93)531, Brussels.

European Commission (1993b), "Medium-term Action Programme to Combat Exclusion and Promote Solidarity: A New Programme to Support and Stimulate Innovation (1994–1999)", Communication from the Commission, COM(93)435, Brussels.

European Commission (1997), "Modernising and Improving Social Protection in the European Union", Communication from the Commission, COM(97)102, Brussels.

European Commission (1999), "A Concerted Strategy for Modernising Social Protection", Communication from the Commission, COM(99)347 final, OJEC, 2000, C 8, Brussels.

European Commission (2002a), "Streamlining the Annual Economic and Employment Policy Coordination Cycles", Communication from the Commission, COM(2002)487 final, Brussels.

European Commission (2002b), *Joint Report on Social Inclusion 2001*, Office for Official Publications of the European Communities, Luxembourg.

European Commission (2002c), "The Lisbon Strategy – Making Change Happen", Communication from the Commission to the Spring European Council in Barcelona, COM(2002)14 final, Brussels.

European Commission (2003a), "Modernising Social Protection for More and Better Jobs: A Comprehensive Approach Contributing to Making Work Pay", Communication from the Commission, COM(2003)842 final, Brussels.

European Commission (2003b), "Structural Indicators", Communication from the Commission, COM(2003)585 final, Brussels.

European Commission (2003c), "Strengthening the Social Dimension of the Lisbon Strategy: Streamlining Open Coordination in the Field of Social Protection", Communication from the Commission, COM(2003)261 final, Brussels.

European Commission (2004a), "Modernising Social Protection for the Development of High-Quality, Accessible and Sustainable Health Care and Long-Term Care: Support for the National Strategies Using the Open Method of Coordination", Communication from the Commission, COM(2004)304 final, Brussels.

European Commission (2004b), *Joint Report on Social Inclusion 2004* (including Statistical Annex), Office for Official Publications of the European Communities, Luxembourg.

European Commission (2004c), "Delivering Lisbon: Reforms for the Enlarged Union", Communication from the Commission, COM(2004)29 final, Brussels.

European Commission (2004d), "Social Inclusion in the New Member States – A Synthesis of the Joint Memoranda on Social Inclusion", Commission Staff Working Paper SEC(2004)848, Brussels.

European Commission (2004e), *Report of the High-Level Group on the Future of Social Policy in an Enlarged European Union*, Office for Official Publications of the European Communities, Luxembourg.

European Commission (2004f), *Perceptions of Living Conditions in an Enlarged Europe*, Office for Official Publications of the European Communities, Luxembourg.

European Commission (2004g), *The Economic Costs of Non-Lisbon: A Survey of the Literature on the Economic Impact of Lisbon-Type Reforms*, Occasional Papers No. 16, Directorate-General for Economic and Financial Affairs, European Economy, Brussels.

European Commission (2005a), "Working Together for Growth and Jobs. A New Start for the Lisbon Strategy", Communication from the Commission, COM(2005)24, Brussels.

European Commission (2005b), "Joint Report on Social Protection and Social Inclusion", Document adopted by the Council on 3 March 2005, Brussels (and Technical Annex to this Report: Commission Staff Working Paper No. SEC(2005)69).

European Commission (2005c), "Report on Social Inclusion 2004. An Analysis of the National Action Plans on Social Inclusion (2004-2006) submitted by the 10 new Member States", Commission Staff Working Paper, SEC(2004)256, Brussels.

European Commission (2005d), "Social Agenda", Communication from the Commission, COM(2005)33 final, Brussels.

European Commission (2005e), "Commission Staff Working Document in support of the Report from the Commission to the Spring European Council (22–23 March 2005) on the Lisbon Strategy of Economic, Social and Environmental Renewal" [see above: European Commission, 2005a], SEC(2005)160, Brussels. [Together with the "Update of the Statistical Annex (Annex 1) to the 2005 Report from the Commission to the Spring European Council - Structural Indicators", available at http://europa.eu.int/growthandjobs/pdf/statistical_annex_2005_en.pdf].

European Commission (2005f), "Sustainable Development Indicators to Monitor the Implementation of the EU Sustainable Development Strategy", SEC(2005)161 final, Brussels.

European Commission (2005g), "The 2005 Review of the EU Sustainable Development Strategy: Initial Stocktaking and Future Orientations", Communication from the Commission, COM(2005)37 final, Brussels.

European Commission (2005h), "Integrated Guidelines for Growth and Jobs (2005–2008)", Communication from the Commission, COM(2005)141 final, Brussels.

European Commission (2005i), "Working Together for Growth and Jobs Next Steps in Implementing the Revised Lisbon Strategy", Commission Staff Working Paper, SEC(2005)622, Brussels.

European Commission (2005j), "Green Paper 'Confronting Demographic Change: A New Solidarity Between the Generations'", Communication from the Commission, COM(2005)94 final, Brussels.

European Commission (2005k), "On the Review of the Sustainable Development Strategy – A Platform for Action", Communication from the Commission, COM(2005)658 final, Brussels.

European Commission (2005l), "Working Together, Working Better: A New Framework for the Open Coordination of Social Protection and Inclusion Policies in the European Union", Communication from the Commission, COM(2005)706 final, Brussels.

European Commission (2005m), "Amended Proposal for a Decision of the European Parliament and of the Council 'Establishing a Community Programme for Employment and Social Solidarity (PROGRESS)'", Communication from the Commission, COM(2005)536 final, Brussels.

European Commission (2006a), "Joint Report on Social Protection and Social Inclusion", Document adopted by the Council on 10 March 2006, Brussels (together with "country profiles").

European Commission (2006b), "Technical Annex to the Joint Report on Social Protection and Social Inclusion", Commission Staff Working Document No. SEC(2006)523, Brussels (together with Annex on Methodological Notes and Statistical Tables).

European Commission (2006c), "Social Inclusion in Europe 2006 (Implementation and Update Reports on 2003–2005 NAPs/inclusion and Update Reports on 2004–2006 NAPs/inclusion)", Commission Staff Working Document No. SEC(2006)410, Brussels.

European Commission (2006d), "Synthesis Report on Adequate and Sustainable Pensions", Commission Staff Working Document No. SEC(2006)304, Brussels.

European Commission (2006e), "Evaluation of the Open Method of Coordination for Social Protection and Social Inclusion", Commission Staff Working Document No. SEC(2006)345, Brussels.

European Commission (2006f), "Time to Move Up a Gear – The New Partnership for Growth and Jobs", Communication from the Commission to the 2006 Spring European Council, Brussels.

European Commission (2006g), "Implementing the Community Lisbon programme: Social services of general interest in the European Union", Communication from the Commission, COM(2006)177 final, Brussels.

European Commission (2006h), "The Situation of Roma in an Enlarged European Union", Brussels, available at http://ec.europa.eu/employment_social/fundamental_rights/pdf/pubst/roma04_en.pdf.

European Communities (ed.) (2004), *Facing the Challenge. The Lisbon Strategy for Growth and Employment*, Report from the High Level Group chaired by Wim Kok, November 2004, Official Publications of the European Communities, Luxembourg.

European Parliament (2005), "Report on Social Inclusion in the New Member States (2004/2210(INI))", Committee on Employment and Social Affairs, A6-0125/2005, Brussels.

Eurostat (2000), "European Social Statistics: Income Poverty and Social Exclusion (1st Report)", KS-29-00-181-EN-C, Luxembourg.

Eurostat (2003), "European Social Statistics: Income Poverty and Social Exclusion, (2nd Report)", KS-BP-02-008-EN-C, Luxembourg.

Eurostat (2005), "The Continuity of Indicators During the Transition Between ECHP and EU-SILC", KS-CC-05-006-EN-N, Luxembourg, available at http://epp.eurostat.cec.eu.int/cache/ITY_OFFPUB/KS-CC-05-006/EN/KS-CC-05-006-EN.PDF.

Expert Group on Household Income Statistics (The Canberra Group) (2001), "Final Report and Recommendations", Ottawa, available at http://www.lisproject.org/links/canberra/finalreport.pdf

Fahey, T., Maître, B. and Nolan, B. (2004), "Housing Expenditures and Income Poverty in EU Countries", *Journal of Social Policy*, Vol. 33, No. 3, pp. 437–54.

Fahey, T., Maître, B., Whelan, C.T., Anderson, R., Domanski, H., Ostrowska, A., Alber, J., Delhey, J., Keck, W., Nauenberg, R., Olagnero, M. and Saraceno, C. (2004), *Quality of Life in Europe: First Results of a new pan-European Survey*, Office for Official Publications of the European Communities, Luxembourg.

Fahey, T. and Smyth, E. (2004), "Do Subjective Indicators Measure Welfare? Evidence from 33 European Countries", *European Societies*, Vol. 6, No. 1, pp. 5–27.

Ferrera, M. (1996), "The 'Southern Model' of Welfare in Social Europe", *Journal of European Social Policy*, Vol. 6, No. 1, pp. 17–37.

Foidart, F., Génicot. G. and Pestieau, P. (1997), "Echelles d'équivalence et allocations familiales", *Cahiers Economiques de Bruxelles*, No. 155, pp. 231–8.

Förster, M. (2004), "Longer-Term Trends in Income Poverty in the OECD Area", *Czech Sociological Review*, Vol. 40, No. 6, pp. 785–805.

Förster, M. (2005), "The European Social Space Revisited: Comparing Poverty in the Enlarged European Union", *Journal of Comparative Policy Analysis*, Vol. 7, No. 1, pp. 29–48.

Förster, M. and d'Ercole, M.M. (2005), "Income Distribution and Poverty in OECD Countries in the Second Half of the 1990s", OECD Social, Employment and Migration Working Papers No. 22, OECD, Paris.

Förster, M., Fuchs, M., Immervoll, H. and Tarcali, G. (2003), "Social Inclusion in Larger Europe: All About Money? Uses, Limitations and Extensions of Income-based Social Indicators", in Förster, M.F. et al (eds), *Understanding Social Inclusion in a Larger Europe – An Open Debate*, Eurosocial 71/03, Vienna.

Fouarge, D. (2003), "Costs of Non-Social Policy: Towards an Economic Framework of Quality Social Policies – and the Costs of Not Having Them", Study for the European Commission, Brussels.

Fouarge, D. (2004), *Poverty and Subsidiarity in Europe*, Edward Elgar, Cheltenham.

Frazer, H. (2005), "The Prospects for the Fight Against Poverty in an Enlarged EU and its Position within the Lisbon Agenda", Paper presented at the EAPN Conference on "The Future of the Inclusion Strategy", Luxembourg, 14 April, available at http://eapn.horus.be/module/module_page/images/pdf/pdf_events/HughFrazer04-05.doc.

Freeman, R.B. (1984), "Longitudinal Analyses of the Effects of Trade Unions", *Journal of Labor Economics*, Vol. 2, No. 1, pp. 1–26.

Frey, B.S. and Stutzer, A. (2002), "What Can Economists Learn from Happiness Research?", *Journal of Economic Literature*, No. 40, pp. 402–35.

Frick, J. and Grabka, M. (2003), "Imputed Rent and Income Inequality: A Decomposition Analysis for Great Britain, West Germany and the U.S.", *Review of Income and Wealth*, Series 49, No. 4, pp. 513–37.

Fusco, A. (2005), "La Contribution des Analyses Multidimensionnelles à la Compréhension et à la Mesure du Concept de Pauvreté – Application Empirique au Panel Communautaire de Ménages", Doctoral dissertation, University of Nice (Sophia Antipolis), available at http://www.ceps.lu/iriss/documents/these_fusco.pdf.

Government of Austria (2003), "Second National Action Plan for Social Inclusion 2003–2005".

Government of Cyprus (2004), "National Action Plan for Social Inclusion 2004–2006".

Government of Denmark (2003), "National Action Plan on Social Inclusion 2003–2005".

Government of Finland (2003), "National Action Plan against Poverty and Social Exclusion for 2003–2005".

Government of Hungary (2004), "National Action Plan on Social Inclusion 2004–2006".

Government of Italy (2003), "National Action Plan on Poverty and Social Exclusion 2003–2005".

Government of Lithuania (2004), "National Action Plan against Poverty and Social Exclusion in 2004–2006".

Government of Luxembourg (2003), "Plan National d'Action pour l'Inclusion Sociale pour le Grand-Duché de Luxembourg, Rapport National 2003–2005".

Government of the Netherlands (2003), "National Action Plan for Combating Poverty and Social Exclusion 2003–2005".

Government of the United Kingdom (2003), "National Action Plan on Social Inclusion 2003–2005", UK.

Gregg, P. and Wadsworth, J. (1996), *Mind the Gap, CEP Discussion Papers 0303*, Centre for Economic Performance, LSE, London.

Guio, A.-C. (2005a), *Income Poverty and Social Exclusion in the EU25*, Statistics in Focus, Population and Social Conditions, 13/2005, Eurostat, Luxembourg.

Guio, A.-C. (2005b), *Material Deprivation in the EU*, Statistics in Focus, Population and Social Conditions, Living Conditions and Welfare, 21/2005, Eurostat, Luxembourg.

Guio, A.-C. and Marlier, E. (2004), "The Laeken Indicators: Some Results and Methodological Issues in New EU Member States and Candidate Countries", *EMERGO, Journal of Transforming Economies and Societies*, Vol. 11, No. 2, pp. 21–48.

Guio, A.-C. and Museux, J.-M. (2006), "The Situation of Children in the EU: Comparison Between Income Poverty and Material Deprivation Approaches", Paper presented at the 29th General Conference of I.A.R.I.W., Joensuu, Finland, 20–26 August, available at http://www.iariw.org/c2006.asp.

Hagenaars, A., de Vos, K. and Zaidi, A. (1994), *Poverty Statistics in the Late 1980s*, Eurostat, Luxembourg.

Hagerty, M.R., Cummins, R.A., Ferris, A.L., Land, K., Michalos, A.C., Peterson, M., Sharpe, A., Sirgy, J. and Vogel, J. (2001), "Quality of Life Indexes for National Policy: Review and Agenda for Research", *Social Indicators Research*, No. 55, pp. 1–96.

Hernanz, V., Malherbet, F. and Pellizzari, M. (2004) *Take up of welfare benefits in OECD countries: a review of the evidence*, OECD Social, Employment and Migration Working Papers No. 17, OECD, Paris.

Hills, J. (2002), "Comprehensibility and Balance: The Case for Putting Indicators in Baskets", *Politica Economica*, No. 1, pp. 95–8.

Hills, J. (2004), *Inequality and the State*, Oxford University Press, Oxford.

Hoelscher, P. (2003), *"Immer musst du hingehen und praktisch betteln" – Wie Jugendliche Armut erleben*, Campus, Frankfurt am Main.

Hoelscher, P. (2004), "A Thematic Study Using Transnational Comparisons to Analyse and Identify What Combination of Policy Responses Are Most Successful in Preventing and Reducing High Levels of Child Poverty", Final report submitted to the European Commission, DG Employment and Social Affairs, Brussels, available at http://europa.eu.int/comm/employment_social/social_inclusion/docs/child_poverty_study_en.pdf.

Horemans, L. (ed.) (2003), *Final Report: European Project on Poverty Indicators Starting from the Experience of People Living in Poverty*, Vlaams Netwerk van Verenigingen waar Armen het Woord Nemen, Antwerp.

Iacovou, M. (2003), *Work-Rich and Work-Poor Couples: Polarisation in 14 Countries in Europe*, Working Paper 45 of the European Panel Analysis Group, University of Essex, Colchester.

Immervoll, H., Levy, H., Lietz, C., Mantovani, D., O'Donoghue, C., Sutherland, H. and Verbist, G. (2004), "The Effects of Taxes and Transfers on Household Incomes in the European Union", For presentation at the conference "The Distributional Effects of Government Spending and Taxation", Levy Institute of Bard College, USA, 15–16 October.

Immervoll, H., Levy, H., Lietz, C., Mantovani, D. and Sutherland, H. (2005), "The Sensitivity of Poverty Rates to Macro-level Changes in the European Union", *Cambridge Journal of Economics*, Vol. 30, No. 2, pp. 181–99.

Immervoll, H. and O'Donoghue, C. (2001), *Imputation of Gross Amounts from Net Incomes in Household Surveys: An Application Using EUROMOD*, EUROMOD Working Paper No. EM/1/01, Department of Applied Economics, Cambridge.

Immervoll, H., O'Donoghue, C. and Sutherland, H. (2000), *An Introduction to EUROMOD*, EUROMOD Working Paper, EM0/99, Department of Applied Economics, Cambridge.

Immervoll, H., Sutherland, H. and de Vos, K. (2001), "Reducing Child Poverty in the European Union: The Role of Child Benefits", in Vleminckx, K. and Smeeding, T.M. (eds), *Child Well-Being, Child Poverty and Child Policy in Modern Nations*, The Policy Press, Bristol.

Indicators Sub-Group of the Social Protection Committee (2004a), "Health and Social Exclusion Related Indicators Used at National Level: Review of National Action Plans for Social Inclusion", Document prepared by the Indicators Sub-Group secretariat for the 30/03/04 meeting of the Indicators Sub-Group, European Commission, Brussels.

Indicators Sub-Group of the Social Protection Committee (2004b), "Overview of Third Level Indicators Used in the NAP/inclusion. Relating to the Social Inclusion of 'Foreigners, Immigrants and Ethnic Minorities' (first discussion on possible common indicators)", Document ISG2004/16.09.2004/2 prepared by the Indicators Sub-Group secretariat for the 16/09/04 meeting of the Indicators Sub-Group, European Commission, Brussels.

Indicators Sub-Group of the Social Protection Committee (2005a), "Indicators of Material Deprivation for Monitoring Poverty and Social Exclusion in the EU", Document ISG/Doc/Feb05/point 6 prepared by Eurostat for the 22/02/05 meeting of the Indicators Sub-Group, European Commission, Brussels.

Indicators Sub-Group of the Social Protection Committee (2005b), "Conclusions of the ISG Meeting of 22 February 2005", European Commission, Brussels.

Indicators Sub-Group of the Social Protection Committee (2005c), "Minutes of the ISG Meeting of 15 June 2005", European Commission, Brussels.

Indicators Sub-Group of the Social Protection Committee (2006a), "Indicators of Material Deprivation and Poor Housing – Update on the Basis of the New 2004 EU-SILC Data and Proposals in the Context of Streamlined EU Indicators", Document prepared by Anne-Catherine Guio for the 12/07/06 meeting of the Indicators Sub-Group, European Commission, Brussels.

Indicators Sub-Group of the Social Protection Committee (2006b), "Proposal for a Portfolio of Overarching Indicators and for the Streamlined Social Inclusion, Pensions, and Health Portfolios", Final document as approved by Social Protection Committee (version adopted by the SPC at their May 2006 Meeting, dated 7 June 2006), European Commission, Brussels.

Irish National Economic and Social Council (2003), "An Investment in Quality: Services, Inclusion and Enterprise", available at http://www.nesc.ie/dynamic/docs/nesc111.pdf

Jeandidier, B. (1997a), "L'analyse des dimensions redistributives des politiques familiales. Des méthodes et des résultats qui stimulent la curiosité", *Recherches et Prévisions*, No. 48, pp. 5–26.

Jeandidier, B. (1997b), "La spécificité des politiques familiales en Europe. Une application menée à l'aide de microsimulations", *Recherches et Prévisions*, No. 48, pp. 27–44.

Jeandidier, B., Bastian, N., Jankeliowitch-Laval, E., Kop, J.-L. and Ray, J.-C. (1995), *Analyse et simulation de politiques de prestations familiales en Europe: une comparaison entre la France et l'Allemagne, la Belgique, l'Irlande et le Luxembourg*, ADEPS-Université, Nancy.

Jeandidier, B. and Reinstadler, A. (2002), "Pauvreté des enfants dans l'Union européenne et transferts sociaux : quels liens entre générosité, ciblage, efficacité, efficience et équité?", in Dupuis, J.-M., El Moudden, C., Gravel, F., Lebon, I., Maurau, G. and Ogier, N., *Politiques sociales et croissance économique*, Vol. 1, Editions L'Harmattan.

Jesuit, D., Rainwater, L. and Smeeding, T. (2002), "Regional Poverty within Rich Countries", in Bishop, J.A. and Amiel, Y. (eds), *Inequality, Welfare and Poverty: Theory and Measurement*, Vol. 9, Elsevier Science, New York.

Johansson, S. (1973), "The Level of Living Survey: a Presentation", *Acta Sociologica*, Vol. 16, pp. 211–19.

Killingsworth, M.R. (1983), *Labor Supply*, Cambridge University Press, Cambridge.

Kuivalainen, S. (2003), "How to Compare the Incomparable: An International Comparison of the Impact of Housing Costs on Levels of Social Assistance", *European Journal of Social Security*, Vol. 5, No. 2, pp. 128–50.

Kutsar, D. (2005), "Speech delivered at the EU Luxembourg Presidency Conference on 'Taking Forward the EU Social Inclusion Process'", Luxembourg, 13–14 June, available at http://www.ceps.lu/eu2005_lu/inclusion/interventions.cfm.

Laroque, G. (2005), "Income Maintenance and Labor Force Participation", *Econometrica*, Vol. 73, No. 2, pp. 341–76.

Laroque, G. and Salanié, B. (2002), "Labour Market Institutions and Employment in France", *Journal of Applied Econometrics*, Vol. 17, pp. 25–48.

Layard, R. (2005), *Happiness: Lessons from a New Science*, Allen Lane, London.

Legendre, F., Lorgnet, J.-P. and Thibault, F. (2003), "Que peut-on retenir de l'expérience française en matière de micro-simulation?", *Economie et Statistique*, No. 160–1, pp. I–XV.

Leibfried, S. (1992), "Towards a European Welfare State? On Integrating Poverty Regimes into the European Community", in Ferge, Z. and Kolberg, J. (eds), *Social Policy in a Changing Europe*, Campus Verlag, Frankfurt am Main.

Lelièvre, M., Marlier, E. and Pétour, P. (2004), "Un nouvel indicateur européen: les travailleurs pauvres", Paper presented at the Conference on "Accès inégal à l'emploi et à la protection sociale", University Paris 1, Matisse, Paris, 16–17 September, available at http://matisse.univ-paris1.fr/colloque-eps/.

Lenoir, R. (1974), *Les exclus*, Seuil, Paris.

Levy, H. (2003), *Child-Targeted Tax-Benefit Reform in Spain in a European Context: A Microsimulation Using EUROMOD*, EUROMOD Working Paper EM2/03, Department of Applied Economics, Cambridge.

Maître, B., Nolan, B. and Whelan, C.T. (2005), "Welfare Regimes and Household Income Packaging in the European Union", *Journal of European Social Policy*, Vol. 15, No. 2, pp. 157–71.

Marlier, E. (2003), "The EU Social Inclusion Process – Where We Were, Where We Are and What We Should Aim At …", in Förster, M.F. et al (eds), *Understanding Social Inclusion in a Larger Europe – An Open Debate*, Eurosocial 71/03, Vienna.

Marlier, E. (2006), "Embedding the Social Inclusion Process in Domestic Policies", Paper presented at the Combat Poverty Agency Conference on "Learning from Europe on Mainstreaming Social Inclusion Through the National Action Plans", Dublin, 11 April.

Marlier, E. and Cohen-Solal, M. (2000), *Social Benefits and Their Redistributive Effect in the EU – Latest Data Available*, Statistics in Focus, Theme 3, 09/2000, Eurostat, Luxembourg.

Matsaganis, M., O'Donoghue, C., Levy, H., Coromaldi, M., Mercader-Prats, M., Rodrigues, C.F., Toso, S. and Tsakloglou, P. (2004), *Child Poverty and Family Transfers in Southern Europe*, EUROMOD Working Paper No. EM2/04, Department of Applied Economics, Cambridge.

Meade, J.E. (1962), *UK, Commonwealth and Common Market*, Hobart Paper No. 17, Institute of Economic Affairs, London.

Melkert, A.P.W. (1997), "Speech by the Minister of Social Affairs and Employment of the Netherlands Mr A.P.W. Melkert", at the "For a Europe of Civil and Social Rights" Conference, Brussels, 4 June, available at http://home.szw.nl/actueel/dsp_persbericht.cfm?jaar=1997&link_id=725.

Micklewright, J. and Stewart, K. (2001), "Child Well-Being in the EU – and Enlargement to the East", in Vleminckx, K. and Smeeding, T.M., *Child Well-Being, Child Poverty and Child Policy in Modern Nations*, The Policy Press, Bristol.

Morley, J., Ward, T. and Watt, A. (2004), *The State of Working Europe 2004*, ETUI, Brussels.

Murat, F. (2004), "Les difficultés des adultes face à l'écrit", *INSEE Première*, No. 959, April.

Nelson, K. (2003), *Fighting poverty. Comparative Studies on Social Insurance, Means-Tested Benefits and Income Distribution*, Stockholm University, Stockholm.

Nolan, B. (1999), "Targeting Poverty", *New Economy*, Vol. 6, No. 1, pp. 44–9.

Nolan, B. and Whelan, C.T. (1996), *Resources, Deprivation and Poverty*, Oxford University Press, Oxford.

OECD (2003), *Taxing Wages*, OECD, Paris.

OECD (2004), *Benefits and Wages*, OECD, Paris.

OECD (2005), *Extending Opportunities: How Active Social Policy Can Benefit Us All*, OECD, Paris.

O'Higgins, M. and Jenkins, S. (1990), "Poverty in Europe: Estimates for 1975, 1980 and 1985, Analysing Poverty in the European Community", *Eurostat News*, Special Edition, Vol. 1.

Osier, G. and Museux, J.-M. (2006), "Variance Estimation for EU-SILC Complex Poverty Indicators using Linearization Techniques", Paper presented at the European Conference on Quality in Survey Statistics, Cardiff, 24–26 April, available at http://www.statistics.gov.uk/events/q2006/agenda.asp.

Oxley, H., Dang, T.-T., Förster, M.F. and Pellizari, M. (2001), "Income Inequality and Poverty Among Children and Households with Children in Selected OECD Countries: Trends and Determinants", in Vleminckx, K. and Smeeding, T.M. (eds), *Child Well-Being, Child Poverty and Child Policy in Modern Nations: What Do We Know?*, The Policy Press, Bristol.

Peña Casas, R. and Latta, M. (2004), *Working Poor in the European Union*, European Foundation for the Improvement of Living and Working Conditions, Office for Official Publications of the European Communities, Luxembourg, available at http://www.fr.eurofound.eu.int/publications/files/EF0467EN.pdf.

Politica Economica (2002), "Indicators for Social Inclusion: Making Common EU Objectives Work", *Politica Economica*, Special Issue, No. 1.

Potůček, M. (2004), "Accession and Social Policy: The Case of the Czech Republic", *Journal of European Social Policy*, Vol. 14, No. 3, pp. 253–66.

Ritakallio, V.-M. (2002), "New Recommendations for Compilation of Statistics Will Change the Cross-National Picture of Poverty in Europe", Paper presented at the EU COST A15 meeting, Urbino, 25 October.

Ritakallio, V.-M. (2003), "The Importance of Housing Costs in Cross-national Comparisons of Welfare (State) Outcomes", *International Social Security Review*, Vol. 56, No. 2, pp. 81–101, available at http://www.ingentaconnect.com/content/bpl/issr;jsessionid=19304f2ipype0.victoria.

Ritakallio, V.-M. and Bradshaw, J. (2005), "Child Poverty in the European Union", Nordic Research Council Project.

Room, G. (ed.) (1995), *Beyond the Threshold*, The Policy Press, Bristol.

Room, G. (2005), "Policy Benchmarking in the European Union: Indicators and Ambiguities", *Policy Studies*, Vol. 26, No. 2, pp. 117–32.

Ruxton, S. and Bennett, F. (2002), *Including Children?*, Euronet, Brussels.

Ryan, M. and Deci, A. (2001), "On Happiness and Human Potentials: A Review of Research on Hedonic and Eudaimonic Well-being", *Annual Review of Psychology*, No. 52, pp. 141–66.

Sakellaropoulos, T. and Berghman, J. (eds) (2004), *Connecting Welfare Diversity within the European Social Model*, Social Europe Series, Vol. 9, intersentia, Antwerp, Oxford and New York.

Santayana, G. (1980) *Reason in Common Sense*, Dover, New York.

Saraceno, C. (ed.) (2002), *Social Assistance Dynamics in Europe*, The Policy Press, Bristol.

Schmähl, W. (2004), "EU Enlargement and Social Security", *Intereconomics*, Vol. 39, No. 1, pp. 1–8.

Sen, A.K. (1985), *Commodities and Capabilities*, North-Holland, Amsterdam.

Silver, H. (1995), "Reconceptualizing Social Disadvantage: Three Paradigms of Social Exclusion", in Rodgers, G., Gore, C. and Figueiredo, J. (eds), *Social Exclusion: Rhetoric, Reality, Responses*, ILO, Geneva.

Social Protection Committee (2001), "Report on Indicators in the Field of Poverty and Social Exclusion", Brussels, available at http://www.europa.eu.int/comm/employment_social/news/2002/jan/report_ind_en.pdf.

Social Protection Committee (2003a), "Opinion of the Social Protection Committee on the Commission's Communication on Strengthening the Social Dimension of the Lisbon Strategy: Streamlining Open Coordination in the Field of Social Protection (COM(2003)261 final)", Brussels, available at http://europa.eu.int/comm/employment_social/social_protection_commitee/streamlining_en.pdf.

Social Protection Committee (2003b), "Common Outline for the 2003/2005 NAPs/inclusion", Brussels, available at http://europa.eu.int/comm/employment_social/social_inclusion/docs/commonoutline2003final_en.pdf.

Social Protection Committee (2006), "Guidelines for Preparing National Reports on Strategies for Social Protection and Social Inclusion", Brussels.

Social Protection Committee and Economic Policy Committee (2006), "Joint Opinion of the Social Protection Committee and the Economic Policy Committee on the Commission Communication on 'Working Together, Working Better: A New Framework for the Open Coordination of Social Protection and Inclusion Policies in the European Union' (COM(2005)706 final)," Brussels.

Špidla, V. (2005), "Speech Delivered at the EU Luxembourg Presidency Conference on 'Taking Forward the EU Social Inclusion Process'", Luxembourg 13–14 June, available at http://www.ceps.lu/eu2005_lu/inclusion/interventions.cfm.

Stewart, K. (2003), "Monitoring Social Inclusion in Europe's Regions", *Journal of European Social Policy*, Vol. 13, No. 4, pp. 335–56.

Sutherland, H. (1997), "Women, Men and the Redistribution of Income", *Fiscal Studies*, Vol. 18, pp. 1–22.

Sutherland, H. (1998), "Les modèles statiques de microsimulation en Europe dans les années 90", *Economie et Statistique*, Vol. 315, No. 5, pp. 35–50.

Sutherland, H. (2001), *EUROMOD: An Integrated European Benefit-Tax Mode*, EUROMOD Working Paper EM9/01, Department of Applied Economics, Cambridge.

Sutherland, H. (2005), "Speech Delivered at the EU Luxembourg Presidency Conference on 'Taking Forward the EU Social Inclusion Process'", Luxembourg 13–14 June, available at http://www.ceps.lu/eu2005_lu/inclusion/interventions.cfm.

Tsakloglou, P. and Papadopoulos, F. (2002), "Aggregate Level and Determining Factors of Social Exclusion in Twelve European Countries", *Journal of European Social Policy*, Vol. 12, No. 3, pp. 209–23.

UK Department for Work and Pensions (2003), *Measuring Child Poverty*, Department for Work and Pensions, London.

UK Department for Work and Pensions (2005), *Households Below Average Income 1994/5–2003/4*, Department for Work and Pensions, London.

UK Department of Social Security (1995), *Piloting Change in Social Security*, Department of Social Security, London.

UNDP (1990), *Human Development Report 1990*, Oxford University Press, Oxford.

UNICEF (2005a), *Child Poverty in Rich Countries*, Innocenti Report Card No. 6, Innocenti Research Centre, Florence.

UNICEF (2005b), "Children and Disability in Transition in CEE/CIS and Baltic States", Innocenti Insight, UNICEF ICDC and UNICEF Innocenti Research Centre, Florence, available at http://ideas.repec.org/p/ucf/innins/innins05-22.html.

UNICEF (forthcoming), *Child Poverty in Perspective: An Overview of Child Well-Being in Rich Countries*, Innocenti Report Card No. 7, Innocenti Research Centre, Florence.

US Department of Health, Education, and Welfare (1969), *Toward a Social Report*, US Government printing Office, Washington, D.C.

Van den Bosch, K. (1998), "Poverty and Assets in Belgium", *Review of Income and Wealth*, Series 44, No. 2, pp. 215–28.

Van den Bosch, K. (2002), "Convergence in Poverty Outcomes and Social Income Transfers in Member States of the EU", Paper for the XV World Congress of Sociology, Brisbane, July.

Vandenbroucke, F. (2002a), "The EU and Social Protection: What should the European Convention propose?", Paper presented at the Max Planck Institute for the Study of Societies, Cologne, 17 June.

Vandenbroucke, F. (2002b), "Foreword", in Atkinson, A.B., Cantillon, B., Marlier, E. and Nolan, B., *Social Indicators: The EU and Social Inclusion*, Oxford University Press, Oxford.

Van der Molen, I. and Novikova, I. (2005), "Mainstreaming Gender in the EU Accession Process: The Case of the Baltic Republics", *Journal of European Social Policy*, Vol. 15, No. 2, pp. 139–56.

Van Doorslaer, E., Koolman, X. and Jones, A.M. (2004), "Explaining Income-Related Inequalities in Health Care Utilisation in Europe: A Decomposition Approach", *Health Economics*, Vol. 13, No. 7, pp. 629–47.

Van Doorslaer, E., Koolman X. and Puffer, F. (2001), "Equity in the Use of Physician Visits in OECD Countries: Has Equal Treatment for Equal Need Been Achieved?", Chapter 11, "Measuring Up: Improving Health Systems Performance in OECD Countries", Proceedings of the Ottawa Conference, November 2001.

Van Doorslaer, E., Masseria C. and the OECD Health Equity Research Group (2004), *Income-Related Inequality in the Use of Medical Care in 21 OECD Countries*, OECD Health Working Papers No. 14, OECD, Paris.

Van Doorslaer, E., Wagstaff, A., van der Burg, H., Christiansen. T., De Graeve, D., Duchesne, I., Gerdtham, U.-G., Gerfin, M., Geurts, J., Gross, L., Häkkinen, U., John, J., Klavus, J., Leu, R.E., Nolan, B., O'Donnell, O., Propper, C., Puffer, F., Schellhorn, M., Sundberg, G. and Winkelhake, O. (2000), "Equity in the Delivery of Health Care in Europe and the US", *Journal of Health Economics*, Vol. 19, No. 5, pp. 553–83.

Van Oorschot, W. (1995), *Realizing Rights. A Multi-Level Approach to Non-Take-Up of Means-Tested Benefits*, Aldershot, Avebury.

Van Praag, B. and Ferrer-i-Carbonnel, A. (2004), *Happiness Quantified: A Satisfaction Calculus Approach*, Oxford University Press, Oxford.

Večerník, J. (1991), "Poverty in Czechoslovakia – A Brief Report Based on Two Surveys", unpublished (available from author).

Večerník, J. (2004), *Structural Tensions in the Interface between the Labour Market and Social Policy in the Czech Republic*, Sociological Studies 0404, Academy of Sciences of the Czech Republic.

Verbist, G. (2002), "An Inquiry into the Redistributive Effect of Personal Income Taxes in Belgium", Doctoral dissertation, University of Antwerp, Antwerp.

Verbist, G. (2005), *Replacement Incomes and Taxes: A Distributional Analysis for the EU-15 Countries*, EUROMOD Working Paper No. EM2/05, Department of Applied Economics, Cambridge.

Verma, V., Lemmi, A., Betti, G., Mulas, A., Natilli, M., Neri, L. and Salvati, N. (2005), "Regional Indicators to Reflect Social Exclusion and Poverty", Report prepared for Directorate-General "Employment, Social Affairs and Equal Opportunities" of the European Commission, available at http://www.unisi.it/ricerca/dip/dmq/verma/Reports/[16]%20Regional%20Indicators%20Social%20Exclusion%20and%20Poverty.pdf.

Vleminckx, K. and Smeeding, T. (2001), *Child Well-Being, Child Poverty and Child Policy in Modern Nations*, The Policy Press, Bristol.

Walker, R. (1995), "The Dynamics of Poverty and Social Exclusion, in Room, G. (ed.), *Beyond the Threshold*, The Policy Press, Bristol.

Whelan, C.T., Layte, R. and Maître, B. (2002), "Multiple Deprivation and Persistent Poverty in the European Union", *Journal of European Social Policy*, Vol. 12, No. 2, pp. 91–105.

Whelan, C.T., Layte, R. and Maître, B. (2004), "Understanding the Mismatch Between Income Poverty and Deprivation: A Dynamic Comparative Analysis", *European Sociological Review*, Vol. 20, No. 4, pp. 287–302.

Whelan, C.T., Layte, R., Maître, B. and Nolan, N. (2001), "Income, Deprivation and Economic Strain", *European Sociological Review*, Vol. 17, No. 4, pp. 357–72.

Whelan, C.T. and Maître, B. (2006), *Measuring Material Deprivation with EU-SILC: Lessons from the Irish Survey*, Working Paper, ESRI, Dublin.

Appendix 1

Tables

Chapter 2 Tables

See overleaf.

Table 2.1a: Some important steps in EU cooperation in the social area between 1993 and the 2004 EU Enlargement to 25 Member States

June 1993	The Copenhagen European Council invites Central and Eastern European countries that so wish to join the EU and adopts the Copenhagen membership criteria
March 1994–June 1996	Hungary, Poland, Romania, Slovakia, Latvia, Estonia, Lithuania, Bulgaria, the Czech Republic and finally Slovenia apply for EU membership [Cyprus, Malta and Turkey applied before 1993]
January 1995	EU Enlargement from 12 to 15 countries (Austria, Finland and Sweden)
October 1997	Signature of the Amsterdam Treaty (which came into force in May 1999), with its new legal base for the fight against social exclusion (Articles 136 and 137)
November 1997	The Luxembourg European Council (Jobs Summit) launches the European Employment Strategy (EES), following on from the introduction of a new title on employment in the Amsterdam Treaty
April 1998	First submission of annual National Action Plans on employment
December 1998	The Council adopts the first Joint Employment Report
January 1999	Completion of the Single European Market and establishment of a single European currency
December 1999	The Council endorses the Commission's Communication on "A Concerted Strategy for Modernising Social Protection" in its Conclusions on "the strengthening of cooperation for modernising and improving social protection" [see Appendix 2a]
March 2000	The Lisbon European Council launches the Lisbon Strategy, the Open Method of Coordination (OMC) and the Social Inclusion Process
December 2000	The Nice European Council adopts the EU common objectives for the Social Inclusion Process, launches the Pensions' Process and adopts the European Social Policy Agenda
February 2001	Signature of the Nice Treaty (which came into force in February 2003)
June 2001	Member States submit their first NAPs/inclusion to the Commission
September 2001	Adoption of the first Programme of Community action to encourage cooperation between Member States to combat social exclusion (five-year programme which started on 1 January 2002)
December 2001	The Laeken European Council endorses a first set of 18 Laeken indicators for social inclusion and the first Joint Inclusion Report; it also adopts the common objectives for the Pensions' Process
March 2002	The Barcelona European Council invites Member States to set "appropriate national targets for significantly reducing the number of people at risk of poverty and social exclusion by 2010" in their next NAPs/inclusion
September 2002	Member States submit their first National Strategy Reports on pensions to the Commission [the second (EU-25) round of national reporting on pensions took place in July 2005]
December 2002	The Council slightly amends the Nice common objectives for social inclusion to stress the importance of setting quantitative targets in National Action Plans on social inclusion (as agreed in Barcelona in March 2002), the need to strengthen the gender perspective in those Plans, and the risks of poverty and social exclusion faced by immigrants
	The Council endorses the Commission's proposal to establish three-year cycles for the policy coordination and synchronisation of the Broad Economic Policy Guidelines and the Employment Guidelines
February 2003	Croatia presents its application for EU membership
July 2003	Member States submit their second NAPs/inclusion to the Commission
October 2003	The Council endorses the Commission's proposal to streamline: i) the various EU social policy processes at EU level (launched as a follow-up of Lisbon) as from 2006; and ii) this "streamlined social protection and inclusion process" with the "streamlined Broad Economic Policy Guidelines and Employment Guidelines"
December 2003	Acceding countries and the Commission sign individual Joint Memoranda on Social Inclusion (JIM), which outline the situation and policy priorities in relation to poverty and social exclusion in the acceding countries
March 2004	Adoption of the second Joint Report on Social Inclusion by the Council
March 2004	The Former Yugoslav Republic of Macedonia presents its application for EU membership

Table 2.1b: Some important steps in EU cooperation in the social area since the 2004 EU Enlargement to 25 Member States

May 2004	EU Enlargement from 15 to 25 countries (Cyprus, the Czech Republic, Estonia, Hungary, Latvia, Lithuania, Malta, Poland, Slovakia and Slovenia)
July 2004	The 10 new Member States submit their first NAPs/inclusion to the Commission, the examination of which being issued in a *Commission's staff report*
October 2004	Launch of the Health Care and Long-Term Care Process, with the first National Strategy Reports to be submitted by Member States to the Commission in April 2005
October 2004	Signature by 25 Heads of State and Government of the *Treaty establishing a Constitution for Europe*[1]
November 2004	The Social Protection Committee starts preparing the mid-term review of the Lisbon process (preparation of the questionnaire to be answered by Member States, etc.)
February 2005	Bulgaria and the Commission sign a *Joint Memorandum on Social Inclusion* (JIM)
February 2005	European Commission's Communication on the Social Agenda covering the period up to 2010
March 2005	In its meeting of 3 March 2005 the EU EPSCO Council of Ministers states: "On the conclusion of the discussion, the President stressed that the Council felt that [...] it was necessary to stress economic growth and job creation without, however, neglecting to provide a framework of action on social protection and inclusion. For the Council, the social agenda submitted by the Commission was an integral part of the Lisbon Strategy. It also recalled that, in its EPSCO formation, the Council had a central role to play in monitoring that strategy."
March 2005	*Spring Summit*, where EU leaders state that "it is essential to [...] re-focus priorities on growth and employment" (par 5), and at the same time reaffirm that "social inclusion policy should be pursued by the Union and by Member States, with its multifaceted approach focusing on target groups such as children in poverty." (par 36)
	The European Council also "welcomes the Commission communication on the social agenda, which will help to achieve the Lisbon Strategy objectives by reinforcing the European social model based on the quest for full employment and greater social cohesion." (par 29)
April 2005	EU Accession Treaty signed by Bulgaria and Romania. These Treaties are to be ratified by the present and future Member States and will then enter into force on 1 January 2007 (except if the Union decides to postpone accession by one year to 1 January 2008).
June 2005	Romania and the Commission sign a *Joint Memorandum on Social Inclusion* (JIM)
December 2005	The Council adopts a revised Accession Partnership for Turkey
March 2006	*Spring Summit*, where the European Council emphasises that "The new strategy for jobs and growth provides a framework where economic, employment and social policy mutually reinforce each other, ensuring that parallel progress is made on employment creation, competitiveness, and social cohesion in compliance with European values." (par 69).
	EU leaders also ask the Commission and the Council to "inform each Spring European Council with the Joint Report on the progress in the area of social protection and social inclusion" (par 70), and reaffirm "the objective of the Partnership for growth and jobs that steps have to be taken to make a decisive impact on the reduction of poverty and social exclusion by 2010" (par 72).
June 2006	The European Council adopts "an ambitious and comprehensive renewed EU Strategy for Sustainable Development [...]. The implementation of this Strategy will be closely monitored and followed up by the European Council on a regular basis." (Presidency Conclusions, par 17)

[1] Updated information on the ratification process in the different Member States can be found on the Council website at the following address: http://www.consilium.europa.eu/showPage.asp?id=735&lang=en&mode=g

---

Table 2.2a: Revised list of streamlined overarching portfolio of indicators as agreed by the SPC on 22 May 2006 – Indicators

Indicator	Definition
1a. At-risk-of-poverty rate **(EU)** + illustrative values of at-risk-of-poverty threshold	Percentage of persons aged 0+ living in households with an income below 60% of national median income (breakdown by age 0-17, 18-64, 65+)
	NB 1: For each country, this indicator has to be systematically analysed by looking at both the proportion of people whose income is below the threshold (60% median national income) and the comparative level (in PPS) of this threshold for an illustrative household type (e.g. single person households)
	NB 2: Indicator likely to be complemented with at-persistent-risk-of-poverty rate once available
1b. Intensity of poverty risk, i.e. "Relative median poverty risk gap" **(EU)**	Difference between the median income of persons aged 0+ living in households with an income below the at-risk-of poverty threshold and the threshold itself, expressed as a percentage of the at-risk-of-poverty threshold (breakdown by age 0-17, 18-64, 65+)
2. S80/S20 Income quintile ratio **(EU)**	Ratio of total income received by the 20% of the country's population with the highest income (top quintile) to that received by the 20% of the country's population with the lowest income (lowest quintile)
3. Healthy life expectancy **(NAT)**	Number of years that a person at birth, at 45 and at 65 is still expected to live in a healthy condition (disability-free life expectancy) (breakdown by gender, and by socio-economic status where available)
	NB: Indicator to be interpreted jointly with life expectancy
4. Early school leavers not in education or training **(EU)**	Share of persons aged 18 to 24 who have only lower secondary education (level 0, 1 or 2 according to the 1997 International Standard Classification of Education - ISCED 97) and have not received education or training in the four weeks preceding the survey (breakdown by gender)
5. People living in jobless households **(EU)**	Proportion of people living in jobless households, expressed as a share of all people in the same age group, separately for those aged 0-17 and 18-59
	(breakdown by gender for 18-59; students aged 18-24 years living in households composed solely of students are counted in neither numerator nor denominator)
	NB: Indicator to be analysed in the light of the distribution of (people living in) jobless households by main household types
6. Projected total public social expenditures **(NAT)**	Age-related projections of total public social expenditures, current levels (% of GDP) and projected change in share of GDP in percentage points to 2010, 2020, 2030, 2040 and 2050
7a. Median relative income of elderly people **(EU)**	Median equivalised income of people aged 65+ as a ratio of income of people aged 0-64
7b. Aggregate replacement ratio **(EU)**	Median individual pensions of those aged 65-74 relative to median individual earnings of those aged 50-59, excluding other social benefits (breakdown by gender)

(continued)

Table 2.2a: Revised list of streamlined overarching portfolio of indicators as agreed by the SPC on 22 May 2006 – Indicators (continued)

Indicator	Definition
8. Self-reported unmet need for healthcare	*To be finalised:* Use, definition and breakdowns yet to be agreed upon once EU-SILC data is available for all 25 Member States (see Section 5.3 for a brief discussion of useful indicators that could be developed on this)
9. At-risk-of-poverty rate anchored at a fixed moment in time **(EU)**	Percentage of persons aged 0+ living in households with an income below the at-risk-of-poverty threshold calculated in 2005 (income reference year 2004), up-rated by inflation over subsequent years (breakdown by age (0-17, 18-64 and 65+, and by gender for people aged 18+)
	NB: Indicator aimed at analysing improved standards of living resulting from economic growth; it might be replaced or supplemented in future by material deprivation or consistent poverty indicators
10. Employment rate of older workers **(EU)**	Persons in employment in age groups 55-59 and 60-64 as a proportion of total population in same age group (breakdown by gender, and by age 55-59, 60-64)
11. In-work poverty risk, i.e. "working poor" **(EU)**	Percentage of individuals who are classified as employed (distinguishing between "wage and salary employment plus self-employment" and "wage and salary employment only") according to the definition of most frequent activity status and who are living in households with an income below 60% of national median income (breakdown by gender)
	NB: Indicator to be analysed according to personal, job and household characteristics; and also in comparison with the poverty risk faced by the unemployed and the inactive
12. Activity rate **(EU)**	Percentage of employed and unemployed people in total population of working age (15-64) (breakdown by age 15-24, 25-54, 55-59, 60-64; and by gender)
	NB: Indicator showing how, on average, the situation in regions differs from the national average; it might be replaced or supplemented by "average exit age from the labour market" when quality issues are resolved
13. Regional cohesion **(NAT)**	Standard deviation of regional employment rates at NUTS (Nomenclature of Territorial Units for Statistics) level 2 divided by the weighted national average (age 15-64)
14. Health	*Yet to be decided* following ISG work on the OMC on health care and long-term care

Notes:

(1) "Income" must be understood as equivalised disposable income. It is defined as the household's total disposable income divided by its 'equivalent size', to take account of the size and composition of the household, and is attributed to each household member including children. The equivalent scale that is used is the modified OECD scale, which gives a weight of 1 to the first adult, 0.5 to any other household member aged 14 and over and 0.3 to any child below the age of 14

(2) The "most frequent activity status" is defined as the status that individuals declare to have occupied for more than half the number of months in the calendar year (see Chapter 2)

(3) "NAT" refers to commonly agreed *national* indicators whereas "EU" refers to commonly agreed *EU* indicators

Source and numbering of indicators: Indicators Sub-Group, 2006b

Table 2.2b: Revised list of streamlined overarching portfolio of indicators as agreed by the SPC on 22 May 2006 – Context Information

Context Information
I. GDP growth
2 Employment rate (by gender)
Unemployment rate (by gender and key age groups)
Long-term unemployment rate (by gender and key age groups)
3. Life expectancy at birth and at 65
4. Old age dependency ratio (current and projected)
5. Distribution of population by household types, including collective households
6. Public debt: current and projected (in % of GDP)
7. Social protection expenditures: current, by function, gross and net (ESPROSS)
8. Distribution of (people living in) jobless households by main household types (same typology of households as that for Secondary Indicator 1a in Table 2.3b)
9. Making work pay indicators: unemployment trap, inactivity trap (esp. second earner case), low-wage trap
10. Net income of social assistance recipients as a % of the at-risk-of-poverty threshold for 3 jobless household types (single, lone parent with 2 children and couple with 2 children) NB: This indicator refers to the income of people living in households that only rely on "last resort" social assistance benefits (including related housing benefits) and for which no other income stream is available from other social protection benefits (e.g. unemployment or disability schemes) or from work
11. At-risk-of-poverty rate before social cash transfers other than pensions (breakdown by age: 0-17, 18-64, 65+)
12. Projected theoretical replacement ratio (income from pensions/earnings from work): Change in projected theoretical replacement ratio (i.e. change in the theoretical level of income from pensions at the moment of take-up related to the earnings from work in the last year before retirement for a hypothetical worker (base case), percentage points, 2004-2050, with information on the type of pension scheme), which is to be presented *together with* change in projected public pension expenditure as a share of GDP, 2004-2050 NB: Results relate to current and projected, gross (public and private) and total net replacement rates, and should be accompanied by information on representativeness and assumptions (contribution rates and coverage rate, public and private)

Note: The indicator on "at-risk-of-poverty rate before social transfers other than pensions" is meant to compare the observed risk of poverty with a *hypothetical measure* of a poverty risk in the absence of all social transfers (other than pensions) all other things being kept equal. In particular, household and labour market structures are kept unchanged. This measure does not take account of other types of transfers which can have an impact on household disposable income such as transfers in kind and tax rebates (for a discussion of this indicator see: Atkinson, Cantillon, Marlier and Nolan, 2002)

Source and numbering of indicators: Indicators Sub-Group, 2006b

Table 2.3a: Revised list of streamlined social inclusion ("Laeken") portfolio of indicators as agreed by the SPC on 22 May 2006 – Primary Indicators

Indicator	Definition
1. At-risk-of-poverty rate **(EU)** + illustrative values of at-risk-of-poverty threshold	Percentage of persons aged 0+ living in households with an income below 60% of national median income (breakdown by age 0-17, 18-64, 65+; and by gender for people aged 18+)
	NB 1: The value of the at-risk-of-poverty threshold (60% median national income) in PPS is to be systematically provided for two illustrative household types: single person households and households with two adults and two children
	NB 2: For each country, this indicator has to be systematically analysed by looking at both the proportion of people whose income is below the threshold (60% median national income) and the comparative level (in PPS) of this threshold for two illustrative household types
2. Persistent at-risk-of-poverty rate **(EU)**	Percentage of persons aged 0+ living in households with an income below the at-risk-of-poverty threshold in the current year and in at least two of the preceding three years (breakdown by age 0-17, 18-64, 65+; and by gender for people aged 18+)
	NB: This indicator will become available as from 2009, when four years of longitudinal data from EU-SILC will be available for the 13 EU countries that launched EU-SILC in 2004. It will be available for all 25 Member States as from 2010 (see Section 5.1)
3. Intensity of poverty risk, i.e. "Relative median poverty risk gap" **(EU)**	Difference between the median income of persons aged 0+ living in households with an income below the at-risk-of-poverty threshold and the threshold itself, expressed as a percentage of the at-risk-of-poverty threshold (breakdown by age 0-17, 18-64, 65+; and by gender for people aged 18+)
4. Long-term unemployment rate **(EU)**	Total long-term unemployed population (=12 months; ILO definition) as a proportion of total active population aged 15 years or more (breakdown by gender)
5. Population living in jobless households **(EU)**	Proportion of people living in jobless households, expressed as a share of all people in the same age group, separately for those aged 0-17 and 18-59 (breakdown by gender for persons aged 18-59; students aged 18-24 years living in households composed solely of students are counted in neither numerator nor denominator)
	NB: This indicator sheds light on an important aspect of social exclusion as it reflects the lack of contact of children and working-age adults with the world of work. It also reflects polarisation of employment across households, and is to be analysed in the light of the distribution of people living in jobless households by household types

(continued)

Table 2.3a: Revised list of streamlined social inclusion ("Laeken") portfolio of indicators as agreed by the SPC on 22 May 2006 – Primary Indicators (continued)

Indicator	Definition
6. Early school leavers not in education or training **(EU)**	Share of persons aged 18 to 24 who have only lower secondary education (level 0, 1 or 2 according to the 1997 International Standard Classification of Education - ISCED 97) and have not received education or training in the four weeks preceding the survey (breakdown by gender)
7. Employment gap of immigrants **(NAT)**	Percentage point difference between the employment rate for non-immigrants and that for immigrants. Immigrants are defined on the basis of the variable "born abroad", with each country deciding whether to include nationals born abroad or not (breakdown by gender)
	NB: This indicator needs to be supplemented by relevant national data covering other key aspects of the inclusion of immigrants
8. *Material deprivation*	*To be developed*
	(breakdown by age 0-17, 18-64, 65+; and by gender)
	(see Sections 5.2 and 5.3 for a brief discussion of useful indicators that could be developed on this)
9. Housing	*To be developed*
	(breakdown by age 0-17, 18-64, 65+; and by gender)
	(it should be recalled that in the meantime, in line with decision of December 2001 Laeken European Council, Member States are expected to report on homelessness, housing costs and decent housing)
10. *Self-reported unmet need for healthcare*	*To be finalised: Use, definition and breakdowns yet to be agreed upon once EU-SILC data is available for all 25 Member States (see Section 5.3 for a brief discussion of useful indicators that could be developed on this)*
11. *Child well-being*	*To be developed (see Section 5.5 for a brief discussion of useful indicators that could be developed on this)*

Notes:

(1) "Income" must be understood as equivalised disposable income. See note to Table 2.2a

(2) "NAT" refers to commonly agreed *national* indicators whereas "EU" refers to commonly agreed *EU* indicators

Source and numbering of indicators: Indicators Sub-Group, 2006b

Table 2.3b: Revised list of streamlined social inclusion ("Laeken") portfolio of indicators as agreed by the SPC on 22 May 2006 – Secondary Indicators

Indicator	Definition
1.At-risk-of-poverty rate **(EU)**	Percentage of persons aged 0+ living in households with an income below 60% of national median income (full breakdown by age (0-17, 18-24, 25-54, 55-64, 65+); breakdown by gender for people aged 18+)
1a. Poverty risk by household type **(EU)**	Percentage of persons aged 0+ living in households with an income below 60% of national median income, in the following household types:
	Households with no dependent children • single person under 65 years of age • single person 65 years and over • single woman • single man • two adults, at least one 65 years or over • two adults, both under 65 years • other
	Households with dependent children (aged 0-17, or 18-24 if inactive *and* living with parent(s) • single parent, one or more dependent children • two adults, one dependent child • two adults, two dependent children • two adults, three or more dependent children • three or more adults with dependent children
1b. Poverty risk by the work intensity of their households **(EU)**	Percentage of persons aged 0+ living in households with an income below 60% of national median income, in different work intensity categories and broad household types. Work intensity is the number of months all working age household members have worked during the income reference year as a proportion of the total number of months they could have worked, with categories ranging from 0 (jobless household) to 1 (full work intensity) (breakdown by age 0-17, 18-64, 65+; and by gender for people aged 18+)
1c. Poverty risk by most frequent activity status **(EU)**	Percentage of adults (aged 18 years or over) living in households with an income below 60% of national median income, in the following most frequent activity status groups: • employment (singling out wage and salary employment) • unemployment • retirement • other inactivity (breakdown by gender)

(continued)

Table 2.3b: Revised list of streamlined social inclusion ("Laeken") portfolio of indicators as agreed by the SPC on 22 May 2006 – Secondary Indicators (continued)

Indicator	Definition
1d. Poverty risk by accommodation tenure status **(EU)**	Percentage of persons aged 0+ living in households with an income below 60% of national median income, in the following accommodation tenure categories: • owner-occupied or rent free • rented (breakdown by age 0-17, 18-64, 65+; and by gender for people aged 18+)
1e. Dispersion around the at-risk-of-poverty threshold **(EU)**	Percentage of persons aged 0+ living in households with an income below 40%, 50% and 70% of the national median income (breakdown by age 0-17, 18-64, 65+; and by gender for people aged 18+)
2. Persons with low educational attainment **(EU)**	Percentage of the adult population (aged 25 years and over) who have only lower secondary education (level 0, 1 or 2 according to the 1997 International Standard Classification of Education – ISCED 97) (breakdowns by age 25-34, 35-54, 55-64, 65+, 25-64; and by gender)
3. Low reading literacy performance of pupils **(EU)**	Percentage of 15-year-old pupils who are at level 1 or below on the PISA combined reading literacy scale (breakdown by gender) NB: Available every 3 years

Notes:

(1) "Income" must be understood as equivalised disposable income. See note to Table 2.2a

(2) The "most frequent activity status" is defined as the status that individuals declare to have occupied for more than half the number of months in the calendar year (see Chapter 2)

(3) "NAT" refers to commonly agreed *national* indicators whereas "EU" refers to commonly agreed *EU* indicators

Source and numbering of indicators: Indicators Sub-Group, 2006b

Table 2.3c: Revised list of streamlined social inclusion ("Laeken") portfolio of indicators as agreed by the SPC on 22 May 2006 – Context Information

Context Information	Definition
1. S80/S20 Income quintile ratio	Ratio of total income received by the 20% of the country's population with the highest income (top quintile) to that received by the 20% of the country's population with the lowest income (lowest quintile)
2. Gini coefficient	Summary measure of the cumulative share of income accounted for by the cumulative percentages of the number of individuals; values ranging from 0% (complete equality) to 100% (complete inequality)
3. Regional cohesion	Standard deviation of regional employment rates at NUTS (Nomenclature of Territorial Units for Statistics) level 2 divided by the weighted national average (age 15-64)
4. Life expectancy at birth and at 65	Number of years a person aged 0 and 65 is still expected to live (breakdown by gender, and by socio-economic status where available)
5. At-risk-of-poverty rate anchored at a fixed moment in time	Percentage of persons aged 0+ living in households with an income below the at-risk-of-poverty threshold calculated in 2005 (income reference year 2004), up-rated by inflation over subsequent years (breakdown by age 0-17, 18-64 and 65+), and by gender for people aged 18+) NB: Indicator aimed at analysing improved standards of living resulting from economic growth
6. At-risk-of-poverty rate before social cash transfers (other than pensions)	Percentage of persons aged 0+ living in households falling below 60% of the median national income (after social cash transfers) on the basis of their income excluding all social cash transfers other than retirement and survivors pensions (see note to Table 2.2b) (breakdown by age, and by gender for people aged 18+)
7. Jobless households by main household types	Distribution of (people living in) jobless households by main household types (same typology of households as that for Secondary Indicator 1a in Table 2.3b)
8. In-work poverty risk	Percentage of individuals who are classified as employed (distinguishing between "wage and salary employment plus self-employment" and "wage and salary employment only") according to the definition of most frequent activity status and who are living in households with an income below 60% of national median income (breakdown by full-time/part-time) NB: This indicator needs to be analysed according to personal, job and household characteristics. It should also be analysed in comparison with the poverty risk faced by the unemployed and the inactive
9. Making work pay indicators	Indicators of unemployment trap, inactivity trap (esp. second earner case), low-wage trap
10. Net income of social assistance as percentage of the at-risk-of-poverty threshold	Income of people living in households that rely solely on "last resort" social assistance benefits (including related housing benefits), and for which no other income stream is available from other social protection benefits (e.g. unemployment or disability schemes) or from work, expressed as a percentage of the 60% median at-risk-of-poverty threshold for their household type. It is calculated for three jobless household types NB: It should help evaluate whether the safety nets provided to those households most excluded from the labour market are sufficient to lift people out of poverty
11. Self-reported limitations in daily activities by income quintiles	Percentage of persons aged 18+ who declare that for at least the last six months, because of health problems, they have not been able to do the activities people usually do (For each quintile: breakdown by age 18-64 and 65+, and and by gender)

Notes: (1) "Income" must be understood as equivalised disposable income. See note to Table 2.2a; (2) The "most frequent activity status" is defined as the status that individuals declare to have occupied for more than half the number of months in the calendar year (see Chapter 2)

Source and numbering of indicators: Indicators Sub-Group, 2006b

Table 2.4: Shortlist of Structural Indicators

Indicator 1	GDP per capita in PPS (General Economic Background)
Indicator 2	Labour productivity per person employed (General Economic Background)
Indicator 3	Employment rate* (Employment)
Indicator 4	Employment rate of older workers (55-64)* (Employment)
Indicator 5	Youth educational attainment (20-24)* (Innovation and Research)
Indicator 6	Gross domestic expenditure on R&D – GERD (Innovation and Research)
Indicator 7	Comparative price levels (Economic Reform)
Indicator 8	Business investment (Economic Reform)
Indicator 9	**At-risk-of-poverty rate after social transfers* (Social Cohesion)**
Indicator 10	**Long-term unemployment rate* (Social Cohesion)**
Indicator 11	**Regional cohesion, i.e. dispersion of regional employment rates* (Social Cohesion)**
Indicator 12	Total greenhouse gas emissions (Environment)
Indicator 13	Energy intensity of the economy (Environment)
Indicator 14	Volume of freight transport relative to GDP (Environment)

Note: * disaggregated by gender

Source: European Commission, 2005e, and Eurostat (http://europa.eu.int/comm/eurostat/structuralindicators)

Table 2.5: Long list of Structural Indicators for social cohesion

Indicator 1	Inequality of income distribution (income quintile share ratio)
Indicator 2	At-risk-of-poverty rate before/after social transfers*
Indicator 3	At-persistent-risk-of-poverty rate*
Indicator 4	Regional cohesion, i.e. dispersion of regional employment rates*
Indicator 5	Early school leavers*
Indicator 6	Long-term unemployment rate*
Indicator 7	Children aged 0-17 living in jobless households Prime-aged adults (18-59) living in jobless households*

Note: * disaggregated by gender

Source: Eurostat (http://europa.eu.int/comm/eurostat/structuralindicators)

Chapter 3 Tables

See opposite.

Table 3.1a: Pattern of social indicators for the 25 Member States - highlighting less than EU median performing countries

	BE	DK	DE	FR	CY	LU	NL	AT	FI	SE	CZ	LT	HU	MT	SI	IE	UK	EE	EL	ES	IT	LV	PL	PT	SK
At-risk-of-poverty rate (60%)	-	--	+	-	-	--	--	-	--	--	--	:	-	:	--	++	+	+	++	++	++	+	+	++	++
Long-term unemployment women	+	--	++	+	-	--	--	--	--	--	+	++	-	+	+		--	++	++	+	++	+	++	+	++
Long-term unemployment men	+	--	++	+	--	--	--	--	-	--	+	++	-	+	+	--	--	++	+	-	+	++	++	-	++
Youth unemployment (15-24)	+	--	-	++	--	--	--	--	-	-	+	-	-	+	-	--	--	+	++	++	++	+	++	-	++
Youth unemployment women (15-24)	+	--	-	+	+	+	--	--	+	-	+	-	-	+	-	--	-	+	++	++	++	++	++	-	++
Youth unemployment men (15-24)	+	--	-	+	--	--	--	--	++	-	++	++	-	+	-	+	+	++	+	+	+	-	++	-	++
Adults in jobless households	++	-	++	+	--	--	+	+	++	::	-	-	++	+	--	++	++	+	-	--	-	--	++	:	+
Children in jobless households	++	-	++	+	--	--	+	--	++	::	+	::	++	+	::	++	++	::	+	--	-	:	:	:	++
Early school leavers women	-	--	+	+	++	++	+	-	-	-	::	::	+	++	::	++	+	:	+	++	++	-	:	++	++
Early school leavers men	-	--	+	+	++	-	+	-	-	--	::	::	-	++	::	+	+	+	++	++	++	+	-	++	--
Life expectancy at birth women	+	-	+	++	+	++	+	++	++	++	-	-	--	+	-	+	+	--	+	++	++	-	+	++	:
Life expectancy at birth men	+	-	+	+	++	+	++	+	-	++	-	-	-	+	-	+	+	--	++	++	++	-	-	++	-
Poverty gap	+	-	++	+	-	++	-	-	-	-	--	-	-	-	-	+	-	+	++	++	++	+	+	++	++
Deprivation on 7-item scale	--	-	+	--	-	--	--	-	-	::	+	-	++	-	-	+	-	++	+	+	-	++	++	++	+

Notes: (1) At-risk-of-poverty rate and poverty gap: income reference year 2003, except for CZ (2002) and MT (2000). Data NL and SK are provisional, see Figure 3.1. (2) Long-term unemployment, youth unemployment, persons in jobless households and early school leavers: 2004. (3) Life expectancy at birth: 2002. (3) Deprivation on 7-item scale: Eurobarometer EU-10 (2002); ECHP (1996). SE not included

Interpretation: Country figures are being compared with the EU-median for each indicator: '-' indicates in the second;'+' in the third;'++' in the fourth quartile;'-' unknown. In borderline cases, the classification is given as + (-) rather than ++ (- -).':' unknown. [Quartiles and median are used for their non-dependency on outliers.]

Data sources for calculations: European Commission, (2006b) – Annex 1c. Statistical Tables; European Commission, 2004f, Table 3 as far as the variable 'Deprivation on a 7-item scale' is concerned.

Table 3.1b: Pattern of social indicators for the 25 Member States – highlighting possible best practices

	BE	DK	DE	FR	CY	LU	NL	AT	FI	SE	CZ	LT	HU	MT	SI	IE	UK	EE	EL	ES	IT	LV	PL	PT	SK
At-risk-of-poverty rate (60%)	-	::	+	-	-	::	-	-	::	::	::	-	-	-	::	++	+	+	++	++	++	+	+	++	++
Long-term unemployment women	+	::	++	+	-	::	-	::	-	::	+	++	-	-	+	::	::	+	++	+	++	+	++	+	++
Long-term unemployment men	+	::	++	+	::	::	-	::	-	::	+	++	-	+	+	::	::	++	+	-	+	++	++	-	++
Youth unemployment (15-24)	+	::	-	++	::	-	::	::	+	-	+	+	-	+	-	::	::	+	++	++	++	+	++	-	++
Youth unemployment women (15-24)	+	::	-	+	::	+	::	::	+	-	+	-	-	+	::	::	::	+	++	++	+	++	++	-	++
Youth unemployment men (15-24)	+	::	-	+	::	-	::	::	++	+	++	++	-	+	-	-	-	++	+	+	+	-	++	-	++
Adults in jobless households	++	-	++	+	++	::	-	+	++	::	-	-	++	+	::	+	++	+	-	+	+	::	++	++	+
Children in jobless households	++	-	++	+	++	::	+	-	++	::	+	-	++	+	::	::	++	-	::	-	-	+	++	::	++
Early school leavers women	-	::	+	+	++	+	+	-	-	-	::	::	-	++	::	+	+	::	+	++	++	+	::	++	::
Early school leavers men	-	-	-	+	++	+	+	::	++	++	::	::	-	++	::	++	++	::	+	++	++	+	::	++	::
Life expectancy at birth women	+	-	+	++	+	++	+	++	++	++	-	--	--	+	-	--	-	--	+	++	++	--	-	-	--
Life expectancy at birth men	+	-	+	+	++	-	++	+	-	++	-	--	--	+	-	+	+	--	++	++	++	--	-	-	-
Poverty gap	+	-	++	-	-	-	-	-	-	-	+	++	++	::	-	-	-	+	++	+	++	+	+	++	++
Deprivation on 7-item scale	::	-	+	::	-	::	::	-	-	::	+	++	++	::	::	+	-	++	+	+	-	++	++	++	+

Notes and interpretation: see Table 3.1a

Data source for calculations: European Commission, (2006b) – Annex 1c. Statistical Tables; European Commission, 2004f, Table 3 as far as the variable 'Deprivation on 7-item scale' is concerned.

Tables

Table 3.2: Breakdowns for the 25 Member States - highlighting less than EU median performing countries (upper part of Table) and subgroups with higher poverty risk than the national average (lower part of Table)

	EU	BE	DK	DE	FR	CY	LU	NL	AT	FI	SE	CZ	LT	HU	MT	SI	IE	UK	EE	EL	ES	IT	LV	PL	PT	SK
Comparison between country figures and EU median																										
At-risk-of-poverty rate (60%)	16.0	-	-	+		-	-	-	-	-	-	-	+	-		-	++	+	+	++	++	++	+	+	++	++
S80/S20 ratio	4.8	=	-	+		-	-	-	-	-	-	-	+	-			+	++	++	++	++	++	++	+	++	++
Employment rate (15-64)	63.3	-	++	+	+	+	+	++	++	+	++	+	+	-	++	+	+	++	++	++	-	-	++	-	++	-
Employment rate women	55.7	-	++	+	+	+	-	++	++	++	++	+	+	-	--	+	+	++	+	-	-	-	+	-	++	-
Employment rate men	70.9	-	++	-		++	++	++	+	+	+	+	+	-	++		++	++	-	+	+	-	-	-	+	-
Employment rate older women (55-64)	31.7	++	++	+	+	++	-	+	-	++	++	+	+	-		-	++	++	++	+	+	+	+	-	++	-
Employment rate older men (55-64)	50.7	--	++	+		++	-	+	-	++	++	+	+	-		-	++	++	+	-	+	+	+	-	++	-
Average labour market exit age	60.7	-	+	+		++		+	-		++	-		-		-	++	+	++		+	+	++		+	-
Comparison between national subgroup figures and national total population figures																										
At-risk-of-poverty women (60%)	6.3	+	=	+	=	+	+	+	+	+	+	=	=	-		+	+	=	+	+	+	=	+	-	=	++
At-risk-of-poverty men (60%)	-12.5	-	-	-	-	-	-	-	=	=	=	=	=	-		+	=	=	-	-	=	-	-	-	=	-
At-risk-of-poverty 0-15 (60%)	25.0	+	++	++	++	-	++	++	+	-	=	+++	+	++	++	-	+	+	+	=	+	++	++	++	+	++
At-risk-of-poverty 16-24 (60%)	31.3	+	+++	++	++	-	-	++	=	+++	+++	=	=	+	++	+	+	+	+	+	-	++	+	=	=	+
At-risk-of-poverty 25-49 (60%)	-12.5	-	-	-	-	-	+	-	-	-	+	=	-	-			-	-	=	-	-	-	=	-	-	+
At-risk-of-poverty 50-64 (60%)	-18.8	-	-	-	-	-	-	-	-	-	+	-	=	-	+	-	-	-	-	-	-	-	-	-	-	+
At-risk-of-poverty 65+ (60%)	12.5	++	+	-	+	+++	-	-	++	++	++	+++	-	-	++	-	+++	++	-	++	++	+++	-	-	++	-
At-risk-of-poverty single women (60%)	62.5	++	+++	++	++	+++	-	-	+++	++	+++	++	++	+	+++	-	+++	++	+++	++	++	++	-	-	+++	+
At-risk-of-poverty Single men (60%)	37.5	+	++	++	++	+++	+	++	+	+++	+++	++	+++	++	+++	+	+++	++	++	++	++	+++	++	+	+++	++
At-risk-of-poverty couple 65 - no child (60%)	-37.5	-	-	-	-	-	-	-	-	-	-	-	-	-	-	-	-	-	-	-	-	-	-	-	-	-
At-risk-of-poverty couple 1 child (60%)	-25.0	-	-	-	-	-	-	-	-	-	-	-	-	-	-	-	-	-	-	-	-	-	-	-	-	-
At-risk-of-poverty couple 2 Children (60%)	-6.3	-	-	-	++	-	=	-	-	-	+	=	-	-	+	+	+	-	-	-	-	++	=	-	-	+
At-risk-of-poverty couple 3 children (60%)	68.8	+	++	++	+++	++	++	+++	++	+	++	+++	+++	+++	+++	-	+	++	++	+++	+++	+++	+++	++	++	+++
At-risk-of-poverty single parents (60%)	112.5	+++	+++	+++	+++	+++	+++	+++	+++	+++	+++	+++	+++	++	+++	+++	+++	++	+++	+++	+++	+++	+++	++	+++	+++
At-risk-of-poverty people at work (60%)	-43.8	+++	+++	+++	+++	+++	+++	+++	+++	+++	+++	+++	+++	+++	+++	+++	+++	+++	+++	+++	+++	+++	+++	+++	+++	+++
At-risk-of-poverty unemployed (60%)	162.5	++	+++	+++	+++	+	+++	-	++	++	+++	+++	++	+++	+++	+++	++	++	+++	++	++	+++	++	+++	++	+++
At-risk-of-poverty pensioners (60%)	0.0	+	++	-	+++	+++	+	+	+	-	++	++	+	+	+	++	++	+++	+++	+++	++	+++	+	+++	+++	+++

Notes: (1) At-risk-of-poverty rate (60%); S80/S20 ratio and Reduction in Poverty Risk by Transfers (excl. pensions): income reference year 2003, except for CZ (2002) and MT (2000), see Figure 3.1 (2) Employment rate (% population aged 15-64) annual average 2004. (3) Employment rate Older Women/Men (55-64 years) annual average 2004 (break in series). (4) Average Labour Market Exit-Age reference year 2004. EU provisional: IT, AT, SI excluded due to missing data (6) 'Lower part of the table: see note (1)

Interpretation: In the upper part of the Table, country figures are classified as follows ' - ' indicates in the first quartile, '-' indicates in the second; '+' in the third; '++' in the fourth quartile; ':' unknown. In borderline cases, the classification is given as + or (–) rather than ++ (- -). In the lower part of the Table, the at-risk-of-poverty rates for different subgroups are compared with the average national at-risk-of-poverty rate. '+' indicates lower risk than national average; '-' higher risk than national average; '++' and '- -' more than 25% respectively lower and higher risk than national average; '+++' 75 % higher than national average. '=' equal to national average. In the upper part of the Table, the 'EU column' represents the EU average of each variable. In the lower part of the Table the EU column represents the percentage by which each subgroup exceeds the EU average at-risk-of-poverty rate

Data source for calculations: European Commission (2006b – Annex 1c. Statistical Tables

Appendix 2a

Six key EU texts on social protection and social inclusion

The Council Resolution on "Combating social exclusion" (Council, 1989a) adopted in September 1989 emphasised that "combating social exclusion may be regarded as an important part of the social dimension of the internal market" and pointed to "the effectiveness of *coordinated, coherent development policies* based on active participation by local and national bodies and by the people involved". It undertook "to continue and, as necessary, to step up the efforts undertaken *in common* as well as those made by each Member State, and to pool their knowledge and assessments of the phenomena of exclusion" and consequently called on the Commission "to study, together with the Member States, the measures they are taking to combat social exclusion" and "to report on the measures taken by the Member States and by the Community in the spheres covered by this Resolution".

Council Recommendation 92/441/EEC of June 1992 (Council, 1992b) on "Common criteria concerning sufficient resources and social assistance in social protection systems" urged EU Member States to recognise the "basic right of a person to sufficient resources and social assistance to live in a manner compatible with human dignity as a part of a comprehensive and consistent drive to combat social exclusion". Practical guidelines suggested to organise the implementation of this right included: "fixing the amount of resources considered sufficient to cover essential needs with regard to respect for human dignity, taking account of living standards and price levels in the Member State concerned, for different types and sizes of household", "adjusting or supplementing amounts to meet specific needs" and "in order to fix the amounts, referring to appropriate *indicators*, such as, for example, *statistical data* on the average disposable income in the Member State, statistical data on household consumption, the legal minimum wage if this exists or the level of prices".

The third text was adopted one month later, in July 1992: Council Recommendation 92/442/EEC on the "Convergence of social protection objectives and policies" (Council, 1992a). Because "comparable trends in most of the Member States may lead to common problems (in particular the ageing of the population, changing family situations, a persistently high level of unemployment and the spread of poverty and forms of poverty)", the Council recommended that this "de facto convergence" should be further promoted by establishing what was termed a "*convergence strategy*" and which consists basically of the identification of "*common objectives*". The Recommendation suggested that these "*fundamental objectives of the Community*" should act as guiding principles in the development of national social protection systems, while stressing that Member States remain free to determine how their systems should be financed and organised. It explicitly identified *social protection and inclusion as an integral part of the European Social Model and of the Community political "acquis"*. As a follow-up of the Recommendation, the Commission published several "Social Protection in Europe" Reports (starting with its 1993 Report; European Commission, 1993a) analysing developments in Member States' systems with reference to the principles identified in the Recommendation.

In March 1997, the Commission published a Communication on "Modernising and Improving Social Protection in the European Union" (European Commission, 1997), which *inter alia* emphasised the emerging consensus that social protection systems, far from being an economic burden, can act as a *productive factor* that can contribute to economic and political stability and that can help EU economies to perform better. When pointing to the necessity of modernising and improving social protection, and to the need to see social protection as a productive factor, the Commission argued that national systems should be adapted to new realities by making better use of the resources available, not by lowering the level of social protection.

The Treaty of Amsterdam, which was signed in October 1997 and came into force in May 1999, provided a *new legal base for the fight against social exclusion* (Title XI "Social policy, education, vocational training and youth", Chapter 1 "Social provisions", Articles 136 and 137).

In July 1999 the Commission issued a Communication on "A Concerted Strategy for Modernising Social Protection" (European Commission, 1999). In its Conclusions of 17 December 1999 on "the strengthening of cooperation for modernising and improving social protection" (Council, 1999), the Council endorsed the *four broad objectives identified by the Commission*: to make work pay and to provide secure income, to make pensions safe and pensions systems sustainable, to promote social inclusion and to ensure high quality and sustainable health care. The Council welcomed "the Commission's analysis of each of them as a basis for further work by a new high-level group"; a group which was indeed subsequently set up and then became today's EU *Social Protection Committee*.

Appendix 2b

Common objectives of the OMC for Social Protection and Social Inclusion as agreed by the March 2006 European Council

(Source: Social Protection Committee and Economic Policy Committee, 2006)

The overarching objectives of the OMC for Social Protection and Social Inclusion are to promote:

A. social cohesion, equality between men and women and equal opportunities for all through adequate, accessible, financially sustainable, adaptable and efficient social protection systems and social inclusion policies;

B. effective and mutual interaction between the Lisbon objectives of greater economic growth, more and better jobs and greater social cohesion, and with the EU's Sustainable Development Strategy;

C. good governance, transparency and the involvement of stakeholders in the design, implementation and monitoring of policy.

The following objectives apply to the different strands of work:

A decisive impact on the eradication of poverty and social exclusion by ensuring:

D. access for all to the resources, rights and services needed for participation in society, preventing and addressing exclusion, and fighting all forms of discrimination leading to exclusion;

E. the active social inclusion of all, both by promoting participation in the labour market and by fighting poverty and exclusion;

F. that social inclusion policies are well-coordinated and involve all levels of government and relevant actors, including people experiencing poverty, that they are efficient and effective and mainstreamed into all relevant public policies, including economic, budgetary, education and training policies and structural fund (notably ESF) programmes.

Adequate and sustainable pensions by ensuring:

G. adequate retirement incomes for all and access to pensions which allow people to maintain, to a reasonable degree, their living standard after retirement, in the spirit of solidarity and fairness between and within generations;

H. the financial sustainability of public and private pension schemes, bearing in mind pressures on public finances and the ageing of populations, and in the context of the three-pronged strategy for tackling the budgetary implications of ageing, notably by: supporting longer working lives and active ageing; by balancing contributions and benefits in an appropriate and socially fair manner; and by promoting the affordability and the security of funded and private schemes;

I. that pension systems are transparent, well adapted to the needs and aspirations of women and men and the requirements of modern societies, demographic ageing and structural change; that people receive the information they need to plan their retirement and that reforms are conducted on the basis of the broadest possible consensus.

Accessible, high-quality and sustainable healthcare and long-term care by ensuring:

J. access for all to adequate health and long-term care and that the need for care does not lead to poverty and financial dependency; and that inequities in access to care and in health outcomes are addressed;

K. quality in health and long-term care and by adapting care, including developing preventive care, to the changing needs and preferences of society and individuals, notably by developing quality standards reflecting best international practice and by strengthening the responsibility of health professionals and of patients and care recipients;

L. that adequate and high-quality health and long-term care remains affordable and financially sustainable by promoting a rational use of resources, notably through appropriate incentives for users and providers, good governance and coordination between care systems and public and private institutions. Long-term sustainability and quality require the promotion of healthy and active life styles and good human resources for the care sector.

Appendix 3

Members of the Steering Committee

Jutta Allmendinger
Director, Institute for Employment Research (IAB)
Munich, Germany

Wilfried Beirnaert
Union of Industrial and Employers Confederations of Europe (UNICE)
Brussels, Belgium

Jos Berghman
Professor, Catholic University of Leuven (KUL)
Leuven, Belgium

Daniela Bobeva
Bulgarian National Bank
Director, Department of International Relations and European Integration
Sofia, Bulgaria

Andrea Brandolini
Bank of Italy
Economic Research Department
Rome, Italy

Mireille Elbaum
Director, Directorate for Research, Studies, Evaluation and Statistics (DREES)
Paris, France

Robert Erikson
Professor, SOFI, Stockholm University
Stockholm, Sweden

Fintan Farrell
Director, European Anti-Poverty Network (EAPN)
Brussels, Belgium

Gilda Farrell
Council of Europe
Head, "Social Cohesion Development Division"
Strasbourg, France

Zsuzsa Ferge
Professor, Eotvos University
Budapest, Hungary

Paolo Garonna
Professor of Political Economy at the University LUISS G. Carli of Rome and
Chief Economist of Confindustria (Confederation of Italian Industrial
Employers)
Rome, Italy

Michel Glaude
European Commission
Director for "Single Market, Employment and Social Statistics", Eurostat
Luxembourg

John Hills
Professor, Centre for Analysis of Social Exclusion (CASE), London School of
Economics and Political Science (LSE)
London, UK

Dagmar Kutsar
Professor, Tartu University
Tartu, Estonia

Erika Kvapilová
National Programme Officer
United Nations Development Fund for Women (UNIFEM), Regional Office
for CEE
Bratislava, Slovak Republic

Edmundo Martinho
President, Institute of Social Security
Lisbon, Portugal

Tom Mulherin
Chair of the EU Social Protection Committee
Brussels (secretary: European Commission), Belgium

Józef Niemiec
Confederal Secretary, European Trade Union Confederation (ETUC)
Brussels, Belgium

Heinz–Herbert Noll
Director of the "Social Indicators Department", ZUMA
Mannheim, Germany

Mark Pearson
OECD
Head, "Social Policy" Division
Paris, France

Martin Potůček
Professor, Head of the "Centre for Social and Economic Strategies", Charles University
Prague, Czech Republic

Odile Quintin
European Commission
Director General, Directorate-General "Employment, Social Affairs and Equal Opportunities"
Brussels, Belgium

Chiara Saraceno
Professor, University of Turin
Turin, Italy

Tomáš Sirovátka
Professor, School of Social Studies, Masaryk University
Brno, Czech Republic

David Stanton
Chairman, Indicators Sub-Group of the EU Social Protection Committee
Brussels (secretary, European Commission) Belgium

Irena Topińska
Associate Professor, University of Warsaw
Warsaw, Poland

István Tóth
Director, TÁRKI
Budapest, Hungary

Frank Vandenbroucke
Vice-Minister-President of the Flemish Government
Professor, Catholic University of Leuven (KUL)
Leuven, Belgium

Edmunds Vaskis
Central Statistical Bureau of Latvia
Deputy Director, "Department of Social Statistics"
Riga, Latvia

Jiří Večerník
Professor, Institute for Sociology
Prague, Czech Republic

Subject index

Note: References to Boxes, Figures and Tables are given in *italic*.

concentration of poverty 65-6
see also at-risk-of-poverty
confirmatory factor analysis 195n
consistency with national sources 63
consistent poverty 52, 174, 201, 205
see also at-risk-of-poverty
consumption versus income indicators 50
context indicators 47, 68, 165
Context Information 43-4, 163, 165, 180-1,
  272, 277
convergence 19, 133, 144, 154-5
correlation between indicators, *81*, 82-3
COSAC 226, 235n
Council (EU Council of Ministers) *see* author
  index
See also Employment, Social Policy, Health and
  Consumer Affairs Council (EPSCO)
country-specific indicators 39-45, 161
country-specific thresholds 65, 152-5, 161, 240
Croatia 24, 31, 145, 192n
cross-country comparisons 84-97, 120, 160, 213
cross-sectional data 62, 103n, 146-7
Cyprus 31, 64, 68, 72, 75-6, 78, 80, 83, 112,
  191n-2n, 211, 233
Czech Republic 31, 64, 67, 69, 76, 78, 80, 86-7,
  90, 99, 103n, 153, 159, 189, 211

D

data access 151, 240
data collection 60-3, 150-1
data quality 61, 151
demonstration projects 231-2
Denmark 61-2, 64, 67-9, 75, 77, 80, 86, 88, 90,
  95, 98, 101-2, 108, 112, 132-3, 139, 145, 155,
  191n, 207, 216, 230
deprivation 3, 10, 78, 156-7, 170, 174-9
see also non-monetary indicators
disability 98, 146, 160, 172
disaggregation 85-6, *281*
dispersion indicators 69, *71*
diversity within EU 4, 67-9
domestic policy and social inclusion embedding
  50, 150, 199, 217-8, 232-4
see also joined-up Government
durables 177-*178*
dynamics of exclusion 3, 179, 219, 242

E

EAPN (European Anti-Poverty Network) 112,
  156, 231
early school leavers 76, 79-84
see also education
ECHP *see* European Community Household
  Panel

economic growth xv, xxiii, 7-8, 21-2, 30, 95,
  269
economic performance and social policy 19-20,
  53
economic strain 178
education 44, 76, 163-4, 205
see also children mainstreaming, early school
  leavers
EES *see* European Employment Strategy (EES)
efficiency frontier 184
efficiency in targeting 88
EHSS (European Health Survey System) 173-4
elderly 47, *115*, 186
embedding *see* domestic policy and social
  inclusion embedding
employment 91-6
employment gap for migrants/non-migrants 44,
  167, 179, 192n, 241
see also migrants, immigrants
employment growth 6-7, 35, 93, 94-6
Employment Guidelines 22-3, 26-30, 37, 45,
  181, 200, 245
see also Integrated Guidelines
employment policies 227
employment rate and poverty risk *91, 94, 96,
  281*
see also at-risk-of-poverty
Employment, Social Policy, Health and
  Consumer Affairs Council (EPSCO) xiv, 1,
  10, 20, 23, 25, 30, 33, 151, 229
see also Council
Employment Strategy *see* European
  Employment Strategy
Enlargement 5, 31-2, 84, 190, 231, *268-9*
  equivalence scales 159-61
  impact on poverty risk 67-9
  implications for indicators 152-61
  Status of EU Reports post Enlargement *24*
environmental indicators, 114
environmental policy xv, xxiii, 8, 22, 36-7, 181,
  227, 230, 237
EPSCO Council *see* Employment, Social Policy,
  Health and Consumer Affairs Council
  (EPSCO)
equal opportunities 8, 35, 55n, 138, 285
see also children mainstreaming, gender
  mainstreaming
equivalence scales 14, 50-1, 73, 98, 159-61, 241
see also income
ESSPROS 48
Estonia 31, 64, 69, 86, 108, 145, 209
ethnic minorities 114-16, 166-7, 179-80, 241
EU Constitution 26, 199, *269*
EU Council of Ministers *see* Council
see also Employment, Social Policy, Health and
  Consumer Affairs Council (EPSCO)

Author index